ULTIMATE
MAC
PROGRAMMING

DAVE MARK

Programmers Press

A Division of IDG Books Worldwide, Inc.

Foster City, CA • Chicago, IL • Indianapolis, IN • Braintree, MA • Dallas, TX

Ultimate Mac Programming

Published by
IDG Books Worldwide, Inc.
An International Data Group Company
155 Bovet Road, Suite 310
San Mateo, CA 94402

Copyright

Library of Congress Catalog Card No.: 94-072744

ISBN 1-56884-195-7

Printed in the United States of America

First Printing, November, 1994
10 9 8 7 6 5 4 3 2

Distributed in the United States by IDG Books Worldwide, Inc.

Limit of Liability/Disclaimer of Warranty

Trademarks

Published in the United States

CREDITS

Vice President and Publisher
Chris Williams

Publishing Director
Trudy Neuhaus

Brand Manager
Amorette Pedersen

Managing Editor
Beth A. Roberts

Project Editor
Elizabeth Rogalin

Copy Editor
Jean Peck

Editorial Assistant
Berta Hyken

Assistant Brand Manager
Kate Tolini

Compositor
Ronnie K. Bucci

Proofreader
Deborah Kaufmann

Indexer
Liz Cunningham

Book Design
Scally Design

Cover Design
Kavish + Kavish

FOR MORE INFORMATION...

For general information on IDG Books in the U.S., including information on discounts and premiums, contact IDG Books at 800-434-3422 or 415-655-3000. For information on where to purchase IDG's books outside the U.S., contact Christina Turner at 415-655-3022.

For information on translations, contact Marc Jeffrey Mikulich, Foreign Rights Manager, at IDG Books Worldwide; fax number: 415-655-3018.

For sales inquires and special prices for bulk quantities, contact Tony Real at 800-434-3422 or 415-655-3048. For information on using IDG's books in the classroom and ordering examination copies, contact Jim Kelly at 800-434-2086.

Ultimate Mac Programming is distributed in Canada by Macmillan of Canada, a Division of Canada Publishing Corporation; by Computer and Technical Books in Miami, Florida, for South America and the Caribbean; by Longman Singapore in Singapore, Malaysia, Thailand, and Korea; by Toppan Co. Ltd. in Japan; by Asia Computerworld in Hong Kong; by Woodslane Pty. Ltd. in Australia and New Zealand; and by Transword Publishers Ltd. in the U.K. and Europe.

INTERNATIONAL DATA GROUP'S PUBLICATIONS

IDG Books Worldwide, Inc. is a subsidiary of International Data Group. The officers are Patrick J. McGovern, Founder and Board Chairman; Walter Boyd, President. ARGENTINA'S Computerworld Argentina, Infoworld Argentina; AUSTRALIA'S Computerworld Australia, Australian PC World, Australian Macworld, Network World, Mobile Business Australia, Reseller, IDG Sources; AUSTRIA'S Computerwelt Oesterreich, PC Test; BRAZIL'S Computerworld, Gamepro, Game Power, Mundo IBM, Mundo Unix, PC World, Super Game; BELGIUM'S Data News (CW); BULGARIA'S Computerworld Bulgaria, Ediworld, PC & Mac World Bulgaria, Network World Bulgaria; CANADA'S CIO Canada, Computerworld Canada, Graduate Computerworld, InfoCanada, Network World Canada; CHILE'S Computerworld Chile, Informatica; COLOMBIA'S Computerworld Colombia, PC World; CZECH REPUBLIC'S Computerworld, Elektronika, PC World; DENMARK'S Communications World, Computerworld Danmark, Macintosh Produktkatalog, Macworld Danmark, PC World Danmark, PC World Produktguide, Tech World, Windows World; ECUADOR'S PC World Ecuador; EGYPT'S Computerworld (CW) Middle East, PC World Middle East; FINLAND'S MikroPC, Tietoviikko, Tietoverkko; FRANCE'S Distributique, GOLDEN MAC, InfoPC, Languages & Systems, Le Guide du Monde Informatique, Le Monde Informatique, Telecoms & Reseaux; GERMANY'S Computerwoche, Computerwoche Focus, Computerwoche Extra, Computerwoche Karriere, Information Management, Macwelt, Netzwelt, PC Welt, PC Woche, Publish, Unit; GREECE'S Infoworld, PC Games; HUNGARY'S Computerworld SZT, PC World; HONG KONG'S Computerworld Hong Kong, PC World Hong Kong; INDIA'S Computers & Communications; IRELAND'S ComputerScope; ISRAEL'S Computerworld Israel, PC World Israel; ITALY'S Computerworld Italia, Lotus Magazine, Macworld Italia, Networking Italia, PC Shopping, PC World Italia; JAPAN'S Computerworld Today, Information Systems World, Macworld Japan, Nikkei Personal Computing, SunWorld Japan, Windows World; KENYA'S East African Computer News; KOREA'S Computerworld Korea, Macworld Korea, PC World Korea; MEXICO'S Compu Edicion, Compu Manufactura, Computacion/Punto de Venta, Computerworld Mexico, MacWorld, Mundo Unix, PC World, Windows; THE NETHERLANDS' Computer! Totaal, Computable (CW), LAN Magazine, MacWorld, Totaal "Windows"; NEW ZEALAND'S Computer Listings, Computerworld New Zealand, New Zealand PC World, Network World; NIGERIA'S PC World Africa; NORWAY'S Computerworld Norge, C/World, Lotusworld Norge, Macworld Norge, Networld, PC World Ekspress, PC World Norge, PC World's Produktguide, Publish& Multimedia World, Student Data, Unix World, Windowsworld; IDG Direct Response; PAKISTAN'S PC World Pakistan; PANAMA'S PC World Panama; PERU'S Computerworld Peru, PC World; PEOPLE'S REPUBLIC OF CHINA'S China Computerworld, China Infoworld, Electronics Today/Multimedia World, Electronics International, Electronic Product World, China Network World, PC and Communications Magazine, PC World China, Software World Magazine, Telecom Product World; IDG HIGH TECH BEIJING'S New Product World; IDG SHENZHEN'S Computer News Digest; PHILIPPINES' Computerworld Philippines, PC Digest (PCW); POLAND'S Computerworld Poland, PC World/Komputer; PORTUGAL'S Cerebro/PC World, Correio Informatico/Computerworld, Informatica & Comunicacoes Catalogo, MacIn, Nacional de Produtos; ROMANIA'S Computerworld, PC World; RUSSIA'S Computerworld-Moscow, Mir - PC, Sety; SINGAPORE'S Computerworld Southeast Asia, PC World Singapore; SLOVENIA'S Monitor Magazine; SOUTH AFRICA'S Computer Mail (CIO),Computing S.A.,Network World S.A., Software World; SPAIN'S Advanced Systems, Amiga World, Computerworld Espana, Communicaciones World, Macworld Espana, NeXTWORLD, Super Juegos Magazine (GamePro), PC World Espana, Publish; SWEDEN'S Attack, ComputerSweden, Corporate Computing, Natverk & Kommunikation, Macworld, Mikrodatorn, PC World, Publishing & Design (CAP), DataIngenjoren, Maxi Data,Windows World; SWITZERLAND'S Computerworld Schweiz, Macworld Schweiz, PC Tip; TAIWAN'S Computerworld Taiwan, PC World Taiwan; THAILAND'S Thai Computerworld; TURKEY'S Computerworld Monitor, Macworld Turkiye, PC World Turkiye; UKRAINE'S Computerworld; UNITED KINGDOM'S Computing /Computerworld, Connexion/Network World, Lotus Magazine, Open Computing/Sunworld; UNITED STATES' Advanced Systems, AmigaWorld, Cable in the Classroom, CD Review, CIO, Computerworld, Digital Video, DOS Resource Guide, Electronic Entertainment Magazine, Federal Computer Week, Federal Integrator, GamePro, IDG Books, Infoworld, Infoworld Direct, Laser Event, Macworld, Multimedia World, Network World, PC Letter, PC World, PlayRight, Power PC World, Publish, SWATPro, Video Event; VENEZUELA'S Computerworld Venezuela, PC World; VIETNAM'S PC World Vietnam.

DEDICATION

This book is dedicated to Deneen and Daniel. LFUEMISFOK?

ACKNOWLEDGMENTS

I'd like to thank some of the people who made this book possible, who gave up their weekends and evenings editing manuscript, debugging code, and, in general, keeping this book on track.

First of all, I'd like to thank the folks whose technical know-how made this book worthwhile. Donald Olson, Greg Anderson, Jim Reekes, Jorg Brown, and Doug McKenna each breathed life into one of the book's chapters. They patiently answered questions, clarified complex concepts, and in general did their best to bring me up to speed in their particular area of expertise.

Next, I'd like to thank Peter Hoddie, Greg Dow, Joe Zobkiw, Leonard Rosenthol, and Steve Michel, the brains behind Chapter 7. I'd also like to extend a special thanks to Donald Olson, Jim Reekes, Doug Baron and Greg Marriott for all the time they spent reviewing both the code and this manuscript. Thanks also to Scott Boyd for moral and technical support above and beyond the call of duty.

I owe a very special thank you to the team that brought this book together: My good friend and confidante Elizabeth Rogalin, copy editor Jean Peck, Deb Kaufmann, Vicki Hochstedler, and the gang at IDG books: Chris Williams, Amy Pedersen, Trudy Neuhaus, Beth Roberts, Berta Hyken, and Ronnie Bucci. Thanks!

The CD at the back of the book was the result of a tremendous effort by Kate Tolini from IDG Books and Berardino Baratta and Greg Galanos from Metrowerks. Kate coordinated all the non-Metrowerks material that appears on the CD. Berardino helped me with some much needed last minute debugging, and Greg put the whole thing together. Great job—and thanks!

Finally, I'd like to thank my family and friends for their patience and support. Stu, thanks for forcing me to take all those music breaks and for introducing me to Frank. Deneen, thanks for everything else—you are the best!

CONTENTS

6 WORKING WITH RESOURCES

WELCOME

Chapter

1

I've been writing about Macintosh programming for about seven years now. When I started, Windows was just another quirky Mac wanna-be that ran on top of DOS, and the Macintosh II represented Apple's state of the art. My Mac II had an enormous 20-meg hard drive, a 13-inch color monitor, and an entire meg of memory! The Mac Toolbox consisted of about 700 routines, all of them documented in the pages of *Inside Macintosh*, volumes I through V. Once you learned the basics of Mac programming and had some experience navigating the pages of *Inside Macintosh*, you were set. At the time, most people programmed in Pascal, although a growing minority was switching to C. Between THINK Pascal and THINK C, Symantec totally dominated the Macintosh development market. Outside of *Inside Macintosh*, the biggest source of Mac technical information was *MacTutor* magazine and a few Mac programming books.

Seven years later and, oh, how things have changed! C and C++ have become the programming languages of choice, and several new minority candidates (Dylan, for one) have started their bids to take over the top spot. While Windows has moved closer to the Mac's ease of use, the Macintosh has embraced the DOS notion of user-created, executable scripts by introducing AppleScript and the Open Scripting Architecture (OSA). *Inside Macintosh*, having coughed out one last behemoth volume, died but has been reborn. The new series is up to 27 volumes and counting. At this point, I'm not sure anyone knows how many routines are found in the Mac Toolbox anymore.

Learning to program the Macintosh used to be a straightforward, if not simple, process. These days, the professional Mac programmer is constantly inundated with new technologies, and the task of keeping up to date can be a full-time job. To make matters worse, the key to understanding these technologies is to bury your nose in the pages of *Inside Macintosh*. Don't get me wrong. I love *Inside Macintosh*. I just don't think that slogging through a thousand-page reference manual is the right way to learn about anything, which is what started me on the *Ultimate Mac Programming* series.

Each chapter in this book focuses on a different technology. All of these technologies have two things in common: They are all important, and they are all not well understood. An example is the topic covered in Chapter 2, Apple events. When I did the research for the Apple events chapter, I found that although most folks knew how to handle the four required Apple events (or at least had some sample code they could fiddle with), very few people progressed beyond that stage. To me, Apple events and the object model are the basis for much of Apple's future Macintosh innovations. Handling the required Apple events is fine, but learning how to make your application scriptable and recordable or allowing a user to write an AppleScript script that manipulates your program's objects, that's where the real action is! From the information in Chapters 2 and 3 and the three *develop* articles in Appendices A, B, and C, you'll learn all that and much more.

Some chapters start at the beginning and ease you into a new technology. Other chapters assume you know the basics and take you to a more advanced point. In either case, once you finish a chapter, you should find the associated *Inside Macintosh* volume much easier to assimilate.

Before I deal with the specifics of what's covered in each chapter, I'd like to explain the process I went through in putting each chapter together. It might appear as if I wrote this book based on my own knowledge of the Mac Toolbox, but, in truth, I served more as a reporter working side by side with experts. Along with each chapter, you'll find a short bio of the real brains behind the chapter. Though I worked very hard to make this book easy to read, much credit goes to these individuals. I owe each and every one of them a debt of gratitude. All the cool stuff is theirs; all the mistakes are mine.

What's in Each Chapter

Now, let's get into specifics. As is the case in all my books, Chapter 1 is a guided tour through the rest of the book. Even if you're eager to dig into your favorite technology, take the time to read this chapter all the way through. It's not very long, and it contains a lot of important info that might even save your life some day (well, maybe not, but read it anyway).

Chapter 2 takes you on a multipart tour of the Apple Event Manager. First, you'll learn about the data structures and functions you'll need to build and send a basic Apple event. Next, you'll learn about the Apple event Object Model, which will let you fold your program's objects into an Apple event and retrieve objects from Apple events that you receive. This chapter is a must-read and is also, I think, the most strategically important in the book.

Chapter 3 takes the concepts presented in Chapter 2 one step further as you learn about the Apple events and objects supported by the new Scriptable Finder. You'll also learn how to compile and execute scripts inside your own applications. Allowing your users to build and execute their own scripts from inside your application gives them incredible power and makes your application both flexible and extensible.

Chapter 4 is a must-read if you're interested in game design. It covers all aspects of playing synchronous and asynchronous sound. You'll get an insider's tour of the Sound Manager, including work-arounds for bugs that have haunted game programmers for years.

Chapter 5 explores the intricate world of trap patching. First, you'll learn the basics by using a sample program that shows you how to communicate between a cdev and an INIT. Then, you'll learn the proper way to patch traps no matter what the situation, including 68K traps called from PowerPC code and vice versa.

Chapter 6 takes you on a post–System 7 tour of the Resource Manager. This chapter assumes you've already spent a fair amount of time working with resources and thus focuses on some issues that many people (myself included) have not always understood well. You'll get into the resource-manipulating routines you should be using these days. You'll look at the process of loading a resource into memory and learn about resource-file search paths and resource maps. Even if you're already familiar with this technology, take the time to read through this chapter — you might discover something new.

Chapter 7 contains a potpourri of tips, tricks, and techniques that I just couldn't find a home for elsewhere in the book. For example, there are two routines that load a QuickTime movie from a file and play the movie in a window, both with and without the classic QuickTime controls.

While Chapters 2 and 3 focus on the mechanics of building, sending, and receiving Apple events and working with Apple's Open Scripting Architecture, Appendices A, B, and C contain articles from *develop* magazine that each take you one step further toward Apple event enlightenment. Each article presents the author's unique views on the strategies you'll need as you design your own Apple events and Apple event objects.

Appendix D is Dave Winer's famous "Nerd's Guide to Frontier." If you've never used the Frontier scripting system, here's a totally painless way to check it out.

Appendix E is an article, originally published in *MacTech* magazine, that teaches you how to build an AppleScript Addition (also known as an OSAX). AppleScript Additions allow you to add your own commands to the AppleScript language.

Appendix F is also a *MacTech* article reprint. This one is from my "Getting Started" column and gives you a leg up on (and a complete program working with) the four required Apple events.

What's on the Disk

My guess is that you've already pulled the CD out of its hermetically sealed plastic covering and cruised its contents. In case you haven't, here's what you'll find on the CD.

For starters, there's a complete, working version of Metrowerks CodeWarrior. This is the same as the shipping version, except that it doesn't let you create new projects or save source code changes. If you've never worked with CodeWarrior, you'll now have an excellent chance to see what all the buzz is about.

As you'd expect, the CD also contains all the source code from the book. You'll find the code in the `Projects` folder. Assuming you have the space, copy the entire folder to your hard drive. Inside the `Projects` folder, you'll find a subfolder for each of the book's programs. Whenever possible, I tried to build each of the book's projects using both Metrowerks C and THINK C. You'll find the Metrowerks files at the main level of each project folder. You'll find the THINK C files in a subfolder named THINK C (what a concept!).

The CD is also loaded with goodies. There are some really cool shareware games (pay the shareware fees, please) as well as a bunch of commercial game demos. These games are to be used as research for your own user interface experimentation and absolutely not as time-wasting fun. Right?

You'll also find a working (I think it expires after a month or two) copy of TCP/Connect II on the CD. TCP/Connect II gives you everything you need to connect to the Internet and puts it all behind a Mac interface. Find the TCP/Connect II folder and read the read-me file. It tells you how to set up a connection to the Internet (you'll need to sign up with a service provider; the read-me tells you how) and gives you a phone number to call if you have any problems. I think that InterCon (the company that makes TCP/Connect II) has the best tech support I've ever encountered, so don't hesitate to call them.

Take some time to look in every folder on the disk. You'll find some cool tool demos (like CMaster from Jersey Scientific and StoneTable from Stone Tablet Publishing) as well as some programs you'll need as you work through the sample programs in the book. If you don't already have AppleScript installed on your machine, take a minute to locate and install AppleScript, the Script Editor, and the Scriptable Text Editor. All of them are on the CD.

CONVENTIONS USED IN THIS BOOK

As you make your way through this book, you'll encounter a few standard conventions that make the book easier to read. For example, technical terms appearing for the first time are displayed in *italics*. Source code appears in a special `code font`.

> Occasionally, you'll come across a block of text set off in a box, like this. These blocks are called *tech blocks* and are intended to add technical detail to the subject currently being discussed. On your first pass through a chapter, feel free to skip over the tech blocks, but do read them eventually.

KEEP IN TOUCH

As always, I'd love to hear from you. If you have any questions (no matter how simple or how complex), your best bet is to reach me via CompuServe's Macintosh Development forum. Once you're on CompuServe, you can get to the forum by typing `GO MACDEV`. Once you're there, post your questions in the *Learn Programming* section (section 11). Be sure to address your questions to `ALL`. If we can't answer your questions, chances are that we'll be able to point you to someone who can. One nice thing about hooking up with MACDEV section 11 (besides our incredibly friendly sysops!) is that you can pick up any book errata and bug fixes in the forum libraries.

    If you have any comments about the book, send them to me at this address:

`74774.3020@compuserve.com`

    In the meantime, let's get started. . . .

APPLE EVENTS, OSA, AND THE OBJECT MODEL

Chapter

2

One of the coolest features that Apple added in its move from System 6 to System 7 was the *Apple event*. Apple events give your applications a powerful, standardized mechanism for interapplication communication. They are incredibly useful.

For example, the Finder might send an Apple event to your application to request that it open a specified document or even a list of documents. Your application might send an Apple event to a personnel database server to ask that it return an employee's address and phone number to your application and package them in a reply Apple event.

The use of Apple events to communicate between applications is only half the story. To truly take advantage of Apple events, you'll want to make sure your application is *OSA (Open Scripting Architecture)* compliant. OSA is an Apple-defined standard that defines the interface between scripting languages and the applications they control.

For example, consider the personnel database server previously mentioned. If the server is OSA compliant, not only can you write an application to send requests to the server using Apple events, but you can also *do the exact same thing* using a script written in an OSA language such as AppleScript or UserTalk. If an application is OSA compliant, anything you can achieve using Apple events, you can also achieve using a script.

Overview—Learning to Read Inside Macintosh

Though Apple events have been available for quite a while, very few applications have taken full advantage of them—and for good reason. The bible on Apple events and the like is *Inside Macintosh: Interapplication Communication*, published by Addison-Wesley. This book is huge, weighing in at close to 1,000 pages. As this size implies, the task of adding Apple event and OSA support to your applications is nontrivial. Many people (myself included) are intimidated the first time they try to take on the Apple Event Manager. In many ways, this task is as complex as when you first learned to work with the Mac Toolbox.

There is hope, however. Just as you eventually got the hang of the Toolbox, with some sample code and a little bit of help, you'll soon be writing Apple event–savvy, thoroughly scriptable applications. To that end, the remainder of this chapter is broken into three main parts:

- First, we'll explore the basics of Apple event theory, including a review of two sample applications, one a client and the other a server. The client will prepare an Apple event, fold in some data, then send it to the server. The server will fool with the data, fold it back into a reply Apple event, then send the reply back to the client. The client will show you how to send an Apple event (and receive a reply), while the server will show you how to properly process and respond to Apple events.

- Next, we'll learn how to make the server scriptable by giving it an 'aete' (Apple Events Terminology Extension) resource. The 'aete' resource describes the scriptable nature of an application to the outside world. Adding an 'aete' resource gives script writers everything they need to control your application from their own scripts.

- Finally, we'll examine the *Object Model*. By working with the routines and data structures that make up the Object Model, your application can allow script writers direct access to the various objects within your application—even when you're writing in a procedural language like C or Pascal.

For example, imagine a word processor that supported the Object Model. It might allow a script writer to open a specific document, select the third word in the fifth paragraph, then make that selection bold. It might allow a script writer to move or resize the program's windows or, perhaps, change the program preferences.

THINK Reference, the THINK Project Manager, and Code Warrior all support Apple events. If you double-click on a Toolbox call in your source code, your development environment sends an Apple event describing the call to THINK Reference. THINK Reference then jumps to the page describing that call and comes to the foreground. How useful! Note that development environments like Code Warrior and the THINK Project Manager also act as Apple event servers since they allow you to do things such as opening a project, removing objects, and then closing the project, all from inside an application or from a script.

The idea here is that if you design your application with Apple events in mind, not only do you gain a powerful interapplication communication mechanism, but you also make your application much more useful to end users by allowing them access to your application's functionality without necessarily going through your user interface.

In short, this chapter's goal is to give you a basic understanding of Apple events. When you're done reading this chapter, you'll know how to add Apple events to your own applications, and, more importantly, documents like *Inside Macintosh: Interapplication Communication* and the *Apple Event Registry* will make much more sense to you.

Let's get started!

PART 1: APPLE EVENTS

UNDERSTANDING APPLE EVENT SUITES

Every Apple event has both a class and an ID. The class, or *suite*, identifies the event's basic category. Examples are the Text suite, the QuickDraw Graphics suite, and the Finder suite. The *event's ID* distinguishes the event from others in the same suite.

> As you'll see in the next section, "Descriptors," when you create an Apple event, you identify the event's class and ID using constants defined in include files like <AppleEvents.h>.

The most commonly supported suite, by far, is the *Required suite*. As this name implies, every application you write should support the Required suite. It features four Apple events:

- **Open Application**—As soon as the Finder launches your application (assuming no documents were selected), it sends this event to indicate that your application should perform its standard start-up tasks, such as opening an untitled document window.

- **Open Documents**—In the Finder, when the user double-clicks one or more document icons, instead of sending an Open Application event, the Finder embeds the document names in an Open Documents Apple event and then sends this event to the application. Your application retrieves the names from the event and opens the specified documents.

- **Print Documents**—When the user selects Print from the Finder's File menu, the Finder first embeds the names of the documents to be printed in an Apple event and then sends this event to your application. If your application was not already running, the Finder will launch it, send it the Print Documents event, then (when your application finishes printing) send it a Quit Application event.

- **Quit Application**—The Finder sends this event to your application to indicate that it is time for your application to quit. When the user selects Shutdown from the Finder's Special menu, the Finder sends this event to all open applications.

When the Apple Event Manager was first released, the Required suite was the only suite available and the Object Model did not yet exist. As the Object Model evolved, new suites evolved along with it. The most important of these suites is the *Core suite*. The Core suite contains the basic events, objects, properties, and elements you'll need to support to implement scripting in your application. If you plan on going beyond the Required suite, you'll definitely need to support at least a subset of the Core suite.

The Core suite contains 16 events. The two most important of these are the *Get Data* and *Set Data* events. Get Data allows you to retrieve the data stored in an object or set of objects, while Set Data allows you to set the data of an object or set of objects. With these two events, you can support many of the tasks a user might want to perform. You'll see an example of Get Data and Set Data later in the chapter, once we dig into the Object Model.

The remaining Core suite events are Clone, Close, Count Elements, Create Element, Delete, Do Objects Exist, Get Class Info, Get Data Size, Get Event Info, Move, Open, Print, Quit Application, and Save. (Print and Quit Application are extensions of the definitions for these events in the Required suite.)

Other suites include the Text suite (for manipulating text objects), the QuickDraw Graphics suite (for manipulating graphic objects), the Table suite (for manipulating tables made up of cells), and the Finder suite (for manipulating Finder objects such as windows and icons).

Each of these suites is described in detail in the document *Apple Event Registry: Standard Suites*, which is also known as "the Registry." For each suite, the Registry lists each of the events that make up the suite, along with the various constants, data descriptions, and instructions you'll need to properly create, send, and respond to each event.

....

You really should get a copy of the Registry. You can buy a loose-leaf edition from APDA (Apple Programmers and Developers

Association) for about $85, but if you have Apple's monthly developer CDs, you'll find the Registry on the *Reference Library Edition,* which appears every three months. You can also find the Registry on the AppleScript Developer's Toolkit CD, as well as on AppleLink.

The next few sections will focus on the Apple Event Manager and the routines and data structures you'll be working with. As you read along, you might want a copy of the Registry by your side. Pick a suite that interests you and, as new structures and routines are introduced, imagine how they relate to the events in that suite.

DESCRIPTORS

The Apple Event Manager's basic data structure is the *descriptor.* When you want to add some data to an Apple event, you'll first place the data inside a descriptor and then use the appropriate Apple Event Manager routine to add the descriptor to the event.

In the Apple event universe, descriptors are everywhere. In fact, the AppleEvent structure itself is a giant descriptor filled with a bunch of other descriptors. Before we talk about the process of creating, sending, and processing Apple events, let's take a look at the four different descriptor types you'll need to know about to build your own Apple events.

The first three descriptor types, AEDesc, AEDescList, and AERecord, provide the building blocks. The fourth type, AppleEvent, brings these types together to form the actual Apple event.

As you read through the next few sections, try not to get too caught up in the details. First, scan through the description of each of the four descriptor types. Then, see how each type is used in the first pair of sample programs. Once you get the basic idea, turn back to this section and reread it in more detail.

The AEDesc

The AEDesc is the most basic of the four descriptor types. It consists of a 4-byte type code, followed by a 4-byte handle (Figure 2.1). The handle points to a pointer that points to some data, while the type code tells you to what kind of data the handle points.

FIGURE 2.1

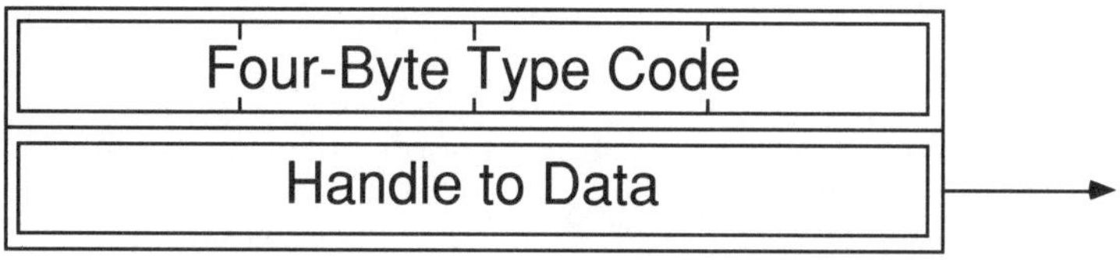

```
┌─────────────────────────────────────┐
│  ┌───────────────────────────────┐  │
│  │     Four-Byte Type Code       │  │
│  ├───────────────────────────────┤  │
│  │       Handle to Data          │  │────────────▶
│  └───────────────────────────────┘  │
└─────────────────────────────────────┘
```

The AEDesc data structure.

The following type codes are from the <AppleEvents.h> include file (you can find them by searching for the string "Apple event descriptor types"):

```
enum {
    typeBoolean = 'bool',
    typeChar = 'TEXT',
    typeSMInt = 'shor',
    typeInteger = 'long',
    typeSMFloat = 'sing',
    typeFloat = 'doub',
    typeLongInteger = 'long',
    typeShortInteger = 'shor',
    typeLongFloat = 'doub',
    typeShortFloat = 'sing',
    typeExtended = 'exte',
    typeComp = 'comp',
    typeMagnitude = 'magn',
    typeAEList = 'list',
    typeAERecord = 'reco',
    typeAppleEvent = 'aevt',
    typeTrue = 'true',
    typeFalse = 'fals',
    typeAlias = 'alis',
    typeEnumerated = 'enum'
};

enum {
    typeType = 'type',
    typeAppParameters = 'appa',
    typeProperty = 'prop',
    typeFSS = 'fss ',
    typeKeyword = 'keyw',
    typeSectionH = 'sect',
    typeWildCard = '****',
    typeApplSignature = 'sign',
    typeSessionID = 'ssid',
```

```
    typeTargetID = 'targ',
    typeProcessSerialNumber = 'psn ',
    typeNull = 'null'
};
```

> The 32 codes just listed are broken into two enumerations because the compiler limits you to 20 items per enum.

As an example, if the type code `typeLongInteger` were found in the first 4 bytes of an `AEDesc`, the `AEDesc` handle would point to a pointer that pointed to a `long`. Note that the 32 codes listed in `<AppleEvents.h>` are by no means the only type codes available. `<AERegistry.h>` contains type codes relating to the events in the Registry. You might want to create your own codes to describe the unique data structures in your own programs. At this point, don't worry about all the different type codes and what they mean. Some of the codes are obvious enough, but some won't make sense until you start working with specific events.

Working with the AEDesc

There are two ways to create an `AEDesc`. The first way is to build one by hand. To do this, start with a handle to the data you want enclosed in the descriptor. Next, define a variable of type `AEDesc`, placing the appropriate type code in the first field and your handle in the second field. Here's the `AEDesc` type definition:

```
struct AEDesc {
    DescType descriptorType;
    Handle      dataHandle;
};
typedef struct AEDesc AEDesc;
```

The second way to create a descriptor is to call `AECreateDesc()`. Here's the prototype:

```
pascal OSErr   AECreateDesc( DescType typeCode, const void* dataPtr,
                   Size dataSize, AEDesc *newAEDescPtr )
```

`AECreateDesc()` allocates a new handle of size `dataSize` and then copies the data pointed to by `dataPtr` into the newly allocated block. Next, the `typeCode` and handle are copied into the `AEDesc` pointed to by `newAEDescPtr`.

> Note that while `AECreateDesc()` *does* allocate the block of memory pointed to by the `dataHandle`, it *does not* allocate the 8 bytes that

make up the descriptor itself. As you see in the sample programs that appear later in the chapter, you'll allocate the 8-byte `AEDesc` and then pass a pointer to it as the last parameter to `AECreateDesc()`.

So, when should you call `AECreateDesc()` and when should you create your `AEDesc` by hand? If you already have a handle to the data you want to embed in your descriptor, go ahead and build the `AEDesc` yourself. If you don't have a handle set up or if you want to copy the data rather than embed the original in the descriptor, call `AECreateDesc()`.

Here's an example that creates a descriptor containing a handle to a `long`:

```
long    myLong = 32L;
AEDesc  myAEDesc = { typeNull, NULL };
OSErr   err;

err = AECreateDesc( typeLongInteger, &myLong,
              sizeof( myLong ), &myAEDesc );
```

The first thing to notice is that `myAEDesc`'s `descriptorType` is initialized to `typeNull` and its `dataHandle` is initialized to `NULL`. Even though you don't have to do this, it's generally a good idea to initialize all of your descriptors in this way, just as you'd initialize a return code or an uninitialized handle or pointer.

As it turns out, if `AECreateDesc()` fails, it will set the descriptor's type code to `typeNull` and its `dataHandle` to `NULL`. This fact shouldn't change your strategy, however. By initializing your descriptors to `{typeNull,NULL}`, you'll be sure that your descriptors are always filled with legitimate values.

The above-mentioned call to `AECreateDesc()` attempts to allocate a block of memory the size of a `long` and places a handle to this memory in `myAEDesc.dataHandle`. If the handle-based, 4-byte block of memory is successfully allocated, the constant `typeLongInteger` is copied into `myAEDesc.descriptorType` and `noErr` is returned. If there isn't enough memory to allocate the block, `AECreateDesc()` returns `memFullErr` and copies `typeNull` into `descriptorType`.

Regardless of whether you used `AECreateDesc()` or built the descriptor by hand, you're responsible for deallocating any memory allocated for `myAEDesc.dataHandle`. You *can* deallocate the handle yourself, but the preferred method is to pass the descriptor to `AEDisposeDesc()`:

```
pascal OSErr AEDisposeDesc( AEDesc *theAEDesc );
```

If the descriptor's `descriptorType` field is set to `typeNull`, `AEDisposeDesc()` will just return `noErr`.

Is there anything wrong with disposing of the handle yourself? In most cases, no. The one case where you must call `AEDisposeDesc()` involves the `AppleEvent` descriptor type, the descriptor used to implement the Apple event itself (we'll get to it in a bit). The reason for this is that the Apple Event Manager maintains an internal list of Apple events it has created so that it can match up Apple event replies with the original Apple event. If you dispose of an Apple event yourself, this list will be wrong.

In a nutshell, it's probably best to call `AEDisposeDesc()` anytime you want to dispose of a descriptor.

The AEDescList

The second of the four descriptor types is the `AEDescList`. The `AEDescList` is a descriptor containing a list of other descriptors. The `AEDescList` consists of a `descriptorType` field and a `dataHandle`, just like the `AEDesc`. The `dataHandle` refers to a block of descriptors, one right after the other.

The block of descriptors is *not* just a sequence of `AEDesc`s, each with a handle to its respective data. Instead, all the descriptors are flattened into one long chunk, with the data stored directly in the sequence rather than accessed via a handle. This format is proprietary, but you can follow it quite easily with a debugger.

`AEDescList`s are typically used when you want to enclose a list of objects in an Apple event. For instance, you might want to pass a list of files or aliases for another application to open or print. You'll find lots of examples of this technique in the Registry. For one example, take a look at the parameter listed in the Open Documents event in the Required suite. You'll also find many similar examples in the Finder suite.

Working with the AEDescList

To create an `AEDescList`, you call `AECreateList()`. `AECreateList()` creates an empty list with the appropriate header. Here's the prototype:

```
pascal OSErr   AECreateList( const void* factoringPtr,
                  Size factoredSize, Boolean isRecord,
                  AEDescList *resultList );
```

If all of the descriptors in your list start with the *exact same data*, you can pass a pointer to this data as the first parameter to `AECreateList()`. The Apple Event Manager will package one copy of this data in the list, thus saving space by not replicating the data in every list item. If you don't want to take advantage of this feature, just pass `NULL` as the first parameter.

The second parameter is the size of the data passed in the first parameter. If you pass `NULL` as the first parameter, pass 0 as the second parameter.

The third parameter is a `Boolean`, indicating whether `AECreateList()` should create an `AEDescList` or an `AERecord`. Pass `false` to create an `AEDescList` (we'll get to `AERecords` in a bit).

The final parameter is a pointer to the created `AEDescList`. Just as you did with `AECreateDesc()`, you allocate and initialize an `AEDescList` and then pass the address of this list on to `AECreateList()`.

Like `AECreateDesc()`, if `AECreateList()` returns an error, the descriptor's type code will be set to `typeNull`.

> Once again, initializing your descriptor to {typeNull,NULL} is a waste if you immediately pass the descriptor to a routine like `AECreateList()` because `AECreateList()` will set the descriptor's fields to appropriate values even if it fails. Nonetheless, I still initialize all my descriptors—just to be safe.

Once you're done with your list, call `AEDisposeDesc()` to deallocate the list. `AEDisposeDesc()` doesn't care what the descriptor's type is. All it does is free up the memory allocated to the descriptor's `dataHandle` and then set the `dataHandle` to `NULL` and the `descriptorType` to `typeNull`.

To add data to the list, you use the routines `AEPutPtr()` and `AEPutDesc()`. If you have a descriptor already built, use `AEPutDesc()` to add the descriptor to the list. If you don't have a descriptor built, don't bother to build one; use `AEPutPtr()` to add the data to the list.

Accessing the descriptors in a list is done by index, just as if the list were an array of descriptors. To retrieve data from the list, you might first call `AECountItems()` to find out how many descriptors are in a list. You could then call `AEGetNthDesc()` (to get a descriptor) or `AEGetNthPtr()` (to get the data directly). Calling `AESizeOfNthItem()` allows you to retrieve both the size and the type of a descriptor. Finally, calling `AEDeleteItem()` lets you delete a descriptor from the list.

The AERecord

The third of the four descriptor types is the AERecord. Like the AEDescList, the AERecord is a descriptor containing a list of other descriptors. While the descriptors in an AEDescList are accessed by index, the descriptors in an AERecord are organized by keyword. While you might refer to the fourth item in an AEDescList, you'd use a predefined keyword, like keyErrorString or keyDirectObject, to retrieve a descriptor from an AERecord.

Here are some keywords from the file <AppleEvents.h> (look for the string "Keywords for Apple event parameters"):

```
enum {
    keyDirectObject = '—',
    keyErrorNumber = 'errn',
    keyErrorString = 'errs',
    keyProcessSerialNumber = 'psn '
};
```

Most of the time, you'll use the keywords provided by the Apple Event Manager or by the Registry. Other times, you'll define your own keywords. Either way, when you add a descriptor to an AERecord, you tag it with a keyword. To retrieve the descriptor from the AERecord, you need to specify the same keyword.

> If you've got a copy of the Registry by your side, take a look at the description of the Get Data event in the Core suite. Of special interest are the headings "Parameters" and "Reply Parameters." As you'll see, each Apple event is really just an AERecord and is organized by keyword. The first parameter (we'll get to parameters and reply parameters later—just bear with me) in the Get Data event is identified by the keyword keyDirectObject. Other parameters are retrieved using different keywords.

Working with the AERecord

Just as you did to create an AEDescList, you call AECreateList() to create an AERecord:

```
pascal OSErr    AECreateList( const void* factoringPtr,
                    Size factoredSize, Boolean isRecord,
                        AEDescList *resultList );
```

To create an AERecord instead of an AEDescList, pass true as the third parameter. AECreateList() creates an empty list with the appropriate header (this time, an `AERecord` header instead of an `AEDescList` header).

To add data to the record, you use either `AEPutKeyDesc()` or `AEPutKeyPtr()`. Do you see the pattern here? If you have a descriptor already built, call `AEPutKeyDesc()`. Otherwise, call `AEPutKeyPtr()`.

To retrieve the data, you use either `AEGetKeyDesc()` or `AEGetKeyPtr()`. You need to specify the same keyword that was used to store the data in the `AERecord`.

The routine `AESizeOfKeyDesc()` takes an `AERecord` and a keyword and returns the type code of the specified descriptor, as well as the size of the data residing in the descriptor. The routine `AEDeleteKeyDesc()` deletes the descriptor specified by the provided keyword. If you want more details, all of the routines we've covered so far can be found in THINK Reference (version 2.0 or later) or in *Inside Macintosh: Interapplication Communication*.

> By the way, you can also access an `AERecord` in the same way you would an `AEDescList`, using routines like `AECountItems()`, `AEGetNthDesc()`, `AEGetNthPtr()`, and `AEDeleteItem()`.

The AppleEvent

The fourth and final descriptor type is the `AppleEvent`. Defined as an `AERecord`, the `AppleEvent` ties everything else together. When you create an Apple event, you call a routine that allocates an `AppleEvent`. Then, depending on the event you're trying to build, you call various routines to add the appropriate *attributes* and *parameters* to the `AppleEvent`.

Attributes identify an Apple event characteristic. For example, the Apple event class (suite), event ID (event within the suite), and target address are all attributes. Parameters, on the other hand, are the data wrapped in the event. For example, when the Finder sends an Open Documents event, it adds a parameter to the event that describes the files to be opened.

> Typically, your focus will be on parameters rather than attributes. For most events, the only attributes you'll work with are the ones you pass to `AECreateAppleEvent()` when you first create your event (we'll talk about `AECreateAppleEvent()` shortly).

The *Apple Event Registry* defines the attributes and parameters needed by each Apple event. As you review the sample code in this chapter, you'll see how to add attributes and parameters to the Apple events that you create. For now, you might want to scan through the Registry to see what types of attributes and parameters are typically used by the events in the standard suites.

Working with the AppleEvent

To create an `AppleEvent`, you call `AECreateAppleEvent()`:

```
pascal OSErr   AECreateAppleEvent( AEEventClass eventClass,
               AEEventID eventID, const AEAddressDesc *target,
               short returnID, long transactionID, AppleEvent
                   *result );
```

The first two parameters define the event's class and ID. You'll normally get these parameters from the *Apple Event Registry*. The constants listed in the Registry are all defined in the include file `<AERegistry.h>`. For example, the constants for the Core suite's Get Data event are `kAECoreSuite` and `kAEGetData`. If you were creating a Get Data event, you'd pass `kAECoreSuite` and `kAEGetData` as the first two parameters to `AECreateAppleEvent()`.

The third parameter to `AECreateAppleEvent()` is a descriptor that defines the target of the Apple event (the application to receive the event). An `AEAddressDesc` is just an alias for the type `AEDesc`. Just like an `AEDesc`, an `AEAddressDesc` has a type code and a handle to the data defined by that type code. The main difference is that an `AEAddressDesc` is restricted to four legal type codes:

- `typeApplSignature` indicates that the data portion of the descriptor contains the target application's signature. In this case, the Apple Event Manager will attempt (when `AESend()` is called) to deliver the Apple event to a running application with a matching signature.

- `typeSessionID` allows you to specify a session ID as the target for an Apple event. Session IDs are generated by the PPC (Program-to-Program Communication) Toolbox. The PPC Toolbox is used by the Apple Event Manager to send Apple events from one program to another. You'll use the PPC Toolbox when you want to communicate without going through the Apple Event Manager. You might do this if you wanted to pass a great deal of data to another application specifically designed to work with yours. The PPC Toolbox is covered in Chapter 11 of *Inside Macintosh: Interapplication Communication*.

- `typeTargetID` indicates that the descriptor contains a Target ID Record, a data structure returned by the routine `PPCBrowser()`. `PPCBrowser()` allows the user to select the target application at run time. `PPCBrowser()` is part of the PPC Toolbox. Here's a code snippet for creating a `typeTargetID` address descriptor:

```
AEAddressDesc           theTargetDesc;
TargetID                myTempTargetID;
LocationNameRec         theLocNameRec;
PortInfoRec             thePortInfoRec;
OSErr                   err;

// Look PPCBrowser() up in Inside Mac:IAC or in THINK
// Reference...
err = PPCBrowser( nil, nil, false, &theLocNameRec,
            &thePortInfoRec, nil, nil );

// bail on error
if ( err != noErr ) return;

// Bundle up the myTempTargetID
myTempTargetID.location = theLocNameRec;
myTempTargetID.name = thePortInfoRec.name;

// Create the address descriptor
theErr = AECreateDesc( typeTargetID, (Ptr)&myTempTargetID,
            sizeof( myTempTargetID ), &theTargetDesc);
```

- `typeProcessSerialNumber` allows you to specify the process ID of the target application. You'll see an example of this in Chapter 3 when we work with the Scriptable Finder. To learn about process IDs, read up on the Process Manager in THINK Reference or in *Inside Macintosh*. One reason to use the `typeProcessSerialNumber` is when you want to send an Apple event to yourself. Here's a code snippet for creating a self-addressed `typeProcessSerialNumber` descriptor:

```
ProcessSerialNumber     thePSN;
AEDesc                  theTarget;

thePSN.highLongOfPSN = 0L;
thePSN.lowLongOfPSN = kCurrentProcess;
theErr = AECreateDesc( typeProcessSerialNumber,
            (Ptr) &thePSN, sizeof(thePSN), &theTarget );
```

You'll definitely need to send Apple events to yourself if you plan on making your application *recordable*. If your application is recordable, users will be able to record all of their actions as a sequence of Apple events. For example, users of a recordable word processor might record a sequence where they open a document, change all occurrences of the Palatino font to Bookman, then save the changes. They might then save the sequence of Apple events generated by these actions as an AppleScript script and rerun the sequence, this time on several files to which they'd like the same changes to apply.

Here's the way recording works. A recordable application divides its functionality into two parts: code that implements the user interface and code that performs the actions designated by the user interface. This second category of code is wrapped in a series of Apple event handlers (we'll get to them soon). When the user takes some action, your user interface code will send an Apple event to your application and ask it to take the appropriate action.

When recording is turned on for a computer, the Apple Event Manager will send copies of all Apple events to the recording application. So, as your recordable word processor sends Apple events to itself in response to user requests to open a document and perform spell checking, the recording application gets copies of these events and saves them as a sequence until recording is turned off.

For more info on making your application recordable, look up "recordable applications" in the index of *Inside Macintosh: Interapplication Communication*. In the meantime, as you read through this chapter, think about what you'll need to do to make your next application completely Apple event driven.

The fourth parameter to `AECreateAppleEvent()` is the return ID, a number that will associate this event with any reply event sent by the receiving application. You can generate your own ID or ask the Apple Event Manager to generate a unique ID for you by specifying the constant `kAutoGenerateReturnID`.

The fifth parameter to `AECreateAppleEvent()` is the transaction ID. Don't confuse the transaction ID with the return ID. Think of the original event and the reply to it as a single chunk. Sometimes, it will take several of these chunks to complete your task. For example, suppose you needed to find out the current value of an object before you could set the object to a new value. The first chunk is the Get Data event that asks for the object's value and the reply that gives you the value. The second chunk is the Set Data event that sets the object's new value. These two chunks together make up a single transaction and must have the same transaction ID. Use the constant `kAnyTransactionID` if this event won't be part of a transaction.

The last parameter to `AECreateAppleEvent()` is a pointer to an uninitialized `AppleEvent`. `AECreateAppleEvent()` will fill out the `AppleEvent` for you using the specified parameters.

As `AECreateAppleEvent()` creates your `AppleEvent`, it adds the attributes you've provided, the event class, event ID, and target descriptor. If your event calls for any additional attributes, you have to add them yourself by using the routines `AEPutAttributeDesc()` and `AEPutAttributePtr()`. On the flip side, you can retrieve attributes from an `AppleEvent` by calling `AEGetAttributeDesc()` and `AEGetAttributePtr()`.

Once your `AppleEvent` is created, you're ready to add your parameters. As you look through the Registry, you'll see the keywords used to add parameters to different Apple events. One keyword you'll consistently encounter is `keyDirect-Object`. If you think of an Apple event as a "verb," the `keyDirectObject` is the "object" of this verb. For example, in the phrase "close the document," "close" is the verb and "document" is the object. In a Set Data event, the direct object specifies the object whose value is to be set.

> *Object specifiers* are important, and we'll address them in the third part of this chapter when we get into the Object Model. For now, just focus on the mechanics of sending and receiving Apple events.

To add a parameter to your `AppleEvent`, call either `AEPutParamDesc()` or `AEPutParamPtr()`, depending on whether or not you have a descriptor already defined. To retrieve a parameter from an `AppleEvent`, call `AEGetParamDesc()` or `AEGetParamPtr()`.

> Interestingly, the "Param" calls share the same series of traps as their respective "Key" calls. For example, `AEGetParamDesc()` and `AEGetKeyDesc()` are aliases for the exact same trap. If you think about it, this makes sense. The "Param" routines deal with keyword-specified `AppleEvents`. The "Key" routines deal with keyword-specified `AERecords`. An `AppleEvent` follows the exact same format as an `AERecord`, albeit with a different `descriptorType`. When it comes to adding or retrieving a descriptor by keyword, there is no difference between the two.

Once your Apple event is completed, you send it by calling `AESend()`:

```
pascal OSErr   AESend( const AppleEvent *theAppleEvent,
                 AppleEvent *reply, AESendMode sendMode,
                 AESendPriority sendPriority, long timeOutInTicks,
                 IdleProcPtr idleProc, EventFilterProcPtr filterProc );
```

The first parameter is a pointer to your AppleEvent. The second parameter is a pointer to a second AppleEvent, which will be filled out and returned to you by the target application if you request it.

To ask for a reply event, pass kAEWaitReply as the third parameter, sendMode. sendMode is a combination of constants from the list in Figure 2.2. You can combine several constants as long as the combination makes sense. If you pass kAEWaitReply, your call to AESend() won't return until the target application fills out a reply event and returns from its processing of the event. kAEQueueReply also requests a reply, but asks that it be sent via your event queue instead of as a parameter.

FIGURE 2.2

sendMode Constants and Their Meaning	
kAENoReply	Sender doesn't want a reply to event.
kAEQueueReply	Sender wants a reply but won't wait.
kAEWaitReply	Sender wants a reply and will wait.
kAENeverInteract	Server should not interact with user.
kAECanInteract	Server may try to interact with user.
kAEAlwaysInteract	Server should always interact with user where appropriate.
kAECanSwitchLayer	Interaction may switch layer.
kAEDontReconnect	Don't reconnect if there is a sessClosedErr from PPC Toolbox.
kAEWantReceipt	Sender wants receipt of message
kAEDontRecord	Don't record this event—available only in version 1.0.1 and greater.
kAEDontExecute	Send event for recording purposes only—available only in version 1.0.1 and greater.

sendMode constants and their meaning.

The constants kAENeverInteract, kAECanInteract, kAEAlwaysInteract, and kAECanSwitchLayer let you specify the level of user interaction permitted between the recipient of the Apple event, also known as the *server*, and the user. If the kAENeverInteract flag is set, you've told the server never to interact with the user. If the `kAECanInteract` flag is set, the server is allowed to interact with the user (perhaps by putting up a dialog) to request additional information concerning the Apple event just received. If the `kAEAlwaysInteract` flag is set, the server can interact with the user with no restrictions. Finally, the `kAECanSwitchLayer` flag determines whether the server interacts directly with the user or goes through the Notification Manager.

> We'll take a closer look at server/user interaction in the next section, "Processing Apple Events."

The fourth parameter to `AESend()`, `sendPriority`, lets you tag your event as normal (`kAENormalPriority`) or high priority (`kAEHighPriority`).

The fifth parameter lets you specify a time-out value in ticks (60ths of a second), which comes into play if you've used either `kAEWaitReply` or `kAEWantReceipt` in the `sendMode` parameter. Most likely, you'll pass either `kAEDefaultTimeout` or `kNoTimeOut`.

The sixth parameter, `idleProc`, is a pointer to a routine that will be executed repeatedly while waiting for a response to your event. This parameter is useful if you've passed either `kAEWaitReply` or `kAEWantReceipt` in the `sendMode` parameter. You might use the `idleProc` to animate a cursor to let the user know that your application is still alive.

The seventh parameter, `filterProc`, points to a routine that you can use to process events (`updateEvts`, for example) while you wait for `AESend()` to return. Again, this parameter is useful if you've passed either `kAEWaitReply` or `kAEWantReceipt` in the `sendMode` parameter.

Once `AESend()` returns, you can use the appropriate routines to extract data from the reply event (if one exists). Listed in the *Apple Event Registry* under the heading "Reply Parameters" are parameters for those events that call for a reply event. Each parameter is identified by a unique keyword that you can use to retrieve the parameter.

PROCESSING APPLE EVENTS

The previous sections showed you how to build and send an Apple event. In this section, we'll look at the other end of the process and focus on the application receiving the Apple event—the server.

Detecting an Apple Event

When you call `WaitNextEvent()` to retrieve an event, you'll typically compare `event.what` against a list of constants such as `mouseDown`, `keyDown`, and `updateEvt`. With the advent of System 7, a new constant has been added to this list. When `event.what` is equal to `kHighLevelEvent`, the event is either a high-level event that you've defined yourself or an Apple event.

> High-level events are events that pass information between applications. Apple events are high-level events that follow the Apple Event Interprocess Messaging Protocol (AEIMP). Low-level events (such as update, activate, and mouse down events) indicate changes to the operating environment made by the user.

Since we won't be defining any custom high-level events, when `event.what` is equal to `kHighLevelEvent`, we'll pass the event along to `AEProcessAppleEvent()`. `AEProcessAppleEvent()` looks at the Apple event's class and ID and dispatches the event to the routine we've designated as the handler for that particular class and ID.

Installing an Apple Event Handler

As you design your program, you'll make a list of all the Apple events your application will handle. For each event, you'll write a routine called an *Apple event handler*. At initialization time, you'll install each Apple event handler by calling the routine `AEInstallEventHandler()`:

```pascal
pascal OSErr    AEInstallEventHandler( AEEventClass eventClass,
                AEEventID eventID, EventHandlerProcPtr handler,
                long handlerRefcon, Boolean isSysHandler );
```

`AEInstallEventHandler()` installs the routine named `handler` as the Apple event handler for all Apple events of class `eventClass` and ID `eventID`. Basically, this means that when you pass an event to `AEProcessAppleEvent()`, `AEProcessAppleEvent()` looks the class and ID up in a table and turns the class and ID into a function pointer. `AEProcessAppleEvent()` then calls this routine.

The fourth parameter to `AEInstallEventHandler()` is a `long` that you can use for your own nefarious purposes. The `long` will be passed on to the handler when it is called. If you don't need the `handlerRefCon`, pass in a value of `0L`.

The last parameter to `AEInstallEventHandler()` lets you install the handler in the system dispatch table rather than your application's dispatch table. Usually, you'll pass `false` as the last parameter to install the handler in your application's dispatch table.

Writing an Apple Event Handler

Each Apple event handler must follow this format:

```
pascal OSErr    MyEventHandler( AppleEvent *appleEventPtr,
                AppleEvent *replyPtr, long refCon );
```

The first parameter points to the Apple event being sent to the handler for processing. The second parameter points to an empty Apple event that you'll use for your reply, if appropriate. The third parameter is the `long` that you passed in to `AEInstallEventHandler()`.

Getting the Required Parameters

Your handler's job is to retrieve the appropriate parameters from the current event, perform whatever action is called for, then construct a reply event if one is called for. Your handler won't actually send the reply event. Instead, it will add the designated parameters to the reply event pointed to by `replyPtr` (the handler's second parameter). When the handler exits, the Apple Event Manager will either return the reply event as a parameter (if `AESend()` was called with the `sendMode` constant `kAEWaitReply`) or will queue the reply as a new Apple event (`kAEQueueReply`).

Take a look through the *Apple Event Registry*. Notice that for a particular event, each of the parameters is marked as either optional or required. Once your handler has pulled all the parameters it thinks it needs, you should verify that no required parameters are remaining by checking to see whether your event has an attribute whose keyword is `keyMissedKeywordAttr`.

If the `keyMissedKeywordAttr` attribute exists, you haven't retrieved all the required parameters and something is definitely wrong. If the `keyMissedKeywordAttr` attribute doesn't exist, you've snagged all the required parameters, although some optional parameters still might be left.

To check for the `keyMissedKeywordAttr` attribute, call `AEGetAttributePtr()`:

```
DescType returnedType;
Size      actualSize;

err = AEGetAttributePtr( appleEventPtr, keyMissedKeywordAttr,
        typeWildCard, &returnedType, nil, 0, &actualSize );
```

The first parameter is the Apple event pointer passed to your handler. The second parameter is the keyword for the attribute you're looking for. The third parameter asks `AEGetAttributePtr()` to match, no
matter the type of the attribute, as long as the keyword is correct.
The fourth parameter will be set to the attribute's type, assuming one
is found.

Since you care only about whether the attribute exists and you
don't care about the attribute's data, you pass 0 for the data buffer
length (sixth parameter) and `nil` for the buffer pointer (fifth parameter).
You also ignore the last parameter, which tells you how many bytes of
data were retrieved (since it would be 0 anyway).

What you do care about is the error code returned. The key error
code is `errAEDescNotFound`. If `AEGetAttributePtr()` returns
`errAEDescNotFound`, you know that you've fetched all the required
parameters.

Interfacing with the User

Earlier in the chapter, we talked about `AESend()`, the `sendMode` parameter, and the flags that tell the server how to handle user interaction. Now
let's consider the same topic from the server's point of view.

Your server can set its user interaction preferences by calling
`AESetInteractionAllowed()`:

```
pascal OSErr AESetInteractionAllowed( AEInteractAllowed level );
```

`AESetInteractionAllowed()` takes a single parameter, either
`kAEInteractWithSelf`, `kAEInteractWithLocal`, or `kAEInteractWithAll`.
`kAEInteractWithSelf` says that the server will interact with the user
only when the client and the server are the same (when the client sends
an Apple event to itself). `kAEInteractWithLocal` says that the server
will interact with the user only when the client and the server are on
the same machine. This setting is the default and is used if you never call
`AESetInteractionAllowed()`. Finally, `kAEInteractWithAll` says that the
server will interact with the user under all conditions.

You can call `AEGetInteractionAllowed()` to retrieve the current user interaction level.

When you're ready to interact with the user, call
`AEInteractWithUser()`:

```
pascal OSErr AEInteractWithUser(long timeOutInTicks, NMRecPtr
nmReqPtr,
                AEIdleUPP idleProc);
```

`AEInteractWithUser()` **checks both the client and the server's pref-erences for user interaction and does the right thing in either case. If the client set the** `kAENeverInteract` **flag (see** `AESend()`**'s** `sendMode` **parame-ter),** `AEInteractWithUser()` **returns the error code** `errAENoUserInteraction`.

If the client set either the `kAECanInteract` **(the default) or the** `kAEAlwaysInteract` **flag,** `AEInteractWithUser()` **then checks the server's** `AESetInteractionAllowed()` **setting. If this setting, combined with the current situation, doesn't allow for user interaction,** `AEInteractWithUser()` **also returns the** `errAENoUserInteraction` **error code.**

If after all this checking, user interaction *is* **allowed,** `AEInteractWithUser()` **brings your application to the front either by posting a Notification Manager request (asking the user to bring the server to the front) or by switching the server to the front (if the** `kAECanSwitchLayer` **flag was set).**

`AEInteractWithUser()` **takes three parameters. If the Notification Manager is used,** `timeOutInTicks` **is the number of ticks you're willing to wait for the user to bring your application to the front. If the time-out is exceeded,** `AEInteractWithUser()` **returns the error code** `errAETimeout`.

The second parameter is a notification request that you fill out if you don't want to use the default provided by the Apple Event Manager. If you want to use the default notification, pass `nil`. **For more informa-tion on the Notification Manager, check out** *Inside Macintosh: Processes*.

The third parameter is a universal procedure pointer. It points to a routine that you provide to handle events while waiting for the user to bring your application to the front.

If the ins and outs of interfacing with the user seem a little muddy, build yourself some sample code and experiment. Once you get used to the different flags, things won't seem so confusing.

AN APPLE EVENT EXAMPLE

Now that we've covered the basics, let's move on to an example. This example is broken into two parts: ReverServer is an Apple event server, designed to respond to three different Apple events; ReverClient is an Apple event client, designed to send the same three events.

Running ReverServer and ReverClient

Go into the `Projects` folder and then into the `Client/Server 1` subfolder. Double-click on the `ReverServer` application. A window containing a single text field will appear (Figure 2.3). The text field shows any text that has been sent to ReverServer via an Apple event.

FIGURE 2.3

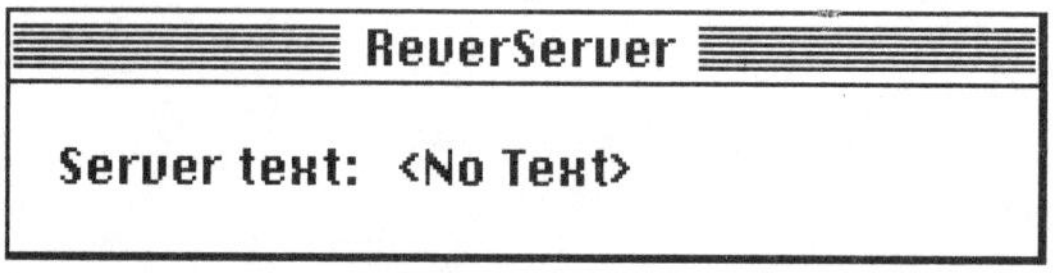

The ReverServer window.

With ReverServer still running, go back into the `Client/Server 1` subfolder and double-click on the `ReverClient` application. A window containing an editable text field and three buttons will appear (Figure 2.4).

FIGURE 2.4

The ReverClient window.

The three buttons represent the three Apple events handled by ReverServer. Set Text adds the text in the text field to an Apple event and sends it to ReverServer. Press the Set Text button. The ReverClient text will appear in the ReverServer window (Figure 2.5).

FIGURE 2.5

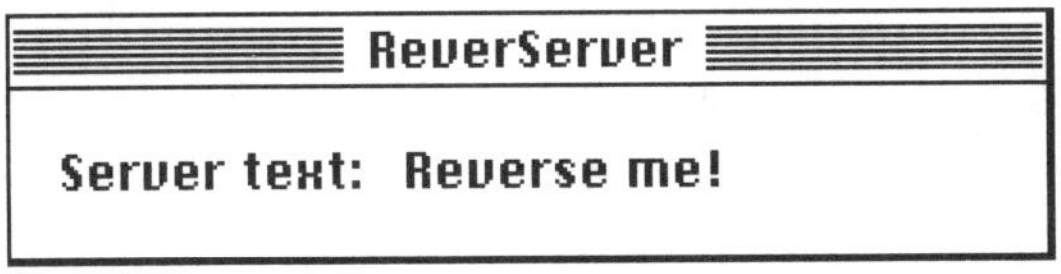

```
========== ReverServer ==========

Server text:  Reverse me!
```

ReverServer, after the Set Text event.

The Reverse button sends an Apple event to ReverServer, asking it to reverse the text in its text field. Press the Reverse button. The ReverServer text string will appear in reverse order (Figure 2.6).

FIGURE 2.6

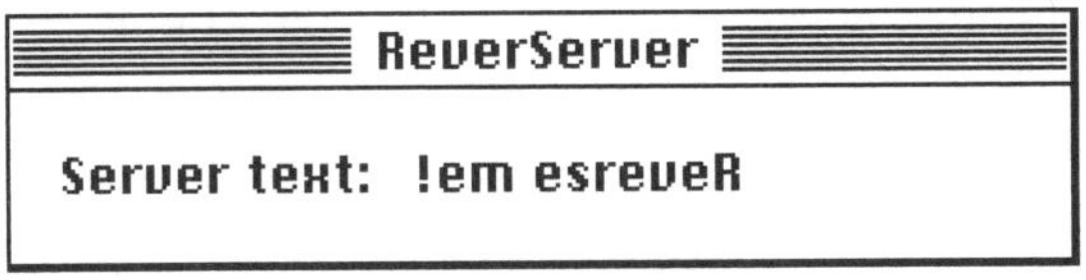

```
========== ReverServer ==========

Server text:  !em esreveR
```

ReverServer, after the Reverse event.

The third button, Get Text, sends an Apple event to ReverServer, asking ReverServer to send its text back via a reply Apple event. When ReverClient receives the reply, it will display the newly received text in its window. Press the Get Text button. The ReverServer text will appear in the ReverClient window's editable text field (Figure 2.7).

FIGURE 2.7

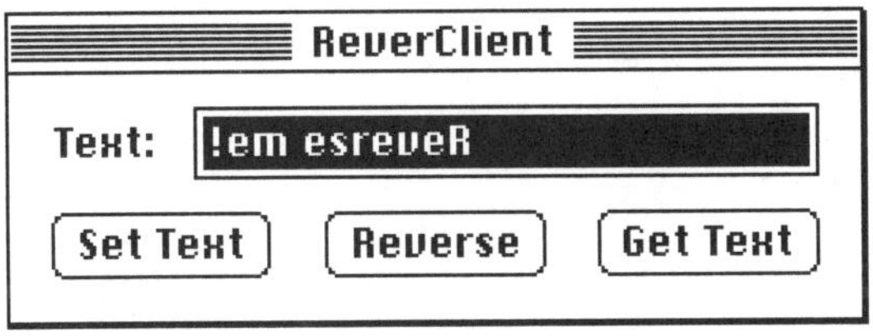

```
========== ReverClient ==========

Text:  [!em esreveR                ]

[ Set Text ]  [ Reverse ]  [ Get Text ]
```

ReverClient, after the Get Text event.

Feel free to play around some with these applications. At the very least, quit ReverServer, then see what happens when you press one of the ReverClient buttons.

In the next few sections, we'll walk through the source code that makes these programs what they are.

THE REVERCLIENT SOURCE CODE

`ReverClient.c` starts with two key `#include`s. `<GestaltEqu.h>` gives us access to `Gestalt()` so that we can make sure that the Apple Event Manager is available on this machine. `<AppleEvents.h>` provides us with the constants, data structures, and function prototypes that we'll need to work with the Apple Event Manager:

```
#include <GestaltEqu.h>
#include <AppleEvents.h>
```

The ReverClient `#define`s are as follows (they'll be discussed as they are used in the code):

```
#define kBaseResID                      128
#define kErrorALRTid            128
#define kAboutALRTid            129
#define kDialogResID            130

#define kVisible                true
#define kMoveToFront            (WindowPtr)-1L
#define kSleep                  60L
#define kNilFilterProc          0L
#define kGestaltMask            1L

#define kOn                     1
#define kOff                    0

#define mApple                  kBaseResID
#define iAbout                  1

#define mFile                   kBaseResID+1
#define iQuit                   1

#define iGetText                1
#define iReverse                2
#define iSetText                3
#define iText                   5

#define kReverServerClass           'Tsrv'
#define kReverServerSignature 'Tsrv'
#define kSetTextID                      'SETT'
#define kReverseTextID              'RVRS'
#define kGetTextID                      'GETT'
```

```
#define kNoIdleProc                    nil
#define kNoFilterProc      nil
#define kMaxTextSize       255
```

As usual, gDone starts off as false and is set to true when it is time to drop out of the main event loop. gDialogPtr points to ReverClient's main dialog window:

```
Boolean    gDone;
DialogPtr  gDialogPtr;
```

Here are the function prototypes:

```
void    ToolboxInit( void );
void    MenuBarInit( void );
void    AEInit( void );
void    SetUpDLOG( void );
void    EventLoop( void );
void    DoEvent( EventRecord *eventPtr );
void    DoDialogEvent( EventRecord *eventPtr );
void    DoAppleEvent( AEEventID idToSend, Str255 theText );
void    HandleMouseDown( EventRecord *eventPtr );
void    HandleMenuChoice( long menuChoice );
void    HandleAppleChoice( short item );
void    HandleFileChoice( short item );
void    DoMessage( Str255 errorString );
void    DoError( Str255 errorString );
```

main() initializes the Toolbox, sets up the menu bar, then calls AEInit() to make sure that Apple events are supported by this configuration:

```
/****************************** main ********/

void  main( void )
{
   ToolboxInit();
   MenuBarInit();
   AEInit();
```

SetUpDLOG() fetches the DLOG resource and EventLoop() enters the main event loop.

```
   SetUpDLOG();

   EventLoop();
}
```

Next comes a standard `ToolboxInit()`:

```
/***************** ToolboxInit ********************/

void  ToolboxInit( void )
{
    InitGraf( &qd.thePort );
    InitFonts();
    InitWindows();
    InitMenus();
    TEInit();
    InitDialogs( 0L );
    InitCursor();
}
```

`MenuBarInit()` **loads the** `MBAR` **resource, calling** `DoError()` **if the resource wasn't found.** `DoError()` **puts up an error alert and then calls** `ExitToShell()`:

```
/***************** MenuBarInit *********************/

void  MenuBarInit( void )
{
    Handle        menuBar;
    MenuHandle    menu;

    menuBar = GetNewMBar( kBaseResID );

    if ( menuBar == NULL )
        DoError( "\pCouldn't load the MBAR resource..." );
```

If the `MBAR` **was found, the menu bar is set up as usual:**

```
    SetMenuBar( menuBar );

    menu = GetMHandle( mApple );
    AddResMenu( menu, 'DRVR' );

    DrawMenuBar();
}
```

`AEInit()` **passes** `gestaltAppleEventsAttr` **to** `Gestalt()` **and then uses** << **to shift** `kGestaltMask` **into position to test whether the** `gestaltAppleEventsPresent` **bit is set:**

```
/****************************** AEInit ********/

void  AEInit( void )
{
```

```
   OSErr   err;
   long    feature;

   err = Gestalt( gestaltAppleEventsAttr, &feature );

   if ( err != noErr )
      DoError( "\pError returned by Gestalt!" );

   if ( !( feature & ( kGestaltMask << gestaltAppleEventsPresent ) ) )
      DoError( "\pThis configuration does not support Apple events..." );
}
```

SetUpDLOG() **loads the** DLOG **resource, makes it the current port, then calls** SelIText() **to highlight all the text in the editable text field:**

```
/****************** SetUpDLOG **********************/

void   SetUpDLOG( void )
{
   gDialogPtr = GetNewDialog( kDialogResID, NULL, kMoveToFront );

   if ( gDialogPtr == NULL )
      DoError( "\pCouldn't load the DLOG resource..." );

   ShowWindow( gDialogPtr );
   SetPort( gDialogPtr );

   SelIText( gDialogPtr, iText, 0, 32767 );
}
```

EventLoop() **does its normal call to** WaitNextEvent(), **but it also includes a call to** TEIdle() **once each time through the loop to keep our modeless dialog's text field cursor blinking properly:**

```
/****************************** EventLoop *********/

void   EventLoop( void )
{
   EventRecord    event;

   gDone = false;
   while ( gDone == false )
   {
      if ( WaitNextEvent( everyEvent, &event, kSleep, NULL ) )
         DoEvent( &event );

      TEIdle( ((DialogPeek)gDialogPtr)->textH );
   }
}
```

Since our window is made up entirely of dialog items, most of the events we care about should be picked up by IsDialogEvent(). The one exception is a mouseDown in the window's drag region, which we pass along to HandleMouseDown():

```
/*********************************** DoEvent****/

void  DoEvent( EventRecord *eventPtr )
{
   if ( IsDialogEvent( eventPtr ) )
   {
      DoDialogEvent( eventPtr );
   }
   else if ( eventPtr->what == mouseDown )
   {
      HandleMouseDown( eventPtr );
   }
}
```

DoDialogEvent() handles events for the modeless dialog:

```
/*********************************** DoDialogEvent****/

void  DoDialogEvent( EventRecord *eventPtr )
{
   short     itemHit;
   short     itemType;
   Handle      itemHandle;
   Rect      itemRect;
   char      theChar;
   DialogPtr   dialog;
   Str255      theText;
```

The following chunk of code first checks to see whether the event in question is a keyDown or an autoKey event:

```
   switch ( eventPtr->what )
   {
     case keyDown:
     case autoKey:
        theChar = eventPtr->message & charCodeMask;
```

If so, it then checks to see whether the command key (⌘) was down when the event occurred. If it was, we call MenuKey() to turn the keypress into its command-key equivalent:

```
        if ( (eventPtr->modifiers & cmdKey) != 0 )
        {
           menuAndItem = MenuKey( theChar );
```

If the menu portion of menuAndItem is not 0, then the keypress was a command-key equivalent, and we pass it on to HandleMenuChoice() and return:

```
    if ( HiWord( menuAndItem ) != 0 )
    {
       HandleMenuChoice( menuAndItem );
       return;
    }
  }
 break;
}
```

If the event made it this far, it wasn't a command-key equivalent, and we pass it on to DialogSelect() for processing. DialogSelect() is the ModalDialog() equivalent for modeless dialogs:

```
if ( DialogSelect( eventPtr, &dialog, &itemHit ) )
{
```

When DialogSelect() returns, itemHit contains the item to which the event relates. We're interested in the dialog's three buttons, which correspond to the three Apple events that we want to send on to ReverServer:

```
switch ( itemHit )
 {
```

If the Set Text button was pressed, we retrieve the text from the editable text field and pass it on to DoAppleEvent(). DoAppleEvent() creates the Apple event specified in the first parameter, adds the text to the event (if the text string is bigger than 0 bytes), sends the event, then retrieves the text from any reply events and returns it in theText:

```
case iSetText:
    // Tell the remote app to use this string
    GetDItem( dialog, iText, &itemType, &itemHandle, &itemRect
);
    GetIText( itemHandle, theText );

    DoAppleEvent( kSetTextID, theText );
    break;
```

Our goal here is to send the text string to ReverServer. We don't expect anything in return, other than a possible error code, and the error codes will be handled inside DoAppleEvent(). As you design your own Apple event strategies, you'll probably want to build a more sophisticated error-handling mechanism.

If the Reverse button was pressed, we call DoAppleEvent() to send the reverse Apple event. Since we don't want any text added to the event, we'll be sure to make theText a zero-length string. Just as with the Set Text event, we don't expect a reply event in response to the Reverse event:

```
case iReverse:
    // Tell the remote app to reverse its string

    theText[0] = 0;
    DoAppleEvent( kReverseTextID, theText );
    break;
```

If the Get Text button was pressed, we send a Get Text Apple event by passing the appropriate event ID to DoAppleEvent(). Since we're not sending any text, we'll pass a zero-length string in theText:

```
case iGetText:
    // Ask the remote app to return its string
    theText[0] = 0;
    DoAppleEvent( kGetTextID, theText );
```

When we send the Get Text event, we do expect a reply event containing ReverServer's current text string. DoAppleEvent() pulls the text out of the reply event and returns it in theText. We pass theText to SetIText() to place the returned text in the editable text field and then call SelIText() to highlight the entire field:

```
        GetDItem( dialog, iText, &itemType, &itemHandle, &itemRect
);
        SetIText( itemHandle, theText );

        SelIText(dialog, iText, 0, 32767 );
        break;
    }
  }
}
```

DoAppleEvent() is where all the action is. The first parameter is the ID of the Apple event to send. But where did this event ID come from? What suite does it belong to?

Most of the Apple events you'll use will come from suites defined in the *Apple Event Registry*. If the need arises, however, you can define your own suites and events. Since we haven't explored the Object Model yet (we'll get to it later in the chapter) and since the Registry events depend on the Object Model, we've defined our own suite and three events within the suite.

You've probably noticed that the various codes used by the Apple Event Manager resemble the 4-byte type codes used by the Resource Manager. Exactamùndo! Same idea. In fact, when you register your application's 4-byte signature with developer services, you also have a handy suite ID guaranteed to be unique.

> Event IDs must be unique within a suite, but they can be reused in different suites. For example, there can be only one 'odoc' event in a single suite, but several suites can feature an event with the ID 'odoc'.

The second parameter to DoAppleEvent() is a pascal string. If the string has a length greater than 0, it will be added to the event. If a reply event is received, any text in the reply event will be returned in theText:

```
/********************************* DoAppleEvent****/

void DoAppleEvent( AEEventID idToSend, Str255 theText )
{
   AEAddressDesc  targetAddrDesc = {typeNull, nil};
   long        targetSignature = kReverServerSignature;
   AppleEvent    event = {typeNull, nil};
   AppleEvent    reply = {typeNull, nil};
   OSErr       err;
   DescType     actualtype;
   Size        actualSize;
```

We start by calling AECreateDesc() to create a descriptor to hold the target address. In this example, we use the signature of the target application to address the Apple event:

```
err = AECreateDesc( typeApplSignature, (Ptr)(&targetSignature),
        sizeof( targetSignature ), &targetAddrDesc );
```

As we discussed earlier, descriptors are made up of a 4-byte type code, followed by a handle to data of that type. In this case, the type code typeApplSignature tells AECreateDesc() that the second parameter is a pointer to a 4-byte application signature. The third parameter says that the second parameter points to a block of 4 bytes. The last parameter is the address of a descriptor we've already allocated. Note that the definition of `targetAddrDesc` also initializes it, using a `typeNull` type code and a `nil` handle.

> It's usually a good idea to start out all of your descriptors in this way. Aside from the fact that `AEDisposeDesc()` is smart enough not to try to dispose of a `typeNull` descriptor, a `nil` handle is always better than an uninitialized handle.

In general, if we run into an error we never expected to get, we call `DoError()`, which puts up an error message and then calls `ExitToShell()`. If the error is a reasonably expected error, we call `DoMessage()` instead, which puts up an error message and returns. This error-handling mechanism is simpleminded and in no way represents the views of the management of this station. Your mileage may vary!

```
if ( err != noErr )
   DoError( "\pError returned by AECreateDesc()..." );
```

With our `AEAddressDesc` in hand, we're now ready to create the actual `AppleEvent` by calling `AECreateAppleEvent()`:

```
err = AECreateAppleEvent( kReverServerClass, idToSend,
                &targetAddrDesc, kAutoGenerateReturnID,
                kAnyTransactionID, &event );

if ( err != noErr )
   DoError( "\pError returned by AECreateAppleEvent()..." );
```

The first parameter uses ReverServer's signature as the Apple event suite code. The first parameter passed to `DoAppleEvent()` specifies the event ID. The event will be addressed to `targetAddrDesc` (which we've set up to send the event to a running application with ReverServer's signature). `kAutoGenerateReturnID` and `kAnyTransactionID` tell the Apple Event Manager to handle the details of generating an ID for the reply event and a transaction ID for this event. Finally, `event` is the `AppleEvent` that we defined at the top of the routine. (Note that `event` was initialized in the same way as `targetAddrDesc`.)

If the pascal string in `theText` is longer than 0, we add it to the event as a parameter by using `AEPutParamPtr()`:

```
if(*theText) // if we have a string longer than 0
{
```

```
   err = AEPutParamPtr( &event, keyDirectObject, typeChar,
           (Ptr)(&(theText[ 1 ])), theText[ 0 ] );

   if ( err != noErr )
      DoError( "\pError returned by AEPutParamPtr()..." );
}
```

> It's important to remember that every parameter and attribute you
> add to an `AppleEvent` must be identified by a keyword. Typically, the
> keyword `keyDirectObject` is used to identify a parameter containing
> the data to be operated on. If you think of an Apple event as a verb,
> the `keyDirectObject` is the verb's object.

We pass `keyDirectObject` as the second parameter to
`AEPutParamPtr()`. (As you look through the Registry, you'll see that the
parameters for each event are listed by keyword.) The third parameter
defines the type of the data being added to the parameter. `typeChar` tells
you that the fourth parameter points to a text string. The number of
bytes in the string is specified by the fifth parameter. This parameter is
important because a `typeChar` string is neither a pascal nor a C string. It
is just a sequence of bytes, with no special length-specifying or terminating bytes.

Once the `AppleEvent` is completed, we're ready to send it by calling `AESend()`:

```
 err = AESend( &event, &reply, kAEWaitReply +
         kAECanInteract + kAECanSwitchLayer,
         kAENormalPriority, kAEDefaultTimeout,
         kNoIdleProc, kNoFilterProc );
```

The first two parameters are the `AppleEvent` and an empty reply
event. (Check out the definition of `reply`. Note that the definition initializes `reply` using a `typeNull` type code and a `nil` handle.) The third
parameter tells the Apple Event Manager that we'd like to wait for a
reply, that the server is allowed to interact with the user, and that the
Apple Event Manager can switch the server to the front at the server's
request. The fourth parameter sets the priority, the fifth specifies the
time-out in ticks waiting for the reply, the sixth and seventh say that we
won't use an idle proc or a filter proc.

> Once you get the hang of the client and server code, try adding calls
> to `AEInteractWithUser()` and `AESetInteractionAllowed()` to the

server and various combinations of flags to the call to AESend() that follows. Think of these programs as a user interface lab designed for your experimentation.

If AESend() can't locate the target application, it returns the error code connectionInvalid. In this case, we put up an error message (there's no need to exit because, most likely, the server just wasn't started yet) and dispose of the three descriptors that we allocated. Notice that AEDisposeDesc() is smart enough to dispose of any type of descriptor, even an AppleEvent:

```
if ( err == connectionInvalid )
{
   DoMessage( "\pServer not running..." );

   AEDisposeDesc( &targetAddrDesc );
   AEDisposeDesc( &event );
   AEDisposeDesc( &reply );
   return;
}
```

If AESend() returns an error other than connectionInvalid, we put up an error message and exit the program:

```
if ( err != noErr )
   DoError( "\pError returned by AESend()..." );
```

Next, we try to retrieve a keyDirectObject from the reply Apple event (as you'll see when we walk through the ReverServer code, this will happen only in response to a Get Text event, with the keyDirectObject parameter holding the ReverServer text):

```
err = AEGetParamPtr( &reply, keyDirectObject, typeChar,
      &actualtype, (Ptr)(&(theText[ 1 ])), kMaxTextSize,
         &actualSize );

theText[0] = actualSize;
```

The first two parameters tell AEGetParamPtr() to retrieve the keyDirectObject parameter. The third parameter says that we want the retrieved data to have a type of typeChar. If we had been retrieving a descriptor instead of a block of text, AEGetParamPtr() would have performed any necessary type coercion to make the data look like the requested type. In any case, the fourth parameter is the parameter's actual type. Since we're retrieving a text string intended as a pascal string, we retrieve the text block starting at the second byte of theText. We fix the length byte next.

The replies to the Set Text and Reverse Events won't have a keyDirect-Object parameter. So, AEGetParamPtr() will return the AEDescNotFound error code. If we get any other kind of error, we display an error message and exit:

```
if (( err != noErr ) && (err != errAEDescNotFound))
   DoError( "\pError returned by AEGetParamPtr()..." );
```

Finally, we dispose of our three descriptors:

```
AEDisposeDesc (&targetAddrDesc);
AEDisposeDesc (&event);
AEDisposeDesc (&reply);
}
```

HandleMouseDown() handles various mouseDown events:

```
/*********************************** HandleMouseDown */

void  HandleMouseDown( EventRecord *eventPtr )
{
   WindowPtr      window;
   short       thePart;
   long        menuChoice;

   thePart = FindWindow( eventPtr->where, &window );

   switch ( thePart )
   {
      case inMenuBar:
         menuChoice = MenuSelect( eventPtr->where );
         HandleMenuChoice( menuChoice );
         break;
      case inSysWindow:
         SystemClick( eventPtr, window );
         break;
      case inContent:
         SelectWindow( window );
         break;
      case inDrag:
         DragWindow( window, eventPtr->where, &screenBits.bounds );
         break;
   }
}
```

HandleMenuChoice() **dispatches all menu selections:**

```
/***************** HandleMenuChoice *******************/

void  HandleMenuChoice( long menuChoice )
{
    short menu;
    short item;

    if ( menuChoice != 0 )
    {
        menu = HiWord( menuChoice );
        item = LoWord( menuChoice );

        switch ( menu )
        {
            case mApple:
                HandleAppleChoice( item );
                break;
            case mFile:
                HandleFileChoice( item );
                break;
        }
        HiliteMenu( 0 );
    }
}
```

HandleAppleChoice() **and** HandleFileChoice() **handle selections from the** ■ **and File menus, respectively:**

```
/***************** HandleAppleChoice *******************/

void  HandleAppleChoice( short item )
{
    MenuHandle  appleMenu;
    Str255      accName;
    short       accNumber;

    switch ( item )
    {
        case iAbout:
            NoteAlert( kAboutALRTid, NULL );
            break;
        default:
            appleMenu = GetMHandle( mApple );
            GetItem( appleMenu, item, accName );
            accNumber = OpenDeskAcc( accName );
            break;
    }
}
```

```
/***************** HandleFileChoice *********************/

void  HandleFileChoice( short item )
{
   switch ( item )
   {
      case iQuit:
         gDone = true;
         break;
   }
}
```

DoMessage() **and** DoError() **use** ParamText() **to display the specified error message in the** kErrorALRTid **alert. The only difference
between them is that** DoError() **calls** ExitToShell()**:**

```
/**************** DoMessage *******************/

void  DoMessage( Str255 errorString )
{
   ParamText( errorString, "\p", "\p", "\p" );

   NoteAlert( kErrorALRTid, kNilFilterProc );
}


/**************** DoError *******************/

void  DoError( Str255 errorString )
{
   ParamText( errorString, "\p", "\p", "\p" );

   StopAlert( kErrorALRTid, kNilFilterProc );

   ExitToShell();
}
```

The ReverServer Source Code

ReverServer.c **starts with the same** #includes **as** ReverClient.c**:**

```
#include <GestaltEqu.h>
#include <AppleEvents.h>
```

We'll get to the ReverServer #defines **as they occur in the code:**

```
#define kBaseResID              128
#define kErrorALRTid      128
```

```
#define kAboutALRTid            129
#define kServerDLOGid           130

#define kVisible                true
#define kMoveToFront            (WindowPtr)-1L
#define kSleep                  60L
#define kNilFilterProc          0L
#define kGestaltMask            1L

#define kOn                     1
#define kOff                    0

#define mApple                  kBaseResID
#define iAbout                  1

#define mFile                   kBaseResID+1
#define iQuit                   1

#define iDisplayText            2

#define kReverServerClass           'Tsrv'
#define kReverServerSignature 'Tsrv'
#define kSetTextID                      'SETT'
#define kReverseTextID                  'RVRS'
#define kGetTextID                      'GETT'

#define kNoTextString           "\p<No Text>"

#define kMaxTextSize            255
```

ReverServer has three globals. gDone is false until we're ready to
drop out of the program. gHasText starts off as false and is true when
ReverServer's current text string is bigger than 0 bytes. gServerDialog
points to the modeless dialog that displays the ReverServer text:

```
Boolean     gDone, gHasText;
DialogPtr   gServerDialog;
```

Here are the function prototypes:

```
void      ToolboxInit( void );
void      MenuBarInit( void );
void      AEInit( void );
void      AEInstallHandlers( void );
pascal OSErr      DoOpenApp( AppleEvent *event, AppleEvent *reply,
                                  long refcon );
pascal OSErr      DoOpenDoc( AppleEvent *event, AppleEvent *reply,
                                  long refcon );
```

```
pascal OSErr      DoPrintDoc( AppleEvent *event, AppleEvent *reply,
                              long refcon );
pascal OSErr      DoQuitApp( AppleEvent *event, AppleEvent *reply,
                              long refcon );
pascal OSErr      DoSetTextEvent( AppleEvent *event, AppleEvent
                                   *reply, long refcon );
void     DoSetText( Str255  theText);
pascal OSErr      DoReverseEvent( AppleEvent *event, AppleEvent
                                   *reply, long refcon );
void     DoReverse( void );
void     ReverseString( Str255 string );
pascal OSErr      DoGetTextEvent( AppleEvent *event, AppleEvent
                                   *reply, long refcon );
void     DoGetText( Str255 string );
void     CreateDialog( void );
void     EventLoop( void );
void     DoEvent( EventRecord *eventPtr );
void     HandleMouseDown( EventRecord *eventPtr );
void     HandleMenuChoice( long menuChoice );
void     HandleAppleChoice( short item );
void     HandleFileChoice( short item );
void     DoUpdate( EventRecord *eventPtr );
void     DoError( Str255 errorString );
```

main() initializes the Toolbox, sets up the menu bar, then checks
for Apple event support. If the Apple Event Manager is present, the dialog is loaded and the main event loop is entered:

```
/****************************** main ********/

void  main( void )
{
   ToolboxInit();
   MenuBarInit();
   AEInit();

   CreateDialog();

   EventLoop();
}
```

Next comes the standard ToolboxInit():

```
/******************************** ToolboxInit */

void  ToolboxInit( void )
{
   InitGraf( &qd.thePort );
   InitFonts();
```

```
   InitWindows();
   InitMenus();
   TEInit();
   InitDialogs( 0L );
   InitCursor();
}
```

MenuBarInit() **looks just like its ReverClient counterpart:**

```
/****************** MenuBarInit **********************/

void  MenuBarInit( void )
{
   Handle        menuBar;
   MenuHandle    menu;

   menuBar = GetNewMBar( kBaseResID );

   if ( menuBar == NULL )
      DoError( "\pCouldn't load the MBAR resource..." );

   SetMenuBar( menuBar );

   menu = GetMHandle( mApple );
   AddResMenu( menu, 'DRVR' );

   DrawMenuBar();
}
```

AEInit() **calls** Gestalt() **to check for Apple event support, just as
it did in ReverClient. This time,** AEInstallHandlers() **is also called so
that we can install handlers for the four required events, as well as for
our own Set Text, Reverse, and Get Text events:**

```
/****************************** AEInit ********/

void  AEInit( void )
{
   OSErr err;
   long  feature;

   err = Gestalt( gestaltAppleEventsAttr, &feature );

   if ( err != noErr )
      DoError( "\pError returned by Gestalt!" );

   if ( !( feature & ( kGestaltMask << gestaltAppleEventsPresent ) ) )
      DoError( "\pThis configuration does not support Apple events..." );
```

```
   AEInstallHandlers();
}
```

AEInstallHandlers() **consists of a sequence of calls to**
AEInstall-EventHandler(), **one for each event we support. Each call to**
AEInstall-EventHandler() **starts with the suite and event ID of the**
event handled by the handler. The third parameter is a pointer to the
handler itself. The Apple Event Manager keeps a table that maps the
suite and event ID to a specific handler. Note that when an Apple event
is passed to AEProcessAppleEvent() (see DoEvent() **shown later in the**
code), the Apple Event Manager looks at the attributes that specify the
event's suite and ID and then looks the suite and ID up in the table to
retrieve and call the event's handler. The fourth parameter is a reference constant, which we didn't use. The fifth parameter tells the Apple
Event Manager to install the handler in the application's event handler
table, as opposed to in the system's event handler table:

```
/****************************** AEInstallHandlers ********/

void  AEInstallHandlers( void )
{
   OSErr err;
```

The first four calls to AEInstallEventHandler() **install handlers for**
the four required Apple events:

```
   err = AEInstallEventHandler( kCoreEventClass, kAEOpenApplication,
           DoOpenApp, 0L, false );

   if ( err != noErr )
     DoError( "\pError installing 'oapp' handler..." );

   err = AEInstallEventHandler( kCoreEventClass, kAEOpenDocuments,
           DoOpenDoc, 0L, false );

   if ( err != noErr )
     DoError( "\pError installing 'odoc' handler..." );

   err = AEInstallEventHandler( kCoreEventClass, kAEPrintDocuments,
           DoPrintDoc, 0L, false );

   if ( err != noErr )
     DoError( "\pError installing 'pdoc' handler..." );

   err = AEInstallEventHandler( kCoreEventClass, kAEQuitApplication,
           DoQuitApp, 0L, false );
```

```
   if ( err != noErr )
      DoError( "\pError installing 'quit' handler..." );
```

The last three calls to AEInstallEventHandler() install handlers for our own Set Text, Reverse, and Get Text events:

```
   err = AEInstallEventHandler( kReverServerClass, kSetTextID,
         DoSetTextEvent, 0L, false );

   if ( err != noErr )
      DoError( "\pError installing set text handler..." );

   err = AEInstallEventHandler( kReverServerClass, kReverseTextID,
         DoReverseEvent, 0L, false );

   if ( err != noErr )
      DoError( "\pError installing text reversing handler..." );

   err = AEInstallEventHandler( kReverServerClass, kGetTextID,
         DoGetTextEvent, 0L, false );

   if ( err != noErr )
      DoError( "\pError installing get text handler..." );
}
```

DoOpenApp(), DoOpenDoc(), DoPrintDoc(), and DoQuitApp() are the handlers for the four required events. Since ReverServer doesn't handle documents, these routines do the absolute minimal acceptable thing—they return noErr:

```
/***************** DoOpenApp ********************/

pascal OSErr   DoOpenApp( AppleEvent *event, AppleEvent *reply,
                              long refcon )
{
   return noErr;
}


/***************** DoOpenDoc ********************/

pascal OSErr   DoOpenDoc( AppleEvent *event, AppleEvent *reply, long
                              refcon )
{
   return noErr;
}


/***************** DoPrintDoc ********************/
```

```
pascal OSErr   DoPrintDoc( AppleEvent *event, AppleEvent *reply,
                                long refcon )
{
   return noErr;
}
```

> Notice that each of these handlers returns an OSErr and is declared
> using the pascal keyword. The pascal keyword is necessary when-
> ever you define a routine that will be called by a Toolbox routine, as
> opposed to by your own code.

```
/***************** DoQuitApp *********************/

pascal OSErr   DoQuitApp( AppleEvent *event, AppleEvent *reply, long
refcon )
{
   SysBeep( 20 );
   gDone = true;

   return noErr;
}
```

Actually, DoQuitApp() does a little more than the absolute minimum. It calls SysBeep() and sets gDone to true, thus causing the program to exit. Why do this? Just to prove a mild point, start up
ReverServer, go to the Finder, and then select ShutDown. That beep you
just heard was in response to a Quit Application Apple event that was
sent by the Finder to all open applications in response to the shutdown
request. You won't hear the beep when you quit ReverServer in the normal way (unless you make your application recordable, that is).

Don't make the mistake of calling ExitToShell() from inside your
Quit Application handler. If you do, your handler will never return to
the Apple Event Manager (which called your handler in the first place),
the Apple Event Manager will get hosed, and strange futuristic sounds
will start emanating from your Mac's speaker (and that's bad, by the
way). Instead, do what DoQuitApp() does. Set a flag and, when control
returns to your program, drop out of your main event loop (or call
ExitToShell() if you prefer).

> The required events are not explained in great detail in this chapter
> because they are covered in so many other sources. You can find
> the basics in Chapter 8 of the *Macintosh C Programming Primer*,

Volume I, Second Edition, published by Addison-Wesley, or in Appendix F of this book. Once you get through those examples, you shouldn't have any trouble following the examples here.

DoSetTextEvent() is called whenever a Set Text event is received. The three parameters are the event, the reply event (all ready for you to add parameters to it), and the reference constant you passed in when you installed the handler:

```
/***************** DoSetTextEvent *********************/

pascal OSErr     DoSetTextEvent( AppleEvent *event, AppleEvent
                                        *reply, long refcon )
{
    DescType    actualtype;
    Size        actualSize;
    Str255        theText;
    OSErr       err;
```

First, we call AEGetParamPtr() to fetch the text from the keyDirectObject parameter. We put the text into theText, starting at the second byte:

```
err = AEGetParamPtr( event, keyDirectObject, typeChar,
    &actualtype, (Ptr)(&(theText[ 1 ])), kMaxTextSize,
        &actualSize );
```

Next, we make the text a true pascal string by placing the string's length in theText's length byte:

```
theText[ 0 ] = actualSize;
```

If we run into any problems, we return the error code returned by AEGetParamPtr():

```
if ( err != noErr )
    return err;
```

Then, we pass the text to DoSetText() to place the text in the dialog's static text field, and we return noErr:

```
DoSetText( theText );

return noErr;
}
```

DoSetText() **starts by retrieving the handle to the dialog's static text item (not the label, but the actual text):**

```
/****************** DoSetText *********************/

void DoSetText( Str255  theText)
{
    short       itemType;
    Handle          itemHandle;
    Rect        itemRect;

    GetDItem( gServerDialog, iDisplayText, &itemType, &itemHandle,
        &itemRect );
```

If theText **has a length of 0 we put the string "**<No Text>**" in the static text field and set** gHasText **to** false**:**

```
    if ( *theText == 0 )
    {
        SetIText( itemHandle, kNoTextString );
        gHasText = false;
    }
```

Otherwise, we put the text in the static text field and set gHasText **to** true**:**

```
    else
    {
        SetIText(itemHandle, theText);
        gHasText = true;
    }
}
```

DoReverseEvent() **is called to handle a reverse Apple event.** DoReverseEvent() **calls** DoReverse() **to reverse the text in the dialog's static text field and then returns** noErr**:**

```
/****************** DoReverseEvent *********************/

pascal OSErr   DoReverseEvent( AppleEvent *event, AppleEvent *reply,
        long refcon )
{
    DoReverse();

    return noErr;
}
```

You might be wondering why DoReverseEvent() does nothing but call DoReverse(). We could easily have embedded the DoReverse() code inside DoReverseEvent(), but we wanted this code to match as closely as possible the code in the third part of this chapter. Each of our three custom Apple events has an associated bottleneck routine that manages the text in the static text field. These routines (DoSetText(), DoReverse(), ReverseString(), and DoGetText()) won't change a bit when we consider the Object Model later in the chapter.

If any text is in the dialog's static text field, DoReverse() will retrieve it, reverse it in place, then place it back in the static text field:

```
/***************** DoReverse *******************/

void  DoReverse( void )
{
    Str255        theText;
    short         itemType;
    Handle        itemHandle;
    Rect          itemRect;

    if ( gHasText )
    {
        GetDItem(gServerDialog, iDisplayText, &itemType, &itemHandle,
                &itemRect);
        GetIText(itemHandle, theText);

        ReverseString( theText );
        SetIText(itemHandle, theText);
    }
}
```

ReverseString() reverses a pascal string in place:

```
/***************** ReverseString *******************/

void  ReverseString( Str255 string )
{
    char  c;
    short i, j;

    for ( i=1, j=string[0]; i<j; i++, j- )
    {
        c = string[ i ];
        string[ i ] = string[ j ];
        string[ j ] = c;
```

    }
}

      DoGetTextEvent() is called whenever a Get Text Apple event is received. DoGetTextEvent() calls DoGetText() to retrieve the text from the dialog's static text field and then calls AEPutParamPtr() to add a keyDirectObject parameter containing the text to the reply Apple event:

```
/***************** DoGetTextEvent *******************/

pascal OSErr      DoGetTextEvent( AppleEvent *event, AppleEvent
                                    *reply, long refcon )
{
   Str255          theText;

   DoGetText( theText );

   return AEPutParamPtr( reply, keyDirectObject, typeChar,
        (Ptr)(&(theText[ 1 ])), theText[ 0 ] );
}
```

      Notice that we are returning the error code returned by AEPutParamPtr(), rather than testing it here and putting up an error dialog if there's a problem. We'll let ReverClient report the problem on its end.

> As you work out the relationship between your client and server, you'll have to decide when it's appropriate for the server to talk to the user and when that responsibility lies with the client.

      DoGetText() retrieves the text from the dialog's static text item. If gHasText is false, we can't just retrieve the text in the static text field because the string "<No Text>" is there. Instead, we just set the string's length byte to 0:

```
/***************** DoGetText *******************/

void DoGetText( Str255 string )
{
   short       itemType;
   Handle         itemHandle;
   Rect        itemRect;

   if ( gHasText )
   {
```

```
        GetDItem(gServerDialog, iDisplayText, &itemType, &itemHandle,
            &itemRect);
        GetIText(itemHandle, string);
    }
    else
        string[ 0 ] = 0;
}
```

CreateDialog() **loads the** DLOG **resource, makes the window visible and the current port, then sets** gHasText **to** false **to indicate that ReverServer has no text at the moment:**

```
/****************** CreateDialog *********************/

void  CreateDialog( void )
{
    gServerDialog = GetNewDialog( kServerDLOGid, NULL, kMoveToFront );

    if ( gServerDialog == NULL )
        DoError( "\pCouldn't load the DLOG resource..." );

    ShowWindow( gServerDialog );
    SetPort( gServerDialog );

    gHasText = false;
}
```

EventLoop() **is like the one in ReverClient, but without the call to** TEIdle() **(since the ReverServer dialog doesn't have an editable text field):**

```
/***************************** EventLoop ********/

void  EventLoop( void )
{
    EventRecord      event;

    gDone = false;
    while ( gDone == false )
    {
        if ( WaitNextEvent( everyEvent, &event, kSleep, NULL ) )
            DoEvent( &event );
    }
}
```

DoEvent() **is pretty standard, with one exception. When we detect the** kHighLevelEvent, **we pass the event on to** AEProcessAppleEvent():

```
/********************************* DoEvent    */

void  DoEvent( EventRecord *eventPtr )
{
   char      theChar;

   switch ( eventPtr->what )
   {
      case mouseDown:
         HandleMouseDown( eventPtr );
         break;
      case keyDown:
      case autoKey:
         theChar = eventPtr->message & charCodeMask;
         if ( (eventPtr->modifiers & cmdKey) != 0 )
            HandleMenuChoice( MenuKey( theChar ) );
         break;
      case updateEvt:
         DoUpdate( eventPtr );
         break;
      case kHighLevelEvent:
         AEProcessAppleEvent( eventPtr );
         break;
   }
}
```

....

Important! If you're going to send or receive high-level events, you *must* set the `HighLevelEventAware` bit in your application's 'SIZE' resource.

....

`HandleMouseDown()`, `HandleMenuChoice()`, `HandleAppleChoice()`, **and** `HandleFileChoice()` **are all the same as their ReverClient counterparts:**

```
/********************************* HandleMouseDown */

void  HandleMouseDown( EventRecord *eventPtr )
{
   WindowPtr     window;
   short         thePart;
   long          menuChoice;

   thePart = FindWindow( eventPtr->where, &window );

   switch ( thePart )
   {
```

```
         case inMenuBar:
            menuChoice = MenuSelect( eventPtr->where );
            HandleMenuChoice( menuChoice );
            break;
         case inSysWindow:
            SystemClick( eventPtr, window );
            break;
         case inContent:
            SelectWindow( window );
            break;
         case inDrag:
            DragWindow( window, eventPtr->where, &screenBits.bounds );
            break;
      }
}


/***************** HandleMenuChoice *********************/

void  HandleMenuChoice( long menuChoice )
{
   short menu;
   short item;

   if ( menuChoice != 0 )
   {
      menu = HiWord( menuChoice );
      item = LoWord( menuChoice );

      switch ( menu )
      {
         case mApple:
            HandleAppleChoice( item );
            break;
         case mFile:
            HandleFileChoice( item );
            break;
      }
      HiliteMenu( 0 );
   }
}


/***************** HandleAppleChoice *********************/

void  HandleAppleChoice( short item )
{
   MenuHandle  appleMenu;
   Str255      accName;
```

```
   short    accNumber;

   switch ( item )
   {
      case iAbout:
         NoteAlert( kAboutALRTid, NULL );
         break;
      default:
         appleMenu = GetMHandle( mApple );
         GetItem( appleMenu, item, accName );
         accNumber = OpenDeskAcc( accName );
         break;
   }
}


/***************** HandleFileChoice **********************/

void  HandleFileChoice( short item )
{
   switch ( item )
   {
      case iQuit:
         gDone = true;
         break;
   }
}
```

In response to an update event, `DoUpdate()` **calls** `DrawDialog()` **to ask the Dialog Manager to update the contents of the dialog. Even though this dialog is technically a modeless dialog, we're not handling any standard dialog events, so this approach will do just fine:**

```
/********************************** DoUpdate    */

void  DoUpdate( EventRecord *eventPtr )
{
   WindowPtr   window;

   window = (WindowPtr)eventPtr->message;

   BeginUpdate(window);
   DrawDialog(window);
   EndUpdate(window);
}
```

`DoError()` **is just like the version in ReverClient:**

```
/***************** DoError ******************/

void  DoError( Str255 errorString )
{
   ParamText( errorString, "\p", "\p", "\p" );

   StopAlert( kErrorALRTid, kNilFilterProc );

   ExitToShell();
}
```

If you're experimenting with the user interaction routines, you might add a call to AEInteractWithUser() before your call to StopAlert(). A better way to play might be to add an Interact with User... item to the client's File menu. When the user selects Interact with User..., have the client create an Apple event (you'll have to design a new one) and send it to the server. When the server gets the event, have the handler call AEInteractWithUser() and then put up an alert or dialog once the server comes to the front.

PART 2: OSA

PROVIDING SCRIPTING SUPPORT

With what you've learned so far, you can do a lot with Apple events. You've learned the steps involved in constructing and sending an Apple event:

- Build an AEAddressDesc descriptor that tells the Apple Event Manager who to send the event to.

- Pass the suite code, event ID, and AEAddressDesc to AECreateAppleEvent() to create the basic AppleEvent.

- Call the appropriate AEPutxxx() routines to add whatever attributes and parameters your event calls for.

- Call AESend() to send the event. At your request, you may receive a reply event. If so, call the appropriate AEGetxxx() routines to retrieve the attributes and parameters you need from the reply.

- Somewhere along the way, call AEDisposeDesc() to dispose of the descriptors you've allocated.

On the flip side, you've also learned how to write and install the Apple event handlers that are called when an application receives an Apple event. Your handler's job is to call the appropriate `AEGetxxx()` routines to retrieve the attributes and parameters it needs from the event. The attributes provide administrative information about the event (such as the event's suite and ID), while the parameters contain the event's data.

Your handler should process the event's data as called for by the event. For example, ReverServer's Set Text handler updated the static text field in its dialog, while the Get Text handler retrieved the text from the dialog, adding it to a parameter in the reply event. When your handler exits, the reply event passed to it will be returned to the event's originator, if requested.

Finally, you've learned that your server has to check in with the Apple Event Manager before it attempts to interact with the user. Be sure you understand how to use routines like `AEInteractWithUser()` and `AESetInteractionAllowed()`.

Adding the 'aete' Resource

There's one more issue to discuss before we move on to the Object Model. You've already seen ReverServer handle Apple events sent to it by another application (ReverClient). Thanks to the addition of a single resource, ReverServer can also respond to events generated by an OSA-compatible scripting language such as AppleScript.

The `'aete'` resource describes the Apple events supported by your application to the scripting universe. In this section, we'll walk through ReverServer's `'aete'` resource and then test the resource by using an AppleScript script.

> Even though you *can* edit your `'aete'` resources using ResEdit, the `'aete'` editor in Resorcerer can't be beat. If your company plans on creating scriptable applications, see if they'll buy a copy of Resorcerer for you. The cost is $256, and this editor is worth every penny! Resorcerer can be ordered directly from Mathemaesthetics; the number is (303) 440-0707.

If you have a copy of Resorcerer, fire it up. If you don't have a copy, follow along as best you can using ResEdit. Figure 2.8 shows the main resource editing window. In the Types: column, click on `aete`. A list of `'aete'` resources will appear, containing a single `'aete'` with a resource

ID of 0. Double-click on the single 'aete' resource that appears. An 'aete' editing window will appear, listing the entire 'aete' resource.

FIGURE 2.8

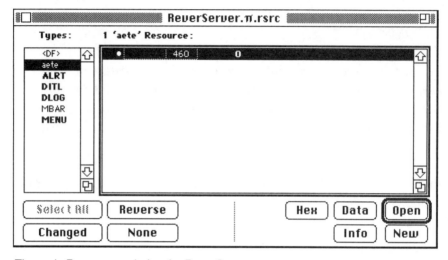

The main Resorcerer window for ReverServer.π.rsrc.

Scroll through the entire resource. Try to get a feel for the different fields that make up the resource. The first three fields are listed in Figure 2.9. Most likely, you won't change them.

FIGURE 2.9

The first three fields in the 'aete' resource.

> The language code specifies the language in which scripts will be written. Your 'aete' resource ID should match this setting. Here, both are set to 0.

Immediately following the first three fields is a cluster of fields for each suite you support. You'll always support the Required suite. The Required suite's fields are shown in Figure 2.10. Notice that there's not much information here—and intentionally so. When you add a suite description to the `'aete'` resource, you only describe the additions and changes you've made to the suite. Since we'll be supporting the Required suite as is, we just added the suite without making any changes to any of its fields.

FIGURE 2.10

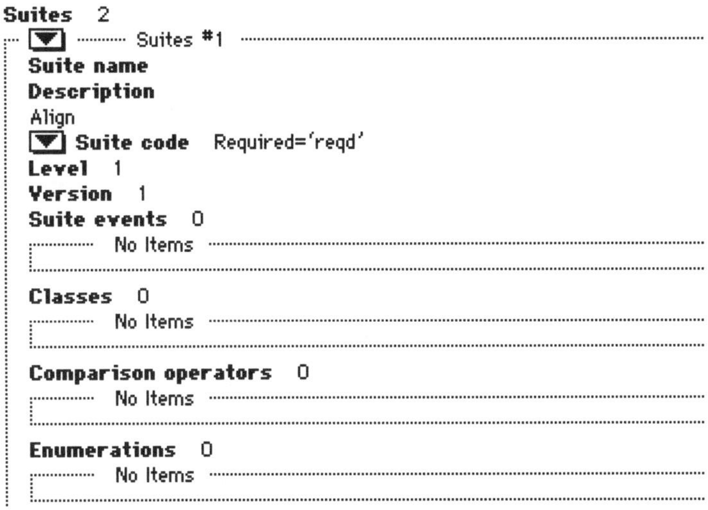

```
Suites   2
··· ▼ ········· Suites #1 ·································································
   Suite name
   Description
   Align
      ▼ Suite code   Required='reqd'
   Level   1
   Version   1
   Suite events   0
     ············· No Items ·····················································

   Classes   0
     ············· No Items ·····················································

   Comparison operators   0
     ············· No Items ·····················································

   Enumerations   0
     ············· No Items ·····················································
```

The fields associated with the required suite.

Before we move on, let's take a quick look at how you add a new suite to an `'aete'` resource in Resorcerer. Select New Resource from the Resource menu. A new `'aete'` resource will appear in the list, and an `'aete'` resource editing window will appear with the three fields shown in Figure 2.9.

Now, drag the arrow in the upper left corner of the window downward. As you drag the arrow, a line will appear. Keep dragging until the line appears right in the middle of the Suites box, as shown in Figure 2.11.

Click the New button in the window's lower left corner. A set of suite fields will appear, and the Suites field will change from 0 to 1. Notice that the Suite code field lists the code for the Required suite. When you support the Required suite with no changes, your suite fields should look just like this.

FIGURE 2.11

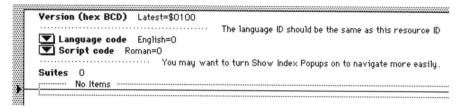

Drag the line down to the Suites field and then click the New button.

Let's get back to 'aete' 0. In addition to the Required suite, ReverServer also supports our custom Text Server suite. We added a new suite in the same way we added the Required suite fields. This time, we filled out all the fields to completely describe the three events in the Text Server suite. Figure 2.12 shows the first few fields. Notice that the Suite code was set to 'Tsrv'.

FIGURE 2.12

```
·············· Suites #2 ··········································
  Suite name   "Text Server"
  Description    "The SetString, ReverseString, and GetString Apple events."
  Align
   ▼ Suite code   'Tsrv'
  Level  1
  Version  1
  Suite events   3
```

The first few fields in the second suite.

Figure 2.13 shows the fields that correspond to the Set Text event. The Event name field is critical. This field gives your event a name, a verb that can be used by a scripting language. When you want to trigger this event from a script, you use the verb SetString, followed by a single parameter, a text string (we'll get to an example soon).

Notice that the Event ID for this event is 'SETT' and that we won't send a reply when we receive this event. Notice also that the Direct parameter preferred type is set to TEXT, indicating that the parameter marked by the keyDirectObject keyword is a text string. The Parameters field is somewhat misleading. It should read Additional parameters, since we've already indicated that SetString takes a direct parameter. If you wanted to add an additional parameter you would drag a line to the middle of the No Items box and click the New button.

FIGURE 2.13

```
┌─────── Suite events #1 ──────────────────────────────────────────────────┐
│  Event name    "SetString"                                               │
│  Description    "Sends the text string to ReverServer..."                │
│  Align                                                                    │
│  ▼ Event class code   'Tsrv'                                             │
│  Event ID   'SETT'                                                        │
│  ▼ Reply type   None='null'                                             │
│  Reply description    "No reply."                                        │
│     15. Reply is optional   On                                           │
│     14. Reply must be list of Items   Off                                │
│     13. Enumerated   Off                                                  │
│   1-12. Reserved   0                                                      │
│      0. Non-verb event   Off                                             │
│  ▼ Direct parameter preferred type   Characters='TEXT'                  │
│  Direct parameter comment    "The string to be passed to ReverServer..." │
│     15. Direct parameter is optional   Off                               │
│     14. Direct parameter is list of items   Off                          │
│     13. Enumerated   Off                                                  │
│     12. Changes state   Off                                              │
│   0-11. Reserved   0                                                      │
│  Parameters   0                                                          │
│  ..........................  (order is significant when parameters are listed without keywords) │
│  ┌──── No Items ──────────────────────────────────────────────────────── │
└───────────────────────────────────────────────────────────────────────── ┘
```

The fields that correspond to the Set Text event.

Figure 2.14 shows the fields for the reverse event. The verb for this event is `ReverString`, and the `Event ID` is `'RVRS'`. When we receive a reverse event, we won't send a reply, and the reverse event has no parameters at all.

FIGURE 2.14

```
┌─────── Suite events #2 ──────────────────────────────────────────────────┐
│  Event name    "ReverString"                                             │
│  Description    "Reverses the text string"                               │
│  Align                                                                    │
│  ▼ Event class code   'Tsrv'                                            │
│  Event ID   'RVRS'                                                        │
│  ▼ Reply type   None='null'                                             │
│  Reply description    "No reply."                                        │
│     15. Reply is optional   On                                           │
│     14. Reply must be list of Items   Off                                │
│     13. Enumerated   Off                                                  │
│   1-12. Reserved   0                                                      │
│      0. Non-verb event   Off                                             │
│  ▼ Direct parameter preferred type   None='null'                        │
│  Direct parameter comment    "No Direct Parameter..."                    │
│     15. Direct parameter is optional   On                                │
│     14. Direct parameter is list of items   Off                          │
│     13. Enumerated   Off                                                  │
│     12. Changes state   Off                                              │
│   0-11. Reserved   0                                                      │
│  Parameters   0                                                          │
│  ..........................  (order is significant when parameters are listed without keywords) │
│  ┌──── No Items ──────────────────────────────────────────────────────── │
└───────────────────────────────────────────────────────────────────────── ┘
```

The fields that correspond to the reverse event.

Figure 2.15 shows the fields for the Get Text event. The verb for this event is GetString, and the Event ID is 'GETT'. The reply will take the form of an Apple event and the reply is *not* optional. The event takes a single parameter, the direct parameter, which is a text string.

FIGURE 2.15

```
·········· Suite events #3 ·································································
 Event name    "GetString"
 Description    "Retrieves the text string from ReverServer..."
 Align
    ▼ Event class code    'Tsrv'
 Event ID    'GETT'
    ▼ Reply type    Apple event='AEVT'
 Reply description
    15. Reply is optional    Off
    14. Reply must be list of Items    Off
    13. Enumerated    Off
  1-12. Reserved    0
    0. Non-verb event    Off
    ▼ Direct parameter preferred type    Characters='TEXT'
 Direct parameter comment    "The text string from ReverServer..."
    15. Direct parameter is optional    Off
    14. Direct parameter is list of items    Off
    13. Enumerated    Off
    12. Changes state    Off
  0-11. Reserved    0
 Parameters    0
 ························    (order is significant when parameters are listed without keywords)
 ·········· No Items ····························································
```

The fields that correspond to the Get Text event.

Finally, the resource ends up with fields that allow you to add Classes, Comparison operators, and Enumerations (**Figure 2.16**). We'll discuss these fields once we get into the Object Model.

FIGURE 2.16

```
 Classes    0
 ·········· No Items ····································
 
 Comparison operators    0
 ·········· No Items ····································
 
 Enumerations    0
 ·········· No Items ····································
```

The final three fields.

Testing the 'aete' Resource

Now, let's take our `aete` resource for a spin. Before you start, be sure that the AppleScript extension is in place. This test will not work without AppleScript up and running.

> The AppleScript extension is called a *scripting component*. A scripting component takes the commands from a script and translates it into the Apple events specified by the script. When you specify that some portion of a script is to be sent to a specific application, the scripting component reads that application's `aete` resource to aid in translating that portion of the script.

Launch ReverServer and then start up the application Script Editor (AppleScript and the Script Editor are both on the CD at the back of the book). Inside the Script Editor, select Open Dictionary... from the File menu. When prompted for a file to open, find and select ReverServer. A window will appear, listing all the events supported by ReverServer. Click on each event to see a description of the event as culled from the `aete` resource.

Now, type this script in the Script Editor's script window and click the Run button:

```
tell application "ReverServer"
   SetString "Reverse Me!!"
end tell
```

The string "Reverse Me!!" should appear in the ReverServer window. Edit the script so that it looks like this:

```
tell application "ReverServer"
   ReverString
end tell
```

Click the Run button. The string in the ReverServer window should reverse itself. Finally, change the script one more time to look like this:

```
tell application "ReverServer"
   GetString
end tell
```

Then, press the Run button again. A result window will appear showing the string "!!eM esreveR". Feel free to launch ReverClient and alternate sending events from both your scripts and ReverClient.

Congratulations. You've mastered your first scriptable application!

PART 3: THE OBJECT MODEL

WORKING WITH REGISTRY OBJECTS AND PROPERTIES

At this point, you've discovered so much about Apple events. You've learned all about descriptors—the heart and soul of every Apple event. You know that there are four basic descriptor types—the `AEDesc`, `AEDescList`, `AERecord`, and `AppleEvent`—and that each starts with a 4-byte `descriptorType` field, followed by a `dataHandle` that leads to the rest of the descriptor.

You've learned that Apple events are really `AERecord`s filled with keyword-specified attribute and parameter descriptors. With luck, you've had a chance to look through the *Apple Event Registry*, and you've seen some of the Apple events that you'll be using. For each event, the Registry lists the event class, ID, and the event's parameters. Some of the parameters are required, and some are optional. When you process an event (via an Apple event handler), you *must* retrieve all the required parameters. Depending on your situation, you might also want to retrieve the optional parameters.

One thing you might have noticed in the Registry is the term *object specifier*. As its name implies, an object specifier describes an object or a set of objects. For example, an object specifier might refer to a window in your program, a paragraph of text in the window, or perhaps a single character within the paragraph. You might use an object specifier to represent a list of files or a group of spreadsheet cells.

An object specifier can also represent a *property*. For example, an object specifier might describe the color of some text or the location of a window.

Confused about the difference between an object and a property? Think about deleting the item in question. If you can delete it (or dispose of it), it's an object. You can delete a character, but you can't delete a character's color or a window's location. Even though you can't delete a property, a property can have an "empty" value. For example, the formula for a cell in a spreadsheet is a property of that cell; the formula can be empty, however.

> It's also interesting to note that a property can contain a value that could be an object. The formula property for the cell just mentioned could be considered a text object.

The vast majority of the events described in the Registry expect you to understand how to build an object specifier, add it to an Apple event, and, on the flip side, how to resolve an object specifier to the object or property it references. The remainder of this chapter will teach you how to do just that. If you don't know much about object programming, relax. Although the Object Model is very much object oriented, you'll have no problem implementing it using languages like C or Pascal.

In the first half of this chapter, we have frequently referred to the *Apple Event Registry,* which you may have had a chance to look through to familiarize yourself with various suites and events. If you don't have a copy of the Registry as yet, go get one (it's on the developer CDs and the AppleScript Developer's Toolkit CD, or you can buy a copy from APDA). If you can't get hold of a copy, grab the yellow pages off your shelf and riffle the pages occasionally (just to keep your fingers in shape until the genuine article arrives).

The Registry starts with an introduction and then proceeds with a series of chapters, each of which focuses on a different Apple event suite. Chapter 2 describes the Required suite; Chapter 3, the Core suite; Chapter 4, the Text suite; and so on.

Each chapter begins with a list of the events in the particular suite, followed by a detailed description of each event. Next are some pages that go into detail on the object classes defined within the suite. Each object class description includes an overview of all of the object's properties, as well as that object's place in the Registry's overall inheritance hierarchy.

If you are not an object programmer, think of the Registry's object classes as a series of predefined constants, each of which represents an object, like a window (the constant cWindow) or a character (the constant cChar). If you want to give the outside world access to your program's windows, chances are you'll make use of the cWindow constant.

Each Registry object class has a set of corresponding property constants. For example, the cChar object class has properties like pColor and pFont, which represent a character's color and font.

If you *are* an object programmer, the Registry's object classes will most likely correspond directly to objects in your application framework.

The inheritance hierarchy defined in the Registry describes the inheritance relationships you'll be working with.

If you are not an object programmer, you can ignore the inheritance hierarchy. When you work with an object specifier, your job is to map the object and property constants to the appropriate data structures in your program.

> When you do secure a copy of the Registry, remember that it can definitely be overwhelming when you first get into it. Start by paging through it to familiarize yourself with the events, objects, and properties that make up each suite. Don't get hung up on the details.

THE CONTAINMENT HIERARCHY

Once you have a basic handle on the Registry, you need to learn how to use the Registry's objects and properties to build object specifiers. To build an object specifier, you must understand the concept of *containment*.

Take a look at this script fragment:

```
the third word in the front window
```

This bit of script represents a single object, a word that happens to be inside a window. More specifically, the word is the third word *contained* in the frontmost window.

Here's another example:

```
the fifth character in the second word in the window named "Untitled"
```

This example refers to a single character that is contained in a word that is, in turn, contained in a window. Figure 2.17 represents this relationship graphically as a containment chain. Notice that there is a separate box for each object in the chain. The top half of each box is the object class. The bottom half of each box tells you how to locate the object in its container by using one of a series of eight "form" keywords.

For example, the keyword `formAbsolutePosition` tells you what position the object is in in its container, either as an offset from the beginning or end of the container or using one of the keywords `kAEFirst`, `kAEMiddle`, `kAELast`, `kAEAny`, or `kAEAll`. In this case, the `cChar` is the fifth character in its container. As you can see by the arrow, the `cChar` is "in" the `cWord`. That is, the `cWord` is the `cChar`'s container.

FIGURE 2.17

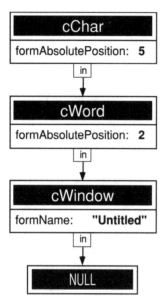

An object specifier showing the fifth character in the second word in the window named "Untitled".

Moving down the containment chain, you can see that the cWord is the second word in its container, which is a cWindow. The cWindow has a NULL descriptor as its container. Since every object has to have a container, a NULL descriptor is the proper way to say that an object is the outermost container.

You may have noticed that the cWindow used the formName keyword instead of formAbsolutePosition. formName allows you to specify an object by name instead of by position. In this example, we've specified a window named "Untitled". (We'll describe the six other "form" keywords later in the chapter.)

A Quick Experiment

Before we get into the details of building an object specifier, let's use the Scriptable Text Editor for a quick experiment. (You'll find the Scriptable Text Editor on the CD that accompanies this book.)

Start up the Scriptable Text Editor and, when the untitled window appears, type in the following text:

```
Here's some sample text for you to work with...
```

Now, launch the Script Editor you used earlier in the chapter and enter the following script:

```
tell application "Scriptable Text Editor"
   the fourth character in the second word in the front window
end tell
```

Run the script by clicking on the Run button. The result window should appear, showing the single character "e". Edit the script, asking for the font property:

```
tell application "Scriptable Text Editor"
   the font of the fourth character in the second word in the front
      window
end tell
```

Run the script again. This time, the string "Geneva" will appear in the result window. Go back into the Scriptable Text Editor, double-click on the second word ("some") and change its font to Chicago.

Go back to the Script Editor and run the script again. The string "Chicago" will now appear in the result window. Once again, edit the script, but change the property "font" to "color":

```
tell application "Scriptable Text Editor"
   the color of the fourth character in the second word in the front
      window
end tell
```

Run the script again. This time, an Execution Error window will appear with the error message "Scriptable Text Editor got an error: No such property". Let's take a look at this experiment from an object specifier viewpoint.

Each time you ran your script, a Get Data Apple event was created. If you look up the Get Data Apple event in the Registry, you'll see that it has one required parameter, an object specifier that tells the receiving application what data is being requested. In the first script, the object specifier described a single character (the fourth character in the second word in the front window). In the remainder of the scripts, the object specifier described a property of this character.

In the last script, you saw what happens when the receiving application can't make sense of your object specifier. In this case, the Scriptable Text Editor didn't support the color property.

Although these scripts won't show you how to create object specifiers, they should give you a better sense of the role they play. As you read through the next few sections, try out each of the script fragments you encounter. Your goal is to be able to map AppleScript script fragments to the appropriate object specifier forms. Once you can do that, you'll be able to build your own object specifiers from scratch.

BUILDING AN OBJECT SPECIFIER

The Apple Event Manager provides a set of routines that simplify the process of working with object specifiers. Together, these routines are known as the *Object Support Library (OSL)*. The OSL provides routines that build an object specifier and, on the flip side, that also resolve an object specifier into the object or property it specifies.

The first OSL routine you'll call is `AEObjectInit()`:

```
pascal OSErr AEObjectInit();
```

As its name implies, `AEObjectInit()` initializes the OSL. `AEObjectInit()` returns three possible error codes. As usual, `noErr` indicates that all is well, `memFullErr` tells you that there isn't enough room in the current heap to initialize the OSL, and `errAENewerVersion` tells you that the Apple Event Manager on this machine is out-of-date (i.e., it doesn't support the OSL yet).

Once you've successfully initialized the OSL, you're ready to build your object specifier. You can build one by hand, but your best bet is to call `CreateObjSpecifier()`:

```
pascal OSErr CreateObjSpecifier( DescType desiredClass,
        AEDesc *theContainer, DescType keyForm,
        AEDesc *keyData, Boolean disposeInputs,
        AEDesc *objSpecifier);
```

> We'll postpone our discussion of each of the `CreateObjSpecifier()` parameters for a few pages. First, let's consider the structure of an object specifier. Then, we can see how the parameters are used to build this structure.

`CreateObjSpecifier()` creates an `AERecord`. If you think back to the beginning of the chapter, you'll remember that an `AERecord` is normally created by calling `AECreateList()`, that it has a `descriptorType` field with a value of `typeAERecord`, and that its `dataHandle` points to a block of keyword-specified descriptors.

When you call `CreateObjSpecifier()`, you get your basic `AERecord`, with two small differences. First, when it creates the `AERecord`, `CreateObjSpecifier()` places the value `typeObjectSpecifier` in the `descriptorType` field (instead of the value `typeAERecord`). Second, `CreateObjSpecifier()` turns its parameters into four descriptors and adds them to the object specifier `AERecord`. These four keyword-specified descriptors completely describe the object and also connect the object to its container.

The Four Object Specifier Descriptors

The four descriptors normally found in an object specifier correspond to the keywords `keyAEDesiredClass`, `keyAEContainer`, `keyAEKeyForm`, and `keyAEKeyData`. `keyAEDesiredClass` tells you the object specifier class or type. `keyAEContainer` is the object's container. `keyAEKeyForm` and `keyAEKeyData` provide extra information about the object and are where the "form" keywords (like `formName` and `formAbsolutePosition` in Figure 2.17) come into the picture.

Remember, you won't add these descriptors to the object specifier yourself. `CreateObjSpecifier()` will build them based on its parameters (we'll get to these parameters in a bit).

Here are some details on the four descriptors found in every object specifier—`keyAEDesiredClass`, `keyAEContainer`, `keyAEKeyForm`, and `keyAEKeyData`.

keyAEDesiredClass

This descriptor describes the object's class or type (most likely, a constant from `<AERegistry.h>`, like `cWindow`, `cChar`, or `cProperty`). The `descriptorType` field is set to `typeType` to indicate that the `dataHandle` field will point to a 4-byte type code. Each of the Registry class constants has a corresponding 4-byte type code. For example, if the `keyAEDesiredClass` is `cWindow`, the `dataHandle` field will point to a master pointer that will point to the 4-byte code `'cwin'` (Figure 2.18).

> If you work with objects that are not in the Registry, then you'll have to design your own codes. Be sure to register them with Apple if you want them added to the Registry.

FIGURE 2.18

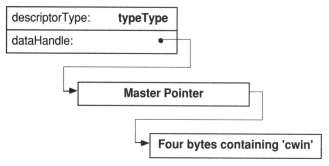

| descriptorType: | **typeType** |
| dataHandle: | ● |

Master Pointer

Four bytes containing 'cwin'

A sample keyAEDesiredClass descriptor.

keyAEContainer

This descriptor describes the object's container. The `keyAEContainer` descriptor's `descriptorType` field has four possible values:

- `typeObjectSpecifier`—In this case, the `keyAEContainer` descriptor is another object specifier, with its own `keyAEDesiredClass`, `keyAEContainer`, `keyAEKeyForm`, and `keyAEKeyData` descriptors. More specifically, this object descriptor is the container of the current object.

  This mechanism is much like the pointers used to hook together a linked list. An object specifier has a container that is also an object specifier. That object specifier has a container that is also an object specifier, and so on. This chain of specifiers will end with a `keyAEContainer` whose `descriptorType` field is set to `typeNull`.

- `typeNull`—If the `keyAEContainer` descriptor has a type of `typeNull`, this object is the top object in the containment hierarchy. If the `descriptorType` is `typeNull`, the `dataHandle` is NULL.

  The `typeNull` container at the top of the containment hierarchy typically represents the application object.

- `typeCurrentContainer`—When an object's container is marked as `typeCurrentContainer`, the object is being used to define a range. For example, the phrase "words 5 through 10 of the front window" defines a range of words, starting with "word 5" and ending with "word 10". (For more info, check out the form keyword `formRange`, given later in the chapter.)

- `typeObjectBeingExamined`—When an object's container is marked as `typeObjectBeingExamined`, the object specifier is part of a test. For example, the phrase "the first word of front window whose font is "Geneva"" involves testing each word in the front window until a word with the font "Geneva" is found. (To learn more about tests and object specifiers, check out the form keyword `formTest`, described later in the chapter.)

keyAEKeyForm and keyAEKeyData

These two descriptors together tell you how to find the current object in its container. Earlier (in Figure 2.17), you got a brief glimpse of the key-forms `formAbsolutePosition` ("the third character") and `formName` ("the window named "Untitled"").

The `keyAEKeyForm` descriptor (Figure 2.19) is a standard `AEDesc`, with a `descriptorType` of `typeEnumerated` and a `dataHandle` that points to a master pointer that points to one of the eight 4-byte form codes—`formPropertyID`, `formName`, `formUniqueID`, `formAbsolutePosition`, `formRelativePosition`, `formTest`, `formWhose`, or `formRange`. The contents of the `keyAEKeyData` descriptor depends on which form code is used.

FIGURE 2.19

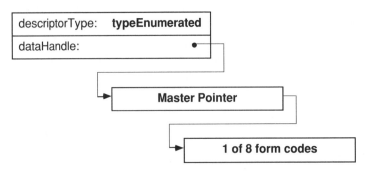

The keyAEKeyForm descriptor.

The Eight Form Codes

formPropertyID

This form tells you that the object specifies a property. The `keyAEKeyData`'s `descriptorType` field is set to `typeType`, and its `dataHandle` field points to a 4-byte property code. For example, the pColor property corresponds to the code 'colr'. You can find the Registry's 4-byte property codes in the file <AERegistry.h>.

formName

This form ties a name to the object. The keyAEKeyData's descriptorType field is set to typeChar (or some other text type). The keyAEKeyData's dataHandle field points to the object's name. This form comes up when an object specifier refers to a named object, like "the window named "Untitled"".

formUniqueID

This form ties an ID to your object. The keyAEKeyData's descriptorType field can be any type that makes sense to your application. The dataHandle field points to a value that serves as a unique ID, differentiating this object from any others. Typically, the formUniqueID is an integral value, although it doesn't have to be.

formAbsolutePosition

If the keyAEKeyData's descriptorType is set to typeLongInteger, the dataHandle points to an offset from the beginning (if positive) or the end (if negative) of the container. For example, this would be the case if you referred to the "third character in the front window".

If the keyAEKeyData's descriptorType is set to typeAbsoluteOrdinal, the dataHandle refers to one of the contants kAEFirst, kAEMiddle, kAELast, kAEAny, or kAEAll.

> The routine CreateOffsetDescriptor() takes a long offset and turns it into a descriptor of type typeLongInteger:
>
> ```
> pascal OSErr CreateOffsetDescriptor( long theOffset,
>                 AEDesc *theDescriptor );
> ```
> You can use CreateOffsetDescriptor() to create your keyAEKeyData descriptor if an offset is called for.

formRelativePosition

This form is used to specify that the object is either the next or the previous of its type in the container. For example, this form comes up in the phrase "the next word in the front window", which, of course, makes sense only if you've already referred to a word in the front window. The keyAEKeyData's descriptorType field is set to typeEnumerated. The dataHandle points to one of the two constants kAENext or kAEPrevious.

formRange

This form indicates that the object specifier is a *range descriptor record*, and it specifies a range of objects. For example, you might have a range descriptor record that defines the object "word 1 through 5 of the front window". You won't build one of these range specifiers by hand. Instead, you'll call `CreateRangeDescriptor()`:

```
pascal OSErr CreateRangeDescriptor( AEDesc *rangeStart,
            AEDesc *rangeStop, Boolean disposeInputs,
            AEDesc *theDescriptor );
```

`CreateRangeDescriptor()` takes two object specifiers as parameters, one that defines the first object in the range and one that defines the last object in the range. The third parameter is `true` if you want `CreateRangeDescriptor()` to dispose of the first two parameters once it is done building the range descriptor record. The fourth parameter is the range descriptor, which is just another form of object specifier.

The six forms we've covered so far can be used to create most of your object specifiers. As an example, Figure 2.20 shows the complete object specifier for the "the fifth character in the second word in the window named "Untitled"", first shown in Figure 2.13. The complete object specifier is actually made up of three object specifiers, one for "the fifth character", one for "the second word", and one for "the window named "Untitled"".

Notice that each of these object specifiers is composed of four descriptors, specified by the keywords `keyAEDesiredClass`, `keyAEKeyForm`, `keyAEKeyData`, and `keyAEContainer`. The object specifier for "the fifth character" tells you that it represents a character by using a `keyAEDesiredClass` of `cChar`. It tells you that it is the fifth character in its container by using the key-form `formAbsolutePosition` with the key-data 5. Finally, its container is itself an object specifier representing "the second word in the window named "Untitled"".

The object specifier for "the second word" uses a `keyAEDesiredClass` of `cWord`, a key-form of `formAbsolutePosition`, and the key-data 2. Its container is the object specifier for "the window named "Untitled"".

The object specifier for "the window named "Untitled"" uses a `keyAEDesiredClass` of `cWindow`, a key-form of `formName`, and the key-data of the string "Untitled". Note that this string is just a series of characters. It doesn't have a leading length byte and doesn't have a terminating '\0' byte. Since "the window named "Untitled"" is the outermost container, its container is a simple NULL descriptor (representing the application object).

formTest and formWhose

These two forms are used in building slightly more sophisticated object specifiers. They come into play when your object specifier involves some kind of test. For example, here's a script that tests to see whether the length of the first word in the front window is 4:

```
if the length of the first word in front window is 4 then
    display dialog "Length is 4"
end if
```

In this case, you're making a comparison test, comparing "the length of the first word in the front window" to the value 4. Here's another example:

```
the first character in the front window whose font is "Geneva"
```

In this case, you're making a series of comparisons, stepping through each character in the front window until you find one whose font is "Geneva".

If your object specifier denotes a comparison test, then you'll use the form formTest. If your object specifier uses the whose form, indicating a test over a range of objects, then you'll use the form formWhose.

Unfortunately, creating formTest and formWhose descriptors and installing the special object counting functions that your program will need to support tests can take up a chapter all by themselves, and there's just not enough room in this book to examine them in detail. However, once you finish this chapter, you should have no problem reading the sections of *Inside Macintosh: Interapplication Communication* that bring these special forms to life.

You'll want to read about *comparison descriptor records* and *logical descriptor records*, as well as *object counting functions* and *object comparison functions*. All of these terms are all in the *Inside Macintosh: Interapplication Communication* index. You should also look up the routines CreateCompDescriptor() and CreateLogicalDescriptor().

Before you dive into testing, read the rest of this chapter, especially the parts on AEResolve() and object accessor routines. Once you understand these two topics, the sections on testing will make much more sense.

FIGURE 2.20

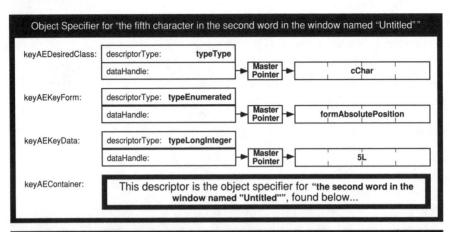

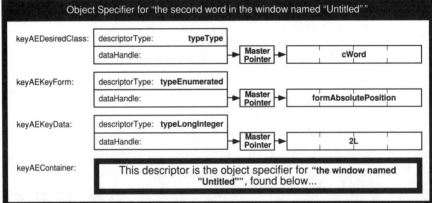

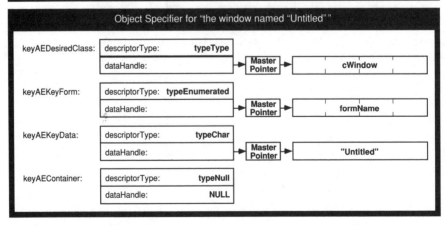

The object specifier for "the fifth character in the second word in the window named "Untitled"".

Calling CreateObjSpecifier()

Now that you have the basic architecture of the object specifier down pat, let's get back to the routine that creates them, `CreateObjSpecifier()`:

```
pascal OSErr CreateObjSpecifier( DescType desiredClass,
        AEDesc *theContainer, DescType keyForm,
        AEDesc *keyData, Boolean disposeInputs,
        AEDesc *objSpecifier);
```

Take a look at the first four parameters. Look familiar? `desiredClass` is a 4-byte object class (most likely, from the Registry). `cChar`, `cWord`, and `cWindow` make perfect sense as values for this parameter.

`theContainer` is either an object specifier or a `NULL` descriptor. If you were going to build the object specifier shown in Figure 2.20 ("the fifth character in the second word in the window named "Untitled""), you'd first build a `NULL` descriptor and then call `CreateObjSpecifier()` to create "the window named "Untitled"" object specifier, using the `NULL` descriptor as `theContainer`. You'd next take the result of this call, `objSpecifier`, and use it as the container when you create the object specifier for "the second word in the window named "Untitled"". Get the idea? You start with a `NULL` descriptor, use it as the outermost container, then keep calling `CreateObjSpecifier()` as you walk along the object containment chain.

The rest of the parameters are as follows: `keyForm` is one of the eight form constants. `keyData` is the `keyAEKeyData` descriptor. `disposeInputs` is `true` if you want `CreateObjSpecifier()` to dispose of the descriptors passed to it once it is done building the object specifier. Finally, `objSpecifier` is the completed object specifier.

ANOTHER EXAMPLE

You've just absorbed a tremendous amount of information. Take some time to reread the last few sections. Start up the Scriptable Text Editor and use the Script Editor to send a few Apple events to the Scriptable Text Editor. Remember to wrap your script inside a `tell` statement:

```
tell application "Scriptable Text Editor"
    — Put your commands here...
end tell
```

As you run your scripts, focus on the Scriptable Text Editor's object containment hierarchy. Try to retrieve objects like `characters`, `words`, and `paragraphs`. Use the Registry's Text suite as a guide, experimenting with the Text suite's objects and properties.

Once you understand the objects handled by the Scriptable Text Editor, take a look at the sample program GetData. You'll find it in the `Projects` folder. If it's not already running, start up the Scriptable Text Editor and type *at least* three words of text in the frontmost window. Now, double-click on the GetData application. An alert should appear, listing the font of the third word in the Scriptable Text Editor's front window.

> If this doesn't happen, check to make sure that the Scriptable Text Editor is still running and that there are at least three words in its frontmost window. You can double-check this by using the Script Editor to run this script:
>
> ```
> tell application "Scriptable Text Editor"
>       the font of the third word in front window
> end tell
> ```
>
> If all goes well, the font of the third word in the Scriptable Text Editor's front window should appear in the Script Editor's result window.

GetData uses the techniques we've just covered to build an object specifier that represents "the font of the third word in the front window," adds the object specifier as a parameter to a Get Data event addressed to the Scriptable Text Editor, sends the event, and displays the result pulled from the reply event.

Let's take a look at the source code.

The GetData Source Code

`GetData.c` starts with several include files. The first three contain the definitions you need to call `Gestalt()` and to access both the Apple Event Manager and the constants that make up the Registry:

```
#include <GestaltEqu.h>
#include <AppleEvents.h>
#include <AERegistry.h>
```

The next two include files give you access to the OSL constants and to routines like `CreateOffsetDescriptor()`:

```
#include <AEObjects.h>
#include <AEPackObject.h>
```

The routines and constants declared in `<AEObjects.h>` and `<AEPackObject.h>` are all part of the Object Support Library. The two files are divided by functionality. If you're writing a client or recordable server, you'll include `<AEPackObject.h>`, which includes everything you need to build object specifiers. If you're writing a server, you'll include `<AEObjects.h>`, which includes everything you need to resolve an object specifier to the object it refers to (we'll talk about resolving object specifiers later in the chapter).

Some development environments require you to include `<AEObjects.h>` even if your application doesn't resolve any object specifiers (as is the case in our current program, GetData). To find out what your development environment does, try to comment out the line.

```
#include <AEObjects.h>
```

in `GetData.c`.

Next come the GetData constants and function prototypes:

```
#define kErrorALRTid          128

#define kDisposeInputs        true

#define kScriptEditSignature  'quil'

#define kNilFilterProc        0L
#define kGestaltMask          1L

#define kNoIdleProc           nil
#define kNoFilterProc         nil
#define kMaxTextSize          255


/***************/
/* Functions */
/***************/

void    ToolboxInit( void );
void    AEInit( void );
void    DoObjectSpecifier( void );
void    DoGetData( AEDesc *objSpecifierPtr );
void    DoMessage( Str255 errorString );
```

```
void      Do2Message( Str255 string1, Str255 string2 );
void      DoError( Str255 errorString );
```

main() **initializes the Toolbox, checks to be sure that Apple events
are supported, then builds and sends the Get Data event:**

```
/****************************** main ********/

void  main( void )
{
   ToolboxInit();
   AEInit();

   DoObjectSpecifier();
}
```

Nothing is new here:

```
/***************** ToolboxInit ********************/

void  ToolboxInit( void )
{
   InitGraf( &qd.thePort );
   InitFonts();
   InitWindows();
   InitMenus();
   TEInit();
   InitDialogs( 0L );
   InitCursor();
}
```

**You saw the following routine in both the client and server sample
programs given earlier in the chapter:**

```
/****************************** AEInit ********/

void  AEInit( void )
{
   OSErr err;
   long  feature;

   err = Gestalt( gestaltAppleEventsAttr, &feature );

   if ( err != noErr )
      DoError( "\pError returned by Gestalt!" );

   if ( !( feature & ( kGestaltMask << gestaltAppleEventsPresent ) ) )
      DoError( "\pThis configuration does not support Apple events..." );
}
```

`DoObjectSpecifier()` starts by building an object specifier that represents "the font of the third word in the front window." We build this object specifier in three stages. First, we build the object specifier that represents "the front window." Next, we use that specifier as a container when we build the specifier that represents "the third word." Finally, we use that specifier as the container when we build the specifier that represents "the font property":

```
/****************************** DoObjectSpecifier *********/

void  DoObjectSpecifier( void )
{
   AEDesc      nullContainer = {typeNull, NULL},
            windObjSpecifier = {typeNull, NULL},
            wordObjSpecifier = {typeNull, NULL},
            fontPropSpecifier = {typeNull, NULL},
            offsetDesc = {typeNull, NULL},
            fontDesc = {typeNull, NULL};
   long     fontType = pFont;
   OSErr    err;
```

The object specifier for "the front window" uses a `keyAEDesiredClass` of `cWindow`, a `NULL` container, a `keyAEKeyForm` of `formAbsolutePosition`, and a `keyAEKeyData` of `1L` to indicate the first, or front window.

We create an offset descriptor record for use with the `formAbsolutePosition` key-form. An offset descriptor record is an `AEDesc` with a `descriptorType` of `typeLongInteger` and a `dataHandle` that points to a master pointer and then to a `long`. This is exactly what is required for the `keyAEKeyData` descriptor when the `keyAEKeyForm` is `formAbsolutePosition` (for a refresher, take a quick look back at Figure 2.20):

```
   err = CreateOffsetDescriptor( 1L, &offsetDesc );

   if ( err != noErr )
     DoError( "\pError creating offset descriptor..." );
```

Next, we call `CreateObjSpecifier()` to create "the front window" object specifier. We pass `cWindow` as the `keyAEDesiredClass`, `nullContainer` as the container, `formAbsolutePosition` as the key-form, and `offsetDesc` as the key-data. We ask `CreateObjSpecifier()` to dispose of the descriptors once it's done with them by passing in `kDisposeInputs`. The completed object specifier is returned in `windObjSpecifier`:

```
err = CreateObjSpecifier( cWindow, &nullContainer,
        formAbsolutePosition, &offsetDesc,
        kDisposeInputs, &windObjSpecifier );

if ( err != noErr )
  DoError( "\pError creating object specifier for 'Front
      Window'..." );
```

Now we repeat this process to create the object specifier for "the third word." This time, we use a value of 3L for the key-data that goes along with `formAbsolutePosition`:

```
err = CreateOffsetDescriptor( 3L, &offsetDesc );

if ( err != noErr )
  DoError( "\pError creating offset descriptor..." );
```

This call to `CreateObjSpecifier()` looks much the same as our last call. This time, we pass in a type of `cWord` instead of `cWindow`, and we pass in the object specifier we just finished creating as the container. The resulting object specifier is returned in `wordObjSpecifier`:

```
err = CreateObjSpecifier( cWord, &windObjSpecifier,
        formAbsolutePosition, &offsetDesc,
        kDisposeInputs, &wordObjSpecifier );

if ( err != noErr )
  DoError( "\pError creating object specifier for
      'Third Word'..." );
```

Our next goal is to build an object specifier that represents "the font property." We use the `formPropertyID` form, which requires a `keyAEKeyData` descriptor that contains a 4-byte property code. We use `AECreateDesc()` to create this descriptor, embedding the `pFont` property code (which we assigned to `fontType` at the top of the routine) in the descriptor:

```
err = AECreateDesc( typeType, &fontType, sizeof( fontType ),
    &fontDesc );

if ( err != noErr )
  DoError( "\pError calling AECreateDesc()..." );
```

Next, we call `CreateObjSpecifier()` to create "the font property" object specifier. We use a class of `cProperty`, "the third word" specifier as a container, `formPropertyID` as the key-form, and the descriptor we just created as the `keyAEKeyData`. The created object specifier is returned in `fontPropSpecifier`:

```
err = CreateObjSpecifier( cProperty, &wordObjSpecifier,
        formPropertyID, &fontDesc,
        kDisposeInputs, &fontPropSpecifier );

if ( err != noErr )
  DoError( "\pError creating object specifier for font
        property..." );
```

> Notice that we build the object specifier by starting at the top, first building the object specifier that has a `NULL` container. We then work our way inward until we get to our ultimate object specifier.

Next, we pass the object specifier on to the routine that creates and sends the Get Data event and, when we're done, dispose of the object specifier:

```
DoGetData( &fontPropSpecifier );

AEDisposeDesc( &fontPropSpecifier );
}
```

`DoGetData()` uses the techniques we've already covered to create a Get Data event, address it to the Scriptable Text Editor, then send the event on its way:

```
/************************************* DoGetData******/

void DoGetData( AEDesc *objSpecifierPtr )
{
   AEAddressDesc   targetAddrDesc = {typeNull, NULL};
   long        targetSignature = kScriptEditSignature;
   AppleEvent     event = {typeNull, NULL};
   AppleEvent     reply = {typeNull, NULL};
   OSErr       err;
   DescType    actualtype;
   Size        actualSize;
   Str255        theText;
```

First, we create the address descriptor, addressing the Apple event to the application whose type is `targetSignature`, which, in this case, happens to be `'quil'`:

```
err = AECreateDesc( typeApplSignature, (Ptr)(&targetSignature),
        sizeof( targetSignature ), &targetAddrDesc );

if ( err != noErr )
  DoError( "\pError returned by AECreateDesc()..." );
```

> Minor trivia: Quill was the pre-release name of the Scriptable Text Editor. The term Quill still appears occasionally in miscellaneous AppleScript and OSA documentation.

Next, we call AECreateAppleEvent() to create the Get Data Apple event. The kAECoreSuite suite code represents the Core suite, kAEGetData is the Get Data event ID, and the event is addressed to the target described in targetAddrDesc. (The rest of the parameters should be familiar from ReverClient, covered earlier in the chapter.) The Apple event is returned in event:

```
err = AECreateAppleEvent( kAECoreSuite, kAEGetData,
                &targetAddrDesc, kAutoGenerateReturnID,
                kAnyTransactionID, &event );

if ( err != noErr )
  DoError( "\pError returned by AECreateAppleEvent()..." );
```

If you have a copy of the Registry handy (and you should!), open it to the page that describes the Get Data event (it's midway through the Core suite). First, check for any required parameters. Get Data has one required parameter, a descriptor of type typeObjectSpecifier associated with the keyword keyDirectObject. Get Data's keyDirectObject parameter describes the object or objects whose data you're looking for. Conveniently, we have an object specifier already built. All we need to do is add it to the Apple event, which is exactly what the call to AEPutParamDesc() does:

```
err = AEPutParamDesc( &event, keyDirectObject, objSpecifierPtr );

if ( err != noErr )
  DoError( "\pError returned by AEPutParamDesc()..." );
```

Next, we call AESend() to send the Get Data event to the Scriptable Text Editor:

```
err = AESend( &event, &reply, kAEWaitReply +
            kAECanInteract + kAECanSwitchLayer,
```

```
                    kAENormalPriority, kAEDefaultTimeout,
                    kNoIdleProc, kNoFilterProc );

if ( err == connectionInvalid )
  DoError( "\pScriptable Text Editor not running..." );

if ( err != noErr )
  DoError( "\pError returned by AESend()..." );
```

> I know I said this earlier in the chapter, but it bears repeating: If you're going to send or receive high-level events, you *must* set the `HighLevelEventAware` bit in your application's `'size'` resource. If you don't set the `HighLevelEventAware` bit, `AESend()` will return the error code `noPortErr (-903)`.

Take another look at the Registry's Get Data entry, this time at the reply parameters. There is one required parameter, a descriptor associated with the keyword `keyAEResult`. When the reply comes back from the Scriptable Text Editor, we use `AEGetParamPtr()` to check for the `keyAEResult` keyword and, if it exists, to save the text from the descriptor in `theText`:

```
err = AEGetParamPtr( &reply, keyAEResult, typeChar,
      &actualtype, (Ptr)(&(theText[ 1 ])), kMaxTextSize,
          &actualSize );
```

If the `keyAEResult` parameter is there, we set `theText`'s length byte and display the returned word using `Do2Message()`:

```
if ( err == noErr )
{
   theText[0] = actualSize;
   Do2Message( "\pThe third word's font is: ", theText );
}
```

If the Scriptable Text Editor can't locate the object you requested (if the front window contained less than three words, for example), the call to `AEGetParamPtr()` returns an error, complaining that it can't find the `keyAEResult` descriptor. In this case, we print an error message (as you work with the Get Data event, you might want to check out the optional `keyErrorNumber` and `keyErrorString` reply parameters):

```
else
{
```

```
      DoError( "\pError returned by AEGetParamPtr()..." );
   }
```

Finally, we dispose of the descriptors we allocated:

```
   AEDisposeDesc (&targetAddrDesc);
   AEDisposeDesc (&event);
   AEDisposeDesc (&reply);
}
```

DoMessage( ) **takes a single parameter, plugs it in as the first**
ParamText( ) **string, then displays the string in an alert:**

```
/**************** DoMessage ********************/

void  DoMessage( Str255 errorString )
{
   ParamText( errorString, "\p", "\p", "\p" );

   NoteAlert( kErrorALRTid, kNilFilterProc );
}
```

Do2Message( ) **does the same thing, but it uses two strings instead**
of one:

```
/**************** Do2Message ********************/

void  Do2Message( Str255 string1, Str255 string2 )
{
   ParamText( string1, string2, "\p", "\p" );

   NoteAlert( kErrorALRTid, kNilFilterProc );
}
```

DoError( ) **does the same thing as** DoMessage( ), **but it exits the pro-**
gram after displaying the message alert:

```
/**************** DoError ********************/

void  DoError( Str255 errorString )
{
   ParamText( errorString, "\p", "\p", "\p" );

   StopAlert( kErrorALRTid, kNilFilterProc );

   ExitToShell();
}
```

An Object Specifier Sandbox

This program was written to give you an environment you can use to run your own nefarious object specifier experiments. Before you move on to the rest of this chapter, take some time to play around with Get Data and Set Data, using the Scriptable Text Editor as your laboratory. See what objects the Scriptable Text Editor supports. What are the limits of its containment hierarchy? Can you retrieve "the third character" from "the second paragraph"? Experiment with different Text suite properties. Try to retrieve the font size of a character. Use Set Data to set a character's font and size. In short, Get Data and Set Data are two incredibly useful and powerful Apple events. Get to know them!

> To see what events and objects are supported by the Scriptable Text Editor, launch the Script Editor and select Open Dictionary... from the File menu and open up the Scriptable Text Editor.

RESOLVING OBJECT SPECIFIERS

So far, we've looked at life through the eyes of a client application. We've used the Object Support Library to build object specifiers representing both objects and properties. We've used the Apple Event Manager to add an object specifier to an event defined in the Registry and to send the event on to another application.

In this section, we'll take a look at the flip side—the process of *resolving an object specifier*. You already know how to install an Apple event handler and how to pull a parameter out of an Apple event. But what do you do if the parameter is an object specifier? How do you follow the object specifier back to the object or property it specifies?

In the GetData program, we created an object specifier, added it to a Get Data Apple event as a parameter, then sent the Get Data event to another application. Suppose you were writing an application that supported the Core suite and the Get Data event along with it. When you're on the receiving end of a Get Data event, you need to retrieve the `keyDirectObject` parameter (the object specifier whose value is being requested) from the event, figure out what object it represents, and place the value of that object in the reply event. Here's what you do.

AEResolve() and Object Accessors

Imagine that your application just received a Get Data Apple event containing an object specifier as a parameter. When the Get Data event arrives, you pass the event to `AEProcessHighLevelEvent()` and `AEProcessHighLevelEvent()` passes it to your Get Data handler. You've seen this process before (see ReverServer).

Your Get Data handler calls `AEGetParamDesc()` to retrieve the object specifier from the Apple event and passes the object specifier to the OSL routine `AEResolve()`. Then, `AEResolve()` parses your object specifier, starting at the outermost container (the `NULL` container) and working its way into the object or property represented by the specifier. Each time it hits a container, `AEResolve()` calls a special routine that you've provided called an *object accessor*.

Consider the object specifier that represents "the third word in the front window" (Figure 2.21). When this specifier is passed to `AEResolve()`, `AEResolve()` starts at the `NULL` container and works its way down to `cWord`, making two object accessor calls along the way. First, it calls the "`cWindow` from `NULL`" accessor, which knows how to retrieve a window from a `NULL` container. The accessor takes information about the container (in this case, `NULL`) and the object located in the container (the first window) and returns a *token*, a descriptor that represents the actual object. In the example, the "`cWindow` from `NULL`" object accessor might return a descriptor containing the frontmost `WindowPtr`, assuming the text in this window was somehow piggybacked off this `WindowPtr`.

FIGURE 2.21

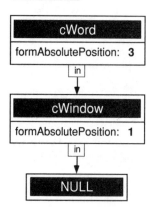

An object specifier for "the third word in the front window."

Second, `AEResolve()` calls the "cWord from cWindow" object accessor, passing in the token returned from the "cWindow from NULL" accessor. The "cWord from cWindow" accessor pulls the `WindowPtr` out of its input token and uses it to get to the window's text. It parses the text, pulls out the third word, embeds it in a descriptor, then returns it as its token.

Once it gets to the end of the containment chain, `AEResolve()` returns the token returned by the last object accessor call—in this case, a descriptor containing the third word in the front window.

Writing an Object Accessor Function

Every object accessor follows the same function prototype:

```
pascal OSErr    MyObjectAccessor( DescType    desiredClass,
                    AEDesc*     containerToken,
                    DescType    containerClass,
                    DescType    keyForm,
                    AEDesc*     keyData,
                    AEDesc*     resultToken,
                    long        refCon );
```

The first parameter, `desiredClass`, is the class of the object you're looking for. In the "cWord from cWindow" accessor, the `desiredClass` is `cWord`. `containerToken` is the token that represents the container. In the "cWord from cWindow" accessor, the `containerToken` is the descriptor containing the `WindowPtr`. The `containerClass` passed to the "cWord from cWindow" accessor is `cWindow`.

`keyForm` and `keyData` tell you how to locate the requested object in the `containerToken`. For example, the `keyForm` and `keyData` passed to the "cWord from cWindow" accessor are `formAbsolutePosition` and 3, which tell you to build a token representing the third word in the window token passed in to the accessor. `refCon` is a reference constant that you provide when you first install the object accessor (you don't have to use the `refCon` if you don't want to).

Once your accessor locates the requested object, you embed it in a descriptor and return the descriptor as `resultToken`. If your accessor finds the requested object, you return a value of `noErr`. If you can't find the object, you return one of the errors defined in `<AERegistry.h>` and `<AppleEvents.h>`. To find the error codes, search for the string "errAE" in both files. Be sure to read the comments to the right of each of the "errAE" constants.

Installing an Accessor Function

You'll install each of your accessor functions at initialization time, at the same time that you install your event handlers. To install an object accessor, you'll first create a universal procedure pointer (using the macro NewOSLAccessorProc()), and then pass it to AEInstallObjectAccessor:

```
pascal OSErr AEInstallObjectAccessor( DescType desiredClass,
          DescType containerType, OSLAccessorUPP theAccessor,
          long accessorRefcon, Boolean isSysHandler);
```

desiredClass is the class of the object you're looking for, and containerType is the descriptorType of the container the object is in. Be sure that this type agrees with the descriptorType field in the token you create for that container.

theAccessor is the universal procedure pointer containing your accessor function pointer. accessorRefcon is a reference constant that you can provide. accessorRefcon will be passed on to your accessor function when it is called. Since one accessor function can be used to handle more than one class or container type, you can use the reference constant to differentiate between them.

The final parameter, isSysHandler, is true if you want to install the accessor in the system accessor dispatch table.

> Object accessors are dispatched from tables in two different places. One table is in your application heap and the other is in the system heap. Normally, AEResolve() calls one of the object accessors in your application heap, based on an object class and container type. If AEResolve() can't find the matching object accessor in your application heap, it tries to find a matching accessor in the system heap. The object accessors in the system heap are available to all the processes running on the same machine.

Calling AEResolve()

Here's the function prototype for AEResolve():

```
pascal OSErr AEResolve( const AEDesc *objectSpecifier,
          short callbackFlags, AEDesc *theToken );
```

The first parameter is the object specifier to be resolved. The third parameter is the token containing the specified object. The second parameter, callbackFlags, is a set of additive flags:

- `kAEIDoMinimum`—When you first get started with `AEResolve()`, you specify this value for `callbackFlags`.

- `kAEIDoWhose`—This flag tells `AEResolve()` to let your application resolve specifiers that use the form `formWhose`. (For more information on this flag, check out the sections "Handling Whose Tests," p. 6-41, and "Writing Object Callback Functions," p. 6-45, in *Inside Macintosh: Interapplication Communication*.)

- `kAEIDoMarking`—This flag tells `AEResolve()` that your application supports marking callback functions, functions that mark Apple event objects with a special token instead of returning a list of matching tokens. (To learn about object marking functions, read the section "Writing Marking Callback Functions," p. 6-53, in *Inside Macintosh: Interapplication Communication*.)

OSL Callback Functions

There are seven *callback functions* that can be installed by an application to enable some of the more advanced capabilities of the OSL. Of the seven, four are more commonly implemented—the compare, count, dispose token, and error descriptor callbacks.

Compare and Count Callbacks

The compare and count callbacks are used by the OSL to resolve the `formTest` and `formWhose` key-forms. A count callback returns a `long` that represents the number of objects of a specified class in a specified container. (To learn how to write an object counting callback, check out the section "Writing an Object-Counting Function," p. 6-48, in *Inside Macintosh: Interapplication Communication*.)

A comparison callback takes two objects and a comparison-operator, performs the comparison on the objects, and returns a `Boolean` indicating whether the comparison was true or false. (To learn how to write an object comparison callback, check out the section "Writing an Object-Comparison Function," p. 6-50, in *Inside Macintosh: Interapplication Communication*.)

Here's a piece of AppleScript that would cause `AEResolve()` to use count and callback functions:

```
first word of paragraph 1 whose style is bold
```

When AEResolve() tries to resolve the object specifier that represents this bit of script, it first calls the accessor to retrieve a token representing paragraph 1 from the NULL container. It next passes this token to the count callback asking for the number of words in paragraph 1. It then repeatedly calls the "word from paragraph" accessor, getting a series of tokens that represent each word in paragraph 1. Each token is passed to the compare callback, checking to see whether the style of the word is bold. When the compare callback returns true, the right token has been found.

Dispose Token and Error Callbacks

If you don't use object marking functions and if you don't have any special token disposal needs, you can dispose of a token by passing it to AEDisposeDesc(). If you do use object marking callbacks or if you need more control over the way a token is disposed of, you can install a dispose token callback function that will be called whenever your application (or AEResolve()) calls AEDisposeToken(). (To learn how to write a dispose token callback function, check out the section "MyDisposeToken," p. 6-99, in *Inside Macintosh: Interapplication Communication*.)

An error callback function provides a way for your application to access the offending container when AEResolve() fails to find a requested object. For example, if you asked for "the fifth word in the second paragraph" and there were only three words in the paragraph, the error callback would provide your application with the address of the token representing "the second paragraph." (To learn how to write an error callback function, check out the section "MyGetErrorDesc," p. 6-100, in *Inside Macintosh: Interapplication Communication*.)

The "Other" Callbacks

The marking callbacks (mark, adjust marks, and get mark token) are used to avoid creating a list of tokens that pass a test when the application already has a scheme for marking or when the resulting token list might not fit in memory. Database applications in particular are likely to use the marking capabilities of the OSL. An object specifier query for "every last name equal to "Smith" whose zip code is 95124" where the database contains all the inhabitants of the State of California would probably create a list of tokens too large to keep in memory. By using marking callbacks, the database application could place marks in the database instead of creating a separate list. (To learn how to write the three marking callback functions, check out the sections "MyGetMarkToken" p. 6-101, "MyMark," p. 6-102, and "MyAdjustMarks," p. 6-103, in *Inside Macintosh: Interapplication Communication*.)

Installing OSL Callbacks

To install any or all of the OSL callback functions, you'll first create the appropriate universal procedure pointer (UPP) for your callback functions and then pass the UPP to `AESetObjectCallbacks()`. If you don't support a particular callback function, pass `NULL` instead of a UPP. Here's the function prototype for `AESetObjectCallbacks()`:

```
OSErr AESetObjectCallbacks( OSLCompareUPP myCompareProc,
                    OSLCountUPP myCountProc,
                    OSLDisposeTokenUPP myDisposeTokenProc,
                    OSLGetMarkTokenUPP myGetMarkTokenProc,
                    OSLMarkUPP myMarkProc,
                    OSLAdjustMarksUPP myAdjustMarksProc,
                    OSLGetErrDescUPP myGetErrDescProcPtr );
```

ONE FINAL EXAMPLE

In the first part of this chapter, we explored a pair of programs called ReverClient and ReverServer. ReverClient supported three Apple events. One event shipped a text string from ReverClient to ReverServer. The second Apple event asked ReverServer to reverse the string in place. The third event asked ReverServer to send the string back to ReverClient. Each of these events was written without the benefit of the Object Support Library and the Registry. The final two programs in this chapter bring ReverClient and ReverServer together with the Object Model. ReverClientOSL and ReverServerOSL should look very familiar to you. The user interface hasn't changed one bit from their non-OSL predecessors.

Running ReverClientOSL and ReverServerOSL

Go into the `Projects` folder and then into the `Client/Server 2` subfolder. Double-click on the `ReverServerOSL` application. A window containing a single text field will appear (Figure 2.22). The text field shows any text that has been sent to ReverServerOSL via an Apple event.

FIGURE 2.22

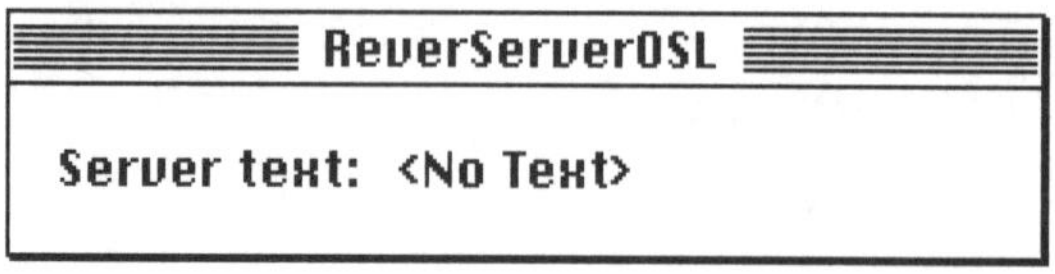

```
▬▬▬▬▬▬ ReverServerOSL ▬▬▬▬▬▬

Server text:  <No Text>
```

The ReverServerOSL window.

With ReverServerOSL still running, go back into the
Client/Server 2 subfolder and double-click on the ReverClientOSL
application. A window containing an editable text field and three buttons will appear (Figure 2.23).

FIGURE 2.23

```
▬▬▬▬▬▬ ReverClientOSL ▬▬▬▬▬▬

Text:  [Reverse me!                ]

[ Set Text ]   [ Reverse ]   [ Get Text ]
```

The ReverClientOSL window.

The three buttons represent the three Apple events handled by
ReverServerOSL. Set Text sends a Set Data Apple event to
ReverServerOSL, asking it to set its pContents property to the text string
embedded in the keyAEData parameter. The pContents property may be
familiar to you if you've spent some time with AppleScript. Here's a sample script that uses the contents property:

```
tell application "Scriptable Text Editor"
    set the contents of front window to "Hello, world!"
end tell
```

> You may have noticed that the pContents constant is in the file
> <AERegistry.h> but not in the Registry itself. pContents was a rela-
> tively late addition to the Registry, so you should look for it in one of
> the Registry errata documents, as a property of cDocument. In gen-
> eral, if you can't find a keyword or constant in the Registry, head for
> the include files. Chances are you'll find what you're looking
> for there.

Press the Set Text button. The ReverClientOSL text will appear in the ReverServerOSL window (Figure 2.24).

FIGURE 2.24

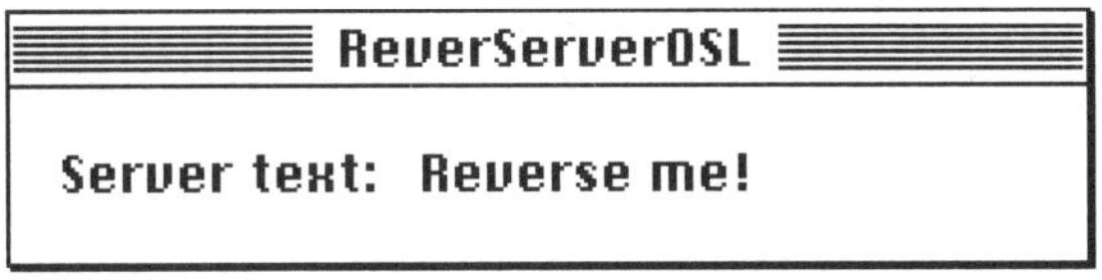

ReverServerOSL, after the Set Data event.

The Reverse button also sends a Set Data Apple event, asking ReverServerOSL to set the pReverse property to a made-up value. When ReverServerOSL gets a request to set its pReverse property, it ignores the data and just reverses its text. Just for fun, here's a script that uses the reverse property:

```
tell application "Scriptable Text Editor"
    set mylist to words in front window
    set mylist to reverse of mylist
end tell
```

Press the Reverse button. The ReverServerOSL text string will appear in reverse order (Figure 2.25).

FIGURE 2.25

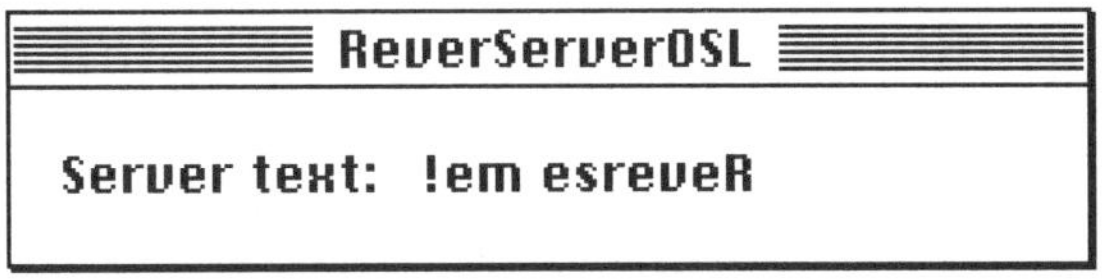

ReverServerOSL, after the pReverse Set Data event.

The third button, Get Text, sends a Get Data Apple event to ReverServerOSL, asking it to send the data associated with its pContents property via a reply Apple event. When ReverClientOSL receives the reply, it will display the newly received text in its window. Press the Get Text button. The ReverServerOSL text will appear in the ReverClientOSL window's editable text field (Figure 2.26).

FIGURE 2.26

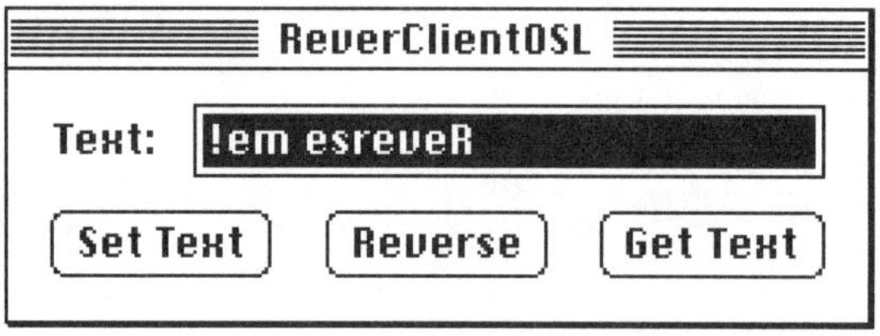

ReverClientOSL, after the Get Data event.

In the next few sections, we'll walk through the source code behind both ReverClientOSL and ReverServerOSL and take a look at the new and improved ReverServerOSL 'aete' resource.

> We've taken the example applications from earlier in the chapter and converted them to be Object Model compliant. We've removed all custom events and are accessing the same data and properties by using the Get Data and Set Data events from the Core suite. This example is very simple. We will neither go into object accessors that return elements of our application nor implement the count and compare procs. Though simple, this example should give you a taste for an Object Model implementation.
>
> Since we've already gone over the basic application code in some detail in prior sections, we'll only discuss the changes that have been made to conform to the Object Model.

The ReverClientOSL Source Code

In the ReverClientOSL version of AEInit( ), we've added a call to initialize the Object Support Library.

```
/******************************* AEInit ********/

void  AEInit( void )
{
   OSErr err;
   long  feature;

   err = Gestalt( gestaltAppleEventsAttr, &feature );

   if ( err != noErr )
      DoError( "\pError returned by Gestalt!" );

   if ( !( feature & ( kGestaltMask << gestaltAppleEventsPresent ) ) )
```

```
      DoError( "\pThis configuration does not support Apple
          events..." );

   // Initialize the Object Support Library
   err = AEObjectInit();
   if ( err != noErr )
      DoError( "\pError initializing Object Support Library..." );
}
```

We've changed DoDialogEvent() in one place, the switch statement that handles the three buttons. The rest of the code is the same with the exception of a few new variables:

```
/************************************ DoDialogEvent****/

void  DoDialogEvent( EventRecord *eventPtr )
{
   OSErr      err;
   short      itemHit;
   short      itemType;
   Handle      itemHandle;
   Rect      itemRect;
   char      theChar;
   DialogPtr   dialog;
   Str255     theText;
   long      menuAndItem;
   AEDesc    theContainer = {typeNull, NULL},
           theData = {typeNull, NULL},
           wantData = {typeNull, NULL},
           objSpecifier = {typeNull, NULL};
   DescType wantTypeData;
   Boolean  boolDisposeInputs = true,
         boolReverseText = true;
   Size      hdlSize;

   switch ( eventPtr->what )
   {
      case keyDown:
      case autoKey:
         theChar = eventPtr->message & charCodeMask;

         if ( (eventPtr->modifiers & cmdKey) != 0 )
         {
            menuAndItem = MenuKey( theChar );

            if ( HiWord( menuAndItem ) != 0 )
            {
               HandleMenuChoice( menuAndItem );
               return;
```

```
            }
        }
        break;
    }
```

Here's the real heart of the client side implementation. For each button in the ReverClientOSL dialog, we create an object specifier by using CreateObjSpecifier() and the formPropertyID form and a descriptor containing the data associated with that property, and then we pass both the object specifier and the data descriptor to DoAppleEvent():

```
if ( DialogSelect( eventPtr, &dialog, &itemHit ) )
{
    switch ( itemHit )
    {
```

For the Set Text button, we build an object specifier that specifies the pContents property and place the text string in the data descriptor theData. We then pass both to DoAppleEvent():

```
        case iSetText:
            // Tell the remote app to use this string
            GetDItem( dialog, iText, &itemType, &itemHandle,
                &itemRect );
            GetIText( itemHandle, theText );
            wantTypeData = pContents;

            err = AECreateDesc( typeType, (Ptr)(&wantTypeData),
                                    sizeof( wantTypeData ),
                                        &wantData );

            err = AECreateDesc( typeChar, (Ptr)(&theText[1]),
                                    *theText, &theData );

            err = CreateObjSpecifier(        cProperty,
                                            &theContainer,
                                            formPropertyID,
                                            &wantData,
                                            boolDisposeInputs,
                                            &objSpecifier ) ;

            DoAppleEvent( kAESetData, objSpecifier, &theData );
            break;
```

For the Reverse button, we build an object specifier that specifies the pReverse property and place a Boolean in the data descriptor theData. Again, we pass both to DoAppleEvent():

```
case iReverse:
    // Tell the remote app to reverse its string

    wantTypeData = pReverse;
    err = AECreateDesc( typeType, (Ptr)(&wantTypeData),
                            sizeof( wantTypeData ), &wantData );

    err = AECreateDesc( typeChar, (Ptr)(&boolReverseText),
                            sizeof(boolReverseText), &theData );

    err = CreateObjSpecifier(        cProperty,
                                     &theContainer,
                                     formPropertyID,
                                     &wantData,
                                     boolDisposeInputs,
                                     &objSpecifier ) ;

    DoAppleEvent( kAESetData, objSpecifier, &theData );
    break;
```

For the Get Data button, we build an object specifier that specifies the pContents property and leave the data descriptor theData as a NULL descriptor. Again, we pass both to DoAppleEvent():

```
case iGetText:
    // Ask the remote app to return its string
    wantTypeData = pContents;
    err = AECreateDesc( typeType, (Ptr)(&wantTypeData),
                            sizeof( wantTypeData ), &wantData );


    err = CreateObjSpecifier(        cProperty,
                                     &theContainer,
                                     formPropertyID,
                                     &wantData,
                                     boolDisposeInputs,
                                     &objSpecifier ) ;

    DoAppleEvent( kAEGetData, objSpecifier, &theData );
```

DoAppleEvent() retrieves the keyDirectObject from the reply event and stores the data in theData. We use BlockMove() to copy the data from theData into a pascal string and then SetIText() to place the string in the editable text field. We call SelIText() to highlight the string:

```
    // Now get the text out of the descriptor
    hdlSize = GetHandleSize(theData.dataHandle);
```

```
            BlockMove(*theData.dataHandle, &theText[1], hdlSize);
            theText[0] = hdlSize;

            GetDItem( dialog, iText, &itemType, &itemHandle,
                &itemRect );
            SetIText( itemHandle, theText );

            SelIText( dialog, iText, 0, 32767 );
            break;
        }
    }
```

Finally, we call AEDisposeDesc() to dispose of all the descriptors (we probably should check all the return codes, but it's been a long chapter, so let's live dangerously:

```
    if( theContainer.dataHandle != NULL)
        err = AEDisposeDesc(& theContainer );
    if( theData.dataHandle != NULL)
        err = AEDisposeDesc(& theData );
    if( wantData.dataHandle != NULL)
        err = AEDisposeDesc(& wantData );
    if( objSpecifier.dataHandle != NULL)
        err = AEDisposeDesc(& objSpecifier );

}
```

The main change to the DoAppleEvent() function is the addition of the parameter theData. theData is an input and output parameter. If the event we're going to send is a Set Data event, the parameter theData contains the value to set the specified property to. If a Get Data event is being set, no input value is provided and the reply is returned in theData:

```
/********************************** DoAppleEvent   */

void DoAppleEvent( AEEventID idToSend, AEDesc theObjectSpecifier,
    AEDesc *theData )
{
    AEAddressDesc   targetAddrDesc = {typeNull, nil};
    long            targetSignature = kReverServerOSLSignature;
    AppleEvent      event = {typeNull, nil};
    AppleEvent      reply = {typeNull, nil};
    OSErr           err;
    DescType        actualtype;
    Size            actualSize;

    err = AECreateDesc( typeApplSignature, (Ptr)(&targetSignature),
            sizeof( targetSignature ), &targetAddrDesc );
```

```
if ( err != noErr )
   DoError( "\pError returned by AECreateDesc()..." );

err = AECreateAppleEvent( kAECoreSuite, idToSend,
                   &targetAddrDesc, kAutoGenerateReturnID,
                   kAnyTransactionID, &event );

if ( err != noErr )
   DoError( "\pError returned by AECreateAppleEvent()..." );

err = AEPutParamDesc( &event, keyDirectObject,
      &theObjectSpecifier );

if ( err != noErr )
   DoError( "\pError returned by AEPutParamPtr()..." );

if(theData->dataHandle != NULL)
{
   err = AEPutParamDesc( &event, keyAEData, theData );
   if ( err != noErr )
      DoError( "\pError returned by AEPutParamDesc()..." );

}
err = AESend( &event, &reply, kAEWaitReply + kAECanInteract +
            kAECanSwitchLayer,kAENormalPriority, kAEDefaultTimeout,
            kNoIdleProc, kNoFilterProc );

if ( err == connectionInvalid )
{
   DoMessage( "\pServer not running..." );

   AEDisposeDesc( &targetAddrDesc );
   AEDisposeDesc( &event );
   AEDisposeDesc( &reply );
   return;
}

if ( err != noErr )
   DoError( "\pError returned by AESend()..." );
```

If an error other than one for a descriptor not found is returned, we report it. If no direct object is contained in the reply, the event requested no reply. We could be paranoid and check the event ID to see whether we should have received a reply, but that might be overkill:

```
err = AEGetParamDesc( &reply, keyDirectObject, typeChar, theData );

if (( err != noErr ) && (err != errAEDescNotFound))
```

```
            DoError( "\pError returned by AEGetParamDesc()..." );

        AEDisposeDesc (&targetAddrDesc);
        AEDisposeDesc (&event);
        AEDisposeDesc (&reply);
}
```

The ReverServerOSL Source Code

In the ReverServerOSL, the changes are more far-reaching. We've replaced the custom Apple event handlers with two event handlers from the Core suite and added one object accessor. The event handlers handle the Core suite event's Get Data and Set Data. The single accessor is the "property from NULL" accessor. We've also added an initialization routine for the OSL and an accessor installation routine called AEInstallAccessors().

For starters, here are the new function prototypes:

```
void     ToolboxInit( void );
void     MenuBarInit( void );
void     AEInit( void );
void     AEInstallHandlers( void );
void     AEInstallAccessors( void );
pascal OSErr DoOpenApp( AppleEvent *event, AppleEvent *reply,
                         long refcon );
pascal OSErr DoOpenDoc( AppleEvent *event, AppleEvent *reply,
                         long refcon );
pascal OSErr DoPrintDoc( AppleEvent *event, AppleEvent *reply,
                          long refcon );
pascal OSErr DoQuitApp( AppleEvent *event, AppleEvent *reply,
                         long refcon );
pascal OSErr DoSetDataEvent( AppleEvent *event,
                             AppleEvent *reply, long refcon );
pascal OSErr DoGetDataEvent( AppleEvent *event,
                             AppleEvent *reply, long refcon );
pascal OSErr AppPropertyFrmNull( DescType    classWanted,
                            AEDesc* container,
                            DescType containerClass,
                            DescType keyform,
                            AEDesc* selectionData,
                            AEDesc* resultToken,
                            long theRefCon );
void     DoReverse( void );
void     DoSetText( Str255  theText);
void     DoGetText( Str255 string );
void     ReverseString( Str255 string );
void     CreateDialog( void );
```

```
void      EventLoop( void );
void      DoEvent( EventRecord *eventPtr );
void      HandleMouseDown( EventRecord *eventPtr );
void      HandleMenuChoice( long menuChoice );
void      HandleAppleChoice( short item );
void      HandleFileChoice( short item );
void      DoUpdate( EventRecord *eventPtr );
void      DoError( Str255 errorString );
```

Take another look at the `AEInstallHandlers()` function. We start
with handlers for the four required events:

```
void  AEInstallHandlers( void )
{
   OSErr err;

   gDoOpenAppUPP = NewAEEventHandlerProc(DoOpenApp);
   err = AEInstallEventHandler( kCoreEventClass, kAEOpenApplication,
          gDoOpenAppUPP, 0L, false );

   if ( err != noErr )
      DoError( "\pError installing 'oapp' handler..." );

   gDoOpenDocUPP = NewAEEventHandlerProc(DoOpenDoc);
   err = AEInstallEventHandler( kCoreEventClass, kAEOpenDocuments,
          gDoOpenDocUPP, 0L, false );

   if ( err != noErr )
      DoError( "\pError installing 'odoc' handler..." );

   gDoPrintDocUPP = NewAEEventHandlerProc(DoPrintDoc);

   err = AEInstallEventHandler( kCoreEventClass, kAEPrintDocuments,
          gDoPrintDocUPP, 0L, false );

   if ( err != noErr )
      DoError( "\pError installing 'pdoc' handler..." );

   gDoQuitAppUPP = NewAEEventHandlerProc(DoQuitApp);
   err = AEInstallEventHandler( kCoreEventClass, kAEQuitApplication,
          gDoQuitAppUPP, 0L, false );

   if ( err != noErr )
      DoError( "\pError installing 'quit' handler..." );
```

Now, we install two more handlers, one for the Core suite's Get
Data event and one for the Set Data event. What happened to the reverse
event? As we said before, when the user presses the Reverse button,

we're going to send a Set Data event asking ReverServerOSL to set its pReverse property to some value (we could have handled Reverse in any number of ways; you might want to try your hand at a different implementation):

```
gDoSetDataEventUPP = NewAEEventHandlerProc(DoSetDataEvent);

err = AEInstallEventHandler( kAECoreSuite, kAESetData,
        gDoSetDataEventUPP, 0L, false );

if ( err != noErr )
   DoError( "\pError installing get data handler..." );

gDoGetDataEventUPP = NewAEEventHandlerProc(DoGetDataEvent);
err = AEInstallEventHandler( kAECoreSuite, kAEGetData,
        gDoGetDataEventUPP, 0L, false );

if ( err != noErr )
   DoError( "\pError installing get data handler..." );

}
```

AEInstallAccessors() **starts by initializing the Object Support Library**:

```
void    AEInstallAccessors( void )
{
   OSErr err;

   // First we initialize the Object Support Library
   err = AEObjectInit();

   if ( err != noErr )
      DoError( "\pError initializing Object Support Library..." );
```

Take a look at the OSL function prototypes in <AEObjects.h>. Notice that each one is followed by a macro containing six hex bytes. For example, the declaration of AEResolve() is followed by the line

```
THREEWORDINLINE(0x303C, 0x0536, 0xA816);
```

These six bytes of code allow you to link your project *without including the OSL library* if and only if you have a version of the Apple Event Manager installed that is later than 1.0.1. In other words, the OSL is built into the most recent versions of the Apple Event Manager.

Here's the catch. Suppose you have an OSL-containing Apple Event Manager installed and you link without the OSL. Now suppose you hand your application to your buddy Clevis, who is running with Apple Event Manager 1.0. Your program crashes, because the OSL isn't available.

This may sound bizarre, but it's true. The solution is to use `Gestalt()` at run time to check for the presence of the Apple Event Manager and then for the presence of the OSL. If the OSL is there, great! Go ahead and be scriptable. If the OSL isn't there, don't make any OSL calls. In short, if the OSL is available, you'll be scriptable; if not, you won't be. One way to do this is to set a global that is `true` if the OSL is present and `false` otherwise.

Of course, you can also link in the OSL and incur the extra overhead. The glue code included with each OSL routine will ensure that the most recent version of the OSL is called. The downside of this strategy is the extra (and, in most cases, unnecessary) memory consumed by the library.

Test for the presence of the Apple Event Manager by calling `Gestalt()` with the gestalt selector `gestaltAppleEventsAttr`. If the `gestaltAppleEventsPresent` bit (bit 0) is set, the Apple Event Manager is installed. Next, use the selector `gestaltAppleEventsAttr` with `gestaltOSLInSystem` (bit 2) to test whether the OSL is installed. If the bit is set, the OSL is installed and your AppleEventManager version is later than version 1.0.1.

Finally, we install the "property from NULL" accessor, which knows how to find a property in a NULL container:

```
// Now add our accessors
gPropertyFrmNullUPP = NewOSLAccessorProc( PropertyFrmNull );

err = AEInstallObjectAccessor(cProperty, typeNull,
                                gPropertyFrmNullUPP, 0, false);
if ( err != noErr )
  DoError( "\pError installing property from null accessor..." );
}
```

Here's our Set Data event handler:

```
pascal OSErr DoSetDataEvent( AppleEvent *event,
                    AppleEvent *reply, long refcon )
{
  OSErr         err;
  Str255        theText;
  AEDesc        target = {typeNull, NULL},
            token = {typeNull, NULL},
```

```
                    data = {typeNull, NULL},
                    stringDesc = {typeNull, NULL};
      long          hdlSize;
```

First, we try to retrieve the `keyDirectObject` descriptor. If we can't find one, we jump to some cleanup code. (Please don't send me any letters complaining about the use of `goto`s in the code. Use 'em or not; it's your call.) When we've successfully extracted the object specifier, we pass it in as a parameter to `AEResolve()`. Notice that since we don't support marking, we set the callback flag parameter to `kAEIDoMinimum` and that since we didn't install any compare or count functions, we don't support ranges or tests either:

```
err = AEGetParamDesc(event, keyDirectObject, typeObjectSpecifier,
   &target);

if (err != noErr)
   goto CLEANUP; // This example uses gotos for exception handling

err = AEResolve(&target, kAEIDoMinimum, &token);  // Resolve ospec.
if (err != noErr)
   goto CLEANUP;
```

After successful resolution of the object specifier, we extract the `keyAEData` parameter, which contains the data we'll set the requested property to. Notice that we used the constant `typeWildCard`, which matches any type. We won't know the type we need until we evaluate the type of the `token` returned by `AEResolve()`:

```
err = AEGetParamDesc( event, keyAEData, typeWildCard, &data );

if( err != noErr)
   goto CLEANUP;
```

Next, we check the `descriptorType` of the token returned by `AEResolve()`. This type will be a property (take a look at `PropertyFrmNull()` later in the code to see why). We switch on all the properties we know about.

The `pName` property refers to ReverServerOSL's name, which is "ReverServerOSL." This doesn't mean very much in Set Data, since you can't set an application's name, but Get Data supports the `pName` property in a more useful way:

```
switch(token.descriptorType)
{
```

```
case pName:
  // Read only property
  err = errAENotModifiable;
  break;
```

The pContents property refers to the contents of the text field. We use the routine AECoerceDesc() to translate a descriptor of one type to produce a new descriptor of the type in the second parameter. In this case, we're turning the data descriptor into a descriptor of typeChar:

```
case pContents:
  // Make sure we have text to work with
  err = AECoerceDesc( &data, typeChar, &stringDesc );

  if( err != noErr)
    goto CLEANUP;
```

If the coercion works, we turn the block of characters into a pascal string and pass the string to DoSetText(), which sets the text field to that string:

```
      // A real pascal-style string please.
      hdlSize = GetHandleSize(stringDesc.dataHandle );
      BlockMove( *stringDesc.dataHandle, &theText[1], hdlSize );
      theText[0] = hdlSize;

      // Now set the text to the new string
      DoSetText( theText );
      break;
```

pReverse just calls DoReverse(), and ignores any data packaged in the Apple event:

```
case pReverse:
  // The data associated with this event is a
  // Boolean value. Since we use the event as a
  // toggle, we'll ignore the data.

  DoReverse();
  err = noErr;
  break;

default:
  err = errAEEventNotHandled;
  break;
}
```

The cleanup is simple. We use `AEDisposeDesc()` to dispose of all our descriptors. Note that since we initialized our descriptors to `{typeNull,NULL}`, there's no need to pre-screen out descriptors before we pass them to `AEDisposeDesc()`:

```
CLEANUP::;
    // Dispose our descriptors
    AEDisposeDesc( &target );
    AEDisposeDesc( &token );
    AEDisposeDesc( &data );
    AEDisposeDesc( &stringDesc );

    return err;
}
```

Next comes our Get Data handler. We follow a similar strategy, pulling the `keyDirectObject` from the event and passing it to `AEResolve()`:

```
pascal OSErr DoGetDataEvent( AppleEvent *event,
                        AppleEvent *reply, long refcon )
{
    OSErr          err;
    AEDesc         target = {typeNull, NULL},
               token = {typeNull, NULL};
    Str255         theString;
    StringPtr      theStrPtr = (StringPtr)&theString;
    Rect           theWindowRect;

    err = AEGetParamDesc(event, keyDirectObject, typeObjectSpecifier,
                        &target);
    if (err != noErr)
      goto CLEANUP;

    err = AEResolve(&target, kAEIDoMinimum, &token);    // Resolve
        ospec.
    if (err != noErr)
      goto CLEANUP;
```

Next, we switch on the token's `descriptorType` field. If we get a request for the `pName`, we use `LMGetCurApName()` to add the current application name to the reply event. If you haven't worked with the universal headers before, `LM` stands for low-memory and signifies a routine that gives you access to the low-memory globals found on 68K Macs:

```
    switch(token.descriptorType)
    {
```

```
case pName:
  // Current applications name
  theStrPtr = LMGetCurApName();

  err = AEPutParamPtr(reply, keyAEResult, typeChar,
                   (Ptr)&theString[1], *theString);
  break;
```

To handle the pContents Get Data request, we get the text from the text field and add it to the reply event:

```
case pContents:
  // Get the text and return it.
  theString[0] = 0;              // Set to zero so we have an empty
                                 // string
  DoGetText( theString );
  err = AEPutParamPtr(reply, keyAEResult, typeChar,
                   (Ptr)&theString[1], *theString);
  break;
```

On pBounds, we return the bounding rectangle of the ReverServerOSL window (note that we won't have access to the bounding rectangle if you hide ReverServerOSL by selecting Hide ReverServerOSL from the Finder's application menu):

```
case pBounds:
  theWindowRect = (*(RgnHandle)((((WindowPeek)gServerDialog)->
                   contRgn))->rgnBBox;

  err = AEPutParamPtr(reply, keyAEResult, typeQDRectangle,
                &theWindowRect, sizeof(theWindowRect));
  break;
```

To test this out, start up ReverServerOSL and use the Script Editor to run this script:

```
tell application "ReverServerOSL"
     bounds
end tell
```

Check your results in the Script Editor's result window.

```
default:
  err = errAEEventNotHandled;
  break;
}
```

```
CLEANUP:;

    // Dispose of our descriptors
    if(target.dataHandle != NULL)
        AEDisposeDesc( &target );
    if(token.dataHandle != NULL)
        AEDisposeDesc( &token );

    return err;
}
```

Finally, here's our `PropertyFrmNull()` object accessor:

```
pascal OSErr PropertyFrmNull( DescType classWanted,
                              AEDesc* container,
                              DescType containerClass,
                              DescType keyform,
                              AEDesc* selectionData,
                              AEDesc* resultToken,
                              long theRefCon )
{
    DescType    propType;
    long        nullValue;
```

`PropertyFrmNull()` builds the token `resultToken`. `resultToken` is a descriptor with a `NULL` `dataHandle` and a `descriptorType` set to the property pulled from `selectionData`'s `dataHandle` field:

```
    nullValue = (long)NULL;

    propType = *(long*)*selectionData->dataHandle;

    return( AECreateDesc( propType, (Ptr)&nullValue,
            sizeof(nullValue), resultToken ) );
}
```

That's it for the code. Next, let's take a look at the modified `'aete'` resource.

The ReverServerOSL 'aete' Resource

Just in case you don't have a copy of Resorcerer handy, this section features a series of snapshots showing the entire `'aete'` resource. The first few fields haven't changed (Figure 2.27).

Figure 2.28 shows the Required suite, which also hasn't changed.

Figure 2.29 gets you into our custom suite, which contains two events.

FIGURE 2.27

Version (hex BCD) Latest=$0100
.... The language ID should be the same as this resource ID
▼ **Language code** English=0
▼ **Script code** Roman=0
.... You may want to turn Show Index Popups on to navigate more easily.

The 'aete' resource, part 1.

FIGURE 2.28

Suites 2
--------- Suites #1 ---------
Suite name "Required Suite"
Description "Terms that every application should support"
Align
▼ **Suite code** Required='reqd'
Level 1
Version 1
Suite events 0
--------- No Items ---------

Classes 0
--------- No Items ---------

Comparison operators 0
--------- No Items ---------

Enumerations 0
--------- No Items ---------

The 'aete' resource, part 2.

FIGURE 2.29

--------- Suites #2 ---------
Suite name "Text Server"
Description "The core events supported by ReverServerOSL."
Align
▼ **Suite code** 'Tsrv'
Level 1
Version 1
Suite events 2

The 'aete' resource, part 3.

Figure 2.30 shows the first event in the suite. The event is based on the Core suite's Get Data event. The reply can include a variety of types, depending on the property requested, so we use `typeWildCard`, which equates to the code '****'. The direct parameter is an object specifier that specifies the property to get. There are no additional parameters.

FIGURE 2.30

```
·········· Suite events #1 ···································································································
Event name    "get"
Description    "Get the data for an object"
Align
  ▼ Event class code   Core='core'
Event ID   'getd'
  ▼ Reply type   Any type (wildcard)='****'
Reply description   "The data from the object"
    15. Reply is optional   Off
    14. Reply must be list of Items   Off
    13. Enumerated   Off
 1-12. Reserved   0
    0. Non-verb event   Off
  ▼ Direct parameter preferred type   Object specifier='obj '
Direct parameter comment   "the object whose data is to be returned"
    15. Direct parameter is optional   Off
    14. Direct parameter is list of items   Off
    13. Enumerated   Off
    12. Changes state   Off
 0-11. Reserved   0
Parameters   0
························· (order is significant when parameters are listed without keywords)
·········· No Items ·······································································································
```

The 'aete' resource, part 4.

Figure 2.31 shows the Set Data event, based on the Core suite's Set Data event. Notice that the reply is set to optional, unlike the Get Data event. Again, the direct parameter is an object specifier that tells you the property whose value you want to change.

FIGURE 2.31

```
·········· Suite events #2 ···································································································
Event name    "set"
Description    "Set an object's data"
Align
  ▼ Event class code   Core='core'
Event ID   'setd'
  ▼ Reply type   None='null'
Reply description
    15. Reply is optional   On
    14. Reply must be list of Items   Off
    13. Enumerated   Off
 1-12. Reserved   0
    0. Non-verb event   Off
  ▼ Direct parameter preferred type   Object specifier='obj '
Direct parameter comment   "the object to change"
    15. Direct parameter is optional   Off
    14. Direct parameter is list of items   Off
    13. Enumerated   Off
    12. Changes state   On
 0-11. Reserved   0
```

The 'aete' resource, part 5.

Figure 2.32 shows the second parameter added to the Set Data event. The first parameter (keyDirectObject) specified the property, and this second parameter (keyAEData) tells you the value to assign to the property.

FIGURE 2.32

```
Parameters   1
.........................   (order is significant when parameters are listed without keywords)
 ─────── Parameters #1 ───────
  Parameter name    "to"
  Keyword  'data'
  Type  '****'
  Description    "the new value"
     15. Parameter is optional   Off
     14. Parameter must be a list of Items   Off
     13. Enumerated   Off
   3-12. Reserved   0
      2. Feminine   Off
      1. Masculine   Off
      0. Plural   Off
```

The 'aete' resource, part 6.

Figure 2.33 lists the custom class we defined for ReverServerOSL. The class has four properties—pName, pContents, pBounds, and pReverse. We could have specified support for the Core suite itself, but we don't support the whole Core suite. Instead, we've defined a custom class that lives in harmony with the Core suite. As long as the property codes and classes associated with each property agree exactly with their Core Suite counterpart, the properties will behave as if they were defined as part of the Core suite.

FIGURE 2.33

```
Classes   1
 ─────── Classes #1 ───────
  Class name    "reverServerOSL Class"
  Class ID  'Tsrv'
  Description    "Our custom Class."
  Properties   4
   ─────── Properties #1 ───────
    Property name    "name"
    ▼ Code   Name='pnam'
    ▼ Class   International text='itxt'
    Description    "the name"
       15. Reserved   Off
       14. Must be a list of items   Off
       13. Enumerated   Off
       12. Readable/writable (off=>read-only)   Off
     3-11. Reserved   0
        2. Feminine   Off
        1. Masculine   Off
        0. Plural   Off
```
The 'aete' resource, part 7.

The first property, pName, is the name of the ReverServerOSL application, which is a value in the 'itxt' class, which corresponds to the Registry class typeIntlText.

Figure 2.34 shows the specs for pContents, which is also in the 'itxt' class. pContents represents the text in ReverServerOSL's text field.

FIGURE 2.34

```
------- Properties #2 -------------------------------------------
Property name    "contents"
 ▼ Code     'pcnt'
 ▼ Class    International text='itxt'
Description    "text of reverServerOSL"
   15. Reserved   Off
   14. Must be a list of items   Off
   13. Enumerated   Off
   12. Readable/writable (off=>read-only)   On
 3-11. Reserved   0
    2. Feminine   Off
    1. Masculine   Off
    0. Plural   Off
```

The 'aete' resource, part 8.

Figure 2.35 shows the specs for pBounds. pBounds is ReverServerOSL's bounding rectangle and is a QuickDraw rectangle.

FIGURE 2.35

```
------- Properties #3 -------------------------------------------
Property name    "bounds"
 ▼ Code     Bounds='pbnd'
 ▼ Class    Quickdraw rectangle='qdrt'
Description    "ReverServerOSL's bounding rectangle"
   15. Reserved   Off
   14. Must be a list of items   Off
   13. Enumerated   Off
   12. Readable/writable (off=>read-only)   On
 3-11. Reserved   0
    2. Feminine   Off
    1. Masculine   Off
    0. Plural   Off
```

The 'aete' resource, part 9.

Finally, Figure 2.36 shows the pReverse property. pReverse uses a type of Boolean just to keep in sync with the Core suite, but we ignore the data associated with pReverse and use it as a trigger to reverse the ReverServerOSL's text.

FIGURE 2.36

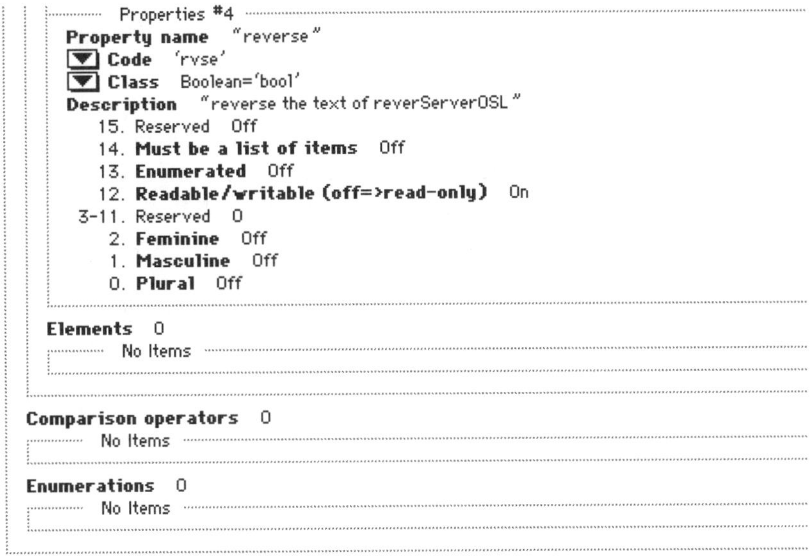

```
  ------- Properties #4 -------
  Property name   "reverse"
  ▼ Code   'rvse'
  ▼ Class   Boolean='bool'
  Description   "reverse the text of reverServerOSL"
     15. Reserved   Off
     14. Must be a list of items   Off
     13. Enumerated   Off
     12. Readable/writable (off=>read-only)   On
  3-11. Reserved   0
      2. Feminine   Off
      1. Masculine   Off
      0. Plural   Off

  Elements   0
  ------- No Items -------


  Comparison operators   0
  ------- No Items -------

  Enumerations   0
  ------- No Items -------
```

The 'aete' resource, part 10.

SUMMARY

We've covered a great deal of material in this chapter. I hope that at this point, you have a handle on the basics of Apple events, the Object Model, and the Apple Event Registry. Your mission now is to go back and dig into *Inside Macintosh: Interapplication Communication*. It should make much more sense to you. Read up on `formTest` and `formWhose` and the different callback functions touched on in this chapter. Play with AppleScript. Write a scriptable application. Learn the difference between the terms *scriptable*, *recordable*, and *attachable*.

In the next chapter, you'll really get some good use from your Apple event construction skills when we get into the Scriptable Finder.

BIOGRAPHY

This chapter was made possible by my good friend, and Apple events maven, Donald Olson. Donald is an engineer at Apple Computer and has been working with Apple events since their infancy. When he is not trying to convince the world that AppleScript is the most important technology to come out of Apple since the introduction of the Mac, Donald hangs out with his wife Theresa and children Matthew and Jessica.

In earlier lives at Apple, Donald has worked on the HyperCard, Apple Event Manager, and AppleScript teams. Now, as a senior software engineer, he is working on the OpenDoc project. If he is not writing code or waiting for compiles to finish, Donald likes to cruise with his family, go for long bicycle rides, and make obnoxious noises with his electric guitar.

APPLESCRIPT AND THE SCRIPTABLE FINDER

Chapter

3

Ever since I learned how to program my Mac, I've wanted to control the Finder. I've had lots of ideas. For example, how about an application that would catalog, compress, and then back up any currently selected volumes, folders, and files? Or perhaps a cdev/INIT combination that would wait for a specific keystroke and then drag the currently selected files and folders to the trash.

Over the years since the Finder made its first appearance, many folks have attempted to master the Finder. The problem was that the Finder wasn't set up to communicate with other Macintosh applications. With the introduction of System 7.5, all that changed. The Finder is now completely scriptable. By using AppleScript, you can create a script to do just about anything you can do in the Finder by hand. By using the techniques you picked up in the previous chapter, you can also control the Finder from within your programs.

In this chapter, we'll begin with a tour of the Scriptable Finder. We'll use the Script Editor to run some sample scripts that take the Finder through a few of its paces. Also, we'll take a quick look at the Finder's Apple Events Terminology Extension ('aete') resource. Finally, we'll explore two sample programs, each of which takes a different approach to communicating with the Finder.

Your first order of business is to get the Scriptable Finder installed. If you're using System 7.5 or later, you're all set. If you can't upgrade to 7.5 for some reason, don't despair. The "Finder Scripting Extension" makes the System 7.1 Finder completely scriptable. You can find it on AppleLink as well as in the AppleScript SDK, available through the Apple Programmers and Developer's Association (APDA).

GETTING TO KNOW THE SCRIPTABLE FINDER

The best way to get to know the Scriptable Finder is to take it for a spin. Start up the Script Editor and select New Script... from the File menu. When the new script–editing window appears, press the Record button. Now, bring the Finder to the front and do some standard Finder things. For example, select a file, duplicate it, and drag the duplicate to the trash. Then, go back to the Script Editor and press the Stop button.

As is the case with any recordable application, the Scriptable Finder translates each user action into the appropriate Apple event and then sends the Apple event to itself. When recording is turned on, the Apple Event Manager sends copies of each Apple event to the application doing the recording—in this case, the Script Editor. The Script Editor then translates the recorded events into the currently selected scripting language.

Some Sample Scripts

Figure 3.1 shows a sample script that I recorded on my Mac. Notice that the whole script is wrapped in a `tell` block to specify that the events generated by the enclosed script should be sent to the Finder. The script starts by telling the Finder to "move to the front" (`activate`). Next, a file is selected and duplicated. Then, the duplicate is dragged to the trash. Check out the verbs associated with each of these actions. For example, the verb `delete` means "place an object in the trash."

FIGURE 3.1

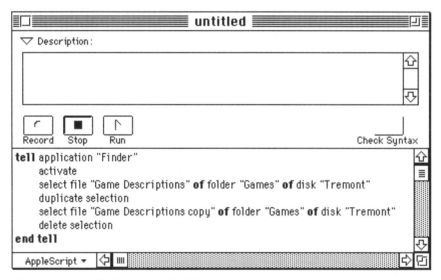

A script recorded in the scriptable Finder.

Notice also the word `AppleScript` located in the lower-left corner of the script editing window. This word designates the scripting language associated with this window. If you click in the lower-left corner, a pop-up menu that lists all of the currently available scripting languages will appear (Figure 3.2). For example, if both AppleScript and Frontier are installed, the pop-up will allow you to select from their respective scripting languages, AppleScript and UserTalk.

FIGURE 3.2

The language pop-up that appears as the result of a click in the lower-left corner of the script editing window.

If you have at least one other scripting component installed (besides AppleScript), you can test this out. If you have a copy of Frontier, just run it and it will install the UserTalk scripting component as part of its start-up process. There's no need to reboot.

Once you have more than one scripting component installed, open a new scripting window and click on the lower-left corner. When the pop-up appears, select UserTalk instead of AppleScript. Next, click the Record button, and then go back to the Finder and repeat your actions. Now, return to the Script Editor and click the Stop button. This time, the script that appears will be in UserTalk (or whatever language you selected) instead of AppleScript (Figure 3.3).

FIGURE 3.3

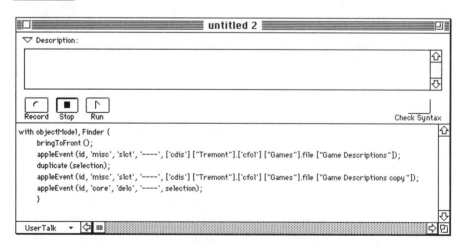

The same recording, using UserTalk instead of Applescript.

Although the examples in this chapter are based on AppleScript, they could just as easily have been based on UserTalk. This flexibility is another example of the power of the Open Scripting Architecture (OSA). Think back to the previous chapter. The OSA allowed us to drive ReverServer from a Script Editor script as well as from an object specifier–generating program like ReverClient. Later in this chapter, you'll learn how to use OSA calls to compile and execute an AppleScript (or any other OSA-compatible language) script from inside your program.

Think about it. With just a few calls, you can give your users the ability to create and run their own scripts from inside your program. For example, you might allow a user to write a script that is executed every time your program starts up. The user might use the script to open a standard set of documents or position windows just so. You can tie a script to any event that makes sense. Take advantage of OSA. Your programs will be much more powerful, and your users will have that much more to brag about!

A Few More Examples

Before we get into the objects that go along with the Scriptable Finder, let's take a look at a few more examples. I created each of the following scripts using the Script Editor's Record button.

This first example checks the "warn before emptying" checkbox in the Trash's Get Info window:

```
tell application "Finder"
    activate
    select trash
    open information window of selection
    select trash
    set warn before emptying of selection to true
    close information window of trash
end tell
```

Notice the verbs select, open, set, and close. You'll see them a lot. Also notice the nouns trash, information window, selection, and warn before emptying. Most of the objects associated with the Scriptable Finder are fairly obvious.

Here's another example:

```
tell application "Finder"
    activate
```

```
    set size of window of disk "Tremont" to {294, 209}
    set position of window of disk "Tremont" to {398, 205}
    set zoomed of window of disk "Tremont" to true
    close window of disk "Tremont"
    set position of disk "Tremont" to {749, 60}
end tell
```

As you can tell, I have a hard drive named "Tremont". First, I dragged in the grow box to resize the Tremont window. Next, I dragged the window to a new location on the screen, clicked in the window's zoom box, then closed the window. Finally, I dragged the hard drive's icon to a new location on the desktop.

Here's one last example:

```
tell application "Finder"
    select file "Finder Script.01"
    open selection
    select file "StuffIt Deluxe™"
    open selection
end tell
tell application "StuffIt Deluxe™"
    activate
    New Archive Pathname "Macintosh HD:Desktop Folder:Archive.sit"
    Stuff Item Pathname "Macintosh HD:Desktop Folder:Finder Script.01"
    Close Archive Pathname "Macintosh HD:Desktop Folder:Archive.sit"
end tell
tell application "Finder"
    close every window
    select {startup disk, folder "Finder Scripting Chap", trash}
    open selection
    set view of window of folder "Finder Scripting Chap" to name
    set view of window of folder "Finder Scripting Chap" to size
    set view of window of folder "Finder Scripting Chap" to kind
    set view of window of folder "Finder Scripting Chap" to icon
    make new folder at folder "Finder Scripting Chap"
    select item "untitled folder" of folder "Finder Scripting Chap"
    set name of selection to "My New Folder"
    select folder "My New Folder" of folder "Finder Scripting Chap"
    make new alias file to selection at folder "Finder Scripting Chap"
    clean up window of folder "Finder Scripting Chap"
end tell
```

First, I double-clicked on a script file, which, as expected, threw me back into the Script Editor and opened the script. I clicked back into the Finder and double-clicked on the application icon for StuffIt Deluxe. StuffIt Deluxe is also recordable. When StuffIt Deluxe came to the front, I created a new archive, added a file to the archive, then closed the archive. I then clicked back into the Finder.

Notice that the script continues to record, even though I switched applications. As long as an application is recordable, its actions will be captured in the script. When you switch gears between applications, a new `tell` block is added to the script.

Back in the Finder, I option-clicked in the frontmost window to close all open windows. Next, I dragged on the desktop, selecting my start-up drive, a folder, and the trash. I then selected Open from the File menu. Next, I selected four different views from the View menu, finally settling on View by Icon.

I created a new folder and then changed the name of the folder to "My New Folder". I selected the folder, made an alias of it, and, finally, selected Clean Up Window from the Special menu.

Basically, anything you can do with the Finder can be captured in a script. Once you know a scripting language like AppleScript or UserTalk, you can create sophisticated scripts that do things like back-up certain portions of your hard drive at regular intervals or create a set of re-creatable desktop snapshots. For example, you might have one set of windows open when you do development and another when you balance your checkbook. With the Scriptable Finder, just turn on recording, set up your windows as you like, then save the new script under the appropriate name.

The Finder's 'aete' Resource

Another way to learn about a scriptable application is to scroll through its `'aete'` resource. As you saw in Chapter 2, Resorcerer does a great job of displaying an `'aete'` in an easy-to-digest format. If you don't happen to have a copy of Resorcerer handy, you can also use the Script Editor to learn about an application's scripting terminology.

Launch the Script Editor and select Open Dictionary... from the File menu. When prompted for a file to open, navigate into the System Folder and open the Finder. The Finder Dictionary window will appear. The window is divided into two panes. The left pane lists the English language terminology that corresponds to each of the Apple events and objects supported by the Finder. Apple events are shown in normal font, and object classes are shown in *italics*.

As you scroll through the items in the left pane, you'll see that the Finder supports Apple events in the Required Suite, the Standard Suite, and the Finder Suite. To find out more about an item, click on it so that its description, built from the `'aete'`, is displayed in the right pane. For example, Figure 3.4 shows a description of the "clean up" Apple event.

FIGURE 3.4

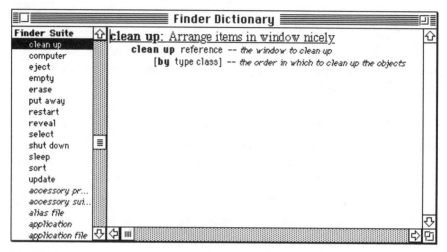

The Finder's 'aete' resource, as seen by the Script Editor's Open Dictionary...
command.

Object and Apple event descriptions embedded in the `'aete'` resource tend to be limited and somewhat hard to read. For example, unless the `'aete'` specifically tells you, there is no easy way to figure out which objects can be used with which events. Hopefully, as more and more people get on board with OSA, they'll take more care in building their application terminology. Until then, the best way to learn is by experimentation: Pick an event and write some scripts.

The *AppleScript Finder Guide*

Finally, the absolute best way to learn about the Scriptable Finder is to read the *AppleScript Finder Guide*. You'll find an electronic copy on the CD that ships with the AppleScript SDK (available from APDA). You can also find it in book form at many technical bookstores. The *Guide* contains descriptions of all the Apple events and object classes supported by the Scriptable Finder. It is well written and absolutely worth reading. Although the concepts in the *Guide* were intended for a scripting audience, the commands and objects it describes correspond directly to the constants defined in the *Registry*'s Finder Suite.

PROGRAMMING THE SCRIPTABLE FINDER

Now that you've had a chance to get to know the Scriptable Finder, let's move on to some programming examples. Each of the next two sample programs takes a slightly different approach to interacting with the Scriptable Finder.

The first program uses the constants defined in the file `<FinderRegistry.h>` to build object specifiers that refer to various Finder objects. These object specifiers are added to various Apple events, such as Get Data and Set Data, and the events are sent to the Finder. As an example, the program sends a Get Data event to the Finder to find the current setting of the "warn before emptying" trash checkbox, and then it sends a Set Data to set the checkbox to its opposite value (checking the box if it is currently unchecked and vice versa).

The second program accomplishes the same ends but uses a completely different technique. This time, a series of scripts is embedded in the program. For example, here's the script that's used to toggle the value of the "warn before emptying" trash checkbox:

```
tell application "Finder"
   set warn before emptying to not warn before emptying
end tell
```

When the corresponding menu item is triggered, the program uses various OSA routines to compile the script and then to execute the script. The program also implements a simple script editor to show you just how simple it is to do.

FINDERSCRIPTER (AE)

The first version of FinderScripter is called FinderScripter (AE) since it is based on Apple events as opposed to scripts.

Running FinderScripter (AE)

Dive into the `Projects` folder, then into the `FinderScripter (AE)` subfolder, and double-click on the `FinderScripter` application. When the menu bar appears, take a look at the items in the Scripts menu (Figure 3.5). Each of these items triggers an Apple event designed to fetch some information from the Finder.

FIGURE 3.5

Scripts	
Name of Front Window	⌘1
Toggle Trash Warning	⌘2
Count of Objects	⌘3
Count of Containers	⌘4
Count of Folders	⌘5
Count of Alias Files	⌘6
Set Creator and Type...	⌘7

The Scripts menu from the Apple event version of FinderScripter.

The first item, Name of Front Window, returns the title of the front-most Finder window. If you don't have any windows open, an error will be reported. Toggle Trash Warning toggles the "warn before emptying" trash checkbox. Here's a cool way to test this item. In the Finder, click on the Trash icon and then select Get Info from the File menu. With the Get Info window in plain sight, go back to FinderScripter and select Toggle Trash Warning, keeping an eye on the checkbox in the Get Info window. You'll actually see the checkbox change state. (I don't know why, but I got a real kick out of this!)

The next four items send a Count Elements event to the Finder, asking it to count the number of objects, containers, folders, or alias files in the current selection. As you'll see when you get to the source code, the routine that constructs the Count Elements event is parameterized so that you can have the Finder count any type of object you like. As you read through <FinderRegistry.h> and the *AppleScript Finder Guide*, try adding different object types to the menu and then count them to be sure that you understand the proper definition of each object type.

To test each of the four counting menu items, select some objects in the Finder and then go back to FinderScripter and choose each of the counting items. As you'll discover, everything you select qualifies as an object. A container is any object that can contain other objects (a folder is a container, a hard drive icon is a container, a file is not a container), and folders and alias files are just what they seem.

The final item in the Scripts menu is Set Creator and Type..., which lets you change the creator and type of every file in the selection (Figure

3.6). Be careful with this item. I'd suggest you make a copy of some files and then experiment with the copies. Once you understand how this bit of source code works, you might want to create a drag-and-drop application that changes anything dropped on it to a specific type. For example, you might create one app that changes anything dropped on it to a TEXT file that launches your favorite word processor. Or you might change ResEdit files dropped on your app to Resorcerer files. Of course, you can also change a file's creator and type using AppleScript, but where's the challenge?

FIGURE 3.6

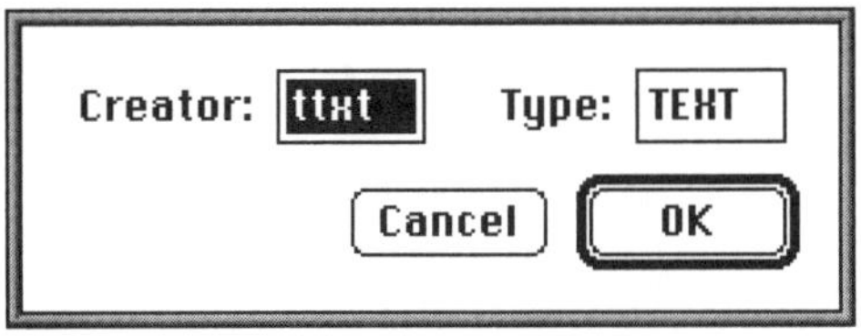

The Set Creator and Type... dialog box.

The FinderScripter (AE) Source Code

The first version of FinderScripter is divided into six separate source code files. FSMain.c starts things off with routines like main() and ToolboxInit(), plus all of the event and menu management routines. FSAEUtils.c contains the routines that build the various Apple events sent by the rest of the program.

FSNameOfFrontWindow.c contains the routines that support the Name of Front Window menu item. FSToggleTrashWarn.c contains the routines that support the Toggle Trash Warning menu item. FSCountSelection.c implements all four counting menu items, and FSSetTypeAndCreator.c implements the Set Creator and Type... dialog.

Let's take a look at the source code.

FinderScripter (AE): FSMain.c

FSMain.c starts with four include files:

```
#include <GestaltEqu.h>
#include <AERegistry.h>
#include <AEObjects.h>

#include "FinderRegistry.h"
```

To find out what any one of them does, comment it out and try rebuilding the application. The fourth include file, `FinderRegistry.h`, is not part of the standard include files that come with your development environment. `FinderRegistry.h` defines all of the constants that make up the *Registry's* Finder Suite. `FinderRegistry.h` contains definitions for `Gestalt()` as well as for the Finder Suite's objects and properties. If you're going to write code that communicates with the Finder, you'll need a copy of `FinderRegistry.h`, so you'll want to either add it to your development environment's `Universal Headers` folder or put a copy in the same folder as your source code.

Next comes the usual cast of #`defines`:

```
#define kBaseResID              128
#define kErrorALRTid            128
#define kAboutALRTid            129

#define kVisible                true
#define kMoveToFront            (WindowPtr)-1L
#define kSleep                  60L
#define kNilFilterProc          0L
#define kGestaltMask            1L

#define kOn                     1
#define kOff                    0

#define mApple                  kBaseResID
#define iAbout                  1

#define mFile                   kBaseResID+1
#define iQuit                   1

#define mScripts                kBaseResID+3
#define iNameOfFrontWindow      1
#define iToggleTrashWarn        2
#define iCountObjects           4
#define iCountContainers        5
#define iCountFolders           6
#define iCountAliases           7
#define iSetTypeAndCreator      9
```

As usual, `gDone` starts life as `false` and will be set to `true` when it's time to drop out of the main event loop:

```
/*************/
/*  Globals  */
/*************/

Boolean     gDone;
```

Here are the function prototypes. The first four are the four external functions called in response to their corresponding menu items. Each of the first four are defined in a separate source code file:

```
/***************/
/*  Functions  */
/***************/


void    NameOfFrontWindow( void ); /* In FSNameOfFrontWindow.c */
void    ToggleTrashWarning( void );      /* In FSToggleTrashWarn.c */
void    CountSelection( long objectClass );   /* In
            FSCountSelection.c */
void    SetTypeAndCreator( void ); /* In FSSetTypeAndCreator.c */
```

The following functions are all found in this source file:

```
void    ToolboxInit( void );
void    MenuBarInit( void );
void    AEInit( void );
void    EventLoop( void );
void    DoEvent( EventRecord *eventPtr );
void    HandleMouseDown( EventRecord *eventPtr );
void    HandleMenuChoice( long menuChoice );
void    HandleAppleChoice( short item );
void    HandleFileChoice( short item );
void    HandleScriptsChoice( short item );
void    DoMessage( Str255 string );
void    Do2Messages( Str255 s1, Str255 s2 );
void    DoError( Str255 errorString );
```

main() starts by initializing the Toolbox and setting up the menu bar. Next, it calls AEInit() to make sure that the Apple Event Manager is installed. Finally, main() drops into the main event loop:

```
/***************************** main ********/

void main( void )
{
    ToolboxInit();
    MenuBarInit();
    AEInit();

    EventLoop();
}
```

ToolboxInit() does its usual thing:

```
/***************** ToolboxInit *******************/

void  ToolboxInit( void )
```

```
{
    InitGraf( &qd.thePort );
    InitFonts();
    InitWindows();
    InitMenus();
    TEInit();
    InitDialogs( 0L );
    InitCursor();
}
```

So does MenuBarInit():

```
/***************** MenuBarInit *********************/

void  MenuBarInit( void )
{
    Handle        menuBar;
    MenuHandle    menu;

    menuBar = GetNewMBar( kBaseResID );

    if ( menuBar == NULL )
        DoError( "\pCouldn't load the MBAR resource..." );

    SetMenuBar( menuBar );

    menu = GetMHandle( mApple );
    AddResMenu( menu, 'DRVR' );

    DrawMenuBar();
}
```

AEInit() **calls** Gestalt() **to make sure that the Apple Event Manager is supported by this configuration:**

```
/***************************** AEInit ********/

void  AEInit( void )
{
    OSErr err;
    long  feature;

    err = Gestalt( gestaltAppleEventsAttr, &feature );

    if ( err != noErr )
        DoError( "\pError returned by Gestalt!" );
```

If the gestaltAppleEventsPresent **bit is not set, we post an error message. Otherwise, we initialize the Object Support Library by calling** AEObjectInit():

```
   if ( !( feature & ( kGestaltMask << gestaltAppleEventsPresent ) ) )
      DoError( "\pThis configuration does not support Apple
            events..." );

   AEObjectInit();
}
```

EventLoop() **makes its usual call to** WaitNextEvent() **and, if an event occurred, passes it on to** DoEvent():

```
/****************************** EventLoop *********/

void  EventLoop( void )
{
   EventRecord    event;

   gDone = false;
   while ( gDone == false )
   {
      if ( WaitNextEvent( everyEvent, &event, kSleep, NULL ) )
         DoEvent( &event );
   }
}
```

DoEvent() **processes mouse and key-based events:**

```
/*********************************** DoEvent   */

void  DoEvent( EventRecord *eventPtr )
{
   char     theChar;

   switch ( eventPtr->what )
   {
      case mouseDown:
         HandleMouseDown( eventPtr );
         break;
      case keyDown:
      case autoKey:
         theChar = eventPtr->message & charCodeMask;

         if ( (eventPtr->modifiers & cmdKey) != 0 )
            HandleMenuChoice( MenuKey( theChar ) );
         break;
   }
}
```

HandleMouseDown() **processes all mouseDown events:**

```
/*********************************** HandleMouseDown */

void  HandleMouseDown( EventRecord *eventPtr )
{
   WindowPtr      window;
   short          thePart;
   long           menuChoice;

   thePart = FindWindow( eventPtr->where, &window );

   switch ( thePart )
   {
      case inMenuBar:
         menuChoice = MenuSelect( eventPtr->where );
         HandleMenuChoice( menuChoice );
         break;
      case inSysWindow :
         SystemClick( eventPtr, window );
         break;
   }
}
```

HandleMenuChoice() **dispatches menu selections, passing them off
to** HandleAppleChoice(), HandleFileChoice(), **or**
HandleScriptsChoice():

```
/****************** HandleMenuChoice **********************/

void   HandleMenuChoice( long menuChoice )
{
   short menu;
   short item;

   if ( menuChoice != 0 )
   {
      menu = HiWord( menuChoice );
      item = LoWord( menuChoice );

      switch ( menu )
      {
         case mApple:
            HandleAppleChoice( item );
            break;
         case mFile:
            HandleFileChoice( item );
            break;
         case mScripts:
            HandleScriptsChoice( item );
            break;
```

```
      }
      HiliteMenu( 0 );
   }
}
```

HandleAppleChoice() **and** HandleFileChoice() **do their normal thing:**

```
/***************** HandleAppleChoice *********************/

void   HandleAppleChoice( short item )
{
   MenuHandle appleMenu;
   Str255     accName;
   short   accNumber;

   switch ( item )
   {
      case iAbout:
         NoteAlert( kAboutALRTid, NULL );
         break;
      default:
         appleMenu = GetMHandle( mApple );
         GetItem( appleMenu, item, accName );
         accNumber = OpenDeskAcc( accName );
         break;
   }
}


/***************** HandleFileChoice *********************/

void  HandleFileChoice( short item )
{
   switch ( item )
   {
      case iQuit:
         gDone = true;
         break;
   }
}
```

HandleScriptsChoice() **dispatches all the selections from the Scripts menu. Notice that** CountSelection() **takes a class constant and then counts the number of objects of that class in the current Finder selection:**

```
/***************** HandleScriptsChoice *********************/

void  HandleScriptsChoice( short item )
```

```
{
   switch ( item )
   {
      case iNameOfFrontWindow:
         NameOfFrontWindow();
         break;
      case iToggleTrashWarn:
         ToggleTrashWarning();
         break;
      case iCountObjects:
         CountSelection( cObject );
         break;
      case iCountContainers:
         CountSelection( cContainer );
         break;
      case iCountFolders:
         CountSelection( cFolder );
         break;
      case iCountAliases:
         CountSelection( cAliasFile );
         break;
      case iSetTypeAndCreator:
         SetTypeAndCreator();
         break;
   }
}
```

DoMessage() **puts up an alert containing the specified pascal string:**

```
/***************** DoMessage ******************/

void  DoMessage( Str255 string )
{
   ParamText( string, "\p", "\p", "\p" );

   NoteAlert( kErrorALRTid, kNilFilterProc );
}
```

Do2Messages() **does the same thing but displays two pascal strings, one right after the other:**

```
/***************** Do2Messages ******************/

void  Do2Messages( Str255 s1, Str255 s2 )
{
   ParamText( s1, s2, "\p", "\p" );

   NoteAlert( kErrorALRTid, kNilFilterProc );
}
```

DoError() **does the same thing as** DoMessage() **but exits back to the Finder after it displays its message:**

```
/**************** DoError ******************/

void  DoError( Str255 errorString )
{
    ParamText( errorString, "\p", "\p", "\p" );

    StopAlert( kErrorALRTid, kNilFilterProc );

    ExitToShell();
}
```

FinderScripter (AE): FSNameOfFrontWindow.c

FSNameOfFrontWindow.c **starts with a pair of** #includes **and a single** #define:

```
#include <ASRegistry.h>      // Additional constants used in
AppleScript.
#include <AEPackObject.h>    // The object specifier building utilities
                            // included in the OSL library

#define kDisposeInputs       true
```

Next come the function prototypes. The first three functions are defined in other source code files; the last two are defined in this file:

```
/**************/
/* Functions */
/**************/

void   DoError( Str255 errorString );  /* In FSMain.c */
void   DoMessage( Str255 string );      /* In FSMain.c */
void   DoGetDataText( AEDesc *objSpecifierPtr, Str255 text );  /* In */
          /* FSAEUtils.c */

void    NameOfFrontWindow( void );
static void   BuildObjectSpecifier( AEDesc *nameOfFrontWindObjSpecPtr
);
```

NameOfFrontWindow() **is called when the user selects Name of Front Window from the Scripts menu:**

```
/***************************** NameOfFrontWindow *********/

void  NameOfFrontWindow( void )
```

```
{
   AEDesc      nameOfFrontWindObjSpec = {typeNull, NULL};
   Str255      name;
```

First, we build an object specifier that represents the name of the frontmost window:

```
BuildObjectSpecifier( &nameOfFrontWindObjSpec );
```

Next, we create a Get Data event, add the object specifier to it, and send the Get Data event to the Finder. DoGetDataText() returns the name of the frontmost window in the parameter name:

```
DoGetDataText( &nameOfFrontWindObjSpec, name );
```

If no window is open, DoGetDataText() returns a null string in name. If a name is returned, we call DoMessage() to display the name in an alert:

```
if ( name[0] > 0 )
   DoMessage( name );
```

Finally, we dispose of the descriptor used to hold the object specifier:

```
AEDisposeDesc( &nameOfFrontWindObjSpec );
}
```

This version of BuildObjectSpecifier() builds an object specifier for the "name of the frontmost window" using the techniques demonstrated in Chapter 2. Notice that BuildObjectSpecifier() is declared as a static void, which limits the scope of this routine to this file, thus allowing us to define additional routines named BuildObjectSpecifier(). As you'll see, we built a BuildObject-Specifier() inside the other source files that implemented menu items as well. (No big deal—just thought you'd be curious.)

```
/****************************** BuildObjectSpecifier ********/

static void BuildObjectSpecifier( AEDesc *nameOfFrontWindObjSpecPtr )
{
   AEDesc      nullContainer = {typeNull, NULL},
               windObjSpecifier = {typeNull, NULL},
               offsetDesc = {typeNull, NULL},
               nameDesc = {typeNull, NULL};
   long        nameProperty = pName;
```

```
OSErr    err;
```

First, we build a specifier representing the front window, which is really a cWindow with a formAbsolutePosition of 1, residing in the NULL container. The NULL container represents the Finder application. The call to CreateOffset-Descriptor() just creates a descriptor with type typeLongInteger and a dataHandle that leads to the value 1L:

```
err = CreateOffsetDescriptor( 1L, &offsetDesc );

if ( err != noErr )
   DoError( "\pError creating offset descriptor..." );
```

Now, we create the object specifier representing the frontmost window by passing the appropriate arguments to CreateObjSpecifier().

```
err = CreateObjSpecifier( cWindow, &nullContainer,
        formAbsolutePosition, &offsetDesc,
        kDisposeInputs, &windObjSpecifier );

if ( err != noErr )
   DoError( "\pError creating object specifier for 'Front Window'..."
);
```

Next, we build a specifier representing the pName property, using the windObjSpecifier as a container. First, we call AECreateDesc() to build a descriptor containing the nameProperty type:

```
err = AECreateDesc( typeType, &nameProperty,
        sizeof( nameProperty ), &nameDesc );

if ( err != noErr )
   DoError( "\pError calling AECreateDesc()..." );
```

Then, we build the "name of" object specifier, using the "frontmost window" specifier as a container:

```
err = CreateObjSpecifier( cProperty, &windObjSpecifier,
        formPropertyID, &nameDesc,
        kDisposeInputs, nameOfFrontWindObjSpecPtr );

if ( err != noErr )
   DoError( "\pError creating object specifier for name property..."
);
}
```

You'll see the description of DoGetDataText() when we get to the source file FSAEUtils.c later in the chapter.

FinderScripter (AE): FSToggleTrashWarn.c

FSToggleTrashWarn.c contains the routines that implement the Toggle
Trash Warning item in the Scripts menu. FSToggleTrashWarn.c starts
with the standard #includes and the same single #define:

```
#include <ASRegistry.h>        // Additional constants used in
                               // AppleScript.
#include <AEPackObject.h>      // The object specifier building utilities
                               // included in the OSL.
#include "FinderRegistry.h"


#define kDisposeInputs       true
```

Next come the function prototypes. The first four are from other
files; the last two are from this file. Notice that BuildObjectSpecifier()
is, once again, defined as a static void:

```
/***************/
/*  Functions  */
/***************/


void    DoError( Str255 errorString );   /* In FSMain.c */
void    DoMessage( Str255 string );      /* In FSMain.c */
Boolean DoGetDataBoolean( AEDesc *objSpecifierPtr );   /* In
             /* FSAEUtils.c */
void    DoSetDataBoolean( AEDesc *objSpecifierPtr,
                        Boolean boolValue );   /* In FSAEUtils.c */


void    ToggleTrashWarning( void );
static void    BuildObjectSpecifier( AEDesc *nameOfFrontWindObjSpecPtr );
```

ToggleTrashWarning() gets called when the user selects Toggle
Trash Warning from the Scripts menu.

```
/***************************** ToggleTrashWarning ********/

void  ToggleTrashWarning( void )
{
   AEDesc      warnObjSpecifier = {typeNull, NULL};
   Boolean     curTrashWarnSetting;
```

First, we build an object specifier that represents the Finder's
pWarnOnEmpty property. The pWarnOnEmpty property is connected to the
"warn before emptying" checkbox in the Trash's Get Info window:

```
   BuildObjectSpecifier( &warnObjSpecifier );
```

Next, we send a Get Data event to the Finder that gets the value of the pWarnOnEmpty property. Then, we pass the opposite value to DoSetData-Boolean(), which sends a Set Data event to the Finder to toggle the value of the pWarnOnEmpty property:

```
curTrashWarnSetting = DoGetDataBoolean( &warnObjSpecifier );
DoSetDataBoolean( &warnObjSpecifier, ! curTrashWarnSetting );
```

Finally, we call DoGetDataBoolean() again to verify that we did, indeed, toggle the pWarnOnEmpty property, and we display an appropriate message. Both DoGetDataBoolean() and DoSetDataBoolean() are described later in the chapter when we go through the source file FSAEUtils.c:

```
if ( DoGetDataBoolean( &warnObjSpecifier ) )
    DoMessage( "\pThe empty trash warning has been turned on..." );
else
    DoMessage( "\pThe empty trash warning has been turned off..." );
```

When we're done, we dispose of the object specifier by calling AEDisposeDesc():

```
    AEDisposeDesc( &warnObjSpecifier );
}
```

This version of BuildObjectSpecifier() builds an object specifier that represents the pWarnOnEmpty property. Note that we could have also built a specifier for the "pWarnOnEmpty property of the pTrash property of the Finder," but since the Scriptable Finder recognizes the "pWarnOnEmpty property of the Finder," why do the extra work?

```
/****************************** BuildObjectSpecifier ********/

static void  BuildObjectSpecifier( AEDesc *warnObjSpecifierPtr )
{
    AEDesc      nullContainer = {typeNull, NULL},
                pWarnDesc = {typeNull, NULL};
    long        warnProperty = pWarnOnEmpty;
    OSErr       err;
```

First, we embed the pWarnOnEmpty property inside a typeType descriptor:

```
    err = AECreateDesc( typeType, &warnProperty,
        sizeof( warnProperty ), &pWarnDesc );
```

```
if ( err != noErr )
    DoError( "\pError calling AECreateDesc()..." );
```

Now, we create the object specifier by passing the appropriate arguments to `CreateObjSpecifier()`:

```
err = CreateObjSpecifier( cProperty, &nullContainer,
        formPropertyID, &pWarnDesc,
        kDisposeInputs, warnObjSpecifierPtr );

if ( err != noErr )
    DoError( "\pError creating object specifier for pWarnOnEmpty..." );
}
```

FinderScripter (AE): FSCountSelection.c

`FSCountSelection.c` contains the routines that implement the four Count... items in the Scripts menu. `FSCountSelection.c` starts with the standard `#include`s and the same single `#define`:

```
#include <ASRegistry.h>        // Additional constants used in
AppleScript.
#include <AEPackObject.h>       // The object specifier building utilities
                               // included in the OSL.
#include "FinderRegistry.h"

#define kDisposeInputs          true
```

Next come the function prototypes. The first two are from other files; the last two are from this file. Once again, `BuildObjectSpecifier()` is defined as a `static void`:

```
/***************/
/*  Functions  */
/***************/

void    DoError( Str255 errorString );    /* In FinderScripter.c */
void    Do2Messages( Str255 s1, Str255 s2 );    /* In FinderScripter.c */

void    CountSelection( long objectClass );
static void    BuildObjectSpecifier( AEDesc *selectionObjSpecifierPtr );
```

`CountSelection()` takes a single parameter, the class of objects to be counted:

```
/***************************** CountSelection ********/

void    CountSelection( long objectClass )
```

```
{
   AEDesc      selectionObjSpecifier = {typeNull, NULL};
   long      selectionCount;
   Str255      countStr;
```

First, we build an object specifier that describes the pSelection property:

```
   BuildObjectSpecifier( &selectionObjSpecifier );
```

Next, we send a Count Elements event to find out how many objects of class objectClass are in the current selection. DoCountElements() is in the file FSAEUtils.c, described later in the chapter:

```
   selectionCount = DoCountElements( &selectionObjSpecifier,
      objectClass );
```

Then, we convert the count to a string and display it.

```
   NumToString( selectionCount, countStr );

   if ( objectClass == cObject )
     Do2Messages( "\pNumber of cObjects selected: ", countStr );
   else if ( objectClass == cContainer )
     Do2Messages( "\pNumber of cContainers selected: ", countStr );
   else if ( objectClass == cFolder )
     Do2Messages( "\pNumber of cFolders selected: ", countStr );
   else if ( objectClass == cAliasFile )
     Do2Messages( "\pNumber of cAliasFiles selected: ", countStr );
```

And finally, we call AEDisposeDesc() to dispose of the memory allocated for the object specifier.

```
   AEDisposeDesc( &selectionObjSpecifier );
}
```

This version of BuildObjectSpecifier() builds an object specifier that represents the pSelection property. The pSelection property refers to the current Finder selection. You can get the current selection by using a Get Data event to get the value of this property, or you can set the selection by sending a Set Data event to set the value of this property:

```
/***************************** BuildObjectSpecifier *********/

static void BuildObjectSpecifier( AEDesc *selectionObjSpecifierPtr )
```

```
{
    AEDesc      nullContainer = {typeNull, NULL},
                pSelectionDesc = {typeNull, NULL};
    long        selectionProperty = pSelection;
    OSErr       err;
```

As we did with the pWarnOnEmpty property, we wrap the pSelection code in a descriptor and then pass it on to CreateObjSpecifier():

```
err = AECreateDesc( typeType, &selectionProperty,
        sizeof( selectionProperty ), &pSelectionDesc );

if ( err != noErr )
    DoError( "\pError calling AECreateDesc()..." );

err = CreateObjSpecifier( cProperty, &nullContainer,
            formPropertyID, &pSelectionDesc,
            kDisposeInputs, selectionObjSpecifierPtr );

if ( err != noErr )
    DoError( "\pError creating object specifier for pSelection..." );
}
```

FinderScripter (AE): FSSetTypeAndCreator.c

FSSetTypeAndCreator.c contains the routines that implement the Set Creator and Type... item in the Scripts menu. FSSetTypeAndCreator.c starts with the same #includes and #define as the other files:

```
#include <ASRegistry.h>       // Additional constants used in AppleScript.
#include <AEPackObject.h>      // The object specifier building utilities
                              // included in the OSL library
#include "FinderRegistry.h"


#define kDisposeInputs        true
```

FSSetTypeAndCreator.c adds a few more #defines:

```
#define kDialogResID          130
#define iCreatorText          4
#define iTypeText             6
#define kNULLStorage          NULL
#define kMoveToFront          (WindowPtr)-1L
#define kNULLFilterProc       NULL
```

Next come the function prototypes. The first four are from other files; the last three are from this file:

```
/**************/
/* Functions  */
/**************/

void      DoError( Str255 errorString );    /* In FSMain.c */
void      DoMessage( Str255 string );       /* In FSMain.c */
void      Do2Messages( Str255 s1, Str255 s2 );   /* In FSMain.c */
void      DoSetDataDescType( AEDesc *objSpecifierPtr, DescType
                       descTypeValue );    /* In FSAEUtils.c */

void      SetTypeAndCreator( void );
Boolean     GetNewTypeAndCreator( OSType *typePtr, OSType
    *creatorPtr );
static void  BuildObjectSpecifier( DescType property, AEDesc
    *propertyObjSpecifierPtr );
```

`SetTypeAndCreator()` **is called when the user selects Set Type and Creator... from the Scripts menu:**

```
/***************************** SetTypeAndCreator ********/

void  SetTypeAndCreator( void )
{
   OSType      newType, newCreator;
   AEDesc      propertyObjSpecifier = {typeNull, NULL};
```

First, we put up a dialog to prompt the user for a new type and creator. If the user presses the Cancel button, `GetNewTypeAndCreator()` **returns** `false` **and we return:**

```
   if ( GetNewTypeAndCreator( &newType, &newCreator ) )
   {
```

If we get a legal type and creator, we first build an object specifier that represents the `pFileType` **property of the** `pSelection` **property of the Finder:**

```
      BuildObjectSpecifier( pFileType, &propertyObjSpecifier );
```

Then, we set the `pFileType` **property to its new value using a Set Data event:**

```
      DoSetDataDescType( &propertyObjSpecifier, newType );
```

Next, we do the same thing for the new creator. `DoSetDataDescType()` **is in the file** `FSAEUtils.c`, **and will be described in just a bit:**

```
        BuildObjectSpecifier( pCreatorType, &propertyObjSpecifier );
        DoSetDataDescType( &propertyObjSpecifier, newCreator );
    }
}
```

GetNewTypeAndCreator() **puts up a dialog to prompt the user for a new creator and type. The dialog defaults to the creator** 'ttxt' **and the type** 'TEXT':

```
/****************************** GetNewTypeAndCreator ********/

Boolean   GetNewTypeAndCreator( OSType *typePtr, OSType *creatorPtr )
{
    Boolean      done;
    DialogPtr    dialog;
    OSErr        err;
    short        itemHit, iType;
    Handle       iHandle;
    Rect         iRect;
    Str255       text;
```

We start by retrieving the DLOG **from the resource fork, turning it into a** DialogRecord:

```
    dialog = GetNewDialog( kDialogResID, kNULLStorage, kMoveToFront );

    if ( dialog == NULL )
        DoError( "\pCould not load DLOG resource..." );
```

Next, we call SetDialogCancelItem() **and** SetDialogDefaultItem() **to tie** command-. **to the Cancel button and return to the OK button, and to draw the default rounded-rect around the OK button. Technically, we should have called** Gestalt() **first to see whether the routines were available and then checked the error codes:**

```
    err = SetDialogCancelItem( dialog, cancel );
    err = SetDialogDefaultItem( dialog, ok );
```

If SetDialogCancelItem() and SetDialogDefaultItem() aren't available, you'll have to draw the border around the OK item yourself. Here's the standard code to do that:

```
GetDItem( dialog, ok, &itemType, &itemHandle, &itemRect );
PenSize( 3, 3 );
InsetRect( &itemRect, -4, -4 );
FrameRoundRect( &itemRect, 16, 16 );
PenSize( 1, 1 );
```

Next, we select the text in the creator field and make the dialog the current port and make it visible:

```
SelIText( dialog, iCreatorText, 0, 32767 );
SetPort( dialog );
ShowWindow( dialog );
```

Here's the main dialog loop:

```
done = false;
while ( ! done )
{
    ModalDialog( kNULLFilterProc, &itemHit );

    switch ( itemHit )
    {
```

If we get a click in the OK button, then we make sure that the creator is exactly 4 bytes long. If it's not, we put up a message and then highlight the text in the creator field:

```
case ok:
    GetDItem( dialog, iCreatorText, &iType, &iHandle, &iRect );
    GetIText( iHandle, text );

    if ( text[0] != 4 )
    {
        DoMessage( "\pThe creator must be four characters
                    long!!!" );
        SelIText( dialog, iCreatorText, 0, 32767 );
    }
    else
    {
```

If the creator field is 4 bytes long, we put the 4 bytes in the return parameter pointed to by `creatorPtr`:

```
*creatorPtr = *((long *)(&text[1]));
```

We then repeat the whole process for the type field:

```
GetDItem( dialog, iTypeText, &iType, &iHandle, &iRect );
GetIText( iHandle, text );

if ( text[0] != 4 )
{
    DoMessage( "\pThe type must be four characters long!!!"
);
```

```
        SelIText( dialog, iTypeText, 0, 32767 );
        }
        else
        {
        *typePtr = *((long *)(&text[1]));
```

If we get a proper type and creator, we set done to true and drop out of the dialog loop:

```
            done = true;
        }
    }
    break;
```

If the click is in the Cancel button, we just drop out of the dialog loop:

```
    case cancel:
        done = true;
        break;
    }
}
```

Once we're out of the loop, we dispose of the dialog and return true if the Ok button is hit, false otherwise:

```
DisposeDialog( dialog );

return (itemHit == ok);
}
```

This version of BuildObjectSpecifier() builds an object specifier that represents either the "creator property of the current selection" or the "type property of the current selection," depending on which is passed in the property parameter:

```
/****************************** BuildObjectSpecifier ********/

static void  BuildObjectSpecifier( DescType property, AEDesc
    *propertyObjSpecifierPtr )
{
    AEDesc      nullContainer = {typeNull, NULL},
                pSelectionDesc = {typeNull, NULL},
                selectionObjSpecifier = {typeNull, NULL},
                propertyDesc = {typeNull, NULL};
    long        selectionProperty = pSelection;
    OSErr       err;
```

First, we build a `typeType` descriptor containing the `pSelection` property:

```
err = AECreateDesc( typeType, &selectionProperty,
    sizeof( selectionProperty ), &pSelectionDesc );

if ( err != noErr )
  DoError( "\pError calling AECreateDesc()..." );
```

Next, we build an object specifier that represents the "selection property of the Finder" by passing the newly created descriptor in to `CreateObjSpecifier()`. Remember, the `NULL` container represents the Finder:

```
err = CreateObjSpecifier( cProperty, &nullContainer,
        formPropertyID, &pSelectionDesc,
        kDisposeInputs, &selectionObjSpecifier );

if ( err != noErr )
  DoError( "\pError creating object specifier for pSelection..." );
```

Then, we use this object specifier as the container for the "creator property" or "type property" specifier:

```
err = AECreateDesc( typeType, &property,
    sizeof( property ), &propertyDesc );

if ( err != noErr )
  DoError( "\pError calling AECreateDesc()..." );

err = CreateObjSpecifier( cProperty, &selectionObjSpecifier,
        formPropertyID, &propertyDesc,
        kDisposeInputs, propertyObjSpecifierPtr );

if ( err != noErr )
  DoError( "\pError creating object specifier for property of
        pSelection..." );
}
```

FinderScripter (AE): FSAEUtils.c
`FSAEUtils.c` contains the routines used to build and send the various Apple events used by FinderScripter. It starts with a single `#include` and a few `#define`s:

```
#include <ASRegistry.h>


#define kFinderType                     'FNDR'
#define kFinderCreator          'MACS'

#define kNoIdleProc                     NULL
#define kNoFilterProc           NULL
#define kMaxTextSize            255
```

Here are the function prototypes. The first two functions are in `FSMain.c`, and the rest are in this file:

```
/***************/
/*  Functions  */
/***************/

void    DoError( Str255 errorString );    /* In FSMain.c */
void    DoMessage( Str255 errorString ); /* In FSMain.c */

void    CreateFinderAddressDesc( AEAddressDesc *finderAddressDescPtr );
void    DoSetDataBoolean( AEDesc *objSpecifierPtr, Boolean boolValue );
void    DoSetDataDescType( AEDesc *objSpecifierPtr, DescType
            descTypeValue);
Boolean DoGetDataBoolean( AEDesc *objSpecifierPtr );
void    DoGetDataText( AEDesc *objSpecifierPtr, Str255 theText );
```

Part of the process of building an Apple event is building an `AEAddressDesc` that contains the address of the Apple event's target application. In this program, we'll address all of our Apple events to the Finder. In the previous chapter, we used the target application's signature to address our Apple event. FinderScripter uses a different approach. It searches the System's process list until it finds the Finder, and then it embeds the Finder's process serial number (PSN) in an `AEAddressDesc` of type `typeProcessSerialNumber`. Either method is fine. Use the one that makes sense for your application.

```
/********************** CreateFinderAddressDesc    */

void CreateFinderAddressDesc( AEAddressDesc *finderAddressDescPtr )
{
    ProcessSerialNumber     psn;
    Boolean                 done = false;
    ProcessInfoRec          procInfo;
    OSErr           err;
```

> A good reason to search for the PSN of the Finder is that other applica-
> tions (At Ease, for example) also have a creator of 'MACS'. The use of
> both the type and creator in our search for the PSN ensures that we're
> really talking to the Finder. Sometimes, you'd rather just send the mes-
> sage to 'MACS' and be happy if whoever is masquerading as the Finder
> understands the event.

We start by initializing `psn` to make sure that our first call to
`GetNext-Process()` retrieves the first process in the process list:

```
psn.highLongOfPSN = 0;
psn.lowLongOfPSN = kNoProcess;
```

Next, we initialize a `ProcessInfoRec` before we pass it to
`GetProcessInformation()`. `GetProcessInformation()` will fill the
`ProcessInfoRec` with information about the process described by the
process serial number in `psn`. Since we're not interested in the Finder's
name or location and we don't need an `FSSpec` that refers to the Finder,
we set these fields to `NULL`. No matter what information you're interested in, you'll always set the `processInfoLength` field to the size of a
`ProcessInfoRec` struct:

```
procInfo.processInfoLength = sizeof( ProcessInfoRec );
procInfo.processName = NULL;
procInfo.processAppSpec = NULL;
procInfo.processLocation = NULL;
```

The following loop steps through each process in the process list,
looking for the Finder:

```
while ( ! done )
{
  err = GetNextProcess( &psn );

  if ( err != noErr )
    DoError( "\pError calling GetNextProcess()..." );
```

Once we hit the end of the process list, `highLongOfPSN` of the PSN
returned will be set to 0 and `lowLongOfPSN` will be set to the constant
`kNoProcess`. In this case, we go through the whole list without hitting
the Finder and we put up an error message:

```
if( (psn.highLongOfPSN == 0) && (psn.lowLongOfPSN == kNoProcess) )
  DoError( "\pGetNextProcess() couldn't find the Finder..." );
```

For every candidate `psn`, we call `GetProcessInformation()` to retrieve the candidate processes' type and signature:

```
err = GetProcessInformation( &psn, &procInfo );

if ( err != noErr )
   DoError( "\pError calling GetProcessInformation()..." );
```

If we find the Finder, we're done:

```
done = ( (procInfo.processType == kFinderType) &&
       (procInfo.processSignature == kFinderCreator) );
}
```

At this point, `psn` holds the process serial number of the Finder. Now all we have to do is embed it in an `AEAddressDesc` of type `typeProcessSerialNumber`:

```
err = AECreateDesc( typeProcessSerialNumber, (Ptr)&psn,
      sizeof( ProcessSerialNumber ), finderAddressDescPtr );

if ( err != noErr )
   DoError( "\pError calling AECreateDesc()..." );
}
```

`DoCountElements()` builds and sends a Count Elements event to the Finder, asking it to count the number of objects of class `objectClass` in the current selection:

```
/******************************** DoCountElements    */

long DoCountElements( AEDesc *objSpecifierPtr, long objectClass )
{
   AEAddressDesc   finderAddressDesc = {typeNull, NULL};
   AppleEvent      event = {typeNull, NULL};
   AppleEvent      reply = {typeNull, NULL};
   OSErr      err;
   DescType   actualType;
   Size       actualSize;
   long       result;
```

First, we build a descriptor containing the address of the Finder:

```
CreateFinderAddressDesc( &finderAddressDesc );
```

Now, we create the Count Elements Apple event:

```
err = AECreateAppleEvent( kAECoreSuite, kAECountElements,
                  &finderAddressDesc, kAutoGenerateReturnID,
```

```
                       kAnyTransactionID, &event );

  if ( err != noErr )
    DoError( "\pError returned by AECreateAppleEvent()..." );
```

The Count Elements Apple event takes two parameters. The first corresponds to the keyword `keyDirectObject` and specifies the set of objects whose elements are to be counted. The routine that called `DoCountElements()` took care of this parameter by building an object specifier containing the `pSelection` property. By adding this object specifier as the `keyDirectObject`, we've asked the Finder to count the elements in its current selection:

```
  err = AEPutParamDesc( &event, keyDirectObject, objSpecifierPtr );

  if ( err != noErr )
    DoError( "\pError returned by AEPutParamDesc()..." );
```

The second Count Elements parameter corresponds to the keyword `keyAEObjectClass` and tells the Finder what class of object it should count. We call `AEPutParamPtr()` to fold `objectClass` into the event as a parameter:

```
  err = AEPutParamPtr( &event, keyAEObjectClass, typeType,
         (Ptr)&objectClass, sizeof( objectClass ) );

  if ( err != noErr )
    DoError( "\pError returned by AEPutParamPtr()..." );
```

Now, we're ready to send the event by calling `AESend()`:

```
  err = AESend( &event, &reply, kAEWaitReply +
         kAECanInteract + kAECanSwitchLayer,
         kAENormalPriority, kAEDefaultTimeout,
         kNoIdleProc, kNoFilterProc );

  if ( err == connectionInvalid )
    DoError( "\pCan't send to the Finder..." );

  if ( err != noErr )
    DoError( "\pError returned by AESend()..." );
```

Next, we retrieve the `keyAEResult` parameter from the reply Apple event, `result`. The `keyAEResult` parameter contains the count, embedded in a `typeLongInteger` descriptor:

```
err = AEGetParamPtr( &reply, keyAEResult, typeWildCard,
        &actualType, (Ptr)&result, sizeof( long ),
        &actualSize );
```

Finally, we dispose of our allocated descriptors and return the count:

```
AEDisposeDesc (&finderAddressDesc);
AEDisposeDesc (&event);
AEDisposeDesc (&reply);

return result;
}
```

DoSetDataBoolean() builds and sends a Set Data event that sets the object described in the object specifier to the Boolean value boolValue:

```
/******************************** DoSetDataBoolean     */

void DoSetDataBoolean( AEDesc *objSpecifierPtr, Boolean boolValue )
{
    AEAddressDesc   finderAddressDesc = {typeNull, NULL};
    AppleEvent      event = {typeNull, NULL};
    AppleEvent      reply = {typeNull, NULL};
    OSErr           err;
```

First, we build an AEAddressDesc descriptor containing the address of the Finder:

```
CreateFinderAddressDesc( &finderAddressDesc );
```

Next, we create a Set Data event:

```
err = AECreateAppleEvent( kAECoreSuite, kAESetData,
                    &finderAddressDesc, kAutoGenerateReturnID,
                    kAnyTransactionID, &event );

if ( err != noErr )
    DoError( "\pError returned by AECreateAppleEvent()..." );
```

A Set Data Apple event takes two parameters. The first is a keyDirectObject and describes the set of objects whose data is to be set. The object specifier pointed to by objSpecifierPtr is already set up to be the keyDirectObject. We add it to the Apple event using AEPutParamDesc():

```
err = AEPutParamDesc( &event, keyDirectObject, objSpecifierPtr );

if ( err != noErr )
    DoError( "\pError returned by AEPutParamDesc()..." );
```

The second Set Data parameter goes with the keyword `keyAEData` and contains the data the object will be set to. In this case, the data is the `Boolean` value in `boolValue`. We add it as a parameter using `AEPutParamPtr()`:

```
err = AEPutParamPtr( &event, keyAEData, typeBoolean,
      (Ptr)&boolValue, sizeof( boolValue ) );

if ( err != noErr )
  DoError( "\pError returned by AEPutParamDesc()..." );
```

Next we send the event using `AESend()`:

```
err = AESend( &event, &reply, kAEWaitReply +
        kAECanInteract + kAECanSwitchLayer,
        kAENormalPriority, kAEDefaultTimeout,
        kNoIdleProc, kNoFilterProc );

if ( err == connectionInvalid )
  DoError( "\pFinder not running..." );

if ( err != noErr )
  DoError( "\pError returned by AESend()..." );
```

Finally, we dispose of our allocated descriptors. Notice that we ignore the reply Apple event. If you want, you can check out the parameters corresponding to the keywords `keyErrorNumber` and `keyErrorString` if they exist:

```
AEDisposeDesc( &finderAddressDesc );
AEDisposeDesc( &event );
AEDisposeDesc( &reply );
}
```

`DoSetDataDescType()` **does the same thing as** `DoSetDataBoolean()`, **except it sets an object's value to data of type** `DescType` **instead of type** `Boolean`:

```
/******************************** DoSetDataDescType   */

void DoSetDataDescType( AEDesc *objSpecifierPtr, DescType
    descTypeValue )
{
   AEAddressDesc    finderAddressDesc = {typeNull, NULL};
   AppleEvent       event = {typeNull, NULL};
   AppleEvent       reply = {typeNull, NULL};
   OSErr         err;
```

Again, we create an `AEAddressDesc` containing the address of the Finder and then create a Set Data Apple event:

```
CreateFinderAddressDesc( &finderAddressDesc );

err = AECreateAppleEvent( kAECoreSuite, kAESetData,
                    &finderAddressDesc, kAutoGenerateReturnID,
                    kAnyTransactionID, &event );

if ( err != noErr )
  DoError( "\pError returned by AECreateAppleEvent()..." );
```

We fold the object specifier in as the `keyDirectObject` parameter:

```
err = AEPutParamDesc( &event, keyDirectObject, objSpecifierPtr );

if ( err != noErr )
  DoError( "\pError returned by AEPutParamDesc()..." );
```

This time, we provide a `DescType` as the `keyAEData`. If the object specifier contains the `pCreator` property, the `DescType` will contain the new creator for the Finder selection. Otherwise, the `DescType` contains the new type for the Finder selection:

```
err = AEPutParamPtr( &event, keyAEData, typeType,
    (Ptr)&descTypeValue, sizeof( descTypeValue ) );

if ( err != noErr )
  DoError( "\pError returned by AEPutParamDesc()..." );
```

Next, we send the Apple event and dispose of any allocated descriptors:

```
err = AESend( &event, &reply, kAEWaitReply +
        kAECanInteract + kAECanSwitchLayer,
        kAENormalPriority, kAEDefaultTimeout,
        kNoIdleProc, kNoFilterProc );

if ( err == connectionInvalid )
  DoError( "\pFinder not running..." );

if ( err != noErr )
  DoError( "\pError returned by AESend()..." );

AEDisposeDesc( &finderAddressDesc );
AEDisposeDesc( &event );
AEDisposeDesc( &reply );
}
```

`DoGetDataBoolean()` **builds and sends a Get Data event that gets the value of the specified** `Boolean` **object:**

```
/******************************** DoGetDataBoolean      */

Boolean DoGetDataBoolean( AEDesc *objSpecifierPtr )
{
   AEAddressDesc   finderAddressDesc = {typeNull, NULL};
   AppleEvent      event = {typeNull, NULL};
   AppleEvent      reply = {typeNull, NULL};
   OSErr        err;
   DescType     actualtype;
   Size         actualSize;
   Boolean      theBool;
```

First, we get the address of the Finder and build a Get Data Apple event:

```
   CreateFinderAddressDesc( &finderAddressDesc );

   err = AECreateAppleEvent( kAECoreSuite, kAEGetData,
                    &finderAddressDesc, kAutoGenerateReturnID,
                    kAnyTransactionID, &event );

   if ( err != noErr )
     DoError( "\pError returned by AECreateAppleEvent()..." );
```

Next, we add the object descriptor describing the object whose value we want as the `keyDirectObject` **parameter and then send the event:**

```
   err = AEPutParamDesc( &event, keyDirectObject, objSpecifierPtr );

   if ( err != noErr )
     DoError( "\pError returned by AEPutParamDesc()..." );

   err = AESend( &event, &reply, kAEWaitReply +
           kAECanInteract + kAECanSwitchLayer,
           kAENormalPriority, kAEDefaultTimeout,
           kNoIdleProc, kNoFilterProc );

   if ( err == connectionInvalid )
     DoError( "\pFinder not running..." );

   if ( err != noErr )
     DoError( "\pError returned by AESend()..." );
```

Next, we retrieve the `Boolean` result from the `reply` event, dispose of our allocated descriptors and return the `Boolean`:

```
err = AEGetParamPtr( &reply, keyAEResult, typeBoolean,
    &actualtype, (Ptr)(&theBool), sizeof(Boolean), &actualSize );

if ( err != noErr )
  DoError( "\pError returned by AEGetParamPtr()..." );

AEDisposeDesc( &finderAddressDesc );
AEDisposeDesc( &event );
AEDisposeDesc( &reply );

return theBool;
}
```

`DoGetDataText()` does the same thing as `DoGetDataBoolean()`, except it gets data from a text object instead of from a `Boolean`:

```
/******************************** DoGetDataText   */

void DoGetDataText( AEDesc *objSpecifierPtr, Str255 theText )
{
  AEAddressDesc   finderAddressDesc = {typeNull, NULL};
  AppleEvent      event = {typeNull, NULL};
  AppleEvent      reply = {typeNull, NULL};
  OSErr       err;
  DescType    actualtype;
  Size        actualSize;
```

As usual, we get the address of the Finder and then build a Get Data event:

```
CreateFinderAddressDesc( &finderAddressDesc );

err = AECreateAppleEvent( kAECoreSuite, kAEGetData,
                    &finderAddressDesc, kAutoGenerateReturnID,
                    kAnyTransactionID, &event );

if ( err != noErr )
    DoError( "\pError returned by AECreateAppleEvent()..." );
```

Now, we add the object specifier as the `keyDirectObject` and then send the event:

```
err = AEPutParamDesc( &event, keyDirectObject, objSpecifierPtr );

if ( err != noErr )
```

```
        DoError( "\pError returned by AEPutParamDesc()..." );

    err = AESend( &event, &reply, kAEWaitReply +
            kAECanInteract + kAECanSwitchLayer,
            kAENormalPriority, kAEDefaultTimeout,
            kNoIdleProc, kNoFilterProc );

    if ( err == connectionInvalid )
        DoError( "\pFinder not running..." );

    if ( err != noErr )
        DoError( "\pError returned by AESend()..." );
```

Next, we retrieve the specified text from the reply event's `keyAEResult` **parameter, coercing it to** `typeChar`. **If we don't get any text (perhaps the object isn't found?), we put up an error message:**

```
    err = AEGetParamPtr( &reply, keyAEResult, typeChar,
        &actualtype, (Ptr)(&(theText[ 1 ])), kMaxTextSize,
            &actualSize );

    if ( err == noErr )
        theText[0] = actualSize;
    else
        DoMessage( "\pError returned by AEGetParamPtr()..." );
```

Either way, we dispose of our allocated descriptors:

```
    AEDisposeDesc( &finderAddressDesc );
    AEDisposeDesc( &event );
    AEDisposeDesc( &reply );
}
```

> I know, I know! I could have combined a lot of the code in `FSAEUtils.c` into a common routine called by all of the Apple event construction routines. I started with the code that way, but I thought it seemed easier to read with all of the code for a single event contained in a single routine. I left out the error checking for the calls to `AEDisposeDesc()` at the end of each routine for the same reason. You'll probably want to bottleneck your Apple event construction in your own code, and you definitely won't want to skimp on your error checking.

FINDERSCRIPTER (SCRIPTS)

The second version of FinderScripter accomplishes the same things as its predecessor but uses a completely different approach. The first

FinderScripter built an object specifier describing the Finder object or property to be accessed, added the specifier to an Apple event, sent the event to the Finder, and then retrieved any return data from the reply event.

Although the first version is about as efficient as you can get in terms of speed, the second version of FinderScripter takes a much simpler approach. Each of the menu items in the Scripts menu is tied to a pascal string containing a script addressed to the Finder. For example, here's the script tied to the Toggle Trash Warning item:

```
tell application "Finder"
    set warn before emptying to not warn before emptying
end tell
```

When a menu item is selected, the associated script is compiled and executed, all courtesy of some simple Component Manager calls. There are a few catches, however. First of all, your program is now dependent on a specific scripting component's being installed. For example, if your scripts are in AppleScript, you won't be able to compile and execute them unless the AppleScript scripting component is installed. If your scripts are in UserTalk, they'll instead be dependent on the UserTalk scripting component, which is automatically installed when you run Frontier.

> If your application allows users to enter their own scripts, you can use the Component Manager to build a pop-up menu of all available scripting languages so that users can script in their language of choice.

Another issue concerns performance. As you'll see when you run the new version of FinderScripter, there is a noticeable delay the first time your application compiles a script. The delay occurs as the Component Manager sets up a scripting environment in your heap and occurs only once per program execution. Since you can hide this delay by compiling a script at start-up, it isn't much of a problem. It's just something you need to be aware of.

The issue of whether to use the Component Manager or the Apple Event Manager is not a simple one. Of course, you'll always use the Apple Event Manager since all of your programs will support the four required Apple events. But which mechanism should you choose when you want your program to communicate with a program such as the Scriptable Finder? As you'll see, the Component Manager provides a flexible and an easy-to-use mechanism for adding scripts to your program. You can even provide a script editor so that users can write their own scripts. If your application is scriptable, your users can even write scripts inside your program that actually control your program. How recursive!

On the other hand, the process of building object specifiers by hand, adding them to Apple events, and then sending the Apple events yourself gives you much tighter control over your interapplication communications. You'll get better performance, and it will be somewhat easier to add your internal objects to your events and to pull objects out of any reply events.

The point here is to master both methods and then use whichever one makes the most sense at a particular point in your application. Start with the goal of making your application scriptable and recordable and of giving the user the ability to tie a script to your program's most important events. If you do that, you'll be way ahead of your competition.

Running FinderScripter (Scripts)

Go into the `Projects` folder, then into the `FinderScripter (Scripts)` subfolder, and double-click on the `FinderScripter` application. When the menu bar appears, take a look at the items in this version of the Scripts menu (Figure 3.7). Each of these items is tied to a script targeted at the Scriptable Finder.

FIGURE 3.7

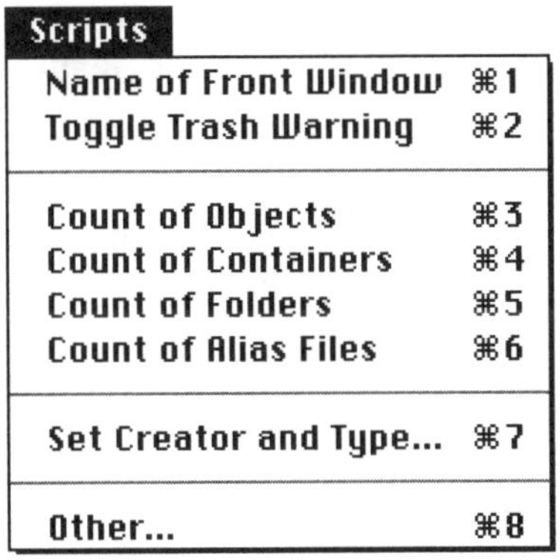

Scripts	
Name of Front Window	⌘1
Toggle Trash Warning	⌘2
Count of Objects	⌘3
Count of Containers	⌘4
Count of Folders	⌘5
Count of Alias Files	⌘6
Set Creator and Type...	⌘7
Other...	⌘8

The Scripts menu from the scripting version of FinderScripter.

The first seven items are identical to the first seven items in the first version of FinderScripter. The last item, Other..., brings up a dialog that allows you to enter your own script, which is then compiled and executed.

Go back to the Finder and make sure that you have at least one window open. Then, return to FinderScripter and select Name of Front Window from the Scripts menu. The first thing you'll see is the "Compiling script" status window that appears in the center of the screen (Figure 3.8). Keep your eye on this window.

After a short delay, the message "Compiling script" will change to "Executing script" and, almost immediately, an alert will appear containing the name of the frontmost Finder window. Click OK to dismiss the alert (the status window will also disappear) and run the script again. Notice that this time the "Compiling script" message changes to "Executing script" almost immediately.

FIGURE 3.8

> **Compiling script...Please wait...**

The "Compiling script" status window.

> If you missed the delay the first time, quit the program and run it again. As mentioned earlier, the delay occurs only once per program execution.

Now, experiment with the other scripts. Notice that some of the menu items (like Toggle Trash Warning) do their thing and then bring up the alert shown in Figure 3.9. This isn't an error. It just means that the Finder didn't return any data as the result of running the script. For example, if you ask for the name of the frontmost window, the Finder returns a text string, but if you tell the Finder to set the "warn before emptying" checkbox, the Finder does it but doesn't return any data.

Spend some time playing with the new version of FinderScripter. You'll notice that the new version of Set Creator and Type... doesn't prompt you for a new creator and type. Instead, it is hard-coded with the creator `'ttxt'` and the type `'TEXT'` for the sake of simplicity. If you like, integrate the creator/type dialog from the first version of FinderScripter with the Set Creator and Type... script found in `FSMain.c` **in the routine** `HandleScriptsChoice()`.

FIGURE 3.9

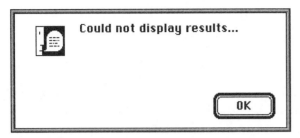

The alert that appears when the Finder doesn't return any particular data as the result of a script.

The last item in the Scripts menu, Other..., brings up a dialog box (Figure 3.10) that allows you to write, compile, and execute your own AppleScript scripts.

One interesting thing about this dialog is the fact that the text that appears in the script editing field is in 10-point Geneva, not your typical dialog size and font. The current version of ResEdit doesn't give you any way to do this, but Resorcerer does.

Just open the resource file in Resorcerer, open the DLOG resource, click on the text-edit item, and then select Colors and Text Styles... from the Item menu. Resorcerer is awesome!

FIGURE 3.10

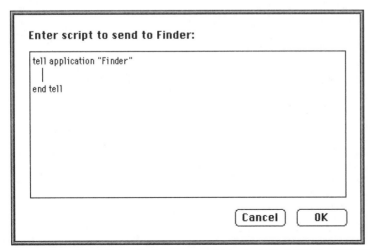

The script editing dialog that appears when you select Other... from the Scripts menu.

The FinderScripter (Scripts) Source Code

The second version of FinderScripter is much simpler than its object specifier-building predecessor. The new FinderScripter project is divided into two source code files, as opposed to the six that made up the first version.

FinderScripter (Scripts): FSMain.c

The file `FSMain.c` hasn't changed much. It still contains all of the event and menu management routines. One difference is in the routine `HandleScripts Choice()`. The new version turns an item selected from the Scripts menu into a pascal string containing a script. The script is passed to the function `ProcessScript()`, which is in the other source code file, `FSOSAUtils.c`:

```
/****************** HandleScriptsChoice ******************/

void  HandleScriptsChoice( short item )
{
    switch ( item )
    {
        case iNameOfFrontWindow:
            ProcessScript( "\ptell application \
\"Finder\"\rname of front window\rend tell" );
            break;
        case iToggleTrashWarn:
            ProcessScript( "\ptell application \
\"Finder\"\rset warn before emptying to not warn \
before emptying\rend tell" );
            break;
        case iCountObjects:
            ProcessScript( "\ptell application \
\"Finder\"\rcount every item of selection\rend tell" );
            break;
        case iCountContainers:
            ProcessScript( "\ptell application \
\"Finder\"\rcount every container of selection\rend tell" );
            break;
        case iCountFolders:
            ProcessScript( "\ptell application \
\"Finder\"\rcount every folder of selection\rend tell" );
            break;
        case iCountAliases:
            ProcessScript( "\ptell application \
\"Finder\"\rcount every alias file of selection\rend tell" );
            break;
        case iSetTypeAndCreator:
```

```
        ProcessScript( "\ptell application \
\"Finder\"\rset file type of every file of selection \
to \"TEXT\"\rset creator type of every file of selection \
to \"ttxt\"\rend tell" );
        break;
```

The item Other... puts up a dialog that lets you enter your own script via a call to the routine `GetAndProcessScript()`, which is also in `FSOSAUtils.c`:

```
    case iOther:
        GetAndProcessScript();
        break;
    }
}
```

This version of `FSMain.c` also contains two utility routines not found in its predecessor. `CreateStatusWindow()` creates a window just large enough to contain a single line of text in 12-point Chicago:

```
/**************** CreateStatusWindow **********/

WindowPtr   CreateStatusWindow( void )
{
    WindowPtr   w;

    w = GetNewWindow( kStatusMsgWindID, kNullStorage,
            kMoveToFront );

    SetPort( w );
    TextSize( 12 );
    TextFont( systemFont );

    return( w );
}
```

`PostStatusMessage()` takes a `WindowPtr` and a `Str255` and centers the string in the window:

```
/**************** PostStatusMessage **********/

void  PostStatusMessage( WindowPtr w, Str255 string )
{
    short   stringWidth, windowWidth;

    SetPort( w );
```

```
stringWidth = StringWidth( string );
windowWidth = w->portRect.right - w->portRect.left;

MoveTo( ((windowWidth - stringWidth)/2) +
        w->portRect.left, 15 );

EraseRect( &w->portRect );
DrawString( string );
}
```

Before we compile a script, we create a status window and post the message "Compiling script...Please wait..." in it. Once the script compiles, we post the message "Executing script...Please wait..." in the same window and then execute the script. When the script is done executing, we dispose of the window with a call to DisposeWindow().

FinderScripter (Scripts): FSOSAUtils.c

The real differences between the old and new FinderScripters are found in this source file. FSOSAUtils.c starts with two extra #includes. <OSAGeneric.h> contains the prototype for the routine OSASetDefaultScriptingComponent(), and <AppleScript.h> contains the definition of the constant kAppleScriptSubtype (we get to both of these in a moment):

```
#include <ASRegistry.h>
#include <AEPackObject.h>
#include <OSAGeneric.h>
#include <AppleScript.h>

#include "FinderRegistry.h"
```

Next comes a series of #defines:

```
#define kScriptDLOGResID     131
#define iScriptText            4
#define kNULLFilterProc      NULL
#define kNULLStorage         NULL
#define kMoveToFront         (WindowPtr)-1L
```

The global gGenericSC will hold a reference to the *generic scripting component*. The generic scripting component is a scripting component, just like the AppleScript and UserTalk scripting components. Instead of being focused on a single language, the generic scripting component is more of a dispatcher. Instead of handling the compilation and execution chores of a traditional scripting component, its job is to route scripting data to the appropriate scripting component. If you send an AppleScript script to the generic component for compilation, it will see to it that the script is sent to the AppleScript component and that the results get back to you. We establish a connection with the generic scripting component in the routine `OSAScriptInit()`:

```
/*************/
/*  Globals  */
/*************/


static ComponentInstance        gGenericSC;
```

Here are the function prototypes. The first four are from `FSMain.c`, and the rest are found in this file:

```
/****************/
/*  Functions  */
/***************/


void      DoError( Str255 errorString );   /* In FSMain.c */
void      Do2Messages( Str255 s1, Str255 s2 );   /* In FSMain.c */
WindowPtr   CreateStatusWindow( void );   /* In FSMain.c */
void      PostStatusMessage( WindowPtr w, Str255 string );
              /* In FSMain.c*/

void      OSAScriptInit( void );
void      GetAndProcessScript( void );
void      ProcessScript( Str255 scriptStr );
Boolean      DoScriptDialog( Str255 scriptStr, short startRange, short
                          endRange );
Boolean      CompileScript( Str255 scriptStr, OSAID *scriptIDPtr,
                      short *startRangePtr, short *endRangePtr );
Boolean      ExecuteScript( OSAID scriptID, short *startRangePtr,
                      short *endRangePtr );
void      DisplayScriptResults( OSAID resultID );
void      ReportScriptError( Str255 message );
void      DescToString( AEDesc *textDescPtr, Str255 string );
void      DescToRange( AEDesc *rangeDescPtr, short
              *startRangePtr,short *endRangePtr );
```

`OSAScriptInit()` is called from `main()`, right before `main()` enters the main event loop. `OSAScriptInit()` establishes a connection with the generic scripting component:

```
/****************************** OSAScriptInit *********/

void   OSAScriptInit( void )
{
   OSAError err;
```

The Component Manager maintains a list of default components for each component type and subtype. In this case, we want to establish a connection with an OSA component (in other words, a scripting component) and, more specifically, the generic scripting component. `OpenDefaultComponent()` returns a pointer to a `ComponentInstance`, a record containing details about this particular component connection:

```
gGenericSC = OpenDefaultComponent( kOSAComponentType,
            kOSAGenericScriptingComponentSubtype );
```

Next, we tell the generic scripting component that we want all scripts sent to the AppleScript component:

```
err = OSASetDefaultScriptingComponent( gGenericSC,
kAppleScriptSubtype );

if ( err != noErr )
    DoError( "\pError calling OSASetDefaultScriptingComponent()..." );
}
```

While it's true that this program supports only AppleScript, with a little bit of work you could easily modify it to support multiple scripting languages.

For example, you can call `CountComponents()` to find out how many OSA components are installed and then use `FindNextComponent()` to step through each of the components. Pass each component to `GetComponentInfo()` and then take a look at the returned component description's `componentSubType` field. If the field is set to `kOSAGenericScriptingComponentSubtype`, you've found a generic scripting component. Otherwise, you've found a real scripting component. In the latter case, the `componentName` returned by `GetComponentInfo()` is the language name supported by the component.

If you want to build a script editor that supports multiple scripting languages, use the method detailed in the previous paragraph to build a pop-up menu of available languages. When users select their language of preference, call `OSASetDefaultScriptingComponent()` and pass a new subtype to your generic scripting component. No matter what the user's language of choice is, the rest of your code remains the same. Just continue sending your scripts to the generic scripting component for compilation.

....

Just as you'd use GetPort() to save your old GrafPort and then later restore the saved GrafPort with SetPort(), you can do the same thing with calls to OSAGetDefaultScriptingComponent() and OSASetDefaultScriptingComponent().

....

GetAndProcessScript() **is called when the user selects Other...**
from the Scripts menu:

```
/******************************* GetAndProcessScript *********/

void    GetAndProcessScript( void )
{
   Boolean      done;
   OSAID        scriptID;
   Str255        scriptStr;
   short        startRange = 30, endRange = 30;       // Range of
                                                      // selection to
                                                      // highlight...
               // Default places cursor in second line of script
                  // so typing
               // automatically starts inside tell statement.
```

Each time you send a script to a scripting component to be compiled, the script is assigned an ID. If this is the first time you're compiling this script, pass in kOSANullScript as a script ID to so advise the scripting component.

The first time the component tries to compile your script, it allocates the memory it needs to track your script's compilation, including the memory it needs to hold the compiled script, once it successfully compiles. The script ID is the key to getting at this memory. If you recompile the same script, be sure to reuse the script ID the component sent you when it first tried to compile your script. Although this isn't strictly necessary, it will save time and memory:

```
   scriptID = kOSANullScript;
```

The following loop calls DoScriptDialog(), which brings up a dialog that prompts the user to enter a script. The script is returned as a pascal string in the parameter scriptStr and is therefore limited to 255 characters. If you design your own script editor, you'll probably want to take a text-edit approach (as opposed to the dialog approach used by DoScriptDialog()) so that the user can build scripts as large as possible:

```
done = false;
while ( ! done )
{
   if ( DoScriptDialog( scriptStr, startRange, endRange  ) )
   {
```

If the script doesn't compile, it is passed back to DoScriptDialog()
and redisplayed in the dialog. When the scripting component reports an
error, it also provides a range of characters to highlight, telling the user
where the error occurred. To start with, we pass 30 as both a
startRange and endRange, placing the cursor on the second line of the
script, right in the middle of the tell statement. Once we have a script
to compile, we pass it to CompileScript():

```
      if ( CompileScript( scriptStr, &scriptID,
                          &startRange, &endRange ) )
      {
```

If the script does compile, we pass the scriptID on to
ExecuteScript(). Notice that we aren't passing a compiled script on to
ExecuteScript(). When the scripting component gets a script ID to
execute, it uses it as an index to retrieve and execute the matching compiled script. Once we execute the script, we drop out of the loop:

```
         if ( ExecuteScript( scriptID, &startRange, &endRange ) )
            done = true;
      }
```

If the script doesn't compile, CompileScript() will display an error
message and return new values for startRange and endRange. At this
point, we go back to the top of the loop and try again. If the Cancel button is pressed, we drop out of the loop:

```
   }
   else
      done = true;
}
}
```

ProcessScript() compiles and executes the script in scriptStr.
Since all the scripts sent to ProcessScript() are canned (and presum-
ably tested), it is assumed that each script will compile with no errors.
When you add your own scripts to the Scripts menu, be sure to test
them before you pass them to this routine!

```
/******************************** ProcessScript *********/

void   ProcessScript( Str255 scriptStr )
{
   OSAID       scriptID;
   WindowPtr    statusWindow;
   short        startRange = 0, endRange = 0;

   scriptID = kOSANullScript;
```

We start by creating a small status window and posting the message "Compiling script...Please wait...":

```
   statusWindow = CreateStatusWindow();
   PostStatusMessage( statusWindow,
     "\pCompiling script...Please wait..." );
```

Next, we pass the canned script to `CompileScript()` along with some dummy values for `startRange` and `endRange` (since all these scripts are going to compile and there won't be any errors to highlight, right?):

```
   if ( CompileScript( scriptStr, &scriptID,
                                &startRange, &endRange ) )
   {
```

Assuming the script compiles, we post the message "Executing script...Please wait..." and then pass the script ID to `ExecuteScript()`. If the script doesn't compile or doesn't execute properly, we post the appropriate message:

```
      PostStatusMessage( statusWindow,
          "\pExecuting script...Please wait..." );
      if ( ! ExecuteScript( scriptID, &startRange, &endRange ) )
         DoMessage( "\pA canned script didn't execute properly..." );
   }
   else
      DoMessage( "\pA canned script didn't compile properly..." );
```

When we're done, we dispose of the status window:

```
   DisposeWindow( statusWindow );
}
```

`DoScriptDialog()` puts up a dialog that lets the user enter a script of up to 255 characters:

```
/****************************** DoScriptDialog *********/

Boolean  DoScriptDialog( Str255 scriptStr, short startRange, short
    endRange )
{
    Boolean      done;
    DialogPtr    dialog;
    OSErr      err;
    short      itemHit;
    short      iType;
    Handle       iHandle;
    Rect       iRect;

    dialog = GetNewDialog( kScriptDLOGResID, kNULLStorage,
        kMoveToFront );

    if ( dialog == NULL )
    DoError( "\pCould not load DLOG resource..." );

    err = SetDialogCancelItem( dialog, cancel );
```

Since we want the ability to include carriage returns in our script, we pass 0 to `SetDialogDefaultItem()`, telling the Dialog Manager we don't want to trap carriage returns. (I've never seen this documented, but it seems to work OK.)

```
    err = SetDialogDefaultItem( dialog, 0 );
```

If a script is passed in (due to a previous compile error, no doubt), we copy it into the text-editing field:

```
    if ( scriptStr[ 0 ] != 0 )  // If we have an existing script...
    {
        GetDItem( dialog, iScriptText, &iType, &iHandle, &iRect );
        SetIText( iHandle, scriptStr );
    }
```

Next, we highlight the specified portion of the script:

```
    SelIText( dialog, iScriptText, startRange, endRange );

    SetPort( dialog );
    ShowWindow( dialog );
```

Here's the main dialog loop:

```
    done = false;
    while ( ! done )
```

```
{
    ModalDialog( kNULLFilterProc, &itemHit );

    switch ( itemHit )
    {
```

If we get a click in the OK button, we retrieve the text in the text-edit field and then check to see whether it's 0 bytes long. If so, we change the OK to Cancel. Either way, we drop out of the loop:

```
        case ok:
            GetDItem( dialog, iScriptText, &iType, &iHandle, &iRect );
            GetIText( iHandle, scriptStr );

            if ( scriptStr[ 0 ] == 0 ) // No text to process...
                itemHit = cancel;

            done = true;
            break;
```

If the click is in the Cancel button, we just drop out of the loop:

```
        case cancel:
            done = true;
                break;
    }
}

DisposeDialog( dialog );

return (itemHit == ok);
}
```

CompileScript() compiles the specified script and, if the script doesn't compile correctly, returns a selection range that tells you where the error is located in the script. Whether an error occurred or not, CompileScript() also returns a script ID that distinguishes this particular script from the others handled by the same scripting component:

```
/***************************** CompileScript ********/

Boolean     CompileScript( Str255 scriptStr, OSAID *scriptIDPtr,
                        short *startRangePtr, short *endRangePtr )
{
    OSErr     err;
    OSAError  errOSA;
    AEDesc      errorDesc = {typeNull, NULL};
    AEDesc      textDesc = {typeNull, NULL};
```

First, we embed the script in a `typeChar` descriptor:

```
err = AECreateDesc( typeChar, &scriptStr[ 1 ], scriptStr[ 0 ],
&textDesc );

if ( err != noErr )
  DoError( "\pError calling AECreateDesc()..." );
```

We pass this script descriptor to `OSACompile()`. The first parameter points to the scripting component we want `OSACompile()` to send the script to (in this case, it's a generic scripting component). The third parameter specifies a series of mode flags (Figure 3.11), much like the mode flags you passed to `AESend()`.

FIGURE 3.11

OSACompile() Mode Flags	
kOSAModeNull	Don't set any mode flags.
kOSAModePreventGetSource	Don't save source with compiled script. Now OSAGetSource() will fail.
kOSACompileIntoContext	Create a script context instead of a compiled script.
kOSAModeAugmentContext	Create a script context and add to any existing context for this script ID.
kOSAModeNeverInteract	Add this flag to AESend() when Apple events for this script are sent.
kOSAModeCanInteract	Add this flag to AESend() when Apple events for this script are sent.
kOSAModeAlwaysInteract	Add this flag to AESend() when Apple events for this script are sent.
kOSAModeDontReconnect	Add this flag to AESend() when Apple events for this script are sent.
kOSAModeCantSwitchLayer	Don't allow kAECanSwitchLayer in AESend()'s for this script.
kOSAModeDoRecord	Don't allow kAEDontRecord in AESend()'s for this script..

The mode flags you can pass to OSACompile().

Two of the mode flag descriptions in Figure 3.11, `kOSACompileIntoContext` and `kOSAModeAugmentContext`, refer to the term *script context*. A script context is any script you compile with one of these flags or via a call to `OSAMakeContext()`. When asked to build a script context, both `OSACompile()` and `OSAMakeContext()` return a context ID.

There are several ways to take advantage of a script context. When you execute a script using `OSAExecute()`, you can pass in a context ID in addition to the script ID. When the script is executed by the scripting component, the top-level data and handlers in the compiled context are also available to the script. In this way, a script context is like a library of pre-compiled utility routines you might add to your project. More importantly, the global data in a context is persistent, providing a mechanism for sharing data between scripts.

You can also build a script context designed to handle a specific Apple event. For example, you might write an "on open" handler and then compile it into a context. When an Open Apple event occurs, your application passes a context ID to `OSADoEvent()`. If the script context has a matching handler, `OSADoEvent()` passes the Apple event to the handler and returns the reply event to the application. If no matching handler is found, `OSADoEvent()` returns the error `errAEEventNotHandled`.

Similarly, the routine `OSAExecuteEvent()` executes a context-based handler in response to an Apple event but, instead of returning a reply event, returns a script ID just like `OSAExecute()`.

To learn more about script contexts, check out the routines `OSAExecuteEvent()` and `OSADoEvent()` as well as the term "script context" in *Inside Macintosh: Interapplication Communication*.

We pass `kOSAModeNull` as the third parameter, telling `OSACompile()` that we don't want any of the mode flags set. The fourth parameter is a pointer to the script ID. If this is a recompile of a previous script, we use the same script ID as the last time. If this is the first compile for this script, we pass in a value of `kOSANullScript` and the scripting component will generate a new script ID for us. We need to keep track of this new ID since that's how we ask the scripting component to execute our newly compiled script:

```
errOSA = OSACompile( gGenericSC, &textDesc, kOSAModeNull,
    scriptIDPtr );

err = AEDisposeDesc( &textDesc );

if ( err != noErr )
  DoError( "\pError calling AEDisposeDesc()..." );
```

If `OSACompile()` encounters an error compiling the script, we first report the error:

```
if ( errOSA == errOSAScriptError )
{
  ReportScriptError( "\pError compiling the script: " );
```

Next, we retrieve the selection range so that when we redisplay the script we can highlight the error. To do this, we call `OSAScriptError()`, telling it we want the range of the error found in the last compile directed to our generic scripting component. The third parameter says that we want the data returned in a descriptor of type `typeOSAErrorRange`, and the fourth parameter is a pointer to that very descriptor:

```
errOSA = OSAScriptError( gGenericSC, kOSAErrorRange,
              typeOSAErrorRange, &errorDesc );

if ( errOSA != noErr )
  DoError( "\pError calling OSAScriptError." );
```

The routine `DescToRange()` (described later) will convert the range descriptor into two `shorts`:

```
DescToRange( &errorDesc, startRangePtr, endRangePtr );

err = AEDisposeDesc( &errorDesc );

if ( err != noErr )
  DoError( "\pError calling AEDisposeDesc." );
```

Once we've retrieved our range, we return `false`, telling the calling routine that a compile error occurred:

```
  return false;
}
```

If `OSACompile()` returns an error that isn't `errOSAScriptError`, something is seriously wrong and we bail out. Of course, you might want to make a little better attempt at a recovery:

```
else if ( errOSA != noErr )
  DoError( "\pError calling OSACompile()..." );
```

If we get here, the script compiled successfully and we let the calling routine know by returning `true`:

```
  return true;
}
```

`ExecuteScript()` takes a script ID and passes it to our generic scripting component for execution:

```
/****************************** ExecuteScript ********/

Boolean ExecuteScript( OSAID scriptID, short *startRangePtr,
                       short *endRangePtr )
{
  OSAID    resultID;
  OSErr    err;
  OSAError errOSA;
  AEDesc   errorDesc = {typeNull, NULL};
```

Here's the call to `OSAExecute()`. The first parameter indicates the scripting component to which the script ID in the second parameter should be sent. The third parameter lets you specify a script context that goes along with this script, assuming you've created one. Since we haven't, we pass in a context ID of `kOSANullScript`:

```
errOSA = OSAExecute( gGenericSC, scriptID, kOSANullScript,
        kOSAModeNull, &resultID );
```

The fourth parameter lets you specify a set of mode flags (Figure 3.12), just as you did when you called `OSACompile()`. Since we don't have any flags to set, we pass a value of `kOSAModeNull`. The last parameter is a result ID we can use to retrieve the result of the script (which we'll do in a second).

FIGURE 3.12

OSAExecute() Mode Flags	
kOSAModeNull	Don't set any mode flags.
kOSAModeNeverInteract	Add this flag to AESend() when Apple events for this script are sent.
kOSAModeCanInteract	Add this flag to AESend() when Apple events for this script are sent.
kOSAModeAlwaysInteract	Add this flag to AESend() when Apple events for this script are sent.
kOSAModeDontReconnect	Add this flag to AESend() when Apple events for this script are sent.
kOSAModeCantSwitchLayer	Don't allow kAECanSwitchLayer in AESend()'s for this script.
kOSAModeDoRecord	Don't allow kAEDontRecord in AESend()'s for this script..

Mode flags for OSAExecute().

If an error occurred, we send it to our own `ReportScriptError()`:

```
if ( errOSA == errOSAScriptError )
{
    ReportScriptError( "\pError executing the script: " );
```

Next, just as we did when we encountered a compile error, we retrieve the error range descriptor and convert it to a pair of `shorts` describing
the range:

```
errOSA = OSAScriptError( gGenericSC, kOSAErrorRange,
            typeOSAErrorRange, &errorDesc );

if ( errOSA != noErr )
    DoError( "\pError calling OSAScriptError." );

DescToRange( &errorDesc, startRangePtr, endRangePtr );
```

```
      err = AEDisposeDesc( &errorDesc );

      if ( err != noErr )
        DoError( "\pError calling AEDisposeDesc." );

      return false;
    }
  else if ( errOSA != noErr )
    DoError( "\pError calling OSAExecute()..." );
```

If we get here, the script executed successfully and we use the
result ID to display the result:

```
  DisplayScriptResults( resultID );

  return true;
}
```

`DisplayScriptResults()` **takes a result ID produced by**
`OSAExecute()` **and displays the results:**

```
/****************************** DisplayScriptResults *********/
void   DisplayScriptResults( OSAID resultID )
{
    OSAError   errOSA;
    OSErr      err;
    AEDesc        resultDesc = {typeNull, NULL};
    Str255        string;
```

`OSADisplay()` **takes the result ID and builds a descriptor containing a human-readable description of the results. The first parameter is
the scripting component that produced the result ID. The second parameter is the result ID. The third parameter is the preferred type of the
resulting descriptor. The fourth parameter is either** `kOSAModeNull` **or**
`kOSAModeDisplayForHumans`. **Use** `kOSAModeNull` **if you plan on using the
result in its raw form or if you plan on parsing the results yourself. Use**
`kOSAModeDisplayForHumans` **if you want** `OSADisplay()` **to format the
results in a human-readable format. Finally, the last parameter is the
descriptor in which the results will be placed:**

```
  errOSA = OSADisplay( gGenericSC, resultID, typeChar,
        kOSAModeDisplayForHumans, &resultDesc );
```

`OSADisplay()` **will return an error if you attempt to display the
undisplayable. For example, toggling the "warn before emptying" checkbox doesn't generate a human-readable result. We put up a message if
we get an error:**

```
    if ( errOSA != noErr )
        DoMessage( "\pCould not display results..." );
    else
    {
```

If the call to OSADisplay() is successful, we use our own
DescToString() to convert the descriptor to a Str255 and then call
Do2Messages() to display it:

```
        DescToString( &resultDesc, string );

        Do2Messages( "\pResult of script: ", string );

        err = AEDisposeDesc( &resultDesc );

        if ( err != noErr )
            DoError( "\pError calling AEDisposeDesc()..." );
    }
}
```

ReportScriptError() calls OSAScriptError() to retrieve an error
generated by a call to OSACompile() or OSAExecute():

```
/****************************** ReportScriptError ********/

void    ReportScriptError( Str255 message )
{
    OSAError errOSA;
    OSErr    err;
    AEDesc       errorDesc = {typeNull, NULL};
    Str255       errorString;
```

Recognize this call to OSAScriptError()? We called it earlier in
the program to retrieve the range of characters brought on by a compile or an execution error. As it turns out, OSAScriptError() can
retrieve lots of things, depending on the value passed as the second
parameter. Your choices are listed in Figure 3.13.

FIGURE 3.13

OSAScriptError( ) Selectors	
kOSAErrorNumber	A short containing a system or scripting component error number.
kOSAErrorMessage	The error message associated with the error number.
kOSAErrorBriefMessage	A shorter version of the message associated with the error number.
kOSAErrorApp	Either the nameor process serial number of the receiving application.
kOSAErrorPartialResult	A partial result returned when AESend() failed.
kOSAErrorOffendingObject	An obeject specifer associated with the object that caused the error.
kOSAErrorRange	A selection range that describes the error in the original source.

The selector constants you can pass to OSAScriptError().

In this case, we retrieve an informative error message using the constant kOSAErrorMessage. The third parameter specifies the descriptor type you'd like the data wrapped in. The fourth parameter is a pointer to the descriptor:

```
errOSA = OSAScriptError( gGenericSC, kOSAErrorMessage,
            typeChar, &errorDesc );

if ( errOSA != noErr )
   DoError( "\pError calling OSAScriptError." );
```

Next, we pass the descriptor to our own DescToString() to retrieve the embedded error message and then display it with Do2Messages():

```
DescToString( &errorDesc, errorString );

err = AEDisposeDesc( &errorDesc );

if ( err != noErr )
   DoError( "\pError calling AEDisposeDesc." );

Do2Messages( message, errorString );
}
```

DescToString() copies the data from a typeChar descriptor into a pascal string and then returns the string in its second parameter:

```
/****************************** DescToString ********/

void   DescToString( AEDesc *textDescPtr, Str255 string )
{
   Size   len;
   short  i;
   char   *stringPtr;
```

First, we verify that we're dealing with a typeChar descriptor:

```
if ( textDescPtr->descriptorType != typeChar )
   DoError( "\pTried to convert a non-typeChar descriptor to a
string!!!");
```

Next, we find out exactly how big the block of characters is and then place that value in the first byte of our pascal string:

```
len = GetHandleSize( textDescPtr->dataHandle );

string[ 0 ] = (unsigned char)len;
```

If there's no data to copy (`len` will never actually be less than 0), we return. If the error message is longer than 255 characters, we just copy the first 255:

```
if ( len <= 0 )
   return;

if ( len > 255 )
   len = 255;   // Clip the string to first 255 characters
```

Now, we lock the handle, copy the block of characters into the pascal string, and then unlock the handle:

```
HLock( textDescPtr->dataHandle );

stringPtr = *(textDescPtr->dataHandle);

for ( i=0; i<len; i++ )
{
   string[ i+1 ] = stringPtr[ i ];
}

HUnlock( textDescPtr->dataHandle );
}
```

`DescToRange()` pulls the two `short`s out of a `typeOSAErrorRange` descriptor:

```
/****************************** DescToRange ********/

void   DescToRange( AEDesc *rangeDescPtr, short *startRangePtr, short
       *endRangePtr )
{
   OSErr    err;
   Size     actualSize;
   DescType returnedTypeCode;
   AEDesc   coercedDesc = {typeNull, NULL};
```

The `typeOSAErrorRange` descriptor is actually just an `AERecord` with two parameters, one corresponding to the keyword `keyOSASourceStart` and the other to the keyword `keyOSASourceEnd`. The problem is that you can't pass a `typeOSAErrorRange` descriptor to `AEGetKeyPtr()` or `AEGetKeyDesc()`. The solution is to coerce our `typeOSAErrorRange` descriptor to an `AERecord` by passing it to `AECoerceDesc()`. The first parameter is a pointer to the original descriptor, the second parameter is the desired type, and the final parameter is the newly created descriptor:

```
err = AECoerceDesc( rangeDescPtr, typeAERecord, &coercedDesc );

if ( err != noErr )
   DoError( "\pError coercing range descriptor to AERecord..." );
```

We can now pass the new descriptor to `AEGetKeyPtr()` to retrieve the two `short` parameters that define the beginning and the end of the range:

```
err = AEGetKeyPtr( &coercedDesc, keyOSASourceStart,
      typeWildCard, &returnedTypeCode, startRangePtr,
      sizeof( short ), &actualSize );

if ( err != noErr )
   DoError( "\pError calling AEGetKeyPtr()..." );

err = AEGetKeyPtr( &coercedDesc, keyOSASourceEnd,
      typeWildCard, &returnedTypeCode, endRangePtr,
      sizeof( short ), &actualSize );

if ( err != noErr )
   DoError( "\pError calling AEGetKeyPtr()..." );

err = AEDisposeDesc( &coercedDesc );

if ( err != noErr )
   DoError( "\pError calling AEDisposeDesc()..." );
}
```

SUMMARY

Chapters 2 and 3 have given you a good head start on the subject of Apple events and the Open Scripting Architecture. Although there's much more to learn, you have most of what you need to bring your programs up to code. Start by making your next application scriptable and then recordable. Spend some time with a scripting language like AppleScript. Dog-ear the pages of *Inside Macintosh: Interapplication Communication*. This technology is incredibly important to Apple's future direction, and now is the time to get on board!

BIOGRAPHY

Greg Anderson (AppleLink: G.ANDERSON) attended the University of California at Santa Cruz, a reputed party school in the redwoods somewhere between San Francisco and Baja. He didn't take advantage of this environment, choosing instead to enroll in difficult classes and study hard, eventually graduating with highest honors in Computer Engineering in 1990. After graduation, most of Greg's colleagues went and got jobs in the real world, but Greg decided it would be more fun to work at Apple instead, and he's been there ever since. Currently, Greg is technical lead of the Finder team, which goes to show he still hasn't learned how to shirk responsibility.

WORKING WITH SOUND

Chapter

4

If you've ever thought about adding sound to your application, this chapter is for you. Even if you've already written Sound Manager-savvy code, keep reading. This chapter not only shows you the right way to work with the Sound Manager, but also shows you some of the tricks you'll need to bypass bugs in the various Sound Manager incarnations your users might have installed on their machines.

To go along with the explanations, Jim Reekes retooled his classic Sound Manager sample program, SoundApp. SoundApp does all kinds of things with sound. It plays sampled sounds and wave table sounds. It plays scales and melodies. It even plays more than one sound at the same time. As you proceed through the chapter, you'll learn your way around the SoundApp code and around the Sound Manager.

> This chapter was originally designed to cover the various technologies involved in writing professional quality games. It became clear there was no way to fit all those concepts in a single chapter. Rather than dedicate this entire book to game programming, we decided to include one game related chapter in each volume. In Volume II, we'll take on the subject of sprites and animation.

RUNNING SOUNDAPP

Since this entire chapter is built around SoundApp, let's take this program for a spin. Navigate over to your Projects folder, move into the SoundApp subfolder, and then launch SoundApp. SoundApp features the usual File and Edit menus. The real action is in the Demos menu (Figure 4.1).

The first item, Check Volume..., brings up an alert that tells you the current volume setting in the Sound control panel (Figure 4.2). The message in this alert makes a somewhat subtle point. It tells you not to change the sound settings from inside your application, but to leave such machinations where they belong—in the Sound control panel.

The remainder of the Demos menu is divided into three sections and lets you make sounds using *square waves*, *wave tables*, and *sampled sounds*. These are the three sound types supported by the Sound Manager.

FIGURE 4.1

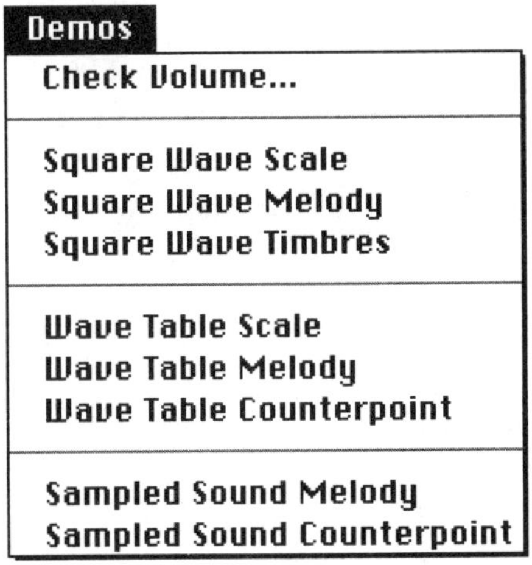

```
┌─────────────────────────────────┐
│ Demos                            │
├─────────────────────────────────┤
│  Check Volume...                 │
│                                  │
│  Square Wave Scale               │
│  Square Wave Melody              │
│  Square Wave Timbres             │
│                                  │
│  Wave Table Scale                │
│  Wave Table Melody               │
│  Wave Table Counterpoint         │
│                                  │
│  Sampled Sound Melody            │
│  Sampled Sound Counterpoint      │
└─────────────────────────────────┘
```

The SoundApp Demos menu.

FIGURE 4.2

The SoundApp Check Volume... alert, which tells you the current setting of the Sound control panel.

Square Waves

Start by listening to the square wave scale, melody, and timbres. The scale is a C Major scale, and the melody is "Promenade" from *Pictures at an Exhibition,* by Mussorgsky. The square wave timbres (pronounced tom-bers) are the range of tones the Sound Manager can produce using square waves. The square wave reminds me of an old Apple II or PC, in the days before sampled sound. Cheesy, yet nostalgic.

Wave Tables

Now, play the wave table sounds. You should hear a definite improvement in sound quality. A wave table is an array of numbers that track a
wave through a single period. The amplitude of the wave is sampled 512
times, and the amplitude of the wave at each point is stored in a 512-byte
array. As you can see in Figure 4.3, negative amplitudes are represented
by the values 0 through 0x80 and positive amplitudes by the values 0x80
through 0xFF, where 0x80 represents an amplitude of 0.

FIGURE 4.3

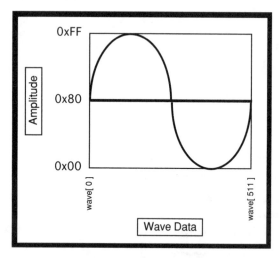

A sample wave table, with 512 amplitudes stored in the 512 bytes of the wave array.

To play a wave table sound, the Sound Manager loops through the
wave array again and again for a specified duration, generating tones that
follow the sound wave embedded in the wave array. Although the wave
in Figure 4.3 looks like a sine wave, you can make a wave table look like
a sine, a cosine, or even a square wave, whichever suits your fancy.

Your wave table can be any size you like. Whatever the table's size,
the Sound Manager will scale your table to fit into a 512-byte array
before it is played. Unless you have a specific reason not to, keep all
wave tables at exactly 512 bytes each to attain the most precise results.

Square waves are just another form of wave table and use data built
into the Sound Manager instead of data provided by you. As you heard,
square waves tend to be harsh, while smoother, sine-shaped waves produce a mellow sound.

Sampled Sounds

In addition to the two sound just discussed, the Sound Manager also supports the recording and playback of sampled sounds. These days, the vast majority of Macintosh sound is sampled sound. Wave table sound is very space efficient, but is not very realistic. Sampled sound is as realistic as you can get, but is costly in terms of disk space and RAM. As Macs increase their standard RAM and hard disk minimums, the fact that sampled sound can get pretty large becomes less and less of an issue.

Back in SoundApp, try out the two sampled sound demos. As you listen to the sampled sound melody, notice how realistic the flute sounds. The flute melody was not recorded as one large sampled sound. Instead, a single flute note was recorded. To create each note in the melody, the Sound Manager played the sampled note at the right pitch.

If you wait long enough, you'll notice that the flute melody is joined by an electric piano. The piano melody was also built from a single sampled note. If you go back and listen to the wave table melody, you'll also hear multiple sounds being played at the same time. Sound Manager versions 3.0 and later support the ability to play an unlimited number of simultaneous wave table and sampled sounds. (Actually, you can play only as many sounds as you can fit in memory, but that's being picky, right?)

More Sampled Sounds

In addition to the demos, SoundApp lets you open a resource file and display and play the file's 'snd ' resources. Select Open from the File menu and then open the file Example Sounds in the SoundApp folder (or open one of your own 'snd ' resource files, if you prefer). A window that lists the 'snd ' resources by name will appear (Figure 4.4).

To play a sound, select it and press one of the buttons on the right. Play Sound plays the sound once, using the correct method. Hyper Play also plays the sound, but this time using the incorrect sampling-rate adjusting method used by HyperCard. To learn more about the HyperCard approach, check out the routine HyperSndPlay() in the file SoundUnit.c.

Play Scale and Play Melody play the sound in a scale and in a melody, respectively. Once you've started a sound, you can stop it by pressing Stop in the sound's status window or by pressing Stop Sound in the list window. Finally, you can add a new sound to the list by pressing Record Sound.

Create a new sound list by selecting New from the File menu and try your hand at creating a few new sounds. Experiment with sounds, scales, and melodies. Try to play a scale based on a long sound and then on a short sound. Try breathy sounds, as well as short, sharp, staccato sounds.

The SoundApp Source Code

Before we get into the technical details of using the Sound Manager, let's take a few minutes to open the SoundApp project and walk through the three SoundApp source code files. SoundApp.c contains main() and the support routines that make up the SoundApp infrastructure (menu-handling code, the main event loop, and so on). SoundUnit.c contains the routines that actually touch the Sound Manager. SoundUnit.h contains the prototypes of the public routines and constants from SoundUnit.c (the routines meant to be called by the outside world). Feel free to use the routines defined in SoundUnit.c in your own programs.

FIGURE 4.4

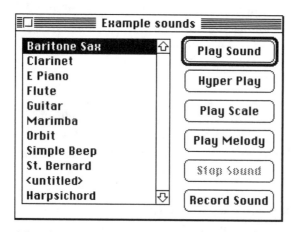

A list of sounds prepared by our leader, Jim Reekes!

Start your code walk-through by opening the file SoundApp.c. The first thing you'll notice is the incredible wealth of comments. Read them! Jim Reekes knows a tremendous amount about Mac programming, and there's something in his comments for even the most experienced Mac programmer. At the beginning of the file, you'll see a series of commentaries covering various strategies involving the different Toolbox managers that Jim used in building SoundApp and ending with the section entitled "Strategies for Sound."

As you look through the code, check out the comment block that precedes each function. As you encounter function calls in the code, chances are that you'll have some questions. Most likely, your questions will be addressed by these function header comment blocks.

SoundApp takes the Sound Manager through its paces and contains some awesome sample code. It's also a great example of a complete Macintosh application, with full error handling, support for the required Apple events, and a look at the right way to work with the most popular Toolbox managers.

When you're reading the SoundApp sources, keep in mind the fact that SoundApp supports all versions of the Sound Manager since version 2.0, all known Mac configurations, and all known data formats. Some of the error checking that goes along with this support might be overkill for your particular application. For example, you might require that your user have the latest version of the Sound Manager installed, and, therefore, you might jettison all the error checking and special casing that goes along with supporting earlier versions of the Sound Manager. On the other hand, SoundApp checks out the format of a particular 'snd ' resource before it plays it. You'll probably want to carry this error-checking code into your own programs. Pay attention to the comments. They'll help you decide what you need and what you don't.

GETTING STARTED WITH THE SOUND MANAGER

As you make your way through the Sound Manager, you'll want to learn about sound channels and sound commands. To produce sound, you first create a sound channel and then send a series of sound commands to the channel. Each command is either executed immediately or placed in the channel's command queue. The sound commands allow you to do things like tying a sampled sound or wave table to a channel and then playing the sound at a specified frequency. You can change a sampled sound's playback rate and adjust its volume, and you can change a stereo sound's left–right balance. We'll get to the master list of sound commands in a bit. First, let's look at the process of creating a new channel.

Creating a Sound Channel

To create a new sound channel, you call SndNewChannel():

```
OSErr SndNewChannel(SndChannelPtr *chan, short synth, long init,
                    SndCallBackUPP userRoutine);
```

The first parameter is a pointer to a sound channel structure. If you pass a `SndChannelPtr` with a value of `nil`, the Sound Manager will allocate a nonrelocatable sound channel structure for you *in the system heap*. If the Sound Manager allocates the memory for you, it will allocate a channel large enough to hold 128 sound commands, which should be plenty.

> You can allocate the memory for your sound channel yourself, but this practice is *not* recommended. As it turns out, the Sound Manager has to allocate additional memory to go along with the channel structure. This additional memory is always allocated in the system heap and is larger than the channel structure. The point is, why go to the trouble of allocating the extra memory and then tracking it (so that you can delete it later) when it won't make much of a difference and will result in memory that is split between two different heaps? Unless you plan on sending more than 128 sound commands to a channel at one time (highly unlikely), it's just not worth it. Let the Sound Manager allocate your channels for you.

The second parameter specifies the type of sound you want to play on this channel. Due to a bug in the old Sound Manager, you need to pass 0 as the sound type (also known as the *synth*). If you know that Sound Manager 3.0 or later is installed, feel free to pass `squareWaveSynth`, `waveTableSynth`, or `sampledSynth`, assuming you know the type of sound you'll be playing on this channel.

The third parameter lets you specify initialization parameters for your channel. Setting this parameter to 0 always works. A common misconception is that setting this parameter to `initMono` will produce a monophonic sound. The truth is that the sound you're using is going to define what happens. If you play a stereo sound, you're going to get stereo output. If you play a mono sound, you're going to get mono regardless of the initialization options you've used.

The final parameter is a pointer to a callback routine you want called whenever the channel executes a `callBackCmd`. You might queue up a sound and then a `callBackCmd` to ask the Sound Manager to call your callback routine when the sound finishes playing. That's how SoundApp knows to close the status window when the sound it was playing completes. If you pass `nil`, all `callBackCmds` for this channel are ignored.

Here's a piece of code that creates a new sound channel:

```
SndChannelPtr        chan;

chan = nil;
err = SndNewChannel( &chan, sampledSynth, 0, nil );

if (err != noErr)
   FailWithNoChannel(err);
```

To dispose of the memory allocated to a channel, call `SndDisposeChannel()`:

```
SndDisposeChannel( SndChannelPtr chan, Boolean quietNow );
```

`chan` is the channel to be disposed. If `quietNow` is `true`, the channel will be disposed of immediately, thus interrupting any currently playing sound. If `quietNow` is `false`, `SndDisposeChannel()` queues up a `quietCmd` and waits for it to execute (and for the queue to empty) before disposing of the channel.

> Sound channel structures feature a `userInfo` field, declared as a `long`. Just as you might hang some memory off a window's `refCon` field, feel free to stick a handle or pointer to your own private storage in the `userInfo` field. Just remember to deallocate the memory before you dispose of the channel.

Allocating Your Own Channel

As mentioned, the default Sound Manager channel is large enough to hold 128 commands at one time. That's a lot of commands. Each command is 8 bytes long. If you plan on creating many channels and each will process only a few commands or if you need a channel that will handle more than 128 commands at one time (highly unlikely) you might want to (shudder!) allocate and initialize your own sound channel.

If you've been reading *Inside Macintosh: Sound*, you may have noticed the sound-channel allocation routine (bottom of p. 2-20). Do not use this code! It has a fatal bug in it. First, it lets you allocate a block of memory the size of a `SndChannel`. But a `SndChannel` includes a block of memory large enough to hold 128 commands (see p. 2-103). That's your first clue that something is not quite kosher. Next, the code allows you to set the sound channel's qLength field. But the command queue has already been allocated. When you pass this block of memory to `SndNewChannel()`, you still have a 128-command queue. If you set

qLength to a value of 128 or less, the only problem is that you won't have
saved any space. If you set qLength to a value larger than 128, you'll be
fine as long as there are never more than 128 commands in the queue.
But when that 129th command shows up, get ready for a long weekend
of hair-pulling, nail-biting, screen-slamming debugging. (Aren't you glad
you decided to allocate your own sound channel?)

Here's some code that will work. The downside is that it duplicates
a system structure and will break if the system changes the format of a
sound channel. So don't read this code. Let the Sound Manager allocate
that channel for you. . . . Still here. OK, here goes.

First, you need to define your own sound channel type:

```
struct MySndChannel
{
    struct SndChannel    *nextChan;
    Ptr                         firstMod;
    SndCallBackProcPtr    callBack;
    long                        userInfo;
    Time                        wait;
    SndCommand                  cmdInProgress;
    short                       flags;
    short                       qLength;
    short                       qHead;
    short                       qTail;
    SndCommand                  queue[ kMyQueueSize ];
};
```

kMyQueueSize is the maximum number of commands your queue
will hold. Next, you allocate a block of memory to hold your custom
channel. If you can't allocate enough memory, bail out.

```
SndChannelPtr       chan;

chan = (SndChannelPtr)NewPtr( sizeof( MySndChannel ) );

if (chan == nil)
    FailWithNoChannel( MemError() );
```

Now, set the qLength field inside the channel so that the Sound
Manager knows how big the queue is:

```
chan->qLength = kMyQueueSize;
```

Finally, pass the channel to SndNewChannel() so that the Sound
Manager can do its thing. If all goes well, your channel should be ready
to mambo:

```
err = SndNewChannel( &chan, sampledSound, 0, nil );

if (err != noErr)
   FailWithNoChannel(err);
```

Sound Commands

Once you've allocated your sound channel, you're ready to send some sound commands. Figure 4.5 lists the sound commands supported by Sound Manager 3.0. Figure 4.6 lists commands that you might encounter in old Sound Manager documentation and that are no longer supported or that no longer make sense. Each of the current commands is documented in detail in *Inside Macintosh: Sound*.

Figure 4.5

Sound Manager Commands	
quietCmd	Stop currently playing sound (Use SndDoImmediate()).
flushCmd	Empty a channel's command queue.
reInitCmd	Reinitialize a sound channel.
waitCmd	Suspend processing in a channel for a specified duration.
pauseCmd	Pause Processing in a channel until resumeCmd is sent.
resumeCmd	Resume processing in a channel.
callBackCmd	Execute a call-back procedure.
syncCmd	Suspend processing in a channel until it is sync'ed with another channel.
availableCmd	Used with the function SndControl() to check for specific Sound Manager feature.
restCmd	Rest a channel for a specified duration.
ampCmd	Change the amplitude (loudness) of the current sound or, if no sound is playing, of the next sound to be played.
timbreCmd	Change the timbre (tone) of a sound. 0 is clear, 254 is buzzy.
getAmpCmd	Returns the current amplitude.
volumeCmd	Set the left and right volumes of a channel.
getVolumeCmd	Returns the current left and right volumes of a channel.
waveTableCmd	Install a wave-table sound in a channel.
soundCmd	Install a sampled sound in a channel.
freqDurationCmd	Play the installed sound at the specified frequency for the specifed length of time. If the sound has loop points, then continue playing the sound until the length of time has expired.
freqCmd	Play the installed sound at the specified frequency. If the sound has loop points, continue playing the sound ad infinitum.
bufferCmd	Play a buffer filled with sampled sound data.
rateCmd	Set the playback rate of the current sampled sound.
getRateCmd	Returns the playback rate of the current sampled sound.

The sound commands supported by Sound Manager 3.0.

To execute a command yourself, you start by building a SndCommand structure:

```
struct SndCommand
{
   unsigned short      cmd;
```

```
   short                     param1;
   long                      param2;
};
```

cmd is the command you want to send. param1 and param2 act as both input and output parameters, depending on the command being implemented. For example, restCmd rests the current channel for a specified duration. param1 contains the rest duration in half-milliseconds (legal values are 0 to 65,535 for Sound Manager 2 and later and are 0 to 32,767 for Sound Manager 1), while param2 is ignored.

FIGURE 4.6

Obsolete Sound Manager Commands	
nullCmd	Do nothing, why bother?
initCmd	Allocates and initializes internal structures, but no longer used by Sound Manager 3.0.
freeCmd	Disposes of internal structures, but no longer used by Sound Manager 3.0.
emptyCmd	Never supported.
requestNextCmd	Never supported.
howOftenCmd	Never supported.
wakeUpCmd	Never supported.
totalLoadCmd	First appeared in SoundManager 2.0, but not accurate. Sound Manager 3.0 returns a constant times the total number of channels (ie., 7% for 1 channel, 14% for 2).
loadCmd	First appeared in SoundManager 2.0, but not accurate. Sound Manager 3.0 returns a constant (ie., 7%).
scaleCmd	Never supported.
tempoCmd	Never supported.
phaseCmd	Never supported.
doubleBufferCmd	Used by SndPlayDoubleBuffer(), do not issue this command directly.
sizeCmd and convertCmd	Both of these were created to support MACE compression in the original Sound Manager. There was a compatibility hack in Sound Manager 2.0 to call the MACE routines directly, but sizeCmd and convertCmd are no longer supported by Sound Manager 3.0.
versionCmd	Used to report on available sound formats, but no longer supported.

Sound Manager commands that are obsolete or that no longer make sense.

Once you've built the command, you can send it to the back of a channel's command queue by calling SndDoCommand():

```
OSErr SndDoCommand( SndChannelPtr chan, const SndCommand *cmd,
                           Boolean noWait );
```

SndChannelPtr is a pointer to the sound channel you'd like to handle the command. cmd is the command you want sent to the channel. noWait is true if you want SndDoCommand() to return immediately with an error when the command queue is full. noWait is false if you want

SndDoCommand() to wait for a command to scroll off the queue instead of returning an error.

Alternatively, you can place your command at the front of the queue by calling SndDoImmediate():

```
OSErr SndDoImmediate( SndChannelPtr chan, const SndCommand *cmd );
```

chan is the channel to which you want the command sent, and cmd is the command you want executed. The command overrides any currently executing waitCmd, pauseCmd, or syncCmd, but it won't interrupt a currently playing sound unless the command is a quietCmd. A quietCmd will stop the currently playing sound.

The Most Popular Commands

Of all the Sound Manager commands, the most popular is bufferCmd, which is used to play a buffer filled with sampled sound data. The second most popular command is probably callBackCmd, which causes the Sound Manager to call the callback routine you installed when you created your channel. You can use callBackCmd to send a signal to your application, indicating the progress of a sound or sequence of commands.

As mentioned earlier, a common technique is to execute a bufferCmd immediately followed by a callBackCmd. When your callback procedure is called, the sound that you were playing has finished. More elaborately, the two commands can be combined to double-buffer a sound that won't normally fit in memory. As an example, QuickTime uses this technique to play the audio portion of a movie. (We'll get to double buffering later in the chapter.)

To see bufferCmd and callBackCmd in action, use SndPlay() to open a file of 'snd ' resources and play one of the sounds. When you click the Play Sound button, SndPlay() issues a bufferCmd, that is immediately followed by a callBackCmd. While the sound is playing, a status dialog is shown. When the sound is done playing, the Sound Manager calls the callback routine, which sets a flag indicating that the sound is finished. Meanwhile, once SoundApp queued its two sound commands, it dropped back into its main event loop. Each time through the loop, it checks the flag, and, if the sound has completed, it disposes of the sound's status dialog.

Here are the specifics. Each time through the main event loop, EventLoop() (inside SoundApp.c) executes these lines:

```
if ( HasSoundCompleted() )
        KillSound();
```

SoundApp maintains a global array of `ChanInfo` structs one for each possible sound channel. The array is accessed via the global `gChanInfo`, declared as a pointer to a `ChanInfo`, a struct defined near the top of `SoundUnit.c`. One of the `ChanInfo` fields is the flag `chanState`, which is set to either `kChanFreeState` or `kChanCompleteState`. `kChanFreeState` indicates that the channel corresponding to the array index doesn't exist and can be created using `SndNewChannel()`. `kChanCompleteState` indicates that the channel exists but is done playing its sound.

`HasSoundCompleted()` steps through each of the channels and returns `true` if none of the existing channels is still playing:

```
pascal Boolean HasSoundCompleted(void)
{
    short    i;
    Boolean        result;

    result = true;

    for ( i = 0; i < kMaxChannels; i++ )
    {
        if ( (gChanInfo[i].chan != nil) &&
            (gChanInfo[i].chanState != kChanCompleteState) )
        {
            result = false;
            break;
        }
    }
    return( result );
}
```

If `HasSoundCompleted()` returns `true`, `EventLoop()` calls `KillSound()`, which frees up all the sound data and channels in use.

More Commands

Another, more complicated sound command is `freqDurationCmd`. `freqDurationCmd` is used in conjunction with a sound that has been installed in a channel and is designed to be used as an instrument. To install a sampled sound in a channel, use the command `soundCmd`. To install a wave table sound in a channel, use the command `waveTableCmd`. Then, to use the sampled sound or wave table sound to play a melody, follow the command with a sequence of `freqDurationCmd`, `quietCmd`, and `restCmds`. (These commands were executed every time you chose one of the options in SoundApp that played a melody.)

The 'snd ' Resource

A `'snd '` resource is a collection of sound commands and sound data. (`'snd'` resource IDs 1 through 8191 are reserved by Apple.) All the rest are fair game. There are many ways to create one. You can record a sampled sound by using the Sound control panel, SoundApp, or commercial applications like SoundEdit and AudioShop.

The Sound control panel and SoundApp both save the sampled sound as a `'snd '` resource. SoundEdit and AudioShop allow you to save your sampled sound in a number of different formats, including that of a `'snd '` resource as well as that defined by the Audio Interchange File Format (AIFF).

> AIFF was developed as a standard file format to exchange sound files with computers that don't support the concept of resources. In addition, AIFF solves the problem of storing an extremely large sound as a resource by allowing you to play sound directly from disk (as opposed to loading a resource into memory and then playing it). To learn more about AIFF and AIFF-C (a version of AIFF that supports compression), check out the routines `SndStartFilePlay()`, `SndPauseFilePlay()`, `SndStopFilePlay()`, and `SndRecordToFile()` in *Inside Macintosh: Sound*.

Each `'snd '` resource begins with a *sound resource header*, which specifies the format of the rest of the resource. The first 2 bytes of the header tell you whether the `'snd '` is format 1 (0x0001) or format 2 (0x0002). Format 2 was created specifically for HyperCard and was basically an experiment gone horribly wrong. Use of format 2 sounds is discouraged (and punishable by They Who Must Be Obeyed). Format 1 sounds can include either wave table data or sampled sound data. Format 2 sounds can include only sampled sound data.

The sound resource header for a format 2 `'snd '` is 4 bytes long. The first 2 bytes indicate format 2 (0x0002), and the next 2 bytes were used internally by HyperCard.

The sound resource header for a format 1 `'snd '` is a little more complex. It starts with the 2 bytes that indicate format 1 (0x0001). The next 2 bytes specify the number of sound types in the `'snd '`. Since a sound channel can handle only one type of sound at a time (either square wave, wave table, or sampled sound), this value is usually 0x0001, indicating that the 'snd ' contains only one type of sound.

If this number is 1 or more, the next 2 bytes indicate the type of the first sound in the resource (1 for square wave, 3 for wave table, and 5 for sampled sound) and the 4 bytes after them contain the initialization options for the channel (see the list in *Inside Macintosh: Sound*).

Take a minute to open up a 'snd ' resource using ResEdit or Resorcerer. Reread the last few paragraphs and identify the sound resource header. If the 'snd ' is format 1, the header is probably 10 bytes long and matches the one shown in Figure 4.7. This example is a format 1 sound, with one sound type—a sampled sound—indicated by the constant 0x0005. The 4-byte constant 0x00000080, which corresponds to the initialization constant initMono, indicates that this sound should be played through both left and right channels. initMono is the default initialization mode.

FIGURE 4.7

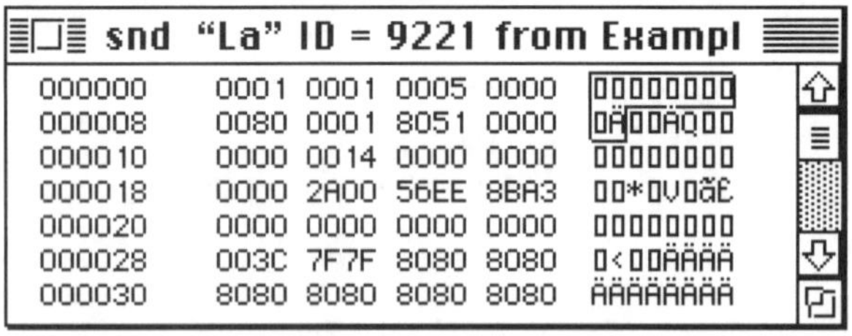

```
┌───────────────────────────────────────────┐
│ ≣▢≣ snd "La" ID = 9221 from Exampl ≣≣≣      │
├───────────────────────────────────────────┤
│ 000000   0001 0001 0005 0000  ⌐⌐⌐⌐⌐⌐⌐⌐  ⇧ │
│ 000008   0080 0001 8051 0000  ⌐Ä⌐⌐Ä⌐Q⌐⌐  ≣ │
│ 000010   0000 0014 0000 0000  ⌐⌐⌐⌐⌐⌐⌐⌐    │
│ 000018   0000 2A00 56EE 8BA3  ⌐⌐*⌐∪⌐ãÉ     │
│ 000020   0000 0000 0000 0000  ⌐⌐⌐⌐⌐⌐⌐⌐  ▓ │
│ 000028   003C 7F7F 8080 8080  ⌐‹⌐⌐ÄÄÄÄ  ⇩ │
│ 000030   8080 8080 8080 8080  ÄÄÄÄÄÄÄÄ   ◱ │
└───────────────────────────────────────────┘
```

A format 1 'snd ', with the sound resource header highlighted.

After the sound resource header, the next 2 bytes indicate the number of sound commands in this resource. The 'snd ' resource in Figure 4.7 contains a single command. Following this command are the commands themselves in blocks of 8 bytes. The first 2 bytes of each command represent the command number, the second 2 bytes param1, and the next 4 bytes param2. The high bit of the command number is called the *offset bit*. If the offset bit is set, the long in param2 is an offset from the beginning of the resource to the sound data. If the offset bit is cleared, param2 contains a pointer to the sound data.

As just stated, the 'snd ' resource in Figure 4.7 contains a single command. The first 2 bytes of the command, 0x8051, tell you that the offset bit is set and that the command is a bufferCmd (0x0051, or decimal

81). This command has a `param2` value of 0x00000014, which is decimal 20, indicating that the sound data starts at byte 21, which happens to be right after the end of the command. In this example, the sound data represents a sampled sound.

> Here's an interesting experiment. Go into ResEdit and create a new resource file. Open the Sound control panel, click on the sound "Wild Eep," copy the sound, and then paste it into your new ResEdit file. Open the `'snd '` resource you just created. You'll notice that the `'snd '` resource contains one sound command, a `bufferCmd` that plays the sampled "Wild Eep" sound. We're going to insert a second `bufferCmd` to the resource, turning the "eep" into an "eep-eep."
>
> First, change the 0001 (second pair of bytes on the second line) to a 0002 to indicate that the resource contains two commands instead of one. Next, change the last 4 bytes of the command from 00000014 to 0000001C to indicate that the sampled sound starts 8 bytes later in the file. Why? Because we're going to insert an extra 8 bytes (the size of a command) in the file. Finally, copy the 8-byte command (starting with 8051 and now ending with 001C) and paste it immediately before the beginning of the existing command. That's it! Close the editing window, click on the `'snd '` resource, and select Try Sound from the snd menu. You should hear your newly created "eep-eep".
>
> If you run into any trouble, check out the file `Wild Eep` in the `SoundApp` folder. It contains before and after versions of the "eep" sound for your parsing pleasure.

Here's a C-code implementation of a `'snd '` resource:

```
struct SndListResource
{
    short           format;
    short           numModifiers;
    ModRef          modifierPart[1];   /* <--Variable-length array*/
    short           numCommands;
    SndCommand      commandPart[1];    /* <--Variable-length array*/
    char            dataPart[1];        * <--Variable-length array*/
};
```

Note that it contains three variable-length arrays, which may or may not be present. The last of these, `dataPart`, points to the beginning of the optional wave or sampled sound data.

The Sampled Sound Header

The content of the block of data at the end of the `'snd '` resource (represented by the field `dataPart`) depends on the sound's type. If the sound is a wave table sound, the block contains the wave table itself. If the sound is a sampled sound, the block is known as a *sampled sound header* or just a *sound header*. (Don't confuse it with the sound resource header, which is at the very beginning of the `'snd '` resource.) If you see the term *sound header*, think sampled sound.

The sampled sound header includes the data that defines the sampled sound, and it also includes some other information, like the sampled sound's sample rate and base frequency.

Here's a C-code implementation of a sound header:

```
struct SoundHeader
{
   Ptr                samplePtr;
   unsigned long   length;
   UnsignedFixed   sampleRate; /*sample rate for this sound*/
   unsigned long   loopStart;  /*start of looping portion*/
   unsigned long   loopEnd;    /*end of looping portion*/
   unsigned char   encode;     /*header encoding*/
   unsigned char   baseFrequency;   /*baseFrequency value*/
   unsigned char   sampleArea[1];
};
```

If `samplePtr` is `nil`, the sampled sound data is accessed using the field `sampleArea`. If not, it points to the sampled sound data. `length` is the length of the sound in bytes. `sampleRate` is the sound's sampling rate and is most likely one of `rate44khz`, `rate22khz`, or `rate11khz`.

`loopStart` and `loopEnd` are the offset in bytes from the beginning of the sampled sound data of the sound's loop points. A *loop point* is a section of the sound that can be repeated indefinitely to extend the duration of a sound. For example, a sampled flute note may start with a little breath exhale, then gather momentum, and, in the middle, will be pretty consistent. At the end of the sound, the flute will tail off and finally die out. The solid section in the middle is a perfect candidate for looping since it is so consistent. By playing it over and over, we can extend the flute note as if the note were much longer than it actually is.

`encode` indicates the encoding method used to generate the sound and is likely one of `stdSH` (8-bit mono), `extSH` (16-bit), or `cmpSH` (compressed). Finally, `baseFrequency` is the sound's original pitch.

Working with a 'snd ' Resource

Understanding the format of a 'snd ' resource allows you to have much more control over the sound process. The simplest way to play a sound is to pass your 'snd ' resource to SndPlay():

```
OSErr SndPlay( SndChannelPtr chan, SndListHandle sndHdl,
                        Boolean async );
```

SndPlay() takes a pointer to a sound channel and a handle to a 'snd ' resource. The third parameter is true if you want the sound played asynchronously or false if you want SndPlay() to return only after the sound finishes playing. If you don't want to create a new channel, pass nil as the first parameter, and SndPlay() will allocate a channel for you. Obviously, this is the simplest way to play a 'snd ' resource.

If, however, you want more control over your sounds, you might want to parse the 'snd ' resource yourself, issuing the commands via calls to SndDoCommand() and SndDoImmediate(). Alternatively, you might use a waveTableCmd or soundCmd to install a sound in a channel and then use a series of freqDurationCmds to play the installed sound as an instrument. If you do handle the sound commands yourself, at some point you'll probably execute a command that requires either a pointer or an offset to the sound data portion of the 'snd ' resource.

For example, suppose you wanted to issue a soundCmd to install a sampled sound in a channel. To construct a soundCmd, you need either a pointer or an offset to the sampled sound header you want to install. If you know that Sound Manager 3.0 or later is installed (because you've checked for it using Gestalt(), perhaps), you can call the routine GetSoundHeaderOffset():

```
OSErr GetSoundHeaderOffset( SndListHandle sndHandle, long *offset );
```

GetSoundHeaderOffset() takes a handle to a 'snd ' resource and returns an offset to the 'snd ' resource's sampled sound header.

Great! But what if you want to issue a waveTableCmd to install a wave table in your channel instead. A waveTableCmd requires both an offset to a wave table as well as the length of the wave table. How will you find this information? Or what if you want to issue a soundCmd, but you don't have access to Sound Manager 3.0 (and thus don't have access to GetSoundHeaderOffset())?

Aha! Jim Reekes to the rescue! Here's a routine that returns the sound's type. If the sound is a sampled sound, it also returns an offset to the sampled sound header. If the sound is a wave table sound, it returns an offset to the wave table as well as the length of the wave table:

```
pascal long GetSndDataOffset( SndListHandle sndHandle,
                short *dataType, short *waveLength )
{
    Ptr        cruisePtr;
    long       sndDataOffset;
    short      synths;
    short      howManyCmds;

    sndDataOffset = 0;          // initialize to defaults
    *dataType = kNoSynth;
    *waveLength = 0;
```

GetSndDataOffset() **takes a** 'snd ' **resource handle and returns an offset to the sound data.** dataType **is the sound's type, and, if** dataType **is equal to** waveTableSynth, waveLength **is the length of the wave table.**

If the handle doesn't point to a resource, we return a value of 0:

```
if (sndHandle == nil)
    return (sndDataOffset);      // return no data
```

Next, we check to be sure the resource wasn't purged:

```
if (*sndHandle != nil)
{
```

If not, we check to see whether the sound is a format 1 'snd ' resource. If so, we bump cruisePtr past the data formats for each sound type. If not, we bump cruisePtr past the first 4 bytes. In either case, cruisePtr now points to the number of commands:

```
    if ((**sndHandle).format == firstSoundFormat)
    {
        synths = (**sndHandle).numModifiers;
        cruisePtr = (Ptr)&(**sndHandle).modifierPart;
        cruisePtr += (sizeof(ModRef) * synths);
    }
    else
        cruisePtr = (Ptr)&((**(Snd2ListHandle)sndHandle).numCommands);
```

We then bump cruisePtr to point to the first command:

```
    howManyCmds = *(short *)cruisePtr;
    cruisePtr += sizeof(howManyCmds);
```

Our goal now is to step through each command looking for either a soundCmd or bufferCmd (in which case, we use param2 to get the offset to the sampled sound header) or a waveTableCmd (in which case, we pull the wave table length from param1 and an offset to the wave table from param2). Notice that we've assumed that the offset bit is always set. If a command uses the offset bit and the command is inside a 'snd ' resource, the offset bit will be set. Why? Because resources are handle based (relocatable) and an offset from the beginning of the resource is the only option that makes sense:

```
do {
    switch (((SndCmdPtr)cruisePtr)->cmd) {

        case soundCmd | dataOffsetFlag:
        case bufferCmd | dataOffsetFlag:
            *dataType = sampledSynth;
            sndDataOffset = ((SndCmdPtr)cruisePtr)->param2;
            howManyCmds = 0;      // done, get out of loop
            break;

        case waveTableCmd | dataOffsetFlag:
            *dataType = waveTableSynth;
            *waveLength = ((SndCmdPtr)cruisePtr)->param1;
            sndDataOffset = ((SndCmdPtr)cruisePtr)->param2;
            howManyCmds = 0;      // done, get out of loop
            break;

        default:                  // catch any other type of cmd
            cruisePtr += sizeof(SndCommand);
            howManyCmds -= 1;
            break;
        }
    } while (howManyCmds >= 1);    // done with all the commands
    }
    return(sndDataOffset);
}
```

Playing a Single Sound Asynchronously

The next example demonstrates the basic instructions that are necessary to play sounds asynchronously. The nice thing about this example is that it makes its point in only a few lines of code. The downside is that it doesn't really do anything useful while the sound is playing, so you'll have to use your imagination to see how it would fit into a real-life application.

First, we create a new sound channel, letting the Sound Manager allocate the memory for us. As mentioned earlier in the chapter, we pass 0 as the sound type to avoid a bug in the pre-3.0 Sound Manager.

Here's the scoop on this bug. Let's say you pass `sampledSynth` to `SndNewChannel()`. The old Sound Manager creates a sound channel initialized for sampled sound. Now suppose you call `SndPlay()` to play a sound that also specifies the `sampledSynth` in its resource. The Sound Manager blindly tries to initialize the channel again, which causes a crash depending on several factors, such as which Memory Manager is running. The older, 24-bit Memory Manager will probably crash, and the 32-bit Memory Manager may not crash at all. The crash may happen when you call `SndDisposeChannel()` because the Sound Manager tries to dispose of a memory object that is already disposed of. This problem is subtle and difficult to debug. The solution: Either require Sound Manager 3.0 or later or always pass 0 as the synth parameter.

We also pass 0 as the third parameter, letting the sound we play determine the initialization parameters. Finally, we pass `nil` as the fourth parameter since we don't have a callback routine at this point. `FailIf()` bails out if `err` is not equal to `noErr`:

```
SCStatus          chanStatus;
SndChannelPtr     chan;
Handle            sndHandle;
OSErr             err;

chan = nil;
err = SndNewChannel( &chan, 0, 0, nil );
FailIf( err != noErr );
```

Next, we load the `'snd '` resource named "Sosumi" and then lock it in memory using `HLock()`. This is necessary because we're using the sound asynchronously and cannot allow it to move in memory while the sound is in use. (This wouldn't be necessary in a synchronous example because the Sound Manager will lock the sound during the call to `SndPlay()`.) In our asynchronous example, `SndPlay()` returns immediately and continues to play the sound:

```
sndHandle = GetNamedResource('snd ', "\pSosumi");
FailIf(sndHandle == nil);

HLock(sndHandle);
```

```
err = SndPlay(chan, sndHandle, true);
FailIf(err != noErr);
```

SndChannelStatus() takes a sound channel pointer and returns an SCStatus structure that tells you what's currently up with the channel. The scChannelBusy field is true if the channel is currently producing sound. We spin in this loop until either an error occurs or the sound ends:

```
do
{
    err = SndChannelStatus(chan, sizeof(chanStatus), &chanStatus);
} while ((err == noErr) && (chanStatus.scChannelBusy));
```

Next, we dispose of the channel. When you called SndPlay(), it initialized the channel to a particulate synthesizer. This means that you cannot call SndPlay() again on this channel since that old Sound Manager bug will happen (unless you know you have Sound Manager 3.0 or later installed). Therefore, SoundApp disposes of each sound channel once it's done playing a sound.

This call to SndDisposeChannel() passes true as its second parameter, telling the Sound Manager to kill the sound immediately. This won't matter if the sound ended normally, but if there was an error, this call will ensure that the sound doesn't go on shrieking forever.

Finally, we unlock the sound and make sure that it is purgeable. In this way, if you need the sound again, it may still be in memory and the Resource Manager will not have to read it again from disk:

```
err = SndDisposeChannel(chan, true);
HUnlock(sndHandle);
HPurge(sndHandle);
```

Now, let's try to figure out how to add asynchronous sound to an application. The first step is to allocate a sound channel. That much we've already covered. We then need to get a sound loaded and locked in memory. We also need to keep track of this sound and the channel so that we can dispose of them after we're done. We need a routine to start the sound playing, and we'll use SndPlay() for this because you already know how it works. The final step is to determine when the sound has finished. This time, instead of polling on chanStatus.scChannelBusy, we'll install a callback routine. Once we've started the sound playing, we queue a callBackCmd so that once the sound ends, the Sound Manager will call our callback routine.

AsynchSndPlay(), as well as the sound utility routines it calls, is in
SoundUnit.c. It takes a sound handle, creates a new sound channel,
queues up the sound, and then installs a callBackCmd:

```
pascal OSErr AsynchSndPlay(SndListHandle sndHandle)
{
    SoundHeaderPtr dataPtr;
    OSErr          theErr;
    long           dataOffset;
    short          sndDataType;
    short          ignore;
```

AsynchSndPlay() starts by calling HoldSnd(). HoldSnd() calls
HLockHi() to lock the 'snd ' resource as high as possible in the heap.
Assuming that works, GetNoSynthChan() is called. GetNoSynthChan() calls
SndNewChannel() to create a new sound channel with no synth and no
initialization parameters (passing 0 as both the second and third parameter) and with the routine DoCallBack() installed as the callback routine
(via the fourth parameter):

```
    theErr = HoldSnd(sndHandle);

    if (theErr == noErr)
    {
        theErr = GetNoSynthChan( &(gChanInfo[0].chan) );
```

Next, we save the resource handle in our global channel array so
that FreeAllChans() can dispose of the resource later:

```
        gChanInfo[0].dataHandle = sndHandle;
```

If the channel is allocated OK, we call GetSynthInfo() to find out
the sound type and initialization parameters embedded in the 'snd '
resource. GetSynthInfo() returns a ModRef struct, which looks like this:

```
struct ModRef
{
    unsigned short              modNumber;
    long                        modInit;
};
```

Think of ModRef as bytes 5 through 10 of a format 1 'snd ' resource.
We save the ModRef's modeNumber field (the sound type) in the global
channel's chanType field. Next, we call GetSndDataOffset() (we walked
through the code earlier). If GetSndDataOffset() identifies the sound as a

sampled sound, we convert the offset returned by `GetSndDataOffset()` to a pointer and then pass this pointer to `SupportedSH()`. `SupportedSH()` checks the sample-sound header pointed to by `dataPtr` to ensure that it is compatible with the current Sound Manager:

```
if ( theErr == noErr )
{
    gChanInfo[0].chanType = GetSynthInfo( sndHandle ).modNumber;
    dataOffset = GetSndDataOffset( sndHandle, &sndDataType,
        &ignore );
    if ( sndDataType == sampledSynth )
    {
        dataPtr = (SoundHeaderPtr)((long)*sndHandle + dataOffset);
        if ( !( SupportedSH(dataPtr) ) )
            theErr = badFormat;
    }
```

All the incredible error checking we just went through is necessary because of the various bugs and missing features in earlier versions of the Sound Manager. If you require that your users have Sound Manager 3.0 or later installed, you can blow off this code. On the other hand, if you want to expand your user base or if you have a driving need to make your life even more complex, take some time to walk through this code, line by line, until you understand why each check is made. Jim's comments are copious and well written, so you shouldn't have too much trouble.

Anyway, with all that out of the way, we're now ready to call `SndPlay()`, asking it to play our `'snd '` resource asynchronously in our new channel:

```
if (theErr == noErr)
{
    theErr = SndPlay( gChanInfo[0].chan,
                    (Handle)sndHandle, kSMAsynch );
```

Assuming that call goes well, we call `SoundComplete()` to queue up a `callBackCmd`, asking the Sound Manager to call our callback function once the sound finishes playing. (We"ll take a look at `SoundComplete()` next).

```
if (theErr == noErr)
            theErr = SoundComplete( gChanInfo[0].chan );
    }
  }
}
```

Assuming we survive all this, we free up our channel and then return:

```
if (theErr != noErr)
  FreeAllChans();
return(theErr);
}
```

`SoundComplete()` **queues up a** `callBackCmd` **in the specified channel:**

```
pascal OSErr SoundComplete( SndChannelPtr chan )
{
    SndCommand     theCmd;
    OSErr          result;
    short          i;
```

First, we create a sound command, setting the `cmd` field to `callBackCmd`. Since `callBackCmd` doesn't take any parameters, we can use `param1` and `param2` for anything we like. (If you set `param1` to a unique value, you can test for it in your callback procedure. Thus, you can use a single callback function to perform different functions depending on the value passed in.) In this case, we set `param1` to `kSoundComplete`, telling the callback function to do what it must, to signal that the sound is complete:

```
theCmd.cmd = callBackCmd;
theCmd.param1 = kSoundComplete;
theCmd.param2 = 0;
```

Next, we step through all the channels to find the one that was passed in as a parameter. If we don't find a match, something is definitely wrong and we return the error `badChannel`. If we find a match, we'll embed a pointer to the channel info structure in `param2`. We do this because of (you guessed it!) another bug in the pre-3.0 Sound Manager that can queue up a `callBackCmd` in our channel by mistake. By embedding unique values in `param1` and `param2`, we ensure that the callback routine can verify that it was called legitimately.

```
for (i = 0; i < kMaxChannels; i++)
{
  if (gChanInfo[i].chan == chan)
  {
    theCmd.param2 = (long)(&gChanInfo[i]);
    break;
  }
```

```
    }
    if (theCmd.param2 == 0)
        result = badChannel;
    else
```

If all goes well, we queue up the `callBackCmd`, placing the command in the back of the channel's queue. Note that if you do ask the Sound Manager to wait, you may cause an infinite loop if the queue never has a command removed from it. For example, if you queue up a `pauseCmd`, no more commands will be processed and commands will eventually fill up the queue. If you then call `SndDoCommand()` with `noWait` set to `false`, the Sound Manager will loop forever waiting for the queue to make some space, which it can't do since it is paused:

```
        result = SndDoCommand( chan, &theCmd, kWait );

    return(result);
}
```

Take a minute to look at the `EventLoop()` routine in `SoundApp.c`. Notice that the `sleep` value passed to `WaitNextEvent()` is altered, depending on whether a sound channel is open or not. If we're playing a sound asynchronously, we want a little more processor time to be sure we catch the sound when it stops playing.

Here's our callback routine. Callback routines take two parameters: the current channel and the command to which the callback is responding. Notice that the callback is declared using the `pascal` keyword. This is mandatory because the Sound Manager follows Pascal calling conventions and `DoCallBack()` is being called by the Sound Manager. You can always declare a routine by using the `pascal` keyword, even when you plan on calling it from inside your own code. The compiler/linker will make sure things work out right. But if you leave off the `pascal` keyword on a routine that is called by the Toolbox, you'll hose the stack (at least):

```
pascal void DoCallBack( SndChannelPtr chan, SndCommand *theCmd )
{
    ChanInfoPtr        info;
```

If this callback is a result of a `callBackCmd` that we posted (and not the result of a Sound Manager bug), `param1` will hold the constant `kSound-Complete` and `param2` will hold a pointer to our channel info structure. If so, we set `chanState` to `kChanCompleteState`, telling our polling code that the sound is done:

```
   if (theCmd->param1 == kSoundComplete)  // if it's my callBackCmd
   {
      info = (ChanInfoPtr)theCmd->param2;
      info->chanState = kChanCompleteState;      // this channel is done
   }
}
```

It's important to note that the callback, like all sound channel commands, is done at interrupt time. Interrupt code is very tricky, and there are strict rules about what can be done in such code. The best rule to follow is to set a flag and then poll to see that this flag is set in your non-interrupt code. SoundApp sets a flag in the ChanInfo struct that signals that this channel has completed. (Interrupt routines are discussed later in the chapter.)

In EventLoop() we poll to see whether all the channel flags are marked as complete, and we then know that all our sounds are complete. That's it for playing sound asynchronously. Next, let's look at the process of playing a scale.

PLAYING A SCALE

Playing a sequence of notes is just like playing a single buffer. The only difference is that playing a sequence of notes uses more sound commands. In the next example, the routines GetSampleChan() and PlaySong() from SoundUnit.c are used together to play a C Major scale. You can hear this effect by choosing a sound from the Example Sounds file and then clicking on the Play Scale button.

The code begins by creating a sound channel and installing an instrument. The example uses a sampled sound, which is the most popular method for playing sound. The first order of business is to allocate a channel initialized for the sampledSynth. This channel will be used asynchronously just like the previous example. We use the same DoCallBack() routine to signal when the channel has completed all commands. Once we successfully allocate a usable channel, we need to install our sound.

Instrument sounds can be any sound that you can sample, such as a trumpet, a flute, a drum, or even a barking dog. If you want to have the sound play a continuous tone during the entire note's duration, then the sound should have loop points. As mentioned earlier, a loop point is a section of the sound that can be repeated indefinitely to extend the duration of a sound. Sounds that can be looped are sounds that have a repeatable portion and, when played over and over, create a seamless tone. Drums and barking dogs cannot be used in this manner. When repeated, they sound staggered and not smooth. But a flute sound can be looped so that the looping portion of the flute sounds like a long sustained note. In this way, you can create sounds that last much longer than the recorded sample, and you can save lots of memory. If the sound does not have loop points, then it will play from the beginning and last until the sound ends or until the specified duration, whichever comes first.

GetSampleChan() creates a new channel using the initialization parameters in init (most likely, 0) and then installs the sound in sndInstrument in the channel:

```
pascal OSErr GetSampleChan( SndChannelPtr *sampleChan, long init,
                            SndListHandle sndInstrument )
{
   OSErr theErr;
```

First, all channels are freed. Then, the new channel is created using SndNewChannel():

```
   FreeAllChans();
   theErr = SndNewChannel(&(gChanInfo[0].chan), sampledSynth,
                          init, GetRoutineAddress(DoCallBack));
```

If we get this far, we call InstallSampleSnd() to install the sound in the channel for use as an instrument:

```
   if (theErr == noErr)
   {
      gChanInfo[0].chanType = sampledSynth;
      theErr = InstallSampleSnd( &gChanInfo[0], sndInstrument );
   }

   if (theErr != noErr)
      FreeAllChans();

   *sampleChan = gChanInfo[0].chan;

   return (theErr);
}
```

InstallSampleSnd() installs the sound handled by sndHandle in the channel described by info:

```
OSErr InstallSampleSnd( ChanInfoPtr info, SndListHandle sndHandle )
{
   SndCommand           theCmd;
   SoundHeaderPtr dataPtr;
   long           dataOffset;
   short          sndDataType;
   short          ignore;
   OSErr          theErr;
```

First, we call HoldSnd() to lock the sound in place:

```
  theErr = HoldSnd( sndHandle );
```

Next, we get the offset to the sampled sound header by calling GetSndDataOffset():

```
  if (theErr == noErr)
  {
     dataOffset = GetSndDataOffset(sndHandle, &sndDataType, &ignore);
```

If the sound type is sampledSynth, and it should be, we convert the offset to a pointer. We use the pointer to verify that the sound uses a standard encoding. If so, we build a soundCmd, embedding the pointer to the sampled sound header in param2. We execute the soundCmd by calling SndDoImmediate(). It doesn't make sense to queue this command (although this would be possible as long as the channel isn't generating sound):

```
     if (sndDataType == sampledSynth)
     {
        dataPtr = (SoundHeaderPtr)((long)(*sndHandle) + dataOffset);

        if (stdSH == dataPtr->encode)
        {
           theCmd.cmd = soundCmd;
           theCmd.param1 = 0;
           theCmd.param2 = (long)dataPtr;
           info->dataHandle = sndHandle;
           theErr = SndDoImmediate(info->chan, &theCmd);
        }
        else
           theErr = badFormat;      //return a bad format error
     }
     else
        theErr = badFormat;      //return a bad format error
```

If there is an error, we unlock the 'snd ' resource and mark it as purgeable. We unlock it because we were the ones who locked it by calling HoldSnd() at the beginning of the routine and, since the error means we won't be playing the sound, there's no reason to keep it locked. We mark the resource as purgeable to be memory friendly in case the sound wasn't marked as purgeable in the resource fork:

```
    if (theErr != noErr)
    {
       HUnlock((Handle)sndHandle);  //and free up the resource
       HPurge((Handle)sndHandle);
    }
  }
  return (theErr);
}
```

Programmers frequently forget to mark their 'snd' resources as purgeable, especially when they copy sounds to the list of sounds in the Sound control panel. Imagine what would happen if you copied a bunch of nonpurgeable sounds into your System and then ran a utility like SoundMaster that tied different sounds to different events. After a while, every sound you used would end up in memory with no chance of being purged. Calling HPurge() on a 'snd ' resource when you're done with it ensures that it doesn't get stuck in memory.

Once your sound is installed in a channel as an instrument, you're ready to play a melody. PlaySong() takes two parameters. The first parameter is the channel with the instrument installed in it. The second parameter is a 'snd ' resource that contains commands, not data. The commands are freqDurationCmds that use the installed instrument to play a melody—in this case, a C Major scale:

```
pascal OSErr PlaySong(SndChannelPtr chan, SndListHandle sndSong)
{
   OSErr theErr;
```

SndDataAvailable() tries to load the resource into memory. If it can't, it returns an error:

```
   theErr = SndDataAvailable(sndSong);
```

SndPlay() is convenient in that it will parse the resource for us and execute each of the commands using SndDoCommand(). We could do this ourselves for better timing and synchronization of the sounds (in a game, for example):

```
if (theErr == noErr)
{
    theErr = SndPlay(chan, (Handle)sndSong, kSMAsynch);
```

Since the commands are all copied into the channel's queue as soon as SndPlay() returns and since the 'snd ' resource contains only commands and no sound data, we can unlock the resource and make it purgeable even though the song is probably not done playing yet:

```
HUnlock((Handle)sndSong);
HPurge((Handle)sndSong);
```

After all of the commands have been queued in the channel, we end with a quietCmd, which is useful for two reasons—one being—you guessed it— an old Sound Manager bug. After the last note has played, if there are no further commands in the queue, the old Sound Manager may continuously loop the note forever. While a sound is playing, the old Sound Manager may crash on some machines if you call SndDisposeChannel(). This is unique to the Sound Manager of System 6 while running on a Macintosh Plus, SE, or Classic:

```
if (theErr == noErr)
{
    theErr = SendQuiet(chan, kWait);// work around bug
```

If all goes well, we call SoundComplete() to queue a callBackCmd to mark the channel as complete once the sound finishes playing:

```
        if (theErr == noErr)
            theErr = SoundComplete(chan);
    }
    else
        theErr = nilHandleErr;        // snd data was not available
}
if (theErr != noErr)
    FreeAllChans();
return (theErr);

}
```

Double Buffering

Double buffering is simply chunking a larger sound into smaller buffers and then playing each of these buffers in order. For example, when you call the Sound Manager routine SndStartFilePlay(), it reads data from disk into two buffers—call them buffer A and buffer B. Once both buffers are filled, buffer A is played. When buffer A is finished, an interrupt occurs to signal that A has completed, and buffer B is played. As B is playing, the Sound Manager reads the next chunk into buffer A. If all goes well, A will be ready before B has finished. When B has completed, the whole process happens again by switching to A. Thus, double buffering is often called *ping-ponging*.

Although most Mac configurations can support double buffering, you should call Gestalt() using the gestaltSoundAttr and check the gestaltSndPlayDoubleBuffer bit. (We'll get into the other Gestalt() bits later in the chapter.)

What if you have a sound that you're creating in real time? For example, you might generate the sound track for an adventure game algorithmically instead of reading it from disk. Fortunately, you can use the same method used by SndStartFilePlay().

SndStartFilePlay() calls a low-level, double-buffering routine called SndPlayDoubleBuffer(). SndPlayDoubleBuffer() was designed to play sounds from disk, but it can be used to produce sound generated in real time by your application. *Inside Macintosh: Sound* describes this routine very well (check out the section "Using Double Buffers," p. 2-68), and even includes some sample code. Instead of repeating that code, let's talk about some of the limitations of SndPlayDoubleBuffer() and how you can work around them.

SndPlayDoubleBuffer() will not allow you to change the sound format once you've started. For example, if the sound starts out as an 8-bit, 11kHz, mono, noncompressed sound, you cannot then play a buffer of compressed, stereo, 22kHz, or 16-bit data. Another limitation is that the two buffers are fixed once you start the sound. The data has to be copied into these buffers. If you have a large sound in memory and are using SndPlayDoubleBuffer(), you'd have to copy portions of it into the two buffers. This copy wastes CPU cycles and memory.

You can use a sequence of bufferCmd and callBackCmds to create double buffering. You start buffer A with a bufferCmd and follow this command with a callBackCmd. You need to mark this callBackCmd in a way that designates it as being the completion of buffer A. For example, set param1 to be the value 1. Then, prepare buffer B so that when buffer A completes, you issue a new bufferCmd and callBackCmd pair for buffer B, this time setting param1 to the value 2. While buffer B is playing, prepare buffer A and repeat the ping-ponging to keep the sound playing.

The important thing here is to have the second buffer ready before you issue the `bufferCmd`. Thus, you always have one buffer ahead of the sound so that when the `callBackCmd` interrupt routine is called, you can immediately switch to the next buffer.

GETTING THE MOST FROM THE SOUND MANAGER

The original Sound Manager shipped with the first Mac II. When System 6 shipped, the Sound Manager included support for all existing machines. Unfortunately, this version of the Sound Manager was plagued with problems. As you've already seen, `SoundUnit.c` includes lots of extra code whose sole purpose is to deal with these bugs. As you read through the SoundApp source code, you'll learn the history of these bugs as well as the work-arounds you'll need to deal with them.

System 6.0.7 included version 2.0 of the Sound Manager. This is the first version that supported multiple sampled sound channels, play from disk, sound input, and MACE audio compression. While not perfect, Sound Manager 2.0 did fix many of the complaints from the previous version. More Sound Manager fixes came in with System 7.0. The current Sound Manager, version 3.0, is part of System 7.5 and is built into the new Mac ROMs. It is also available for any System 7 user as an extension. If you want your programs to require Sound Manager 3.0 (and there's nothing wrong with that), contact Apple's software licensing department so that you can include this extension with your product.

Sound Manager 3.0 provides an entirely new architecture for supporting sound hardware. This is the only version that supports a digital signal processing (DSP) chip and 16-bit sound recording hardware. The new Sound Manager supports all data formats on all hardware platforms. It allows you to write your own plug-in audio compression/decompression components (codecs). The new Sound Manager was a complete code rewrite and has been highly optimized. In many cases, the new version performs more than 2–3 times more efficiently. It also provides a better mixing algorithm that doesn't cause the channel's volume to drop as drastically as the previous version did. The new version also doesn't restrict sound channels to the modes that it used to. For example, you can now open a sampled sound channel along with a square wave channel and play both of them together. The previous version allowed for only one or the other, but not both at the same time.

Gestalt() and the Sound Manager

To determine which features of the Sound Manager are currently available, call Gestalt() using the selector gestaltSoundAttr:

```
long  response;

err == Gestalt( gestaltSoundAttr, &response );
```

Different bits in response tell you whether different Sound Manager features are installed.

Here are the flags you can use to test these bits:

- gestaltStereoCapability is set if the sound hardware is capable of producing stereo sound. This is generally available through the external audio jack or headphone port. The internal speaker may or may not include both the left and right signals.

- gestaltStereoMixing is set if the internal speaker will allow both the left and right signals to be heard when playing a stereo sound.

- gestaltSoundIOMgrPresent is set if Sound Manager 2.0 or later is present. This flag also specifies that sound input is available. If this flag is not set, then you cannot call any Sound Manager routine that uses the _SoundDispatch trap, such as SndStartFilePlay().

- gestaltBuiltInSoundInput is set when the machine has built-in sound input hardware.

- gestaltHasSoundInputDevice is set when a sound input device is available. This flag is different from gestaltBuiltInSoundInput in that it can be set on a machine that does not have built-in sound input support.

- gestaltPlayAndRecord is set if the machine can support input and output at the same time. On some machines, the sound hardware cannot do both together, and, in this case, input has a higher priority. So, if you're playing a sound and then you start to record, the output will stop so long as the sound input driver is open.

- gestalt16BitSoundIO is set if the sound hardware is 16-bit capable. This flag is also useful in determining an optimal sample rate for your sound. If the machine has 16-bit hardware, then it will have an output rate that is a multiple of the audio standard of 44.1kHz. Otherwise, 8-bit hardware uses the old Macintosh rate of 22kHz (which is actually 22,254.54545 hertz).

- `gestaltStereoInput` is set if the input hardware has stereo support.

- `gestaltLineLevelInput` is set if the input hardware supports line-level input. There are basically two input levels: one for a microphone and one for line input. The two inputs have different impedance requirements. Line level refers to external audio equipment such as a stereo receiver or the audio outputs of an audio CD player.

The following flags were introduced as part of Sound Manager 3.0:

- `gestaltSndPlayDoubleBuffer` is set if `SndPlayDoubleBuffer()` is supported.

Originally, *Inside Macintosh* stated that `SndStartFilePlay()` and `SndPlayDoubleBuffer()` were supported only on machines that had the Apple Sound Chip (ASC). This statement implied that you needed to pass `gestaltHardwareAttr` to `Gestalt()` and test whether the `gestaltHasASC` flag was set. Wrong! On the 840AV machine, the sound hardware is not the ASC, but is a DSP chip instead. The `gestaltHasASC` bit is not set, but both of the routines are supported. When Sound Manager 3.0 is installed, new `gestaltSoundAttr` flags are added to help developers determine whether these routines are available. If you want to determine if these two routines are available, first check for Sound Manager 3.0 by calling `SndSound-ManagerVersion()`. If the `majorRev` value returned is 3 or greater, then you can test the `gestaltSndPlayDoubleBuffer` flag. Otherwise, use the `gestaltHasASC` flag. Also, before you can call `SndSoundManagerVersion()`, you need to make sure that the `_SoundDispatch` Sound Manager support traps are available, which can be done by testing the `gestaltSound-IOMgrPresent` bit.

- `gestaltMultiChannels` is set if the Sound Manager can support more than one sound channel at the same time. Although Sound Manager 2.0 supported this as a new feature for sampled sound channels, there was no way to test for this feature. You had to test for the Sound Manager version and then assume multichannel support was present. There is now a flag to test for this feature, but this flag is set only by Sound Manager 3.0 and later.

- `gestalt16BitAudioSupport` is set if the Sound Manager can provide support for 16-bit audio data. This flag is different from `gestalt16BitSoundIO` in that you may be running on a machine that has 8-bit hardware but the Sound Manager can convert 16-bit data to 8.

A Pitch for Using 'snd' Resources

There are alternatives to implementing your program's sounds as 'snd' resources. You can pull your sounds from a file, or you can even come up with your own proprietary resource format designed to help you compose sound on the fly.

The real advantage to using the 'snd' resource is the same advantage that any resource provides: You can alter the application without modifying the code. If you find that the sound in question isn't giving the user quite the effect it should have, then you can simply paste in a new sound and test it again. This is something that can be done during user testing in a laboratory, without requesting that the programmer recompile the code and send out a different version to be tested. Also, it's really nice if the sounds have good names and if the program uses GetNamedResource() instead of making assumptions about the resource IDs. Not only is this helpful for the marketing and user-testing staff, but also folks like me have fun changing the sounds of their software, and if you use named sound resources, it really makes it easier for users to customize their games!

The disadvantages are, well, I can't think of any!

Sound Channel Flags and Fields

Do not attempt to modify or examine any of the fields of the sound channel. The only part of the structure that belongs to you is the userInfo field. Other than this, restrict your channel access through the appropriate Sound Manager routines. Some programmers read a sound channel's qHead and qTail, and, much worse, some actually write to these fields. The use of these fields is not documented and is subject to change. Any use of these fields may cause your software to fail in the future.

The Initialization Options

A channel's initialization options are supposedly used to set channel features like panning, mono versus stereo, and so on. The truth is that these values do nothing. The real thing is determined by the sound you're playing. If you open a mono channel and then attempt to play a stereo sound, you'll hear the true stereo sound exactly as described by the sound header.

There is only one initialization option that currently matters, and it is the initNoInterp option, which determines the quality of sample rate conversion. If you're playing sound that is at the native rate of the hardware (22kHz sound on 22kHz hardware), then there is no sample rate conversion, which means that `initNoInterp` doesn't matter. But if you're playing a sound at some other rate, then the sound has to be rate converted. If the `initNoInterp` option is set, the Sound Manager will use a quicker algorithm, which uses less CPU overhead, at the expense of quality. Try experimenting with setting this flag when you open the channel. Note that you can change this option anytime you wish by using the `reInitCmd`.

The Trouble with SndPlay()

Throughout this chapter, you've seen code that has to do special error checking to avoid bugs in the old Sound Manager. This problem is especially true of code that works with `SndPlay()`. For example, once `SndPlay()` initializes a channel to play a particular type of sound asynchronously, you can no longer call `SndPlay()` on this channel. Thus, if you want to use `SndPlay()` more than once, you need to loop around calls to `SndNewChannel()`, `SndPlay()`, and `SndDisposeChannel()`, which, if you just play the occasional sound, is not a problem and, given how easy `SndPlay()` is to use, represents the ideal solution. But if your plans call for rapid-fire sounds with pinpoint timing, the extra overhead may be too limiting.

The main reason programmers cling to `SndPlay()` is that the prospect of parsing their `'snd '` resources is intimidating. Since you now have the code to do the parsing for you (`GetSndDataOffset()`, for example), this concern should no longer be a factor. On the other hand, you can license the latest version of the Sound Manager from Apple and include it with your application and then use `Gestalt()` in your initialization code to make sure it is installed. The new version of the Sound Manager is 100% bug free. Well, OK, maybe not. But it does fix all the old Sound Manager gremlins, so you don't have to special-case your code all over the place and can use `SndPlay()` to your heart's content.

If you do use a pre-3.0 version of `SndPlay()`, consider this problem: A sound is playing and you need to start a new one. Since the old one is playing asynchronously, you have to decide to either stop the old one or wait until it's done. Generally, you'll want to stop the old one. This means you need to issue two commands, `flushCmd` and `quietCmd` with `SndDoImmediate()`, before starting the new sound.

Here's another detail that has caught a few developers by surprise. In using `SndPlay()` asynchronously, you have to lock the sound resource handle while the sound is playing. As you've already seen, this means you have to keep track of this handle so that, when the sound is done, you can unlock the handle or, preferably, restore its state with HSetState() and then, since sounds tend to be large, probably mark the handle as purgeable. All of this additional code is necessary to support asynchronous sound. So what has this high-level routine SndPlay() done for you? Basically, only one thing: It has parsed the sound and issued all of the commands it contained to the sound channel.

If you do plan on supporting asynchronous sound, which you should, then you have to either poll for the sound to finish or use an interrupt routine. I'm always in favor of avoiding interrupt code whenever possible, but if you use SndPlayDoubleBuffer() (and, therefore, SndStartFilePlay(), which calls it), a polling routine just isn't practical. Since double buffering keeps a channel constantly busy processing first one buffer and then another, the scChannelBusy flag will always be set. Double buffering is one case where you'll have to bite the bullet and work at the interrupt level.

One final thought: In the future, SndPlay() may be asynchronous when passed a nil channel. Thus, adding asynchronous sound to your application will be simple. Currently, if you ask SndNewChannel() to allocate a channel for you, the async parameter of SndPlay() is ignored. In the future, this may not be the case, so pass the value that you really want.

SndAddModifier()
Prior to Sound Manager 3.0, the 'snth' resource contained the code used by a channel to produce sound. With the release of Sound Manager 3.0, the 'snth' resource is no longer used. The routine SndAddModifier() was used by SndNewChannel() to add this resource to the channel. Since the 'snth' resource is dead, SndAdd-Modifier() is now pointless. Moreover, it will do the wrong thing. Prior to 3.0, it blindly added the 'snth' resource to the channel without checking which one was already installed. This led to crashes when you tried to play sounds or when you tried to call SndDisposeChannel(). With Sound Manager 3.0 installed, this routine doesn't do much of anything. Some applications have been relying upon it to establish the type of channel they want, either the sampled sounds, wave table sounds, or square wave sounds. Instead of passing the type to SndNewChannel(), they passed 0 and then call SndAddModifier(). Because of this dependency, SndAddModifier()

continues to set the channel's type. As the Sound Manager moves away from channel types, however, even this will probably change.

In future versions of the Sound Manager, channel types will no longer be an issue. The goal will be to interpret any sound command for any channel. For example, the wave table channel currently will return an error if you issue a bufferCmd. The plan is that, instead of an error, it should just play the sound. This means there will be no more channel "modes" that require specific knowledge by the programmer as to their behavior. As an example, in Sound Manager 3.0.2, if you use the SndPlay() routine, it will play any type of 'snd ' resource on any channel you pass to it. If you create a channel for sampled sounds, for instance, you can use SndPlay() to hear the System alert sound "Simple Beep." "Simple Beep" is actually a square wave sound and, when passed to SndPlay() prior to Sound Manager 3.0.2, would have returned an error.

What You Can Do at Interrupt Level

The same old rules about interrupt-level code apply to Sound Manager interrupt routines. Interrupt routines cannot access relocatable memory objects such as unlocked handles. You cannot call the Memory Manager to dispose of objects, to allocate, or to alter a handle's state. You cannot access a low-memory global or, more importantly, call a Toolbox routine that needs one. This last rule is particularly problematic. There is no list of which routines will use a low-memory global. For example, FrontWindow() doesn't allocate or move memory, but it uses system globals that are not valid at interrupt level. There is a list of routines that *Inside Macintosh* publishes that are allowed at interrupt level. This list is a small percentage of the Macintosh routines.

Finally, on a 68K machine, when your interrupt routine is called, your A5 globals are no longer being pointed to by register A5. Thus, if you want to access one of your application's globals, you have to restore register A5 to point to your globals and then, when you're done, restore A5's current value. You might put your register A5 value into param2 of callBackCmd so that you can access your application's globals. A better, nonmachine-dependent option is to put the address of the data you want to access in param2 instead.

You can call SndDoCommand() and SndDoImmediate() at interrupt level as long as you use a command that isn't going to break one of the rules just stated. This means you can use freqCmd, freqDurationCmd, `callBackCmd`, and just about every other command that is defined, but you may not be able to use `soundCmd` or `bufferCmd`. These last two commands may allocate memory if the sound you want to play is in a different format than that for which the channel was prepared. As an example, if you're playing 8-bit sounds and then issue a `bufferCmd` on a 16-bit sound, this command will cause the Sound Manager to allocate memory. The same is true if you play a new sound that is compressed.

If you plan on using `callBackCmd` to play sounds, there's one thing you should know about `soundCmd`. Normally, `soundCmd` establishes the sound you're going to play using `freqCmd` or `freqDurationCmd`. If you just want to play a sound and don't want to play it as an instrument, you might think that `soundCmd` is of little use. But, in fact, it is very useful! When you issue `soundCmd`, all of the necessary memory and components for playing that sound are created. Thus, if you want to play a 16-bit sound and want it to play as soon as possible, issue `soundCmd` right after creating the channel. Then, when you want to hear the sound, issue `bufferCmd`. At this point, the channel is prepared for 16-bit data and will be able to immediately play it. This technique is also necessary if you're going to attempt to play sounds of a different format at interrupt level. Since channels are initially created for 8-bit data, the first 16-bit sound issued to the channel will cause it to allocate new structures and load components from disk, which isn't something that can be done at interrupt level.

`SysBeep()` will allocate memory. It calls `SndNewChannel()`, `SndPlay()`, and `SndDisposeChannel()`. It should be obvious to you by now that you can't call `SysBeep()` at interrupt level. Calling `SysBeep()` used to be a debugging technique, but you cannot do this from an interrupt handler, a video blanking (VBL) task , or a Time Manager task.

Avoiding Clicks

You may sometimes hear a click or pop when you start a sound playing. The click or pop often happens when the Sound Manager turns on the sound hardware. The noise is generally caused when the current sound starts at a different level than that of the last sound that was played. For example, if the very last sample ended with a high amplitude and the next sample you play begins at the zero-crossing point or a low amplitude, you'll hear a popping sound as the speaker makes the transition between the two disjointed samples. This popping sound may be heard without starting a new sound. Just the fact that the very last sample was at a nonzero crossing may cause the speaker to click as it returns to its resting position (Figure 4.8).

FIGURE 4.8

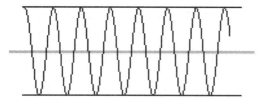

A sound wave moving from a high amplitude back down toward the zero-crossing point. If the sound ends this way, you may hear a click as the speaker jumps back to its resting position.

To avoid these clicks, you should end your very last sound with a buffer of silence to set the speaker at its resting position. After you play a sound, if no other sound is being played, then play one buffer of silence. Play the buffer of silence when you know you have nothing else to play. The buffer has to be only about 2K of 22kHz data and will help the sound hardware to stabilize. Play this buffer in addition to ending your buffers at a zero crossing (Figure 4.9). Otherwise, you might end up with a pop when you start your buffer of silence!

FIGURE 4.9

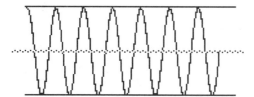

A sound wave that ends at a zero crossing. This positioning helps to avoid a clicking or popping noise.

Choosing the Best Format

Since most Mac hardware is still based on the original 22kHz rate, any sound that is not sampled at this rate has to be converted. The process of sample rate conversion has to take place in real time. This constraint limits the quality of the audio that a particular machine can produce. The conversion algorithm requires a mathematical formula to be applied to every single sample. This conversion process has been optimized using typical cases of audio play. The most commonly used sound on the Macintosh today is 8-bit mono, 11kHz or 22kHz sample rate. If the hardware is at 22kHz, no conversion has to take place for a sound that is also at the 22kHz sampling rate. But if the sound is sampled at 11kHz, then the Sound Manager has to "up-sample" the sound into a 22kHz format. Normally, this process would require math instructions that would slow the process, but if the up sampling is an integral ratio (in this example, 1:2), then the Sound Manager has optimized code to handle this. For other rates that are not an even multiple, the Sound Manager's sample-rate conversion routines have to perform more math, which makes them the most costly of all the sample rate conversions.

Audio Compression

Sixteen-bit sound involves a large amount of data. Compressing this data means less data and less use of RAM. If you're going to play sound from disk (typically, 16-bit sound takes up too much RAM to do anything else), compressed sound means fewer disk accesses. Since a large amount of data is now being distributed on CD-ROM, getting the data into memory is a slow process. It's getting better with faster hard drives and faster CD-ROM players, but it's still much slower than the overhead of playing the sound. The point is that, in many cases, playing a compressed sound from disk is actually faster than playing the same sound uncompressed. You'll have to consider the amount of overhead that decompressing will cost you. If the time spent decompressing the sound is greater than reading it from disk, then you've lost the advantage.

In addition, the quality of the compression technique has to be considered. You use 16-bit sound because it provides high-quality sound. You don't want to choose a compression technique that will effectively reduce this quality to a level that could have been provided by 8-bit sound. You should consider 8-bit, 11kHz, mono sound as one type of compression. You can also create your own audio compression, if you're so inclined. An article by Kip Olson in Apple's *develop* magazine shows how you can write your own audio codec. Check it out ("Make Your Own Sound Components," Issue 20).

8-Bit versus 16-Bit Hardware

Most of the current Macs use 8-bit sound hardware, but things are changing. The Quadra 840AV and 660AV machines include a DSP, which uses 16-bit hardware. The Power Macs also use 16-bit hardware, but without the DSP. What may appear as a serious limitation is not. In fact the PowerPC chips are so powerful that the DSP just isn't necessary. As we go to press, Apple is hard at work on a native PowerPC version of the Sound Manager. Increased speed and efficiency are important, but they're not the only goal. The real advantage will be the improvement in audio quality that results from the new versions of the sample-rate conversion code.

Obviously, 16-bit hardware will be able to produce higher-quality sound than 8-bit hardware. As mentioned earlier, there's a cost that goes along with this increase in quality. Creating 16-bit content will cost you in performance due to the higher sampling rates used. There's also a cost in size, both in RAM and hard drive space.

Since 16-bit audio is generally reserved for musical content, it is recorded in stereo. If you compare the storage requirements of commonly used Mac sound (8-bit, 11kHz, mono) to a 16-bit, 44.1kHz, stereo sound, you'll find that the higher quality will cost you 16 times the storage. Unless storage isn't an issue, you might consider the compromise of 16-bit, 22kHz, mono sound, which is also very good quality.

QuickTime 2.0 and Sound Manager 3.1 or later support a new audio compression format, the International Multimedia Association (IMA) standard. The IMA format is a 4:1 compression used to support 16-bit audio. It will also become a standard part of the Sound Manager 3.1 release, and you will not need to require QuickTime 2.0. If you're considering 16-bit data or high-quality sounds, you should look into the new IMA format because it is 16-bit sound that is 4 times smaller than the original sound. By using the 16-bit IMA format, you can deliver one source for sound data that works on both 8- and 16-bit Macintosh computers. This is also an effective format for 8 bit machines since it is half the size of the same sound recorded in 8 bit. Since decompressing the audio data requires more CPU time, you have to measure the performance cost and determine what data format is best for your needs.

22 Kilohertz Versus 22050 Hertz

A sound's sample rate determines its frequency range. If you desire audio that contains the frequency range of human hearing (up to

20kHz), then you need to use the standard 44.1kHz sample rate used by today's compact discs. According to the Nyquist theorem, you have to use a sampling rate twice that of the desired highest frequencies. If you sample audio at 22kHz, then the highest frequencies that can be present in the audio will be half that, or 11kHz.

The Mac's sample rate of 22kHz is not half that of the commonly used 44.1kHz rate. The sample rate found in most Macintoshes is based on the original Mac 128K hardware. It used a sound driver that was based upon the Mac's video blanking (VBL) rate of 60 times a second (actually, closer to 59.xxxx). The hardware contained a small buffer for audio data, which was 370 bytes in size. This led to a sampling rate of 22.2545454kHz, which became known as 22kHz on the Mac. Since the compact disc sampling rate is 44.1kHz, half would be 22.050kHz. The difference between these two rates becomes important when we consider that the Sound Manager has to convert all sound data to the native rate of the hardware.

In the `Sound.h` header file, you'll find the two constants `rate22050hz` and `rate22khz`. These constants represent the two rates for half of 44.1kHz and the old Macintosh sampling rate. The question is, which one are you going to use? Of course, you can use any rate you want, but essentially these are the two basic rates of the hardware. The other rates are multiples of these two. For the most optimal performance and quality, you want to use a rate that is a multiple of the hardware rate. The two rates can be distinguished by 8-bit and 16-bit hardware. All of the 8-bit machines use `rate22khz` for the hardware output rate. All of the 16-bit machines will use a multiple of 44.1kHz which makes `rate22050hz` the preferred choice. If you're trying to choose a sample rate that works best on all machines, you'll have to make a decision based on the trade-offs. The differences in `rate22050hz` and `rate22khz` are very minimal as far as frequency content, and I don't think the average listener will be able to tell the difference.

The real issue is whether or not the target machine will have to perform sample rate conversion on the data in order to play it back. If you choose `rate22050hz`, you'll get the best performance and quality on 16-bit hardware such as the 840AV and Power Macs. But this same data will have to be rate converted on the 8-bit machines, and the 8-bit machines are less powerful. Therefore, the performance and quality will cost you. Conversely, using `rate22khz` audio on the 8-bit machines is the most efficient and gives you the best quality. This same data played back on 16-bit machines will have to be rate converted, but these machines are more powerful, so the performance cost is less. Also, these machines will have better sample-rate conversion routines, so the quality should be better as well.

Of course, you don't have to use only one sample rate. If you're generating the audio in real time, such as a music synthesizer would, you can create the audio at either rate. If you're delivering your content on a CD-ROM, you have the advantage of being able to store both formats. Then, you can decide at run time which samples to use, either `rate22050hz` or `rate22khz`. This gives you the best performance and quality for all machines. Using a sample rate higher than 22kHz would make sense only for 16-bit machines. Since all 8-bit machines are 22kHz playback rate, a higher rate of data would have to be down-sampled, which loses the higher frequencies that you've recorded. Also, the higher data rate means more memory and more copying, which equates to having more CPU cycles spent in performing audio.

SUMMARY

You've absorbed a lot of information in this chapter, much of which detailed the trade-offs you have to make when you work with the Sound Manager. Do you require that the newest version of the Sound Manager be installed, or do you fill your code with all the bug fixes necessary to ensure that your code will work with older versions? Which sampling rate should you support? Should you use compression? If so, which method?

The answers to these questions almost always involve trade-offs. Although the trade-offs were presented here, your decisions will be the result of experience and the particulars of your situation. Hopefully, with the information in this chapter and *Inside Macintosh: Sound*, you'll be able to make the right choices.

BIOGRAPHY

Jim Reekes studied music composition and theory in college and never took a single computer science or engineering class because he believed they would only pollute his brain. He taught himself programming, beginning with the Apple II and moving on to the Macintosh 128K in 1984, using assembly language because he couldn't afford the Lisa development system. He began working in Apple's Developer Technical Support group (MacDTS) in 1988. He took over responsibility for the Sound Manager during System 7 beta (so you can't blame that one on him!) and last year finished the new Sound Manager 3, which was a complete rewrite to "make it suck less." One thing he has learned while at Apple is that there's a fine line between having an amazing insight and having a bad attitude. Amazing insight occurs when you withhold your opinion until someone asks for it.

Jim has been collecting progressive rock and electronic music recording since 1970. He grew up in Pomona, California, during the 1960s and 1970s and can remember when Frank Zappa performed in local bars on Mission Boulevard and Cucamonga was a vineyard. Jim thinks Frank was the most influential composer of his time. He wishes programming didn't drain his brain so much so that he could spend more time in his MIDI studio creating sound you've never heard before.

PATCHING TRAPS

Chapter

5

Trap patching is one of the most complex and misunderstood of all Macintosh programming techniques. Patching traps is cool; if you patch the right trap, you can do some amazing things. And patching traps is what allows a program like QuicKeys to detect a specific key press no matter what application is in the foreground.

But patching traps the right way is an extremely difficult undertaking. What really makes it hard is the lack of documentation on the subject. There are no books on trap patching and no articles either (at least none that I am aware of). There is a chapter on the Trap Manager in *Inside Macintosh: Operating System Utilities* but, while fairly well written, it focuses on technical implementation details with little in the way of strategic guidance. Simply put, if you want to patch traps, you're on your own. Until now, that is.

This chapter takes you through the process of patching traps from the ground up. We'll start by exploring the trap mechanism and learn exactly what patching a trap means and why you'd want to do such a thing. Along the way, we'll look at some sample code and examine some important strategic issues you'll need to be aware of as you write your own trap-patching code.

Before we move on to the chapter itself, there's one more detail we need to cover. When this book was in its planning stages, I talked to a lot of developers and asked them what topics they wanted me to cover in this series. Patching traps seemed to be on everyone's list. My next goal was to find out everything I could about patching traps. I talked to everyone I knew who knew anything about the subject. The one thing that became clear to me is that there is no consensus on the right way to do this. Everyone I spoke with had their own style, and there was clearly conflict between these styles. So I turned to Jorg Brown for help.

Jorg has a lot of experience patching traps as well as a tremendous amount of experience supporting trap-patching in the real world (check out the list of products in his bio). I asked Jorg to take on the task of explaining this most complex of topics from his perspective. Fortunately for me, Jorg agreed. As you read this chapter, bear in mind that this is our first attempt to document something that hasn't really been covered before. If you have any comments, gripes, or suggestions, please email them to me (74774.3020@compuserve.com) and I will try to get them into the next edition of this chapter. That being said, I'd now like to turn the author's quill over to Jorg…

An Introduction to Traps

In the days before the Macintosh, the most popular personal computer was the Apple II. Like most computers, the Apple II had a ROM. As had become the industry practice, the Apple II ROM contained the code needed to start up the computer, as well as some nice utility routines. Savvy developers knew where these routines lived in ROM and accessed them directly whenever necessary.

As they were planning the Macintosh, Apple wanted to follow this same design. However, there were several problems with programs jumping directly into the ROM to access utility routines. First off, during development the ROMs were constantly changing, so jumping directly into ROM just wasn't practical. In addition, with only 64K of RAM to work with (this was bumped to 128K just before the Mac was released), space was at a premium, and at 6 bytes of code per call, jumping directly into ROM was RAM-intensive. Finally, some parts of the OS changed so frequently that they never made it into ROM, so jumping to these routines was out of the question. Apple needed an alternative.

The solution Apple arrived at was the *trap*, a mechanism that allowed developers to access Macintosh OS routines without having to know where they were. By using traps, Apple was able to replace what would have been 6-byte long JSR or JMP instructions directly into ROM with 2-byte long "A-line instructions." For example, without using traps, calling the QuickDraw routine MoveTo would have required something akin to "JSR $40814EBA." On the other hand, while using traps the A-line instruction $A893 performs the same function in one-third the space.

How the Trap Mechanism Works

Traps are made possible by the Motorola 680x0 exception handling architecture. Every instruction executed by the 680x0 has the potential to generate an exception. Examples of 680x0 exceptions are the bus error, address error, illegal instruction, and zero divide. When an exception occurs, the processor saves a small amount of information about what caused the exception on the stack, looks the exception up in a special table known as the *exception vector table*, and retrieves the address of a routine designed to handle that exception. It then jumps to that routine.

If you are interested in the details, get a copy of the 680x0 *Programmer's Reference Manual* from Motorola and read the chapter on Exception Processing.

The exception type of interest in this chapter is the *line 1010 emulator* exception. This exception occurs whenever an instruction that starts with the four bits 1010 gets executed. Since 1010 is equivalent to the hex digit A, these instructions are known as *A-line instructions*, and the exceptions they cause are known as *A-line exceptions*. Since the terms "trap" and "exception" are often synonymous, both the instructions and the exceptions they generate are sometimes known as *A-traps*, or just plain *traps*.

As is the case with any other exception, there is an entry in the exception vector table for the A-line exception. When your Mac starts up, the operating system places the address of the routine it wants to have handle all A-line exceptions into the A-line exception vector. This routine is known as the *trap dispatcher*.

The trap dispatcher maintains two tables, known as *trap dispatch tables*. These tables take the information embedded in a trap instruction and return the address of a routine that corresponds to that instruction. One of these tables contains a list of 256 Operating System routines and the other a list of 1,024 Toolbox routines. Each address in the table is 32 bits long and may point to either ROM or RAM. Once the trap dispatcher retrieves the address of the routine that corresponds to the current trap, control is transferred to that routine.

As they were originally designed, the Operating System routines were intended for use by the operating system and the Toolbox routines for the general Macintosh programmer. Since then the distinction between the two has become blurred, but the design has not changed.

The Format of an A-Line Instruction

By definition, the leftmost four bits (bits 12 through 15) of an A-trap are always 1010. The fifth bit (bit 11) indicates to which of the two dispatch tables the trap belongs. This bit is important not just because it differentiates between the two tables, but because the calls in the Toolbox dispatch table pass their parameters on the stack while the Operating System calls pass their parameters using registers (there are a few exceptions to that rule but that's beyond the scope of this chapter). The fifth bit lets the trap dispatcher locate the proper routine and tells it the proper way to pass information to that routine.

Stack-based traps use A-traps $A800 through $AFFF and follow the format shown in Figure 5.1. In a stack-based, Toolbox trap the fifth bit is always set. The sixth bit (bit 10) is called the *auto-pop bit* and tells the trap dispatcher whether to treat the A-trap as if it were a JMP instruction (if the bit is set), or a JSR instruction (if it is clear). This was done to accommodate certain development environments which used an intermediate routine (called a *glue routine*) when making Toolbox calls. The auto-pop bit is almost never used and is ignored by most development environments.

FIGURE 5.1

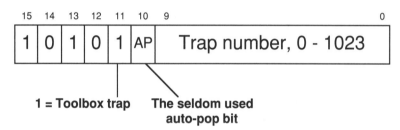

Format of the stack-based Toolbox traps.

The remaining 10 bits contain a trap number ranging in value from 0 to 1023. This is an index into the Toolbox trap dispatch table.

Register-based traps use A-traps $A000 through $A7FF and follow the format shown in Figure 5.2. In a register-based Operating System trap, the fifth bit is always cleared. The sixth and seventh bits are known as flag bits. The meaning of the flag bits depends on the Operating System routine being called. As an example, if the trap represents a call to a Memory Manager routine, bit 8 specifies which heap any allocated memory should come from (if the bit is clear, the memory is allocated in the current heap zone; if the bit is set, the memory is allocated in the system heap zone) and bit 9 specifies whether any allocated memory should be cleared to 0 (done if the bit is set).

The eighth bit indicates whether the called routine returns a value in register A0. If the bit is cleared, the trap dispatcher saves off register A0, calls the routine associated with the trap, then restores the saved A0.

If the bit is set, the value of A0 returned by the trap routine is left in A0. Regardless of the setting of this bit, registers D1, D2, A1, and A2 are saved off before calling the routine and restored afterward.

FIGURE 5.2

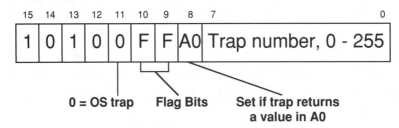

Format of the register-based Operating System traps.

The remaining 8 bits contain a trap number ranging in value from 0 to 255. This is an index into the Operating System trap dispatch table.

A Little History

At this point you might be wondering, why the difference between the two kinds of traps? Wouldn't it be easier just to have 4,096 (based on a 12 bit trap number) ROM entry points, with an A-trap format like that shown in Figure 5.3?

FIGURE 5.3

15	14	13	12	11	0
1	0	1	0		Trap number, 0 - 4095

A generic A-trap instruction assuming a single trap dispatch table.

To answer this question, it is important to hark back to 1982, when the trap mechanism was being laid in place. At the time, the Mac was designed to have only 64K of RAM, 22K of which was reserved as screen memory. Andy Hertzfeld was telling Microsoft that it was all right to assume there would never be more than a megabyte of RAM in any Macintosh (since that was then an unheard of amount of RAM) and flatly stated that no one would ever need more than 4 megabytes. QuickDraw, the Mac's imaging code, was being recoded from Pascal to assembly so that it could fit in ROM. With only 42K of RAM left over, it was imperative that none of it be wasted. If there had been 4,096 trap table entries, the trap dispatch table alone would have consumed 16K, more than a third of the available RAM!

The decision was made to limit the trap dispatch table to 512 entries, which was very reasonable—at the time there were less than 512 ROM routines. Limiting the trap table to 512 entries left 3 extra bits in each A-line instruction (when compared to the 4,096-entry format). Surely a use could be found for those extra bits?

While the majority of the routines in the Mac ROMs use stack-based, Pascal calling conventions, there were other assembly language routines that used registers of the 68000 to pass their parameters. For these routines, extra housekeeping was often necessary, since many of the registers had to be saved away before calls and restored afterward. Since the trap mechanism was already replacing 6-byte long JSR instructions with two-byte long A-line instructions, an idea struck: Even more code could be saved if CPU registers didn't have to be saved and restored by hand, if somehow the A-line exception handler could do some of the work automatically, as part of the dispatching function it already performed.

That's the story behind bit 11, the bit that specifies whether a trap uses the stack or registers to pass parameters. If the bit was zero, the trap mechanism went through additional work to save off registers A1, A2, D1, and D2, made the call, then restored those registers. A-line instructions with this bit clear represented calls to register-based ROM routines, while instructions with this bit set represented calls to stack-based ROM routines. Since register-based routines were predominantly found in the operating system, and stack-based routines were predominantly part of the Toolbox, A-line instructions with this bit clear are known as *OS traps*, and instructions with this bit set are known as *Toolbox traps*.

As time went on, Apple took this even further: For some OS traps, it was also useful to save off register A0, so for OS traps, an additional bit was used to indicate whether A0 should be saved and restored along with all the rest. Similarly, for Toolbox traps, there were occasions where rather than an A-line instruction simulating a JSR instruction, it was useful to simulate a JMP instruction. This was because, in 1983, most development environments were designed to use JSRs to glue code, which could call the ROM, rather than emitting A-line instructions in the code they generated. Rather than force all the existing compilers to recode, A-traps that simulate JMP instructions worked perfectly as glue.

> If you are new to assembler, you might want to check out one of the many 68000 assembler books as you go through this chapter. There's an excellent introduction to assembly language in Scott Knaster's classic *How to Write Macintosh Software* (Appendix A).

A Quick Tour of the Trap Dispatch Tables

OK, now let's put all the pieces together and explore the trap tables, from highest to lowest.

FIGURE 5.4

15	14	13	12	11	10	9							0
1	0	1	0	1	1			Trap number, 0 - 1023					

A-line instructions $AC00 through $AFFF.

A-line instructions $AC00 through $AFFF (Figure 5.4) are a shorthand for jumping directly to a stack-based Toolbox routine. The trap dispatcher handles them as if they were a JMP instruction, fetching the address of the Toolbox routine in question and jumping directly there. For example, embedding trap $AC73 in your code is the same as the assembler instruction `JMP SetPort`.

FIGURE 5.5

15	14	13	12	11	10	9							0
1	0	1	0	1	0			Trap number, 0 - 1023					

A-line instructions $A800 through $ABFF

A-line instructions $A800 through $ABFF (Figure 5.5) are a shorthand for calling (as opposed to jumping to) a stack-based Toolbox routine. The trap dispatcher handles them as if they were a JSR instruction, pushing the address of the instruction immediately following the A-trap on the stack, and then jumping to the Toolbox routine. As an example, embedding trap $A873 in your code is the same as `JSR SetPort`.

FIGURE 5.6

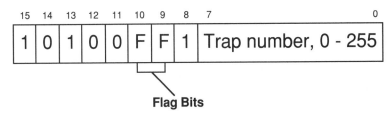

Flag Bits

A-line instructions $A100-$A1FF, $A300-$A3FF, $A500-$A5FF, and $A700-$A7FF.
The four possible values for the 2 flag bits give us this range.

A-line instructions in the range $A100-$A7FF (Figure 5.6) with the result-in-A0 bit set are shorthand for calling a register-based OS routine. The trap dispatcher saves registers A2, D2, D1, and A1 onto the stack, then calls the routine in question using JSR, restores the registers, and returns. On entry to the routine, registers A2, D2, and D1 have been modified by the trap mechanism: A2 points to the instruction immediately following the A-trap, the low 16 bits of D1 contain the A-trap instruction, and D2 is undefined. In addition, for efficiency reasons there is an extra long word on the stack, just after the registers. The reason register D1 is set up this way is so the routines can examine the bits of D1 and determine how the two flag bits have been set. For example, the trap for `NewPtr()` is $A11E, but the trap for `NewPtrSys()`, which is the same except that it always allocates its memory in the system heap, is $A51E. The way that the `NewPtrSys()` routine determines that it should use the system heap is to test bit 10 of D1 on entry.

Trap $A51E is basically the same as:

```
movem.l    D1-D2/A1-A2,-(a7)
move.w     #$A51E,D1
JSR        NewPtr
movem.l    (a7)+,D1-D2/A1-A2
```

The differences are that the stack is slightly different in layout, and A2 actually contains the address of the `NewPtr()` trap. It is worth noting at this point that the code sequence above would be 18 bytes long, whereas using the trap uses only 2 bytes. You can see how important the trap dispatcher is in saving RAM!

FIGURE 5.7

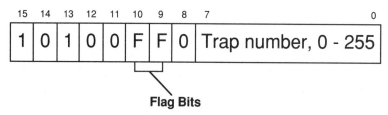

A-line instructions $A000-$A0FF, $A200-$A2FF, $A400-$A4FF, and $A600-$A6FF. The four possible values for the 2 flag bits give us this range.

A-line instructions in the range $A000-$A6FF (Figure 5.7) with the result-in-A0 bit clear are shorthand for calling a register-based OS routine. The trap dispatcher saves registers A2, D2, D1, A1 and A0 onto the stack, then calls the routine in question using JSR, restores the registers, and returns. These traps are handled exactly as the result-in-A0 case in Figure 5.6 except that A0 is saved and restored by the trap dispatcher. D1, D2, and A2 are set up and used the same way, and the same extra long word sits on the stack, unused.

Thus, trap $A41E is basically the same as:

```
movem.l     D1-D2/A0-A2,-(a7)
move.w      #$A41E,D1
JSR         NewPtr
movem.l     (a7)+,D1-D2/A0-A2
```

Again, the difference is that the stack is slightly different in layout, and A2 actually contains the address of the NewPtr() trap. Note that you would never use trap $A41E, because the NewPtr() trap returns its result in register A0, and using $A41E instead of $A51E causes A0 to be restored to the value it had before NewPtr() was called. Hence the trap dispatcher would destroy the return value you were looking for if you used $A41E.

PATCHING TRAPS

The designers of the original Mac had several goals in mind when they created the trap mechanism. Primarily, they saw traps as a way to reduce code size. In addition, they needed to ensure that developers didn't directly access ROM, so burning new ROMs wouldn't invalidate existing software. Finally, they needed a way to patch the ROMs so bug fixes could be introduced without redistributing the ROMs.

Assume for a moment that you work at Apple and you've just found out about a bug in the latest version of NewPtr() in ROM, and it's your job to fix it. The bug is this: if NewPtr() is called with a size less than 4 bytes, the heap gets corrupted. Suppose further that you know that NewPtr() resides in ROM at location $40809122. Since all calls to NewPtr() go through the trap dispatcher, you might patch the NewPtr() address located in the Operating System trap dispatch table, making it point to your own bug-fixing routine instead. This routine would first check the parameter to NewPtr(). If it was 4 or more, it would just jump to the real NewPtr() at $40809122 in ROM. If the parameter was less than 4, it would call the real NewPtr() with a parameter of 4, then call SetPtrSize() to reduce the block of memory down to the requested size. Here's an assembly language snippet that does just that:

```
ourNewPtr:
      cmp.l    #4,d0   ; are we about to hit the bug?
      blt.s    @1  ; if requestedSize of block >= 4, we're fine.
      jmp      $40809122

@1:  move.l   d0,-(a7)  ; otherwise, save the old size,
      move.l    #4,d0     ; use 4 instead,
      jsr       $40809122    ; and call the original trap.
      tst.l     d0    ; was there an error?
      beq.s     @5    ; no error, go ahead.
      addq      #4,a7      ; if there was an error, forget the
                                  old d0
      rts          ; and return

@5:  move.l   (a7)+,d0          ; if there was no error, set the
                                    block size
        _SetPtrSize      ; to the correct value,
        rts           ; and return
```

There—we've done it. Now, NewPtr() works as advertised for anyone calling it, and the bug in the ROM is avoided. Because the trap mechanism exists, this fix can be made at virtually any time, and from that moment on, any application calling NewPtr() is automatically shielded from the bug.

The Trap Manager

The example you just saw was a patch applied to the NewPtr() trap. What you didn't see was how the patch was applied. Fortunately, the

Operating System provides a set of routines to get and set entries in the two trap dispatch tables. These routines are known collectively as the *Trap Manager*.

There are two routines you'll use to fetch an address from a trap dispatch table: GetOSTrapAddress() and GetToolTrapAddress(). Both of these routines take a single parameter: a two byte trap number. Both of these routines return a long containing the address of the routine associated with the trap number. By retrieving the address of a Toolbox or Operating System routine, you can call it or jump to it from within your patching code, or restore the address to its rightful place in the trap dispatch table when you are ready to deinstall the patch.

There are two routines you'll use to set an address in a trap dispatch table: SetOSTrapAddress() and SetToolTrapAddress(). Both of these routines take a pair of parameters a long containing the address to be placed in the table and a short containing the trap number which indicates the position in the table at which the address will be stored.

Finally, there is a special routine, called Unimplemented(), which you'll never call. The address of Unimplemented() is stored in both trap dispatch tables any place where there is no routine defined to go along with a particular trap number. For example, if the Toolbox trap dispatch table (which has room for up to 1,024 entries) currently contains the addresses of 1,000 valid Toolbox routines, the remaining 24 entries in the table will each contain the address of the routine Unimplemented(). If you want to find out if a Toolbox or Operating System routine is available on the current configuration, you can call either GetOSTrapAddress() or GetToolTrapAddress() to fetch the address of the routine in question, then call the same routine to fetch the address of Unimplemented(). Compare the two results. If they are the same, you know the routine you are looking for is unimplemented.

Before we move on to the next section, there are two other points worth making now. First, when you set the address in one of the trap dispatch tables to a routine, make sure that routine is locked in memory until its address is removed from the table.

Second, it's important to note that every application maintains its own copy of the two dispatch tables. That means that whenever any application patches a trap, that trap is only patched for that application. In other words, if two different applications patch the same trap, the patches won't collide. The only way to patch a trap so that it's patched in all applications is to patch it before any applications are launched, and the only way to do that is from an extension (which we'll do in just a minute).

Why Patch Traps?

If you're Apple and want to fix a bug in your code, patching traps is great. Apple also patches traps that were never implemented in the ROM, hence patching them into existence when they weren't there before. But why would anyone else want to patch traps? Here are a few reasons.

Suppose you're playing a game, and it seems slow to you. So you start randomly hitting the interrupt button, and find out that the game, for whatever reason, keeps calling CopyBits() with image sizes of 8 by 8 pixels. If you could only special-case that size within CopyBits(), you could sure speed up the game...

Or suppose you don't feel like purchasing an electricity-wasting wall clock, and you want your computer to show you the time. But you don't like Apple's Alarm Clock desk accessory, because you keep accidentally hiding it. If you could get the Mac to call your code periodically, you could draw the time in the menu bar...

Or suppose you wanted to write some code that would examine every keyDown in every application to detect when a specific keystroke was entered. You might write an extension that patched SystemEvent() to watch for the keystroke of interest. As it turns out, you're about to see an extension that does just that.

THE BEEPER EXTENSION

The previous example showed how Apple might patch a trap. However, you're probably more interested in how you might patch a trap, so that's what this section is about. We're going to create an extension that patches the Operating System trap SystemEvent(). The patch will examine every event that occurs, looking for a sequence of four consecutive keystrokes that spell "beep." When that happens, the extension beeps.

Before we get to the code, it might be helpful to take a look at the process of loading an extension.

How Extensions Load

Way back in the Mac's early days, as part of its normal startup process, the system loaded, locked, and executed all resources of type 'INIT' found in the System file. Whenever Apple wanted to add new patches, or add new start-up behavior, it added another 'INIT' resource to the System file. Alas, when third parties wanted to add new patches, they had to do exactly the same thing. This became problematic after a while, since upgrades of Apple system software would often attempt to add new 'INIT' resources with the same resource ID as third parties, and the results were often disastrous.

To avoid this problem, Apple invented the "INIT 31" mechanism. The idea behind INIT 31 was that, once all of Apple's patches had loaded, the INIT with resource ID 31 would be executed. INIT 31 searched the System folder for files of type 'INIT', opened each file, and executed any INIT resources found. Although Apple prefers to call these files extensions, old habits die hard and most folks still call them INITs.

Testing the Beeper Extension

Go into the Projects folder and open the Beep.INIT subfolder. Drag the file Beeper INIT on top of your System Folder icon. When you let go, the Finder should ask you if it can move Beeper Init into the Extensions folder. Click OK, then restart your Mac. When your Mac finishes booting, the Beeper Init extension should be loaded. Before you do anything else, type the word "beep" (without the quotes). When you do, your Mac should beep at you. If it doesn't, verify that Beeper Init made it into your Extensions folder and, if you have an extensions manager installed, that Beeper Init is enabled. If all else fails, try typing a command key equivalent like ⌘C or ⌘A, an equivalent that is tied to a menu item that is currently enabled, then type "beep" again. Our beep detection algorithm is fairly simple and only detects the characters "beep" at the beginning of the keyboard buffer. Executing a command key equivalent clears the buffer.

Once you are done beeping, be sure to remove Beeper Init from the Extensions folder, since our next project replaces it with a cdev/INIT combination and we don't want the two projects fighting each other.

The Beep.Init Project

Open the Beep.INIT folder and launch the Beeper.68K project file. Figure 5.8 shows the Project preferences pane. Notice that the project is being built as an INIT resource with an ID of -4048 (this ID becomes important in our next example) and a resource name of Beeper. The resource will be saved in a file named Beeper INIT. The file will have a creator of 'Beep' and a type of 'INIT' (standard for extensions).

FIGURE 5.8

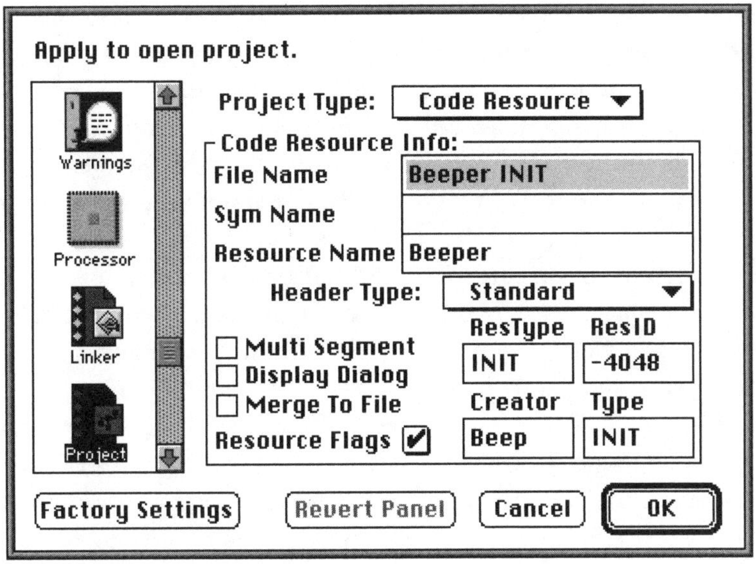

Apply to open project.

Project Type: [**Code Resource** ▼]

┌ **Code Resource Info:** ─────
File Name [**Beeper INIT**]
Sym Name [ ]
Resource Name [Beeper]
Header Type: [**Standard** ▼]

☐ **Multi Segment**   ResType   ResID
☐ **Display Dialog**   [INIT]   [-4048]
☐ **Merge To File**   Creator   Type
Resource Flags ☑   [Beep]   [INIT]

(Factory Settings)   (Revert Panel)   (Cancel)   (**OK**)

The Project preferences pane from CodeWarrior Lite.

Figure 5.9 shows the Resource Flags pop-up menu from the Project preferences pane. The resource attribute settings are critical. They specify that when the INIT is loaded, it is loaded in the System heap and then locked.

FIGURE 5.9

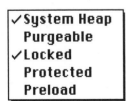

The Resource Flags pop-up menu from CodeWarrior Lite's Project preferences pane.

On this last point, you may be asking yourself why the "system heap" attribute would matter. After all, why would an INIT *not* want to load into the application heap? To answer this question, it's important once again to hark back again to the origins of INITs. Think back to 1985...

When a Macintosh first starts up and you hear the familiar gong, there is no MultiFinder heap and no Finder. In fact, there isn't even an application heap. There's just the system heap, starting right after the low-memory globals, and the stack, somewhere in the middle of memory. Then the system file is opened up, and all manner of strange and wonderful processes happen. After that, the application heap is created, starting right where the system heap stops. From then on, the system heap can no longer expand. At this point, the Macintosh is ready to start up the Finder. It is at this point that INITs are loaded.

Believe it or not, in the early days, INITs had to be careful about how they used the system heap, since there may not have been enough space there to load! Well-written INITs detected this low-memory situation and included code that increased the size of the system heap, and then re-initialized the application heap again! Fortunately for us, System 6 introduced code that did all this automatically. One thing we still have to worry about is that for backward compatibility reasons, the system still provides two heaps for INITs. Anything we leave in the system heap stays there forever, and anything we leave around in the application heap is liable to be discarded as soon as our INIT code returns. It's important to keep in mind this distinction between the "permanent" system heap and "temporary" application heap when writing the portion of our INIT that runs at boot time.

Beeper.main.c

After you are done admiring your preferences, take a look at the source file `Beeper.main.c`. The first thing you'll see is the requisite include files:

```
#include <Events.h>
#include <Resources.h>
#include <Memory.h>
#include <ToolUtils.h>
```

Since we're using Metrowerks, and it needs special access to register A4 for accessing its globals, we'll need to include a special header file:

```
#include <A4Stuff.h>
```

If we were using THINK C, it also needs special access to register A4 for accessing its globals, but we'd do it slightly differently:

```
#pragma parameter __D0 SetA4(__D0)
pascal long SetA4(long newA4) = 0xC18C;

#define SetCurrentA4() SetA4((long)&main)
```

Both methods contain declarations for two important functions. SetCurrentA4() sets up register A4 so that access to globals occurs properly, and returns the old value of A4. SetA4() sets register A4 to whatever is passed in. The idea is simple: At the beginning of a function, we set up register A4 to point to our globals, and at the end of the function, we restore it to its original value. This may seem like an odd way to use globals. Once again, it's time for a little history lesson.

In the dark ages, circa late 1985, support for writing code other than applications, in any development environment, wasn't terribly helpful. Whereas applications could be multi-segment, could be object-oriented, and could easily access their own globals, code resources could do none of these things. For every development environment other than MPW, code resources were merely an afterthought. Since code resources were most often extremely small, multi-segment issues weren't that important, and objects at the time were still of debatable value; access to globals was the only pressing matter at the time. The reason code resources didn't have their own globals was that most compilers revolved around using register A5 as a pointer to all globally accessible data. Trouble was, when a code resource was being run, A5 still pointed to the globals of whatever application was currently being executed. Some writers went ahead and used A5 anyway, being very careful to switch to their A5 while their code was executing, and making sure A5 got restored when they exited.

This approach generally works, but is fraught with peril because QuickDraw also uses register A5 to point to its own globals. Not only did these writers have to change A5's value, they had to make sure that the new A5 pointed to the same four bytes that the old A5 contained. Other people got around the problem by storing all their globals in a position where code ought to be; they would declare a function with nonsense code in it, just to take up space, and then store and retrieve values from that space. This is a much better approach, but it's hard to support and reeks of bad technique. The folks at Symantec finally came up with a better solution: they decided to use register A4 to access globals when building code resources. Applications don't get confused by a changing A5, and QuickDraw doesn't get confused, so that's the technique we'll use. It does have the drawback that the code thus generated will tend to be slightly larger, because the number of available address registers for the compiler to use has dropped by one, but this is mostly negligible.

The rules for making this work for the world of single-segment code resources in THINK C with Custom Headers turned on are quite simple: any time access to global space is desired, register A4 must contain the address of the function `main()`. The second declaration, for `SetCurrentA4()`, does this for us. In the Metrowerks environment, a separate magic function is used, called `SetCurrentA4()`, and it is set up as appropriate by the linker.

You may be wondering why the difference in approach between THINK C and Metrowerks. True, THINK C and Metrowerks both use register A4 to access globals. But THINK C loads the value of A4 with the beginning of the code resources. The result of this is that efficient access to global variables requires that the total size of code plus global variables is less than 32K. This is because the most-efficient register-indirect addressing mode on the 680x0 references an offset of -32K to 32K from an address register. The folks at Metrowerks balked at this limit, and they load the value of A4 with something closer to the beginning of the code resource, plus 32K. This extra bias allows code size plus data size to be 64K, with no loss of efficiency, except that we have to call a linker routine, `SetCurrentA4()`, to set up A4 properly.

The next thing we'll need in our example is a global variable to keep track of the old trap address for each trap that we'll patch, and a definition for each replacement trap that we plan to install. We'll also have to decide which of the various Macintosh traps to patch. What we need to do to intercept our user typing "beep" is to intercept their incoming keystrokes. The best way to catch incoming events, from typing (`keyDown` events) to mousing (`mouseDown` and `mouseUp` events) to window activity (`updateEvt`, `activateEvt`) is to patch a routine called `SystemEvent()`. This is because any event that is not a null event will get passed to the Toolbox routine `SystemEvent()` before it is passed on to a desk accessory or application. Let's review how all this happens.

User activity (mouse and keyboard events) is detected by the ADB manager of the Macintosh. When a user clicks the mouse or taps the keyboard, an interrupt-driven task calls an OS routine named `PostEvent()` to tell the OS that the user has taken an action. This event is placed inside a small queue called the event queue. The event stays in this queue until later, possibly much later, an application calls `GetNextEvent()`, or calls `WaitNextEvent()` (which calls `GetNextEvent()`). `GetNextEvent()` in turn calls `GetOSEvent()`, and `GetOSEvent()` is the routine which actually removes the event from the event queue. When `GetNextEvent()` sees the event from `GetOSEvent()`, it then localizes the event (that is, `GetNextEvent()` changes two- and three-key sequences into single events), checks to see if the event belongs to the system or a desk accessory, filters the event, and finally, returns the event to the application. The way that it checks to see if the event belongs to the system or a desk accessory is to call a trap named `SystemEvent()`, and the way it filters the event is to pass it through the function pointed to by a low-memory global named `jGNEFilter`.

So why is this important, and why do we pick `SystemEvent()` as the place to grab our events? Well, if we patched the `PostEvent()` trap, we could catch all incoming keystrokes as they came in. And if we patched `GetOSEvent()`, we could catch all keystrokes as they were about to be delivered to applications. Trouble is, at that point some of the events aren't correct, because at the `PostEvent()`/`GetOSEvent()` level, no internationalization routines have run. So at that point if a user types the letter "ö", it comes across instead as two characters — """ and "o". If we try to patch ourselves in using the `jGNEFilter` low-memory vector, then we end up with an INIT that doesn't work in desk accessories, because `GetNextEvent()` calls `SystemEvent()`, and `SystemEvent()` passes the event on to a desk accessory, *before the event is filtered*. So when a user types "beep" into their Note Pad, we would never see any of the keystrokes. So of all the myriad ways to hook ourselves in, `SystemEvent()` works best.

There is also a secondary reason, one that you should keep in mind whenever you patch a trap: `SystemEvent()` is listed by Apple as a routine which may move or purge memory. `PostEvent()` and `GetOSEvent()`, on the other hand, are listed as routines that *do not* move or purge memory, safe to call at interrupt time. Now, the additional behavior we wish to cause is a beep, and the most logical way to do that is to call the Toolbox routine `SysBeep()`, which as part of its functioning may have to read the current beep from the system file, hence moving memory. So, if we had patched `PostEvent()`, and tried to call `SysBeep()` from there, we would potentially be moving or purging memory from inside `PostEvent()`, even though `PostEvent()` is documented as not doing so. This would often cause crashes, since the operating system calls `PostEvent()` at interrupt level, when memory can not only not be moved, but may be in flux — the memory manager may be in the middle of rearranging the system heap when the user types a key, and calling `SysBeep()` at that instant would be disastrous!

The upshot is, whenever you patch a trap that is defined as moving or purging memory, you can do almost anything you like. When you patch a trap defined as *not* moving or purging memory, you can't move or purge memory yourself, and you can only call other traps that do not move or purge memory. And if you patch a trap defined as not moving or purging memory, *and* being callable from interrupt level, you should also be careful to call only other traps that also are declared that way.

OK, now back to our definitions. `SystemEvent()` is declared in the Apple header file `<Desk.h>` as:

```
pascal Boolean SystemEvent(EventRecord *theEvent) = 0xA9B2;
```

Since this is the trap we wish to replace, we'll declare our own routine with the same parameters, as well as a global variable which we'll use to point to the default implementation of the `SystemEvent()` patch:

```
pascal Boolean (*gOldSystemEvent)(EventRecord *theEvent);

static pascal Boolean BeeperSystemEvent(EventRecord *theEvent);
```

There's only one problem. Pascal `Boolean`s, which can take up as little as only one bit in Pascal, actually take up two bytes when used as a stack return value. If we were to use the above definitions, our patch wouldn't work correctly, because when the operating system checks for `SystemEvent()`'s return value, it actually checks the result as if it were expecting a 16-bit value, not just a `Boolean`. There really is no reason for this; it is a bug, and this isn't true of all traps, but you'll always be safer using `short`s instead of `Boolean`s when declaring return values from traps. So rather than using `Boolean`s, we'll redeclare our functions like this:

```
pascal short (*gOldSystemEvent)(EventRecord *theEvent);

static pascal short BeeperSystemEvent(EventRecord *theEvent);
```

At this point, we've declared everything we need to write our entire installation routine. It looks like this:

```
void main(void)
{
    long      oldA4;
    THz       oldZone;
```

```
   // Set up A4, so we can access our globals.
oldA4 = SetCurrentA4();

   // Set the current zone to the system zone.
oldZone = GetZone();
SetZone(SystemZone());

   // We need to detach our code, so that we stay around.
DetachResource(GetResource('INIT', -4048));

   // Remember the old implementation of SystemEvent.
gOldSystemEvent = (void *) GetToolTrapAddress(0xA9B2);

   // Patch ourselves in.
SetToolTrapAddress((ProcPtr) &BeeperSystemEvent, 0xA9B2);

   // Restore the old zone again
SetZone(oldZone);

   // And restore the value of A4 on the way out.
SetA4(oldA4);
}
```

The call to SetA4() at the beginning and end of main() are standard; you should make these at the beginning and end of any routine you write where you need access to your globals and when A4 isn't necessarily set up for you. Since we access gOldSystemEvent, we need to set up A4 for global access. We'll see these again later.

The next two lines save away the old zone, and set the current zone to the system zone. In this case, that's not necessary, but it's a good idea in general, so that any data we allocate on a permanent basis is allocated to the system heap.

The call to DetachResource() may seem mysterious at first. What's going on here is that our code is part of a resource file, and that resource file is closed once we have loaded. Any time a resource file is closed, all of its resources are disposed of. So in order to keep our code from being thrown away, we need to tell the resource manager to dissociate our code from the resource file we loaded from, so that we can stay around. The call to make that dissociation is DetachResource().

The next line is basic to any trap patch we make — we need to make a note of how SystemEvent() used to work, so we can probably piggy back off that behavior. Consulting either MacsBug or the file Traps.h, we find that the trap number of SystemEvent() is $A9B2. Since its trap number is greater than $A7FF, we need to call GetToolTrapAddress() to find its old implementation. (For traps numbered $A7FF or lower, we would use GetOSTrapAddress().)

The next line is very similar and just as basic: we call the corresponding routine SetToolTrapAddress() so that from now on, when the system or anyone else calls SystemEvent(), our code is executed.

And that's it — it's just that easy! Of course, we need to define our trap, but that's surprisingly easy, too. We'll isolate our custom behavior into a routine called HandleKeyDown(), and our patch will call that. Our patch looks like this:

```
static void HandleKeyDown(short modifiers, long eventMessage);

pascal short BeeperSystemEvent(EventRecord *theEvent)
{
        // Set up A4, so we can access our globals.
    long        oldA4;
    short       result;

    oldA4 = SetCurrentA4();

        // Check for keyDown events, and pass them to HandleKeyDown:
    if (theEvent->what == keyDown) {
        HandleKeyDown(theEvent->modifiers, theEvent->message);
    }

        // Call the old SystemEvent:
    result = gOldSystemEvent(theEvent);

        // And restore the value of A4 on the way out.
    SetA4(oldA4);

    return result;
}
```

As you can see, our patch isn't so different from code you might find in an application to handle an incoming event. The difference is, we have to set up A4 on the way in and restore it on the way out, so we can access our globals.

The last thing we need now is the routine to handle keyDown events. First, we define some storage to hold our typing buffer:

```
enum { kMaxKeysRecorded = 8 };

    // The last 8 keystrokes are recorded as a p-string in gLastKeys:
char    gLastKeys[kMaxKeysRecorded + 1];
```

And finally, the actual code for handling keystrokes:

```
static void HandleKeyDown(short modifiers, long eventMessage)
{
    char              *lastkeys;        // keep the address of
                                        // gLastKeys in a local
                                        // variable because we access
                                        // it so often
    lastkeys = gLastKeys;

        // If the user types command-O or command-V, our buffer is
        // invalid,
        // and we certainly shouldn't record the keystroke!
    if (modifiers & cmdKey) {
        lastkeys[0] = 0;
        return;
    }

        // if it's a backspace, back up over one of our recorded keys.
    if ('\b' == (char)eventMessage) {
        if (lastkeys[0] != 0) {
            lastkeys[0]—;
    }
    return;
    }

        // if it isn't, add the new key to the end of what we've
        // recorded.
        // first, if we're about to overflow, throw away one old key.
    if (lastkeys[0] == kMaxKeysRecorded) {
        BlockMove(&lastkeys[2], &lastkeys[1], kMaxKeysRecorded - 1);
        lastkeys[0]—;
    }

        // then, store the new typed character:
    astkeys[0]++;
    lastkeys[lastkeys[0]] = eventMessage;

        // have we accumulated "beep"?
    if (lastkeys[0] == 4) {
        if (RelString((unsigned char *)lastkeys, "\pbeep", false,
            true) == 0) {
            SysBeep(8);
            lastkeys[0] = 0;
        }
    }
}
```

There's nothing at all special about this routine, but keep in mind three things: First, since it uses the global variable gLastKeys, A4 must be set up prior to this routine being called. Second, it calls three traps: `BlockMove()`, `RelString()`, and `SysBeep()`. The first two don't move or purge memory, and can be called at interrupt routine, but the third *may* move or purge memory. Thus, `HandleKeyDown()` may move or purge memory. Therefore, `HandleKeyDown()` can only be called from within a trap patch for a routine that moves or purges memory. Finally, note that we haven't been careful to preserve any temporary registers inside our patch. Fortunately, in the case of `SystemEvent()`, this is not necessary. However, in the case of other traps which we might wish to patch, particularly OS patches, which rely on registers to pass parameters, it would be necessary. See the "Gotchas" section for more details.

WRITING A CONTROL PANEL

Now that we've written ourselves an extension, we should feel pretty pleased. Yet, there is something missing. That hallmark of the Macintosh, the user interface, is still totally missing. We have what has been called the ultimate user interface: none. We need a way to control our extension. It's time once again for a history lesson...

The INIT mechanism didn't exist until System 3.0, and until System 4.0, there was no easy way to configure INITs. In Systems up to and including 3.0, there were no *control panels*, but a single control panel, adjusting almost every adjustable item in the Macintosh. And the Control Panel was a desk accessory. So authors of extensions had to find interesting and creative ways of controlling their creations. The most straightforward were applications. The least straightforward either had hidden hotkeys to reveal their interfaces, or listed themselves in the menu but weren't real DAs. Or they really were DAs, in which case they didn't copy easily from machine to machine, and so on. The creativity and rapidity with which extension authors came up with bad ideas for user interface access spurred Apple to action.

So, in System 4.0, Apple finally solved some of this mess; they added hooks into the Control Panel DA. The idea was that programmers could, with minimal pain, give their creations an interface to the world, in a common way, in a common place. INITs, which could previously get by with as little as a single resource (like ours just did), became much more complicated, not just for their user interface, but for many other reasons as well.

Control Panel Resources

There are five resources required by even the most basic control panel. To identify the control panel, it must have an icon. This is implemented as an 'ICN#' resource with an ID of -4064. It is technically neither needed or used under System 7.0; however, it is required under System 6.0 because the Control Panel desk accessory draws its icons based on this resource.

To identify on what machines a control panel can run, it must have a 'mach' resource, that is, a machine mask. The way that the 'mach' resource and the ROM flags interact to provide this description is somewhat convoluted, but all you really need to know is this: If your control panel can run on any Macintosh, your 4-byte 'mach' resource should be 0xFFFF0000. If you can't run on the original 128K or 512K Macs because of their ROMs, but you can run on anything else, your 'mach' resource should be 0x7FFF0000. If you require Color QuickDraw and/or other facilities not present on Macs prior to the Mac II, your 'mach' resource should be 0x3FFF0000. And if your requirements are not as simple, your 'mach' resource should be 0x0000FFFF; in this case, your control device function (discussed later) will be called, and it can programatically determine whether it can run on whatever Macintosh it finds itself on.

When a control panel is opened, a window appears with controls in it very much like a dialog. In fact, the items within the window are specified from a 'DITL' -4064 resource, as though there were a 'DLOG' resource with that number. This resource specifies all the items which will be seen by the user when the control panel is active.

Since there is no corresponding 'DLOG' resource for the required 'DITL' resource, there is no way for the system to determine the appropriate size of the control panel. For this reason, there is an 'nrct' resource with an ID of -4064 that determines the size of the area the user will see where the items from 'DITL' -4064 will be drawn. Why, you may wonder, did Apple choose the 'nrct' resource format rather than just a straightforward 'DLOG' resource? Well, the 'nrct' resource gets its name because it contains a number of rectangles; this is historically due to the way old control panels were laid out: a number of rectangles containing within themselves one or maybe two controls, which altogether became a panel of controls — a control panel. Since the original control panel, the user interface has evolved so much that most Apple control panels no longer resemble a bunch of rectangles, but the functionality is still there to ensure compatibility, and hence we are stuck with this bizarre 'nrct' format. For our purposes, all this resource serves to do is to define the size of our control panel as it appears in the Finder.

Finally, a 'cdev' code resource with an ID of -4064 serves as the guts of the Control Panel code of System 6, as well as the System 7 Finder. This code is called as the control panel opens and closes, and as the user plays with the items in the Control Panel window. The majority of the new code we need to write will be part of this resource, but before we design the code to handle the interface, we'll need to modify our INIT code.

Communicating with the Extension

For the purpose of our simple example, we'll only use a control panel to turn our extension on and off and change the text the extension looks for. Of course, we can't do this just yet, because even if we wrote a control panel for this purpose, we have no way of communicating any of our user's changes to our extension.

How the heck do we get two totally separated pieces of code to talk to each other? As it turns out, there are lots of solutions to this problem. One way is to search through memory looking for some sort of signature information. Another way is to install a trap patch and look for special parameters. These are both bad ideas, but were surprisingly common, before Apple implemented Gestalt().

Gestalt() is one of the seven wonders of the world. Like the Munger() Toolbox call, it is a simple idea with surprising flexibility and power. As originally devised, Gestalt() was implemented so that programs could pass in a four-character code and query the operating system about available functionality. If you call Gestalt() with a paarmeter of 'sysv', for example, you'll retrieve the current System version. If you call Gestalt() with a parameter of 'vers', you'll retrieve the version number of Gestalt() itself. If you call Gestalt() with 'vm', you can determine if virtual memory is active. On today's Macintoshes, more than 80 selector calls can be passed to Gestalt() for the purpose of retrieving information.

This alone does not make Gestalt() special, however; like the trap table, what's great about Gestalt() is that it is extensible. Developers can define their own selectors to override Apple's selectors and, in fact, this is precisely what we will do. That way, our INIT can register itself with Gestalt(), and our control panel code can call Gestalt() and get information back about where the INIT is.

Testing the Control Panel

Before we dive into the code to see how you register with `Gestalt()`, or how the user interface works, let's take the control panel for a spin. Go to the `Projects` folder and open the `Beep.cdev` subfolder. Drag the `Beeper` file onto your System Folder icon. When you let go, you will be asked if it is OK to move `Beeper` into the `Control Panels` folder with all the other control panels. Click OK and restart your computer. Once you are back up and running, type "Beep" (without the quotes) just to verify that the INIT portion of `Beeper` got installed properly (you should hear a beep). If all goes well, dive into the `Control Panels` folder (inside the `System Folder`) and double-click on the `Beeper` control panel. The window shown in Figure 5.10 should appear.

Play with the control panel. Replace the word "Beep" with something more imaginative like "Beeblebrox" or "Dweezil." Close the control panel and verify that it responds to your change. If not, type a working command-key equivalent (like ⌘A or ⌘C) and try again. Open the control panel again, click on the Off radio button, and close the control panel again. Verify that Beeper is ignoring your typing. Now let's get to the control panel code.

FIGURE 5.10

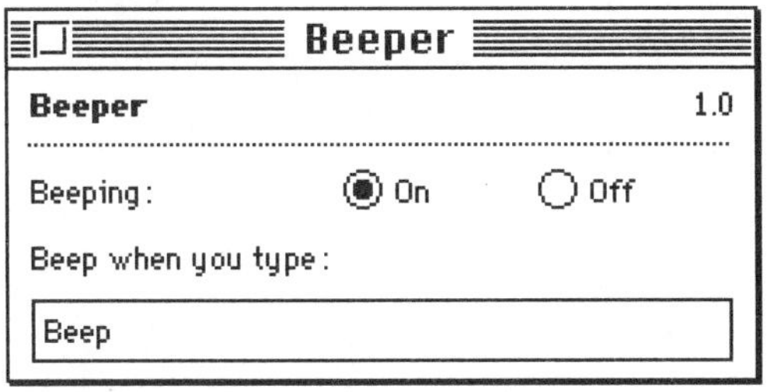

The Beeper control panel.

The Beeper Code

Before we register ourselves with `Gestalt()`, we need to step back and ponder what data we need to share between the INIT and the cdev. So that the code for the control panel and the extension can both access the same set of information, we'll create a new header file, `Beeper.h`, and start it with common information:

```
#ifdef THINK_C
    #pragma parameter __D0 SetA4(__D0)
    pascal long SetA4(long newA4) = 0xC18C;

    #define SetCurrentA4() SetA4((long) &main)
#else
    #include <A4Stuff.h>
#endif

#define kSystemEventTrapNumber 0xA9B2
#define kGestaltTrapNumber 0xA0Ad
#define kUnimplementedTrapNumber 0xA89F
#define UnimplementedTrapAddress
GetToolTrapAddress(kUnimplementedTrapNumber)

typedef unsigned char uchar;
```

Our main file, which we'll rename `Beeper.INIT.c` to avoid confusion, now starts off with:

```
#include <Events.h>
#include <Resources.h>
#include <Memory.h>
#include <ToolUtils.h>

#include <A4Stuff.h>
```

For this simple example, all our control panel really needs to do is be able to access the globals of our INIT code. Since we'd like to be able to turn it on and off, and set the "trigger" string, we'll define a simple global structure in `Beeper.h`:

```
typedef struct BeeperGlobals {
    long        BeeperOn;
    Str31       BeepString;
} BeeperGlobals;
```

We'll have to do a slight bit of recoding to use this structure instead of our hard-wired "Beep" string, but it will come easy. The first step in recoding is to define these globals and fill in default values. This is trivial in C, and looks like this (in `Beeper.INIT.c`):

```
// some sane defaults in case we can't find our prefs.
BeeperGlobals       gBeeperGlobs = {
    1, // on by default
    "\pBeep"
};
```

We'll need the default values of this global so that when we use our control panel, we'll have something to start with.

Next, we need to pay attention to what we store there. Rather than:

```
// Check for keyDown events, and pass them to HandleKeyDown:
    if (theEvent->what == keyDown) {
        HandleKeyDown(theEvent->modifiers, theEvent->message);
    }
```

We'll instead use:

```
// Check for keyDown events, and pass them to HandleKeyDown:
    if (gBeeperGlobs.BeeperOn && theEvent->what == keyDown) {
        HandleKeyDown(theEvent->modifiers, theEvent->message);
    }
```

This way, setting `BeeperOn` to zero will turn off our patch code. Next, since we can handle more characters in our trigger string, we change:

```
enum { kMaxKeysRecorded = 8 };
```

into

```
enum { kMaxKeysRecorded = sizeof(gBeeperGlobs.BeepString) };
```

Finally, this hard-wired test will never do:

```
    // have we accumulated "beep"?
if (lastkeys[0] == 4) {
    if (RelString((unsigned char *)lastkeys, "\pbeep", false, true)
        == 0) {
        SysBeep(8);
        lastkeys[0] = 0;
    }
}
```

Instead, we'll use:

```
    // have we accumulated our trigger string?
if (lastkeys[0] == gBeeperGlobs.BeepString[0]) {
    if (RelString(lastkeys, gBeeperGlobs.BeepString,
        alse, true) == sortsEqual) {
        SysBeep(8);
        lastkeys[0] = 0;
    }
}
```

Now that we've made our trap patch code dynamic, it's time to wire ourselves up to `Gestalt()`. To register ourselves with `Gestalt()`, we'll need a four-character code. More specifically, we need to pick out a four-character code that does not conflict with any of Apple's own four-character codes, or any third-party software. This is easier than it would appear, since Apple never uses any uppercase characters in their codes. The most sure-fire way of picking a unique code is to pick the same one that we use as our creator code for our control panel file. That way, when we register our creator code with Apple's developer services group (to assure uniqueness for our Finder icons), we also (pretty much) guarantee uniqueness for our `Gestalt()` selectors. To underscore the point, we'll make a `#define` constant for our selector, `kDTS_Signature` in our `Beeper.h` header file: (Note: `kGestaltGetInitGlobals` is for later us.)

```
#define kDTS_Signature 'Beep'
#define kGestaltGetInitGlobals 'glob'
```

To register ourselves with `Gestalt()`, we need to pass `Gestalt()` the address of a routine with the following interface:

```
static pascal OSErr BeeperGestalt(OSType selector, long *_response);
```

This may seem strange at first. You would think that to register with `Gestalt()`, you would say something like "Hey, `Gestalt()`, whenever anyone passes in a selector of `Beep`, please pass them this value in return." Instead, what you do say is, "Hey, `Gestalt()`, whenever anyone passes in a selector of `Beep`, call this routine, and pass it `Beep` as the first parameter, and I will tell you what to respond with." There are two reasons for this.

The first is that Apple uses this routine to register multiple `Gestalt()` selectors with a single routine; by having it accept the `Gestalt()` selector as a parameter, we could distinguish between multiple incoming `Gestalt()` requests.

The more important reason is that the response to some `Gestalt()`s may change as the system finishes loading, so a static selector passed to `Gestalt()` isn't as useful as being able to pass a function that can return different results at different times.

We'll turn this even more to our advantage, however. Our `Gestalt()` routine looks like this:

```
static pascal OSErr BeeperGestalt(OSType selector, long *response) {
    long    oldA4;
    OSErr   err = noErr;

        // Set up A4, so we can access our globals.
    oldA4 = SetCurrentA4();

    switch (selector) {
        case kGestaltGetInitGlobals:
            *response = (long)&gBeeperGlobs;
            break;
    case kDTS_Signature:
        *response = (long)ourGestaltUPP;
        break;
    case gestaltVersion:
        *response = 0x0100; // ver. 1.0 Gestalt interface for Beeper
        break;
    default:
        err = gestaltUnknownErr;
        break;
    }

        // Restore the value of A4 on the way out.
    SetA4(oldA4);
    return err;
}
```

What we're doing is allowing our own Gestalt() mechanism to be
extensible. In response to our 'Beep' selector, rather than returning anything immediately useful, we simply return the address of our Gestalt()
routine. From there, we can add extra information. One selector,
kGestaltGetInitGlobals, will return us the address of our globals (the
whole reason we're doing all this). Just as important, however, another
selector, gestaltVersion, will return the version of this Gestalt() interface. This is critical because our users will pull dirty tricks on us. One
particularly obnoxious trick is that our users will use version 1.0 of our
Beep control panel, then drop version 2.0 over it, and double-click on
the 2.0 control panel to see what's new. The version 2.0 control panel
will call Gestalt() and end up talking to the version 1.0 INIT code.
Without some way for the INIT code to respond with its version number, we'd never know there was a potential for serious conflict.

So now that we've got our selector, and our Gestalt() routine,
how do we register ourselves with Gestalt()? It's very simple, just one
extra call inside our main routine:

```
      // now install our gestalt selector, which sets up a mechanism
      // for our control panel to talk to us and at the same time
      // makes sure we're not loading twice.
   if (NewGestalt(kDTS_Signature, ourGestaltUPP) != noErr) goto
      initFailed;
```

As the comment suggests, there are actually two things going on here. First, we are registering ourselves with `Gestalt()`, so that future calls to Gestalt with a selector code of "Beep" will vector off into our code. Second, `Gestalt()` is checking to make sure that no other software has registered "Beep". If there is a conflict, `NewGestalt()` will do nothing and simply return an error. This is critically important because of our tricky users. Some particularly tricky users, the "power users," like to rename their extensions and control panels. They then forget they have done this, reinstall software they already have, and wind up with two copies of the same control panel in their system folder. We want to be sure to detect and avoid this situation before it causes any unexpected problems. By using `NewGestalt()`, this check is automatic.

There is one last change we need to make to our INIT code. In order for our preferences to be saved if our user restarts the Macintosh, we need to save them somewhere. The ideal place is to create our own preferences file inside the System 7 `Preferences` folder. For the sake of brevity, we will take the easy way out and simply add a preferences resource to our control panel. Our INIT needs to look for it and read the information inside it. Therefore we'll add a new local variable, and a code snippet, to `main()`:

```
   BeeperGlobals    **bgh;

   bgh = (BeeperGlobals **)Get1Resource('pref', -4048);
   if (bgh != 0 && GetHandleSize((Handle)bgh) ==
sizeof(gBeeperGlobs)) {
       gBeeperGlobs = **bgh;
   }
```

Note the level of error-checking: You should always assume that any place you store preference information is unsafe and prone to modification. At best, preference change size and format on a regular basis as your code evolves. At worst, your preferences will become corrupted beyond hope, and you had better be able to deal with the situation gracefully!

Getting the Control Panel to Talk to the Extension

Now that our INIT code is wired for sound, we can finally plunge head first into the task of writing our control panel engine. The first thing we'll need to do is design our control panel's interface to the world. Using our favorite resource editor, we can easily create a control panel interface (resource 'DITL' -4064, remember?) for turning on and off our INIT, and allowing our user to change the trigger string. Note that most of the items in this resource are window dressing to make it look good. The only items our control panel will concern itself with are items 1, 2, and 3, the two radio buttons and the text entry area (Figure 5.11).

FIGURE 5.11

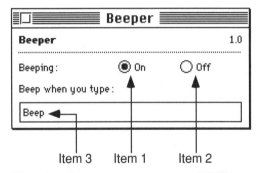

The critical items in our control panel 'DITL'.

The beginning of our control panel code, in addition to reflecting the requisite include files, reflects the three items :

```
#include <Events.h>
#include <Resources.h>
#include <Memory.h>
#include <Devices.h>
#include <Dialogs.h>
#include <OSUtils.h>
#include <ToolUtils.h>
#include <GestaltEqu.h>

#include "Beeper.h"

// dialog items for our control panel:

enum {
    kBeepingOn = 1,
    kBeepingOff = 2,
```

```
    kBeepText = 3
};
```

Global variables are few in this simple control panel; half are there just so we don't have to make repetitive calls to GetDItem() to get information about specific items:

```
BeeperGlobals    *gInitGlobals, **gPrefsResource;

ControlHandle    gOnButton, gOffButton;
Handle           gTextBox;
```

The first of these, gInitGlobals, will contain either zero (if our extension was not loaded when the Macintosh most recently started up), or the address of our extension's globals. This way, we can directly alter them whenever we like.

The second of these, gPrefsResource, is simply a handle to our preferences resource.

The last three are the handles returned by GetDItem(). Having them around as globals makes it easy to get at them whenever it's necessary, with a minimum of fuss.

A good, quick shell for any control panel code, and one we'll build upon, is this:

```
pascal long main(short message, short Item, short numItems, short
    CPanelID,
    EventRecord *theEvent, register long cdevValue, DialogPtr
        CPDialog)
{
    long    oldA4;

    oldA4 = SetCurrentA4();

    if (message == initDev) {
        // do some initialization.
        if ( fubar ) { // the initialization went wrong
bad_problem:cdevValue = cdevGenErr;
        } else {
         cdevValue = 237;   // any unique positive number should do.
        }
    } else if (cdevValue == 237) { // handle non-initDev messages
                    // only if initialization succeeded.
        switch (message) {
            case closeDev:
                    // write out preferences information, dispose
                    // of any temporary storage, etc.
```

```
            break;
      case hitDev:
            Item -= numItems;
                  // handle an item our user has clicked upon:
            break;
      case nulDev:
                  // background activities
            break;
      }
   }

   SetA4(oldA4);
   return cdevValue;
}
```

If you've never written a control panel before, this will take a bit of explanation. Control panels, like desk accessories and unlike applications, are not in charge of their own destiny. In an application, the main() routine is called at the start, before even the Toolbox is initialized, and when main() exits, the application shuts down. In a control panel, by contrast, the main() routine is repeatedly sent various messages to handle. This function, called the *control device function*, can choose to shut down its control panel window, but the more likely scenario is that the user or the Finder makes the choice, and the control panel has no choice in the matter.

Another difference is that, whereas an application's main() takes no parameters, control panels take seven parameters. The first and most important is message, an integer with (currently) 15 possible values. By numerical value, here are the messages along with recommended responses to them:

macDev = 8

This message is only sent if your 'mach' resource contains the value 0x0000FFFF; if you receive this message, don't assume anything about the values of any other parameters, and return either 0 if you can't run on the Macintosh you find yourself on, or 1 if you can. Beeper doesn't handle this message because its 'mach' resource does not contain 0x0000FFFF.

initDev = 0

This is the first message most control panels receive. This message is sent after the control panel's window has been constructed, but while the window is still hidden. Technically, this window is a modeless dialog, since it has all the properties of a dialog box, including items, default buttons, and automatic text handling.

The only valid parameters in this case are `message`, `numItems`, and `CPDialog`, and you should ignore all the others. `CPDialog` will point at your still-hidden control panel window, and `numItems` will contain the number of items in the modeless dialog that aren't yours.

"What do you mean, not mine?" you may ask. Well, it's history time again.

Recall that, under System 6, all control panels existed within the control Panel desk accessory. The left side of this desk accessory contained a scrolling list of icons, whereas the right side was dedicated to individual control panels. To achieve the magic of a dialog where some of the items (the list of icons and its scroll bar, among others) stayed around and some of them changed (everything on the right), Apple wrote some extremely obtuse code capable of dynamically removing and installing items into the control panel's window. This caused a minor problem for developers because while their `'DITL'` -4064 resource might have contained a button as item #1, by the time this item list was added to Apple's scrolling list of icons, the button ended up as item # 5 or so. To get at the button, you code has to know what the offset was between the item numbers in the `'DITL'` and the item numbers when the control panel was in use. This offset is stored in the `numItems` parameter.

When you receive this message, you should load any resources you need, perform any initialization you need, and generally make sure that everything is in order. If there is a problem, return one of three numbers:

- Return `cdevGenErr` if there is a problem so serious that you believe that attempting to display an error message to the user might result in a crash. If you can't load a 4-byte preferences resource, for example, it's a good bet that your control panel is corrupted, or that memory is so low that you should just shut yourself down while you can. Alternately, if you wish to display a custom error alert, display it, and then return `cdevGenErr`.

- Return `cdevMemErr` if you run out of memory and wish the Finder to alert the user to this condition.

- Return `cdevResErr` if you can not find a resource you are looking for. For example you should return `cdevResErr` if you can't find a system resource that doesn't exist on minimal system installations, or a resource of your own that might reasonably be missing.

After the `initDev` message, whatever result your control device function returns to the Finder will be passed in next time as the `cdevValue` parameter. If we didn't have access to our own globals, it would be a good idea to create a handle to a global structure, and return it as our function result, so that we could then access it in the future through the `cdevValue` parameter. Since we do have access to globals, this is unnecessary, so all we do is return an arbitrary but fairly large number to indicate that we have successfully loaded.

Under System 7, returning any of the three error codes causes the control panel to be immediately closed, possibly with an error dialog displayed afterward. Under System 6, the same thing happens, but (for reasons unknown to the author) the control device function may continue to receive other messages. There is no suggested action for these messages, so it is best to ignore them. In our example, we ignore messages other than `initDev` if the `cdevValue` is not exactly equal to our arbitrary large number.

In `Beeper`'s case, we need some extra temporary variables:

```
OSErr    err;
short    kind;
Rect     r;
Str255   text;
pascal OSErr (*BeeperGestalt)(OSType selector, long *response);
long          versionCheck;
```

The first thing we need to do in `Beeper` to handle `initDev` is load in our preferences resource:

```
if (message == initDev) {
    gPrefsResource = (BeeperGlobals **)Get1Resource('pref',
        -4048);
    if (!gPrefsResource) {
        // if we can't load our preferences resource
        // something is seriously wrong.
bad_problem:
        cdevValue = cdevGenErr;
    } else {
        // ... go further
    }
```

Once we've loaded it into memory, to protect us from ourselves, we should make sure it's not marked purgeable, and that it's the right size.

```
    } else {
        HNoPurge((Handle) gPrefsResource);

            // make sure that our prefs resource is the correct
            // size.
```

```
SetHandleSize((Handle) gPrefsResource,
    sizeof(BeeperGlobals));
if (GetHandleSize((Handle) gPrefsResource) !=
    sizeof(BeeperGlobals))
goto bad_problem;
```

One of the biggest causes of control panel crashes, even in commercial control panels, is insufficient error handling that causes crashes when preferences get corrupted. The lines of code just illustrated are not overkill. As your own preferences grow and get more complicated, make sure you can handle any errors in format. If you store your preferences in a separate file in the Preferences folder, be sure that version 1.0 of your product can handle version 2.0's preferences, and vice versa. This is a good idea for applications, but it's critical in the case of trap patching, because of the nature of this sort of system software. An application that crashes when launched is annoying, but the operating system can handle it gracefully a good portion of the time. A control panel that crashes at boot time is seen as a Macintosh that can no longer be turned on, since some users don't know they can disable extensions by holding down the Shift key at boot time. At worst, memory problems caused by trying to access data past the end of a too-small preferences resource can cause serious data corruption as your code accidentally overwrites disk caches and the like. *Always* check preferences carefully!

Next, our control panel needs to find the INIT code in memory, check for the version number, and get access to the global data:

```
err = Gestalt(kDTS_Signature, (long *)&BeeperGestalt);
if (err == noErr) {
    err = BeeperGestalt(gestaltVersion, &versionCheck);
    if (versionCheck != 0x0100) err = -1;
    if (err == noErr) {
        err = BeeperGestalt( kGestaltGetInitGlobals,
                (long *)&gInitGlobals  );
    }
}
if (err != noErr) {
    gInitGlobals = 0;
} else {
    // if our INIT portion loaded, make sure our prefs
    // resource matches its settings.
    **gPrefsResource = *gInitGlobals;
}
```

The first line uses the Gestalt() mechanism to simultaneously determine whether or not our INIT code has loaded and get the address of our private `Gestalt()` routine. If there is no error, then we know the code loaded, but we still must check again to make sure that the version of code running as the INIT is the same as the version of our control panel. So we make a call to our private `Gestalt()` routine to check the version. If that call succeeds, *and* the version number is what it ought to be, then we know we are safe to proceed, and we make the final call to get the address of the INIT's global preferences data.

The last line assures that gInitGlobals points nowhere if there are any errors, and if and only if everything went OK, then we update our preferences resource to match whatever the INIT preferences are. This is important in case we happen to be on a bootable CD-ROM or other locked media: we want to be sure that the user can use our control panel and change and save settings instead of resetting them every time our control panel is opened.

Now that all of our low-level initialization is completed, we can take care of our more mundane user interface housekeeping. We set up our `ControlHandle` global variables:

```
GetDialogItem(CPDialog, numItems + kBeepingOn,  &kind,
              (Handle *) &gOnButton,  &r);
GetDialogItem(CPDialog, numItems + kBeepingOff, &kind,
              (Handle *) &gOffButton, &r);
GetDialogItem(CPDialog, numItems + kBeepText,   &kind,
              &gTextBox,  &r);
```

And then we set up our text entry field:

```
BlockMove((**gPrefsResource).BeepString, text, sizeof(text);
SetDialogItemText(gTextBox, text);
SelectDialogItemText(CPDialog, numItems + kBeepText, 0, text[0]);
```

Note that every time we pass one of our constant item numbers to a dialog manager function that expects an item number, we first offset the item number by `numItems`. This is necessary for System 6 compatibility, and may become necessary again in future system versions.

Finally, we set `cdevValue` to indicate successful initialization, and update our buttons:

```
cdevValue = 237; // any positive number should do.
goto updateButtons;
```

(`updateButtons` isn't important here; it's merely a common section of code that updates our two radio buttons properly before exiting our control device function.)

hitDev = 1

If you receive a `hitDev` message, it means that the user has clicked on one of the items in your control panel. This is somewhat different than handling `mouseDowns` inside of an application, since any control tracking will already have been handled for you automatically. So where you might call `TrackControl()` for a `mouseDown` in an application, in a control panel you can assume that all of this has been done for you already.

In our case, if we get a `hitDev` message on either of our buttons, it means the user has clicked on one of them, the Finder has tracked the click, and the user has released the mouse without moving away first. The code is:

```
            case hitDev:
                Item -= numItems;
                if (Item == kBeepingOn || Item == kBeepingOff) {
                    (**gPrefsResource).BeeperOn = (Item == kBeepingOn);
updateButtons: SetCtlValue(gOnButton,   (**gPrefsResource).BeeperOn);
                    SetCtlValue(gOffButton, !(**gPrefsResource).BeeperOn);
                }
                break;
```

Note that the incoming `Item` parameter has to be adjusted downward by `numItems` before we can compare it with any of our item constants.

If our user clicks inside the text field, `TEClick()` will automatically be called and some of the text will possibly be highlighted, all before we will be called. However, nothing the user does with the mouse inside the text field has any effect on the preferences, so we don't need to handle that case.

keyEvtDev = 7

`keyEvtDev`, unlike `hitDev`, is called *before* the event is handled. Also unlike `hitDev`, the `Items` field in this case should be ignored. Usually, you shouldn't take action based on `keyEvtDevs`; instead, your control device function should use the opportunity to filter the event, for example to prevent the user from typing letters into a numeric text field. If you wish to handle the key event yourself, and you want to make sure that the Finder does not process the event for you, set `theEvent->what` equal to `nullEvent`. If you do not do this, the key press will be processed in addition to the action taken by your control device.

undoDev = 9, cutDev = 10, copyDev = 11, pasteDev = 12, and clearDev = 13

These five message will be sent to you in direct response to a menu selection in the Finder that maps to one of these five basic editing primitives.

For the sake of simplicity our example does not include code to handle them; if you wish to do so, you can do so easily by calling the Toolbox functions `DialogCut()`, `DialogCopy()`, `DialogPaste()`, and `DialogDelete()`. In the case of `DialogPaste()`, you should pre-flight the call to make sure the user isn't trying (accidentally, one would hope) to paste an inordinately large amount of text. Proper implementation of `undoDev` is left as an exercise to the reader.

updateDev = 4, activDev = 5, and deactivDev = 6

These three messages correspond directly to their corresponding event types. Like `hitDev`, appropriate behavior for your dialog, such as updating controls, redrawing text, and activating and deactivating text entry fields, will already have occurred by the time you get this message. Unless you include user items as part of your dialog, it is probably safe to ignore all three messages.

nulDev = 3

Just like the nullEvent returned by `GetNextEvent()`, this message indicates that nothing has happened, and your control panel should take the time to perform periodic duties. If you are leaving the processing of `keyDown` events to the Finder, the `nulDev` message gives you a chance to see the results.

In `Beeper`'s case, we use `nulDev` to examine our text field and adjust our globals appropriately:

```
case nulDev:
    GetIText(gTextBox, text);
    if (text[0] > 31) text[0] = 31;
    BlockMove(text, (**gPrefsResource).BeepString,
        sizeof((**gPrefsResource).BeepString));
    if (gInitGlobals) {
        *gInitGlobals = **gPrefsResource;
    }
    break;
```

Note that when we copy the string into our preferences resource, we do so according to the size of the string in the preferences resource. The idea is, if we change the size of `BeepString` in our preferences structure, this size calculation prevents us from destroying other sections of preferences by accident. Again, preference upkeep is a major problem for control panels; any time you can insert code like this, which prevents data structure changes from causing crashes, do it!

closeDev = 2

If the user closes your window, this is how you will be notified. This is the time to write out any preferences data, and dispose of any memory you had allocated to your control panel. In our case, this isn't much:

```
case closeDev:
    ChangedResource((Handle) gPrefsResource);
    break;
```

Note that you don't necessarily receive a `closeDev` message when your control panel closes. For example, if the Finder "unexpectedly quits," you will not receive a `closeDev` message. More important, if you return a `cdevGenErr`, `cdevMemErr`, or `cdevResErr`, you won't receive a `closeDev` event either.

TRAP PATCHING "GOTCHAS"

Before we get into the real gotchas, here's a warning: Apple's official position on trap patching is that you should avoid it if at all possible. It hurts performance (especially on the PowerPC), it can get hairy, and most important, all trap patching code is likely to break under Copland (Apple's next major OS release). If Copland does change the way traps are patched, we'll update this chapter (or add a new chapter, if necessary) to reflect the new order. And now back to our gotchas.

Up until now we've covered the basics of trap patching. Unfortunately, trap patching is like English spelling: there are only a handful of rules, with a truckload of exceptions and gotchas. Although this list is not exhaustive, here are some of the more common gotchas in patching traps.

Register Usage

One of the most common problems with trap patches, especially OS patches, is making the wrong assumptions regarding registers. Here are three rules that will let you avoid these problems:

1. *Try not to alter the contents of any registers in your patch, unless that is specifically what you are trying to do.*

    The most common pitfall here is when you make a patch to a Toolbox routine, thinking that since the routine in question is a stack-based routine, you can call code that changes the values of

registers A0, A1, D0, D1, and D2. You may not think you're changing these, but if your patch calls C or Pascal code, the compiler of
that code may use those registers, and you need to protect against
that. For example, you might have a problem patching `LoadSeg()`
or `LoadResource()`, which are documented as preserving all registers. If you change any of them, you could get into trouble. In
addition, all Resource Manager calls are documented as preserving
A1, D1, and D2.

2. *Do not depend on register results of traps after they have run.*

It turns out that most File Manager traps that accept the address of
a parameter block in A0 also return with A0 still pointing at that
parameter block. However, neither *Inside Macintosh* nor Apple
guarantees this to be true, and there are cases, especially with File
Sharing turned on, where this isn't true. If you are the one making
the call, the built-in register saving of the trap dispatcher will
restore this register for you, but if you are patching a file manager
call, you'll need to save A0 away before you make the call, and
then restore it again afterward if you'd like to access the parameter block. The same goes for memory manager traps, among many
others: Remember, when you call an OS trap, it's the trap dispatcher that saves A0–A2 and D1–D2, not the trap, so when your
patch calls the original, you can't count on any of these registers
to remain the same.

3. *Don't mess with A5.*

A5 is not just a register pointing to application globals; it is also the
pointer to QuickDraw's global pointer, and some applications make
trap patches that reference A5. If you must change A5, you should
make sure that the `long` that your new A5 points to is the same as
the one the old A5 points to, and you should be extremely careful
which traps you call. For example, some Claris applications patch
`TECut()`, `TECopy()`, and `TEPaste()`, and those patches assume that
A5 is Claris's A5. If A5 is something else when these routines are
called, you will likely corrupt the heap or crash the machine out-
right. Worse yet, sometimes you aren't even changing A5, and the
machine crashes. Suppose, for example, that you've used the
`jGNEFilter` hook to put up a dialog. And suppose further that
you've gone through the trouble of supporting the Clipboard in this
dialog. When you call `TECut()` in MacWrite II, A5 will be
MultiFinder's A5, because MultiFinder sets it to that before it runs
`jGNEFilters`. Since MultiFinder's A5 is not Claris's A5, your dialog

will crash. The solution is to set A5 to the low-memory global CurrentA5 before you put up your dialog, or before you call these routines. And, of course, you'll have to restore it when you're done.

Avoiding Infinite Loops Due to Recursion

Whenever a patch of yours calls another trap, be aware that someone else's patch for the trap you're calling may call the trap you're patching. When this happens, your patches will call each other ad infinitum. Just as important, make sure that the trap you're calling doesn't sometimes call the trap you're patching! For example, if you patch DrawString() to call DrawMenuBar(), you will crash the machine.

Stack Space

This is a particularly hard-to-catch problem, because its effects may not be obvious until long after the problem code has run. Basically, you need to be aware that some traps, like InitGraf(), SetRect(), and even GetNextEvent(), sometimes get called when there is a very small amount of stack space left. If your patch, or any routine or traps it calls, uses a lot of stack space, it will either corrupt the heap or cause a system error when run. It doesn't hurt to call StackSpace() just to be sure you're not going to cause this sort of problem.

File System Problems

Sometimes you may want to patch a file system trap, and in that patch you may want to call another file system trap. Worse yet, you may assume that calling the file manager at interrupt time is not a problem because *Inside Macintosh* says that file manager traps don't move memory. You have to be aware of some problematic scenarios.

If you can avoid it, don't patch the file system. Most of the problems people run into when patching the file system are caused by bad assumptions about the way the file system works. Unlike, for example, QuickDraw, where only one call can happen at a time, and where every routine is documented as possibly moving memory, the file system rarely moves memory and is safe to call at interrupt time. This makes the file system very nice from the point of view of an applications programmer, because it can be called at almost any point, but problematic from our point of view. The reason it is problematic is that in any patch to the file system, we can only call other Toolbox and OS routines that don't move memory and are safe to call at interrupt time. This limits our ability to perform meaningful tasks within our file system patches.

And since it is possible to have multiple file manager calls pending at any given time, through the asynchronous file manager routines, it is sometimes true that a seemingly innocuous file manager call takes an inordinate amount of time. Since the file manager is partially constructed as a FIFO queue, making one synchronous call causes all asynchronous calls to complete first! So if you patch an asynchronous file system call, you should only issue other asynchronous calls, if any, to avoid unexpected program delays.

Worse, when file sharing is on, this changes. All synchronous calls to the file manager are changed into asynchronous calls under file sharing. This allows calls to complete out of order. Worse yet, when these calls complete, their original file manager routine is often re-entered. So if you were watching for, say, `PBDelete()`, you might see the same file get deleted twice!

Most of the time, the only reason you'll want to patch the file system is to watch for changes being made, so you can update, for example, file lists that you may be keeping track of. In this case, it is best to have your patches set some kind of global flag you can check at a later time. This is the only file system patch technique that is truly safe.

Be aware that even if you don't patch the file system, calling the file system from another trap may be problematic. Any trap documented as being OK to call during interrupts probably will be. If you patch one of these traps, you may be called in the middle of a file manager trap, so you had better not do anything that causes the file manager to be executed again, or it may lock. If you write a small INIT that records all trap calls, for instance, don't write anything to disk inside your patch(es), and if you must do this, at least check to see that `FSBusy` is not set, and that there is nothing in the file queue.

Finally, if your patch calls the resource manager, be aware that someone else's patch, or the current application, may have set the low-memory global `ResLoad` to false. If this is the case, your calls to `GetResource()` won't succeed, and calls to display a dialog, or even to `NewMenu()`, won't work properly because they all assume that `ResLoad` is set.

Unwanted Side Effects and Surprising Dependencies
All flavors of `GetResource()` clear the `ROMMapInsert` global. Many traps change the current `GrafPort`. `AddResMenu()` sets `ResLoad`. If you make a patch to a trap that has no side effects, and you call a trap that does, you may cause some interesting behaviors. Some traps have dependencies

that may not be documented. For example, `InsertMenu()` works fine whether or not `ResLoad` is set, but there are a surprising number of third-party INITs that patch `InsertMenu()`, assuming `ResLoad` is set. If you patch, say, `AddResMenu()`, and your patch calls `InsertMenu()`, you may transfer this dependency onto `AddResMenu()`, with the effect that a program that counted on `AddResMenu()` setting `ResLoad` will now crash. It's worth taking some time and thinking about ways that a careless application programmer might make calls that work fine without your patch, but don't work fine once the patch is installed. Just so you know, the `AddResMenu()` scenario presented here actually happened.

Dependencies You Didn't Think You Had

Going a little further in this line of thinking, here's an actual line of source code from a shipping control panel:

```
if (WWExist != 0 || Launched <= 0 || MBarHeight <= 0 || ResLoad == 0 ||
    MenuList == 0 || *MenuList == 0 || (**MenuList).lastMenu == 0 ||
    StackSpace() < 2048) return;
```

This line of code greatly increased the reliability of the control panel in question. In this case, the control panel unknowingly made lots of assumptions about the state of the Macintosh. First, the Window Manager was assumed to have been initialized, which meant that a menu bar had been created. Second, the code assumed that extensions were done loading and that applications were now running. Third, the code assumed that the menu bar was visible and had menus in it. Fourth, the `ResLoad` flag was assumed to have been set. Fifth, the code assumed that there was at least 2K of available stack space. This extra code takes care of these assumptions and makes the control panel much more reliable.

Similarly, the same program makes this check prior to launching a program:

```
Boolean OK_to_Launch(void) {
    WindowPeek wp;

    wp = (WindowPeek) FrontWindow();
    if (wp && wp->windowKind == 2 && GetWVariant(wp) == 1) return
false;
    return (true);
    }
```

It's not a good idea to launch a program if MultiFinder won't switch to it once it's launched, so if a dialog is the frontmost window, it's a good idea to wait until it goes away.

ADVANCED TOPICS

So far, our sample code has patched a relatively benign trap, `SystemEvent()`. `SystemEvent()` is benign because it is a stack-based call and follows normal high-level register-saving conventions. The `SystemEvent()` patches in the sample code are perfectly compatible with both PowerPC and 680x0 machines. However, there are some traps you won't be able to patch due to their register usage, and some traps that, when patched with 68K code, may cause serious performance loss on Power Macs. This section descibes the changes necessary to address these issues.

Revamping the Code to Support the PowerPC

Rewriting our code to run properly on the PowerPC is surprisingly easy. All we have to do is follow these simple rules:

- All of our code that deals with access to our globals (such as `SetA4()`, `SetCurrentA4()`, and so on) is unnecessary.

- Any time we take the address of any part of our code for the purpose of letting the Toolbox or OS call it, we must create a Universal Procedure Pointer (UPP).

- Any time we call part of the Toolbox or OS code through a function pointer rather than official glue, we must go through `CallUniversalProc()`.

In general, to understand what's involved in moving to PowerPC, it's helpful to understand a little of what's going on behind the scenes. This subject is discussed in more detail in *Inside Mac: PowerPC System Software*, but a little foreword is in order before we continue.

When Apple implemented the "mixed mode" portion of the operating system for Power Mac, they didn't just want PowerPC to be an optimized way of coding the same old 68K routines. In order to realize the true power behind PowerPC, Apple had to allow developers to write PowerPC code in such a way as to maximize its speed. This is a bigger distinction than it might seem because of PowerPC considerations such as the "red zone" and parameter-passing conventions very different than those of the 680x0. As a result, what might have been implemented as a small difference between emulating 68K code, and running native PowerPC code that was just mimicking the actions of 68K code, albeit faster, was implemented as a full-blown two-context task-switching nanokernel.

In case these terms confuse you, don't worry; all you have to remember is this: The best way to think of the Power Macintosh's Mixed Mode environment is as two separate processors, one 68LC040 and one PowerPC. At any given time, only one of these processors is processing, while the other is halted. The way control passes to the PowerPC CPU is through the `MixedModeDispatch()` trap ($AAFE), and the way control passes to the 680x0 is through the `CallUniversalProc()` routine.

In real life, of course, no Power Mac has a 680x0 chip on-board. But that's irrelevant; from our software's point of view, it really is there.

There's one other important detail: For compatibility reasons, 68K code has the luxury of not having to worry whether it's calling 680x0 or native code. If it did, none of the old applications or extensions would work at all. But obviously you can't execute PowerPC code as if it were 68K code, so what do you do? In the mixed-mode environment, any time that the address of PowerPC code is used, it has to be surrounded by a `MixedModeDispatch()` trap ($AAFE) so that 68K code calling it will switch properly. `NewRoutineDescriptor()` is the name of the routine that wraps the `MixedModeDispatch()` trap around PowerPC code, and returns a pointer (called a `UniversalProcPtr()`) that is safe to be called both from PowerPC and 680x0 code.

Of course, PowerPC code cannot directly call a `UniversalProcPtr()`as if it were PowerPC code, which is why it's important that every time a PowerPC routine calls a function indirectly through a `UniversalProcPtr()`, it uses `CallUniversalProc()`.

The most important part of how this affects us is that all the entries in the trap table are assumed by the Power Mac to point to 680x0 code. So, any time that we call through the trap table, or through the result of `GetTrapAddress()`, we have to use `CallUniversalProc()`. And any time that we put the address of one of our routines into the trap table through `SetTrapAddress()`, it is critical that we put in the result of a `NewRoutineDescriptor()` call instead.

Let's take a look now at the first of our changes. For best results, we'll use a header file called `Beeper.h` to summarize all the structures and definitions that are common between our INIT and our control panel.

First in our common header are the definitions for use in accessing our globals:

```
#ifndef powerc
    #ifdef THINK_C
        #pragma parameter __D0 SetA4(__D0)
        pascal long SetA4(long newA4) = 0xC18C;

    #define SetCurrentA4() SetA4((long)&main)
    #else
        #include <A4Stuff.h>
    #endif
#else
    #define SetCurrentA4() 0
    #define SetA4(x) 0
#endif
```

Under PowerPC, neither SetCurrentA4() nor SetA4() need do anything; however our existing code assumes they return a result, so we must return zero.

The rest of our header contains the usual common header information, none of which is changed for the purposes of PowerPC:

```
#define kDTS_Signature 'Beep'
#define kGestaltGetInitGlobals 'glob'

#define kSystemEventTrapNumber 0xA9B2

typedef unsigned char uchar;

typedef struct BeeperGlobals {
    long      BeeperOn;
    Str31     BeepString;
} BeeperGlobals;
```

We'll need to change the beginning of Beeper.INIT.c as well to reflect the new header file:

```
#include <Events.h>
#include <Resources.h>
#include <Memory.h>
#include <ToolUtils.h>
#include <GestaltEqu.h>
#include <Errors.h>

#include "Beeper.h"
```

Because `SystemEvent()` is implemented in 68K on most Macintoshes, and we'll need our patch (which is native PowerPC) to call the original, and to use `CallUniversalProc()` in order to access it. Since `CallUniversalProc()` needs to know what the parameters to `SystemEvent()` are in order to properly translate them from PowerPC to 68K, we'll define them after the `SystemEvent()` definitions:

```
pascal short (*gOldSystemEvent)(EventRecord *theEvent);

pascal short BeeperSystemEvent(EventRecord *theEvent);

enum {
    uppSystemEventProcInfo = kPascalStackBased |
            RESULT_SIZE(kTwoByteCode) |
            STACK_ROUTINE_PARAMETER(1, kFourByteCode)
};
```

Likewise, we need an extra line for `Gestalt()` as well:

```
SelectorFunctionUPP ourGestaltUPP;

static pascal OSErr BeeperGestalt(OSType selector, long *_response);
```

This deserves a little more explanation: our `Gestalt()` call can return the address of our `BeeperGestalt()` routine, but its address would be a pointer to PowerPC code, so we have to create a `UniversalProcPtr()`. You might think we would create this `UniversalProcPtr()` inside of the `Gestalt()` routine, but this would create and allocate in memory a new `UniversalProcPtr()` every time we were called. Since we need to create a `UniversalProcPtr()` for our `Gestalt()` routine anyway, it's best that we keep it around as a global.

The next thing we need has to do with the Metrowerks environment. It's somewhat magical that we are able to compile our code into PowerPC and put it in a resource, yet be called from 68K code as if we were written in 680x0. Behind the scenes, what's happening is that Metrowerks is adding a `RoutineDescriptor` at the beginning of the code that contains the `MixedModeDispatch()` trap necessary to translate our parameters from 68K to PowerPC. Of course, to do that properly, the `RoutineDescriptor` must contain information about what the parameters are, so they can be properly converted. The way Metrowerks handles this is that the Metrowerks linker looks for a global variable declaration for `_procinfo`, which we'll define as follows:

```
#ifdef powerc
    // for Metrowerks' linker, this defines the interface for main().
    ProcInfoType __procinfo = kCStackBased | RESULT_SIZE(kNoByteCode);
#endif
```

Because INIT code neither takes parameters nor returns results, this is unexpectedly simple. In the case of our control device function, it is markedly more complicated. But we'll come to that later.

In our main routine, the changes we need to make center around `BeeperGestalt()` and `BeeperSystemEvent()`. We used to take their addresses and blithely pass them to `NewGestalt()` and `SetToolTrap-Address()`, respectively, but this violates rule two of converting our code: Any time we take the address of any part of our code for the purpose of letting the Toolbox or OS call it, we must create a `UniversalProcPtr()`.

We already have a global `UniversalProcPtr()` for our `Gestalt()` routine; we'll need a local one for `BeeperSystemEvent()`. Our local variables now look like this:

```
long                oldA4;
BeeperGlobals       **bgh;
UniversalProcPtr    newSystemEventAddress;
THz                 oldZone;
```

We'll need to allocate our routine descriptors as soon as we can, since they will be critical to the successful functioning of our INIT. So, right after we set the current zone to the system zone, we call:

```
ourGestaltUPP = NewSelectorFunctionProc(BeeperGestalt);
if (ourGestaltUPP == 0) goto initFailed;

newSystemEventAddress = NewRoutineDescriptor(
                            (ProcPtr) &BeeperSystemEvent,
                            uppSystemEventProcInfo,
                            GetCurrentISA());
if (newSystemEventAddress == 0) goto initFailed;
```

All that is left now is to use `ourGestaltUPP` in place of `&BeeperGestalt`, and `newSystemEventAddress` in place of `&BeeperSystemEvent`. Our `NewGestalt()` call becomes:

```
if (NewGestalt(kDTS_Signature, ourGestaltUPP) != noErr) goto
    initFailed;
```

Our `SetToolTrapAddress()` call becomes:

```
SetToolTrapAddress(newSystemEventAddress, kSystemEventTrapNumber);
```

And our `Gestalt()` routine's self-referencing return becomes:

```
case kDTS_Signature:
    *response = (long)ourGestaltUPP;
    break;
```

There is now only one change left to do, and is to do with rule #3: Any time we call part of the Toolbox or OS code through a function pointer rather than official glue, we must go through `CallUniversalProc()`.

Because of this, we have to change the way we call the old `SystemEvent()` patch. We can't just call it directly anymore because what we got back from `GetToolTrapAddress()` was a `UniversalProcPtr()` and, most likely, 680x0 code. Instead, we have to go through `CallUniversalProcPtr()` so that we correctly switch from PowerPC native code to 68K code whenever necessary.

```
    // Call the old SystemEvent:
#ifndef powerc
    result = gOldSystemEvent(theEvent);
#else
    result = CallUniversalProc((UniversalProcPtr)gOldSystemEvent,
                uppSystemEventProcInfo,
                theEvent);
#endif
```

And that's all! With a minimum of hassle, our INIT is now native. Changes to make our control panel run native are even easier, since our control panel never needs to pass the address of one if its own routines anywhere. We have the obligatory `_procinfo` for Metrowerks:

```
#ifdef powerc
        // for Metrowerks' linker, this defines the interface for
        // main().
    ProcInfoType __procinfo = kPascalStackBased
            | RESULT_SIZE(kFourByteCode)
            | STACK_ROUTINE_PARAMETER(1,  SIZE_CODE(sizeof(short)))
            | STACK_ROUTINE_PARAMETER(2,  SIZE_CODE(sizeof(short)))
            | STACK_ROUTINE_PARAMETER(3,  SIZE_CODE(sizeof(short)))
            | STACK_ROUTINE_PARAMETER(4,  SIZE_CODE(sizeof(short)))
            | STACK_ROUTINE_PARAMETER(5,
                SIZE_CODE(sizeof(EventRecord *)))
```

```
             | STACK_ROUTINE_PARAMETER(6,  SIZE_CODE(sizeof(long)))
             | STACK_ROUTINE_PARAMETER(7,
                      SIZE_CODE(sizeof(DialogPtr))));
#endif
```

Most changes have to do, not surprisingly, with our Gestalt() function, whose declaration changes from:

```
pascal OSErr (*BeeperGestalt)(OSType selector, long *response);
```

to:

```
SelectorFunctionUPP ourGestaltUPP;
```

Note that SelectorFunctionUPP is defined in <GestaltEqu.h> to be a UniversalProcPtr()under PowerPC, yet matches our old declaration under 680x0. It's always a good idea to check for this kind of convenience and use it where possible, because it allows you to write code that compiles under 680x0 and PowerPC without modification and without a lot of #ifdef powerc directives. Along with the definition of SelectorFunctionUPP, <GestaltEqu.h> also provides a macro that allows us to call through our Gestalt() function pointer both on 680x0 and PowerPC and have it work correctly. Our calls to Gestalt() thus change only slightly, from:

```
err = Gestalt(kDTS_Signature, (long *)&BeeperGestalt);
if (err == noErr) {
    err = BeeperGestalt(gestaltVersion, &versionCheck);
    if (versionCheck != 0x0100) err = -1;
    if (err == noErr) {
        err = BeeperGestalt( kGestaltGetInitGlobals,
                    (long *)&gInitGlobals  );
}
}
```

to:

```
err = Gestalt(kDTS_Signature, (long *)&ourGestaltUPP);
if (err == noErr) {
    err = CallSelectorFunctionProc(ourGestaltUPP,
                gestaltVersion, (long *)&versionCheck);
    if (versionCheck != 0x0100) err = -1;
    if (err == noErr) {
        err = CallSelectorFunctionProc(ourGestaltUPP,
                kGestaltGetInitGlobals,
                (long *)&gInitGlobals  );
```

```
          }

      }
```

And that's it! We can now build ourselves a completely native control panel with native patches.

But there are some problems. This section of the chapter was written as a how-to guide to show you how to write native patches if you want to do so. There are, however, some serious issues to keep in mind that may keep you from ever actually doing any of this.

The first issue is 68K compatibility. The PowerPC version of this code runs great on Power Macs, but crashes on 68K machines. In order to work properly on both types of machines, that is, in order to be a "fat" control panel, we would have to build the main code as 68K, with a small header that dispatches to our native code, probably best stored in a separate native resource, if we find ourselves on a Power Mac. If we didn't do this, the code would never be shippable, since the vast majority of our users will own 680x0, not PowerPC, CPUs for quite some time.

Even if we do that, which at least would move the code to the level of commercial shippability, there is the question, What's the point? Take the control panel code: it's only called from the Finder, and currently the Finder isn't native. When the code gets run, it immediately makes calls to GetDialogItem(), Gestalt(), and other traps, all of which are not native. As a result, the overhead of switching back and forth between execution of PowerPC code and 680x0 code overcomes any speed advantage we might see from code being written on PowerPC. Since PowerPC code is larger than 680x0 code, and since having both PowerPC code and 680x0 code is *much* larger than just 680x0 code, and since it would run slower when native, the net result is slower, larger code. There are simply no advantages to going native in our control panel. Likewise, our INIT code gains no speed advantage by running native, and our patch code also slows down the system by being native because, unlike certain other traps (notably, QuickDraw and the Memory Manager), SystemEvent() is a 680x0 trap called almost exclusively by 680x0 code. Let's be a little more specific. Without our patch installed, the usual case for a call to SystemEvent() is depicted in Figure 5.12.

With the 680x0 version of our INIT installed, the situation becomes a little more unwieldy (Figure 5.13).

FIGURE 5.12

A typical call to an unpatched SystemEvent().

And if the PowerPC version of our trap is installed, the situation becomes so convoluted that it is impossible to draw:

- 680x0 code calls `SystemEvent()`.

- The trap dispatcher looks up the address of `SystemEvent()`, and finds it pointing to our code.

FIGURE 5.13

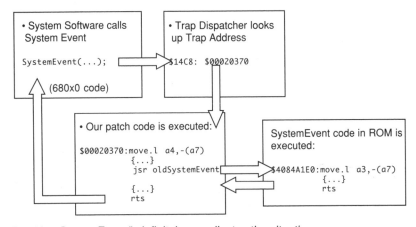

Patching SystemEvent() definitely complicates the situation.

- Execution begins at our routine descriptor, the first word of which is $AAFE, or `MixedModeDispatch()`, and this causes a switch from 680x0 to PowerPC. This switch consumes on average the same time as 50 680x0 instructions.

- Our code executes in PowerPC. If the event coming through is a `keyDown` event, we make a call to `RelString()`, which is a register-based OS trap that is not currently native. Our call is handled by glue, which calls `CallUniversalProc()` to handle the transition.

This switch consumes the equivalent time of another 50 680x0 instructions.

- In the case of a `keyDown` event, execution continues, now in 680x0, through `RelString()`. When `RelString()` returns, it returns to the `CallUniversalProc()` glue, consuming another 50 680x0 instructions. If `RelString()` returns `true`, and we decide to beep, we have to consume the 50-instruction hit twice more to make the call to `SysBeep()`, although in this case the time wastage is vastly overcome by the time to create and play the sound.

- Now that we're done calling `HandleKeyDown()`, it's time to call the original trap. We use `CallUniversalProc()`, which consumes the equivalent time of 50 680x0 instructions, then calls the original trap. When the trap returns, it returns back inside of `CallUniversalProc()`, which consumes 50 more 680x0 instructions, before returning to the end of our patch.

- As we return, we return to the Mixed-Mode Dispatcher, which consumes a final 50-instruction time hit before returning to the original `SystemEvent()` caller.

To put this in perspective, note that if the event coming through is not a `keyDown` event, our 680x0 patch executes a total of 28 extra instructions. By contrast, our PowerPC patch consumes an overhead of approximately 200 68K instructions, and that's not counting the time it takes to execute the native patch code!

The Upside

There is one upside to all this mess: every argument concerning time reverses itself in the case of native traps called by native code. For example, the Toolbox trap `StdLine()` is almost always called from the ROM inside of native QuickDraw. If we were to patch `StdLine()` with similar 680x0 code, we would add a 228 680x0-instruction overhead to every call, whereas our native patch would add approximately the overhead of only 200 PowerPC instructions, or roughly 20 to 30 680x0 instructions. So, if you know in advance that the trap you're patching is native, it pays to have a native patch as well.

Fat Traps

One way to avoid the downside of extreme overhead if your patch doesn't happen to match the architecture (680x0 versus PowerPC) of the routine it's patching is to make a *fat patch*. A fat patch is a patch that forks off at the beginning of its code into either 68K code or PowerPC code, depending on the architecture of its caller. Fat patches are created with a routine called `NewFatRoutineDescriptor()`, which is described in *Inside Macintosh: PowerPC System Software*. Briefly, while fat traps may seem like a good idea, and while their overhead to PowerPC callers is the same as native traps, there is some extra overhead for 68K callers in determining which fork of the trap to take. It's left to you to figure out whether this might ever be of any real benefit to you; for what it's worth, the author has found few cases where a performance benefit would be significant; it is usually just as efficient to determine ahead of time whether the old patch is native or not, and simply patch native traps with native code, and 680x0 code with 680x0 patches.

Patching an OS Trap on 68K

`SystemEvent()` is one of the easiest traps to patch, since it is a stack-based trap, documented as not preserving any scratch registers, and since it may move memory. This means any patch we make to it can also move memory and use scratch registers, and we can write the patch in C. Finally, since `SystemEvent()` is not called often, and is usually called from 680x0 code and is written in 680x0 code, there are no PowerPC issues, nor are there any serious performance issues involved with patching it.

The situation becomes much more difficult when we start trying to patch OS traps, where we can't write our patches in C, can't use scratch registers, and where performance can be critical. So let's give it a try. The code here is not on the CD-ROM included with this book, for fear that you might actually use it. Please understand that this example is meant only to give you a feel for what's involved, not to set an example for how to patch OS traps in general. If you can avoid it, don't patch OS traps; in fact, if you can, patch only those traps that can move memory, avoid patching traps that preserve a lot of registers, and don't patch traps which are called often. `GetResource()` and all the various flavors thereof are traps to avoid patching, because of the time penalty you will impose on the entire Macintosh, which relies on calling `GetResource()` frequently.

> If you are not familiar with assembly language, this is not the place to learn; patching traps is far too dangerous for a first-time project. You should already have a good working knowledge of assembly language before attempting to patch low-level OS traps.

Now that you've been warned, here's the challenge: to implement the bug fix described at the top of this chapter. We assume that NewPtr() functions incorrectly for allocation sizes less than 4. We want to patch NewPtr() so that calls to it with sizes greater than or equal to 4 are untouched, while calls with sizes less than 4 are converted to calls with a size of 4, followed by a SetPtrSize() call. If NewPtr() were a stack-based call, our patch would look something like:

```
pascal void *NewPtr(long size) {
    long    oldA4;
    void    *result;

    oldA4 = SetCurrentA4();

    if (size >= 4) {  // for values greater than or equal to 4, just
                      // call the old NewPtr.
        result = gOldNewPtr(size);
    } else {
        result = gOldNewPtr(4);  // for values less than 4,
                                 // allocate 4
        if (result != 0) {           // and if the allocation succeeded,
            SetPtrSize(result, size);  // then size it down.
        }
    }

    SetA4(oldA4);

    return result;
}
```

Now that we've defined the problem, let's go for the solution: First, we'll need to define a new constant that represents the NewPtr() trap number:

```
#define kNewPtrTrapNumber 0xA01E
```

We'll need two new declarations in Beeper.INIT.c:

```
void *(*gOldNewPtr)(short flags, long size);

void *BeeperNewPtr(short flags, long size);
```

And some new installation code in main():

```
// Remember the old implementation of NewPtr.
gOldNewPtr = (void *) GetOSTrapAddress(kNewPtrTrapNumber);
```

```
    // Patch ourselves in.
SetOSTrapAddress((void *)&BeeperNewPtr, kNewPtrTrapNumber);
```

In order to make this as general as possible, we'll break the patch apart into three additional routines (in addition to `BeeperNewPtr`). The patch itself follows this structure:

* Determine if we need to patch this particular call.

* If we do not, simply continue execution at the old trap address.

* If we do, make any adjustments necessary and call the real trap.

* Do any necessary post-processing.

* Return to the original caller.

The structure of the three additional routines we'll use is:

```
typedef struct PreFlightRegisters {
    long    register_d0;
    long    register_d1;
    long    register_d2;
    long    register_a0;
    long    register_a1;
} PreFlightRegisters;

typedef struct PostNewPtrRegisters {
    long    register_d0;
    long    register_d1;
    long    register_d2;
    long    register_a0;
    long    register_a1;
    long    register_a4;
    long    original_d0;
} PostNewPtrRegisters;

static short PreFlightNewPtr(PreFlightRegisters *pfr);

static void PostNewPtr(PostNewPtrRegisters *pnpr);

static void JumpOldNewPtr(void);
```

The first routine, `PreFlightNewPtr()`, gets a first look at the arguments being passed in. Based on the registers on entry, `PreFlightNewPtr()` will either return 0, meaning not to patch this call, or 1, meaning to call the trap with the new register values (if any), and then call `PostNewPtr()`. Since `PreFlightNewPtr()` is high-level, it almost writes itself:

```
static short PreFlightNewPtr(PreFlightRegisters *pfr)
{
    if (((unsigned long)pfr->register_d0) >= 4) { // if asking for 4
                                                  // or more,
        return 0;                          // don't patch
    }
    pfr->register_d0 = 4; // if less, adjust the size parameter
                          // to equal 4,
    return 1;                             // and call the real trap.
}
```

By allowing `PreFlightNewPtr()` to return 0, we give ourselves a way to avoid additional overhead, because in this case, while we intercept the call to the original `NewPtr()`, we do not intercept the return. A patch that does not intercept the return from the original trap is called a *head patch*, whereas a patch that does intercept the return from the original is called a *tail patch*. Head patches are generally preferable to tail patches because of the reduced overhead, and also because they are virtually undetectable. See *Inside Macintosh: OS Utilities*, the Trap Manager section for a better description of the side effects of head patches versus tail patches.

The second routine, `PostNewPtr()`, is only called once the original patch has taken place, and only if `PreFlightNewPtr()` had returned 1. `PostNewPtr()` takes any actions that are necessary after the original trap takes place; in our case, it needs to conditionally set the returned pointer's size to 4 if the call to `NewPtr()` succeeded.

```
static void PostNewPtr(PostNewPtrRegisters *pnpr)
{
    if (pnpr->register_d0 == noErr) {
        SetPtrSize((void *)pnpr->register_a0, pnpr->original_d0);
    }
}
```

The third routine is necessary in order to provide a way to jump to the original `NewPtr()` routine without affecting any registers. In the head patch case, we will be jumping into it, whereas in the tail patch case, we will be calling it, so that when it returns we can perform additional actions.

```
static asm void JumpOldNewPtr(void)
{
    subq.l    #4,a7
    movem.l      d0/a0/a4,-(a7)
```

```
      sr        SetCurrentA4
      move.l    gOldNewPtr,12(a7)
      movem.l   (a7)+,d0/a0/a4

rts
}
```

Note the `asm` keyword in the function declaration; this keyword tells
Metrowerks that the entire routine is written in assembly language. We
start out by reserving space on the stack for the old address of `NewPtr()`;
this way, executing the `rts` instruction causes control to transfer there.
Next, we must get the old address of `NewPtr()` and put it onto the stack.
We can't just fetch it directly, since register A4 hasn't been set up, and we
don't have access to our globals. Once A4 has been set up, we can
retrieve the old address. Yet it's not even that simple, since the
Metrowerks' routine to set up A4 properly disturbs registers D0 and A0.
So we must save off all the registers (D0, A0, and A4), call the routine to
set up A4, and only then can we retrieve the old address of `NewPtr()`.
Once we have it, we restore D0, A0, and A4, and the `rts` instruction takes
us where we want to go.

The final routine is our patch, with comments in-line:

```
asm void *BeeperNewPtr(short flags, long size)
{
      move.l d0,-(a7)                    // save the original size
                                         // parameter.

      movem.l d0/d1/d2/a0/a1/a4,-(a7)    // save the incoming registers
      jsr    SetCurrentA4                // set up access to our globals

      pea    (a7)                        // see if we need to patch this
                                         // call

      jsr  PreFlightNewPtr
      addq   #4,a7

      tst.w    d0                        // if PreFlightNewPtr returns 1,
                                         // we
      bne.s    @TailPatch                 // must tail patch.

      movem.l  (a7)+,d0/d1/d2/a0/a1/a4   // otherwise restore registers,
      addq     #4,a7                     // discard the copy of size,
      jmp      JumpOldNewPtr             // and jump through to the
                                         // original.

@TailPatch:
      movem.l  (a7)+,d0/d1/d2/a0/a1/a4   // adjust the registers
                                         // according to how PFNP
```

```
                                        // may have changed them.

        jsr     JumpOldNewPtr           // call the original trap

        movem.l    d0/d1/d2/a0/a1/a4,-(a7) // save the new registers
        jsr     SetCurrentA4            // set up access to our globals

        pea     (a7)                    // perform post-processing
        jsr     PostNewPtr
        addq    #4,a7

        movem.l    (a7)+,d0/d1/d2/a0/a1/a4 // adjust registers according
                                        // to PNP
        addq    #4,a7                   // discard the copy of size,

        rts                             // and return to the original
                                        // caller.
}
```

Again, while this may not be the optimal way to perform this patch, it does follow all possible precautions given the patch we need to make, and you can copy the same shell routines (BeeperNewPtr(), JumpOldNewPtr()) for use in patching any other OS trap, while changing only the high-level C code for PostNewPtr() and PreFlightNewPtr().

Patching an OS Trap on PowerPC

Now that we've patched an operating system routine via assembly language, let's explore the same issue from the point of view of a native trap. Due to the nature of the patch, the code must be entirely separate. Starting once again from a code base of the Beep.cdev folder from the CD-ROM with this book, let's add the native NewPtr() patch.

Like the 68K version of this patch, we'll need to define a new constant for the NewPtr() trap number in our header file:

```
#define kNewPtrTrapNumber 0xA01E
```

And we'll need three new declarations in Beeper.INIT.c:

```
void *(*gOldNewPtr)(short flags, long size);

void *BeeperNewPtr(short flags, long size);
```

And some new installation code in main():

```
// Remember the old implementation of NewPtr.
gOldNewPtr = (void *) GetOSTrapAddress(kNewPtrTrapNumber);
```

```
    // Patch ourselves in.
SetOSTrapAddress((void *)&BeeperNewPtr, kNewPtrTrapNumber);

enum {
    uppNewPtrProcInfo =
    kRegisterBased |
    RESULT_SIZE(kFourByteCode) |
    REGISTER_RESULT_LOCATION(kRegisterA0) |
    REGISTER_ROUTINE_PARAMETER(1, kRegisterD1, kTwoByteCode) |
    REGISTER_ROUTINE_PARAMETER(2, kRegisterD0, kFourByteCode)
};
```

Unlike the `ProcInfo` constant for `SystemEvent()`, `NewPtr()`'s
`ProcInfo` constant is quite complex; register-based calls always are.
However the constant itself is quite straightforward. `NewPtr()` is a trap
which takes a size parameter in D0 and returns a pointer in A0.
Additionally, as we mentioned in the beginning of this chapter, register
D1 contains certain flag bits that can distinguish various flavors of
`NewPtr()`, such as `NewPtrSys()` and `NewPtrClear()`. Since register D1
contains exactly the trap word, we could distinguish the flavors ourselves simply by comparing D1 with the trap word listed in Apple's
glue. For example, `NewPtr()`'s declaration in `<Memory.h>` is:

```
extern pascal Ptr NewPtr(Size byteCount)
 ONEWORDINLINE(0xA11E);
```

whereas the declaration of `NewPtrSys()` is:

```
extern pascal Ptr NewPtrSys(Size byteCount)
 ONEWORDINLINE(0xA51E);
```

So if the flags parameter to `BeeperNewPtr()` were equal to $A51E, it
would indicate that the system heap variant of `NewPtr()` had been called.
The next part of our native patch defines and sets up a local variable
similar to `newSystemEventAddress`. The local variables now look like:

```
    long                oldA4;
    THz                 oldZone;
    BeeperGlobals       **bgh;
    UniversalProcPtr    newSystemEventAddress;
    UniversalProcPtr    newNewPtrAddress;
```

And the calls to fill them in are:

```
    newSystemEventAddress = NewRoutineDescriptor(
                            (ProcPtr) &BeeperSystemEvent,
```

```
                                        uppSystemEventProcInfo,
                                        GetCurrentISA());
    if (newSystemEventAddress == 0) goto initFailed;

    newNewPtrAddress = NewRoutineDescriptor(
                                (ProcPtr) &BeeperNewPtr,
                                uppNewPtrProcInfo,
                                GetCurrentISA());
    if (newNewPtrAddress == 0) goto initFailed;
```

And the calls to install them are:

```
    // Remember the old implementation of SystemEvent and NewPtr.
    gOldSystemEvent = (void *)
        GetToolTrapAddress(kSystemEventTrapNumber);
    gOldNewPtr = (void *) GetOSTrapAddress(kNewPtrTrapNumber);

    // Patch ourselves in.
    SetToolTrapAddress(newSystemEventAddress, kSystemEventTrapNumber);
    SetOSTrapAddress(newNewPtrAddress, kNewPtrTrapNumber);
```

So far, so good. Now for the patch code. Unlike the 68K case, the PowerPC code is amazingly simple. This is because our routine descriptors are doing most of the work that we have to do by hand on 68K. In fact, the PowerPC code for an OS patch close resembles what the code would have been like had NewPtr() been a Toolbox trap:

```
void *BeeperNewPtr(short flags, long size) {
    void  *result;

    if (size >= 4) { // for values greater than or equal to 4, just
                     // call the
                     // old NewPtr.

    return (void
*)CallOSTrapUniversalProc((UniversalProcPtr)gOldNewPtr,
                        uppNewPtrProcInfo, flags, size);

    } else {        // for values less than 4, allocate 4

    result = (void
*)CallOSTrapUniversalProc((UniversalProcPtr)gOldNewPtr,
                        uppNewPtrProcInfo, flags, 4);

    if (result != 0) {              // and if the allocation succeeded,
        SetPtrSize(result, size);  // then size it down.
        }
    }
```

```
    return result;
}
```

The big difference is that rather than use CallUniversalProc(), we must call CallOSTrapUniversalProc(). And that's it — we're done! Other than that caveat, and the tediousness of proper uppProcInfo construction, it is basically just as easy to patch OS traps under PowerPC as it is to patch Toolbox traps.

There is one detail that happens to be hidden, however, and you may run into it if you patch traps in native PowerPC. Even though the code we are executing is native code, all 680x0 registers are still "live." What this means is, if you patch a trap such as LoadResource(), which is defined as preserving all registers, with native code, and in your code you call, for example, TickCount(), then when LoadResource() returns, any registers changed by TickCount() will remain changed, and your patch will cause your Macintosh to start crashing. If you really want to patch LoadResource() with a patch that calls TickCount(), you have to be careful to preserve any registers which TickCount() alters beforehand, much the same way as we had to do with the 680x0 version of our NewPtr() patch. To make this easy, the following code will allow you full access to all 68K registers except the stack:

```
typedef struct AlmostAll68KRegs {
    long    DRegs[8];
    long    ARegs[7];
} AlmostAll68KRegs;

    // movem.l    d0-d7/a0-a6,([4,a7])
long    _Get68KRegs[2] = {0x48F77FFF, 0x01610004, 0x4E754E75};

    //  movem.l    ([4,a7]),d0-d7/a0-a6
long    _Set68KRegs[2] = {0x4CF77FFF, 0x01610004, 0x4E754E75};

enum {
    upp68KRegsProcInfo = kCStackBased | RESULT_SIZE(kNoByteCode) |
            STACK_ROUTINE_PARAMETER(1, kFourByteCode)
};

void Get68KRegs(AlmostAll68KRegs *regs) {
    CallUniversalProc((void *)_Get68KRegs, upp68KRegsProcInfo, regs);
}

void Set68KRegs(AlmostAll68KRegs *regs) {
    CallUniversalProc((void *)_Set68KRegs, upp68KRegsProcInfo, regs);
}
```

What these two routines do is use the Mixed Mode Manager to switch over to 680x0, get or set all 15 settable registers, and return. As an example of when they might be useful, consider this scenario: Let's say that all we wanted to do is figure out how much time was being spent inside LoadResource(). Our patch would look like this:

```
long gTicksInLoadResource;

void BeeperLoadResource(Handle r) {
    AlmostAll168KRegs      regs;
    long                   start, stop;

    Get68KRegs(&regs);
    start = TickCount();
    CallUniversalProc((UniversalProcPtr)gOldLoadResource,
                    uppLoadResourceProcInfo, r);
    stop = TickCount();
    gTicksInLoadResource += (stop - start);
    Set68KRegs(&regs);
}
```

If we didn't save and restore the registers, this patch would surely crash the machine.

Finally, there is one caveat: because Get68KRegs() and Set68KRegs() require mode switches, each consume the equivalent of approximately 100 680x0 instructions to execute. Compared to crashing the Mac, this is a small price to pay, but compared to finding other ways to solve your problems, these are very slow routines. If we were using the above routine only for our own personal use, and were never planning to ship the code, we could avoid the use of TickCount() altogether by reading the low-memory Ticks global:

```
long gTicksInLoadResource;

void BeeperLoadResource(Handle r) {
    long                   start, stop;

    start = *(long *)0x16A; // read ticks before call
    CallUniversalProc((UniversalProcPtr)gOldLoadResource,
            uppLoadResourceProcInfo, r);
    stop  = *(long *)0x16A; // read ticks after call
    gTicksInLoadResource += (stop - start);
}
```

This would give us much more accurate timing results as well.

SUMMARY

Well, that's about it. You've just completed a whirlwind tour of the Trap Manager and some general theories and strategies involved in patching traps. I know that the material was rough in places, but we wanted to err on the side of too much material rather than too little.

Before we close, there are a few things worth remembering. Don't patch traps unless you absolutely have to. Patching traps is one great way to make code that crashes and is incompatible with the universe at large. Most likely, the rules for patching traps will change completely with the release of Apple's next major OS revision, Copland. Chances are good that any trap patching code you write will break under Copland, so if you must patch, patch carefully and try to isolate that portion of your design so you can respond to any changes Copland dictates.

BIOGRAPHY

Jorg Brown has been programming computers since the age of 10, when he worked on a Southwest Technical 6800 kit computer. At age 17 he became the youngest person ever to graduate with an electrical engineering degree from Colorado State University. Despite 7 straight-A semesters, he managed to flunk 2 of 3 computer science courses, and for almost a year after graduation, his highest-paid position was at a pizza delivery business. From there things only got better—in the years since he landed a real job, he has written code for 5 Eddy-award-winning products: THINK Pascal, THINK C, Now Utilities, Now Contact, and his most recent joint effort, RAM Doubler. If there is one thing that amazes Jorg, it's how closely high-tech products reflect the personalities of their creators. "There are those to whom a computer is a computer, for whom a spreadsheet is a spreadsheet, but when you really dig into the guts of a machine like the Apple II, or a Macintosh, it becomes clear that certain products were labors of love. I'd been hacking on the Mac for 8 years before I ever met Andy Hertzfeld, but after 2 minutes of talking with him, it was like we'd grown up together. In a way, we had."

WORKING WITH RESOURCES

Chapter

6

Like most Mac programmers, my earliest Mac programming experiences included a little tinkering with the Resource Manager. I started with a 'WIND' and a call to GetNewWindow(). Next, I moved on to 'MENU', 'DLOG', 'ALRT', and 'DITL' resources, along with the Toolbox routines that brought them to life. I learned about icon families and application signatures, about file types and creators. I even learned how to create my own resource types and how to modify my resources and write them back out to disk.

This chapter assumes you've been down a similar path and have already spent some time with the Resource Manager. So, instead of starting from scratch, we'll skip routines like GetNewWindow() and focus on some Resource Manager issues that many people (myself included) have found to be unclear. We'll first look at the process of opening, creating, and closing a resource file. We'll learn about the resource-file search path and the routines that allow you to find the resources you need, when you need them. We'll then consider the process of loading a resource from a file into memory and the five resource attributes that affect this process. Finally, we'll examine the sample program StringLister, which brings the concepts in this chapter together.

WORKING WITH RESOURCE FILES

Let's start by looking at the process of working with resource files, updated to reflect the changes brought on by System 7.

Every Macintosh file has both a *data fork* and a *resource fork* (Figure 6.1). Although a file's data fork and resource fork share a single catalog entry, they are usually thought of as separate files and are opened separately.

The data fork is just a stream of 0 or more bytes (0 bytes means the data fork is empty). It doesn't follow any special format and can contain any data you like.

Like the data fork, the resource fork can be empty. When a program like ResEdit complains that a file has no resource fork, it's really saying that the resource fork is empty. In order for a resource fork to be a legitimate resource file, it needs three things: a resource header, a set of 0 or more resources, and a resource map. The *resource header* contains offsets that get you to the resources and to the resource map. The *resource map* describes each of the file's resources and is the real key to the puzzle.

FIGURE 6.1

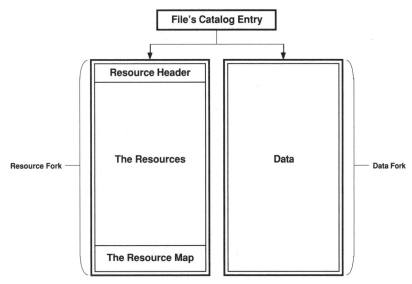

A file, showing both the data fork and the resource fork.

According to *Inside Macintosh*, a resource fork can contain, at most, 2,727 resources; the total size of a resource file cannot exceed 16MB; also as a rule of thumb, you shouldn't create more than 500 or so of the same resource type in the same resource fork. Current implementations of the Resource Manager store resources as linear lists and consequently, cannot access them randomly. This fact can really affect performance, especially when you write loops using `GetIndResource()` or `Get1IndResource()` because these routines have to scan the entire list for the given type in order to reach the resource with the index you provide. For more information, check out the Macintosh Tech Note *M.OV.Managerial Abuse*.

The resource map contains an entry for each resource in the file. A resource's entry contains information about the resource (such as its type, ID, and name) as well as an offset that specifies the resource's location within the file. Unless you're writing a resource editor, you won't have any use for the resource map in its disk-based form.

When your application opens a resource file, the file's resource map is copied into your application's heap. The memory-based copy of the resource map is just like the disk-based original, with one major difference. While the disk-based map uses an offset to each resource location, the memory-based copy replaces each offset with a handle that tells you whether the resource is currently loaded and, if so, tells you where to find it in memory. If the handle is `nil`, the resource hasn't been loaded yet. If the handle points to a master pointer with a value of `nil`, the resource was loaded, but has now been purged. Finally, if the master pointer is not `nil`, it points to the resource's location in memory.

Opening a Resource File

When your application starts up, you automatically have access to two sets of resources: the resources from the System file and the resources from your application file. If you need access to any other resources, you'll have to open the resource file yourself, using Resource Manager routines like `FSpOpenResFile()` and `HOpenResFile()`. Although there *are* other ways to open a resource file, these two calls should provide for all your resource-file opening needs.

Here's the prototype for `FSpOpenResFile()`:

```
short FSpOpenResFile( FSSpec *specPtr, SignedByte permission );
```

> When you're using a Resource Manager routine that does not return an error code (such as `FSpOpenResFile()`), call `ResError()` immediately after calling the routine in question:
>
> ```
> short ResError( void );
> ```
>
> `ResError()` returns an error code that describes the last Resource Manager routine called. To repeat, call `ResError()` immediately! Otherwise, other Toolbox routines may call the Resource Manager and replace the result you think you're getting.

`FSpOpenResFile()` opens the resource fork of the file described by the `FSSpec` parameter. The `FSSpec` was introduced as part of System 7's rewrite of the Standard File package. Before System 7, when you prompted the user for a file name you used the routines `SFGetFile()` and `SFPutFile()`. Under System 7, you'll call `StandardGetFile()` to ask the user to select a file and `StandardPutFile()` to allow the user to name a file. Both of these routines turn the user's reply into an `FSSpec`. `FSpOpenResFile()` is the perfect way to open a resource file selected by the user using either `StandardGetFile()` or `StandardPutFile()`.

Here's the prototype for `HOpenResFile()`:

```
short HOpenResFile( short vRefNum, long dirID,
        ConstStr255Param fName, char permission);
```

As you can see, `HOpenResFile()` lets you specify, as parameters, all the information that would normally be wrapped inside an `FSSpec`.

Creating a Resource File

If your resource file doesn't already exist, you can create a new one by calling `FSpCreateResFile()` or `HCreateResFile()`. It's important to note that a call to `HCreateResFile()` or `FSpCreateResFile()` *will* create a resource file, but *won't* open the file. You still must to open the file with a call to a routine such as `HOpenResFile()` or `FSpOpenResFile()`.

Here's the prototype for `FSpCreateResFile()`:

```
void  FSpCreateResFile( const FSSpec *specPtr, OSType creator,
            OSType fileType, ScriptCode scriptTag );
```

The first parameter is an `FSSpec` that specifies the name and location of the file. The next two parameters specify the file's creator and type. The last parameter specifies the local script code. Pass `nil` as the fourth parameter to specify the Roman script system.

Here's the prototype for `HCreateResFile()`:

```
void HCreateResFile( short vRefNum, long dirID,
            ConstStr255Param fileName );
```

Once again, this version is handy if you don't have an `FSSpec` allocated.

Closing a Resource File

No matter what method you use to open your resource file, you can close the file by passing its file reference number to `CloseResFile()`. Here's the prototype:

```
void CloseResFile( short rfRefNum );
```

When you use `CloseResFile()` to close a resource file, all the memory used by all the resources in the file is freed up. Of course, the resources in this file are no longer available, so be sure you don't make use of any handles that refer to these now-defunct resources.

Understanding the Resource-File Search Path

The Resource Manager maintains a list of each of your application's open resource files. The list always starts with the System file and your application file. When you open a resource file, it's added to the end of the list. When you close a resource file, the file is removed from the list.

One of your resource files is always known as the *current resource file.* When your application starts up, the application file is the current resource file. When you open a resource file, the newly opened file becomes the current resource file. You can call the routine UseResFile() to mark any open resource file as the current resource file. Here's how this works.

Each time the Resource Manager looks for a resource (say, in response to a GetResource() call), it searches each file in the application's open resource file list, *starting with the current resource file* and working backward through the list, stopping when either the resource is found or when the first file in the list (the System file) is searched.

This algorithm has an interesting (that is, bizarre) side effect. Suppose your application starts up and then opens resource file A. Figure 6.2 shows the Resource Manager's search path at this point. When you call GetResource(), the Resource Manager will first search file A for the requested resource, then your application's resource fork, and finally the System file (assuming it didn't find the resource already).

Figure 6.2

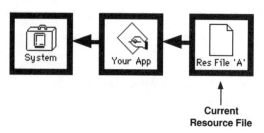

A sample search path, with three open resource files.

Now suppose you call UseResFile(), passing it your application file's file reference number (you'll see how to find this number later in this chapter). Figure 6.3 shows the new search path. Now when you call GetResource() the Resource Manager skips file A entirely!

Fine. You can live with this situation, right? But wait! Now suppose you open yet another resource file, named B. Figure 6.4 shows the new search path. Remember, you just opened B; you didn't call UseResFile() again. Not only is B now in the path, but A is back in as well.

FIGURE 6.3

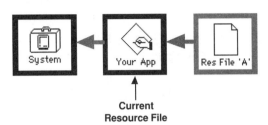

Current
Resource File

The search path after the application file is made the current resource file.

FIGURE 6.4

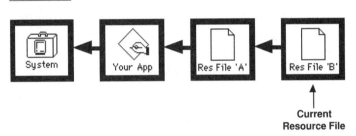

Current
Resource File

The search path after resource file B is opened.

The point is that when you made the application file the current resource file, resource file A wasn't deleted from the resource file list. When you opened resource file B, it was placed on the list right after A. At the same time, the current resource file pointer was reset to point to B, bringing A back into the search path.

> By the way, you can pass 0 to `UseResFile()` to make the System file the current resource file.

Calling Some Search Path–Related Routines

Why mess with your application's resource search path? The Resource Manager provides a set of routines designed to limit its search to the current resource file. For example, `Get1Resource()` is the "current resource file" version of `GetResource()`.

Suppose you design a custom resource to hold a window's size and location. Each time you create a new document, you add a 'wpos' resource with ID 128 to the document, describing the document's last screen position. When the user moves or resizes the document, you update the 'wpos' to reflect the new position. You might also add a 'wpos' with ID 128 to your application to store a document's default size and location.

Given that more than one document is open, how do you find a specific document's 'wpos' resource? How do you get to the application's 'wpos'? The answer, of course, is to call UseResFile().

At start-up, find your application's file reference number and squirrel it away somewhere. To get to the application's 'wpos' resource, pass the file reference number to UseResFile() and then make this call:

```
Handle   wposHandle;

wposHandle = Get1Resource( 'wpos', 128 );
```

When you open a document, you'll probably open its data fork to access the document's data, but you'll also have to open the resource fork to get at the document's 'wpos' resource. To retrieve a document's 'wpos' resource, pass its resource fork reference number to UseResFile() and then make your call to Get1Resource().

> A file's resource fork file reference number is never the same as its data fork file reference number. To open a data fork, use routines like FSpOpenDF() or HOpenDF(). To open a resource fork, call FSpOpenResFile() or HOpenResFile().

Some other "current resource file"–specific routines are as follows. Get1NamedResource() looks in the current resource file for the resource with the specified type and name. Call Count1Resources() to find out how many resources of a specified type are in the current resource file. Call Get1IndResource() to get one of those resources.

Here's some code that counts the number of 'PICT' resources in the current resource file and then retrieves and does something creative with each 'PICT':

```
short    count, i;
Handle   pic;

count = Count1Resources( 'PICT' );

for ( i=1; i<=count; i++ )
{
   pic = Get1IndResource( i );
   DoSomethingCreative( pic );
}
```

Adding a Resource to the Current Resource File

When you create a new resource, you'll need a handle to a block of memory containing the resource data, as well as the resource's type, ID, and name (if any). You can ask the Resource Manager to generate a unique ID for you by calling either UniqueID() or Unique1ID().

UniqueID() generates an ID that is unique across all open resource files (including the System file). Unique1ID() generates an ID that is unique in the current resource file. Once you generate the ID, you pass it, the resource's handle, and the resource type and name on to AddResource().

Here's a routine that turns a string into a 'STR ' resource and then adds the 'STR ' to the current resource file:

```
void  MakeStringResource( Str255 string );
{
   short    resID;
   Handle   resHandle;

   resHandle = NewHandle( (Size)( string[0] + 1 ) );

   for ( i=0; i<=string[0]; i++ )
      (*resHandle)[i] = string[ i ];

   resID = Unique1ID( 'STR ' );

   AddResource( resHandle, 'STR ', resID, string );
      /* Used the string as the 'STR ' name, though this
         adds to the size of the resource file. */
}
```

It's important to note that the resource's handle is just an ordinary handle before the call to AddResource(). AddResource() converts the handle to a "resource handle" (one that is recognized by the Resource Manager). By calling AddResource(), you transfer ownership of this block of memory to the Resource Manager.

Do not call DisposeHandle() on a resource handle. Remember, the Resource Manager owns all resource handles. If you free a resource handle, you're setting yourself up for a hard-to-track-down bug if the Resource Manager frees up the same handle.

Fortunately, the tool DoubleTrouble can catch this double-dispose in the act. DoubleTrouble, an INIT (written by Greg Marriott), kicks in each time DisposeHandle() is called. It compares the handle being freed to the handles already on the free list. If the handle has already been freed, DoubleTrouble drops into the debugger with an appropriate error message. You will find DoubleTrouble on Apple's monthly developer CDs (in the *Tool Chest Edition*). Check it out.

The call to `AddResource()` adds the resource to the resource map of the *current resource file*. Therefore, you must be sure that you've called `UseResFile()` or that the file in question is the most recent resource file you've opened.

The call to `AddResource()` *doesn't* write the resource out to a file, but it *does* mark the resource as having been changed (see the `resChanged` attribute, discussed later in the chapter). When the program exits, the resource will be written out to disk. If you want the resource written to disk immediately, pass the resource handle to `WriteResource()`.

`AddResource()` sets the `resChanged` attribute bit and clears all the others. Use `GetResAttrs()` and `SetResAttrs()` to set whichever bits you like before you call `WriteResource()`. We'll consider the resource attributes later in the chapter.

WHERE TO SAVE YOUR RESOURCE FILES

Imagine this scenario: You've just finished your newest work of genius, a brilliantly addictive game called Virtual Dentist. Before you send your golden master to the duplicators, you throw a copy on the server, daring Arjun and Priya, your quality assurance experts, to find even the smallest of bugs. Ha!

Here's where you stumble. You implemented the game's preferences as a sequence of resources, *saving these resources in the application file itself.* Suppose Arjun logs on to the server via AppleShare, runs the application, and then makes changes to the preferences. Per your design, the preference changes are saved in the application file on the server. Then, Priya logs on to the server, runs the application on her machine, and changes and saves the preferences. See the problem? Priya is going to clobber Arjun's preferences.

As you've probably guessed, the answer here is to use your application's resource fork for read-only resources. If a resource is user modifiable, you should store the resource in one of two places. First, if the resource is related to a specific document, store the resource in the

document's resource fork. For example, you might store a document
window's last position and size in the document's resource fork.

> Another reason to make resources stored in the application file read-only has to do with a user's backup strategy. If the application file never changes, the user will never need to back it up (except, perhaps, by making a copy of the original floppies).
>
> If all of a user's applications are stored in a single folder, that folder should be exempt from backup, thus freeing the user to back up documents, not applications!

Second, if the modifiable resource is at the application level, it
belongs in the `Preferences` folder, found inside the user's System Folder.
To find the `Preferences` folder, call `FindFolder()`:

```
#include <Folders.h>

OSErr    err;
short    foundVRefNum;
long     foundDirID;

err = FindFolder( kOnSystemDisk, kPreferencesFolderType,
    kCreateFolder,  &foundVRefNum, &foundDirID );
```

You should call `FindFolder()` any time you want to find a specific
System-related folder. The first parameter lets you specify a volume reference number, but you'll typically use the constant `kOnSystemDisk`. The
second parameter is a constant that specifies the folder of interest. All
the current folder constants are listed in Figure 6.5. The third parameter
is a constant that tells `FindFolder()` to create the folder if it doesn't
already exist (use `kDontCreateFolder` if you don't want to create the
folder). The fourth and fifth parameters are the folder's volume reference number and directory ID (which are returned by `FindFolder()`).

Once you find the `Preferences` folder, pass the volume reference
number and directory ID, along with your preferences file name, to
`FSMakeFSSpec()`:

```
OSErr FSMakeFSSpec( short vRefNum, long dirID,
    Str255 fileName, FSSpec *specPtr );
```

`FSMakeFSSpec()` turns the first three parameters into an `FSSpec`
(pass a pointer to your `FSSpec` as the fourth parameter) which you can
then pass to `FSpCreateResFile()` or `FSpOpenResFile()`.

FIGURE 6.5

FindFolder Constants	
kAppleMenuFolderType	Apple Menu Items
kControlPanelFolderType	ControlPanels
kDesktopFolderType	Desktop Folder
kExtensionFolderType	Extensions
kPreferencesFolderType	Preferences
kPrintMonitorDocsFolderType	PrintMonitor Documents
kWhereToEmptyTrashFolderType	Shared, Network Trash
kTrashFolderType	Single-user Trash
kStartupFolderType	Startup Items
kSystemFolderType	System Folder
kTemporaryFolderType	Temporary Items

FindFolder() constants and the folders they represent.

If you need more than one preferences file, create a directory in the `Preferences` folder by first calling `FSMakeFSSpec()` to create an `FSSpec` containing the directory name and info and then passing the `FSSpec` to `FSpDirCreate()`:

```
OSErr FSpDirCreate( FSSpec *specPtr, ScriptCode scriptTag,
                    long createdDirIDPtr );
```

The first parameter is a pointer to your newly created `FSSpec`. The second parameter is the same script code that you passed to `FSpCreateResFile()` (remember, pass nil for the default, Roman script system). `FSpDirCreate()` creates the new directory and returns a pointer to the new directory ID in the third parameter. You can use this directory ID to create an `FSSpec` for each of your preferences files.

Finding Your Application File

When you create a resource file in the `Preferences` folder, you get the information you need to build your `FSSpec` from `FindFolder()`. When you prompt the user for a document to open or save, you get the `FSSpec` directly from `StandardGetFile()` or `StandardPutFile()`. If you're opening a file in response to an Apple event, you get the `FSSpec` from the Apple event itself (see Chapter 2 for more info).

Although you'll probably never have a need to open your application's resource fork (since it's already opened for you), there are several cases where you might need to specify your application file's location. For example, if you want to make your application file the current

resource file, you must pass its resource file reference number to
`UseResFile()`.

One way to find your application's resource file reference number
is to call `CurResFile()` at initialization time (before you open any other
resource files), storing the return value in a global you can access later:

```
short CurResFile( void );
```

As its name implies, `CurResFile()` returns the file reference number of the current resource file.

An even better way to find your application file is to call
`GetAppParms()`:

```
void  GetAppParms( Str255 apName, short *resRefNumPtr,
                        Handle *parmsHandlePtr );
```

`GetAppParms()` returns information about your application in three
different parameters. The first parameter contains the name of your
application file. The second parameter contains the application's
resource file reference number, which you should store in a global for
later use. Finally, the third parameter is a handle to a block of Finder
information.

> The Finder information dates back to pre–System 7 days and con-
> tains information about the files selected in the Finder when your
> application was launched. Ignore this info and support the Required
> Apple event suite instead.

If you ever want to open your application file (or a file in your
application file's folder) explicitly, you'll need the file's volume reference
number, directory ID, and file name. You can get your application's file
name from `GetAppParms()`. The other two will take a bit of work.

First, you can turn a file reference number into a volume reference
number (the volume the file resides on) by passing it to `GetVRefNum()`:

```
OSErr GetVRefNum( short fRefNum, short *vRefNumPtr );
```

Then, given the file and volume reference numbers, you can call
`PBGetFCBInfo()` to get the file's directory ID:

```
OSErr PBGetFCBInfo( FCBPBPtr pbPtr, Boolean async );
```

Like all the PB calls, you have to allocate and fill in a parameter
block (in this case, an `FCBPBRec` struct) and then pass a pointer to the

parameter block as the first parameter. Here are the fields you need to set:

- Set `FCBPBPtr->ioCompletion` to `nil`.

- Set `FCBPBPtr->ioNamePtr` to `nil`.

- Set `FCBPBPtr->ioVRefNum` to the volume reference number you got from `GetVRefNum()`.

- Set `FCBPBPtr->ioRefNum` to the file reference number returned by `GetAppParms()`.

- Set `FCBPBPtr->ioFCBIndx` to 0.

When you get the parameter block back, the `FCBPBPtr->ioFCBParID` field will have the directory ID you're looking for. Now that you have your file's name, directory ID, and volume reference number, you can call routines like `HOpenResFile()` and `HCreateResFile()`.

RESOURCE ATTRIBUTES

At the beginning of the chapter, we talked about the resource map found in every resource file. In addition to a resource's type, ID, and name, each entry in the resource map contains eight attribute flags. Two of the flags are private. The other six correspond to the constants `resChanged`, `resPreload`, `resProtected`, `resLocked`, `resPurgeable`, and `resSysHeap` (Figure 6.6).

FIGURE 6.6

Resource Attributes	
resChanged	1 if ChangedResource() called since last time resource written back to disk
resPreload	1 if resource should be loaded as soon as resource fork is opened
resProtected	1 if resource is not to be modified
resLocked	1 if resource's handle should be locked when resource is loaded
resPurgeable	1 if resource's handle should be marked as purgeable when loaded
resSysHeap	1 if resource should be loaded into system heap instead of application's heap

Six resource attributes.

When you create a resource using ResEdit or Resorcerer, you can set five of the six resource attributes using checkboxes in each resource's Info window. Figure 6.7 shows a Resorcerer Info window with five checkboxes for `resPreload`, `resProtected`, `resLocked`, `resPurgeable`, and `resSysHeap`. The missing attribute is `resChanged`. Since you set `resChanged` to indicate that you've modified a resource, it doesn't make sense to set it in the file.

FIGURE 6.7

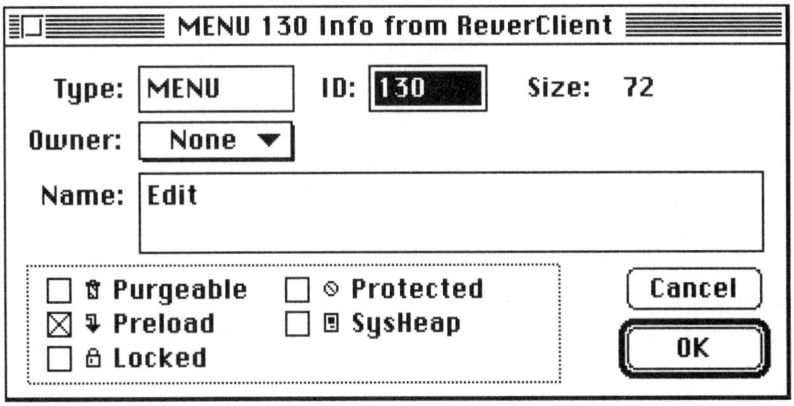

A Resorcerer Info window with five of the six resource attribute checkboxes.

Figure 6.8 shows a ResEdit Info window. Notice that ResEdit has the same five checkboxes as Resorcerer, plus an additional Compressed checkbox. The Compressed checkbox corresponds to one of the two private bits in the attribute byte. The System sets this bit when a resource is stored in a proprietary compressed format. The checkbox is for informational purposes only. You can't set the checkbox yourself (go ahead, try it!).

> Just because the Resorcerer screen shot doesn't show a Compressed checkbox, don't be fooled. When Resorcerer opens a resource file, it checks to see whether at least one resource has the compressed bit set. If it finds one, it shows the compressed attribute in all displays that list attributes (in a resource's Info window, for example).

Before we get to the resource attributes, let's take a quick look at the process of loading a resource into memory.

FIGURE 6.8

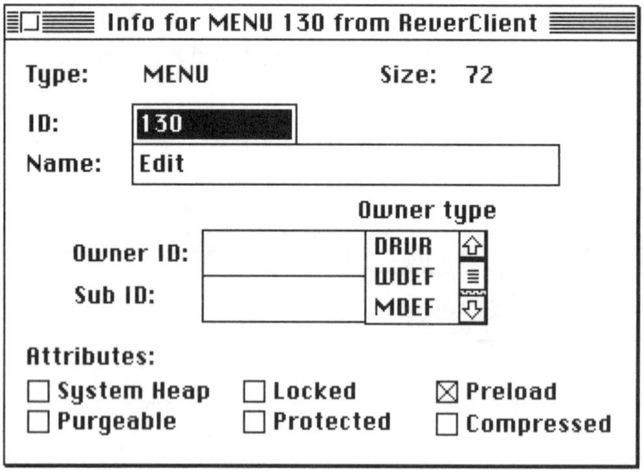

A ResEdit Info window, with the same five checkboxes as Resorcerer, plus a private, Compressed checkbox.

Loading a Resource

Before the Resource Manager loads a resource, it first examines the resource's handle in the resource map in memory. If the handle is `nil`, the resource has not yet been loaded. In this case, the Resource Manager checks the resource map in memory to see how large a block of memory is needed to accommodate the resource. The Resource Manager then allocates a handle of the right size and reads the resource in from disk.

Once the resource is read in, the handle is added to a table in the resource map. Once the handle is added to this table, the Resource Manager owns the handle. As mentioned earlier, you should never call `DisposeHandle()` on a handle owned by the Resource Manager.

The proper way to remove a resource from memory is to pass the resource's handle to `ReleaseResource()`. `ReleaseResource()` deallocates the handle and *removes it from the table in the resource map*. Next, `ReleaseResource()` sets the resource's handle in the resource map in memory to `nil`. Once a handle is passed to `ReleaseResource()`, you shouldn't use it again.

If you want to convert a resource to a regular handle and *remove the resource from the resource map*, call `DetachResource()`. Once you call `DetachResource()`, you're responsible for the handle and can dispose of it at your leisure. Just like `ReleaseResource()`, `DetachResource()` removes the handle from the resource file's table of resource handles. Unlike `ReleaseResource()`, `DetachResource()` doesn't deallocate the handle first.

Both `ReleaseResource()` and `DetachResource()` set the resource's handle in the resource map to `nil`.

If the handle is not `nil`, the Resource Manager follows the handle to its master pointer. If the master pointer is `nil`, the resource has already been loaded and added to the resource handle table. It has been purged by the Memory Manager. In this case, the Resource Manager will have to reload the resource.

Notice that calling `ReleaseResource()` is slightly more memory efficient than purging a resource. `ReleaseResource()` releases the memory as well as the master pointer. Purging leaves the master pointer allocated and sets its value to `nil`.

Finally, if the handle is not `nil` and the master pointer is not `nil`, the Resource Manager knows that the resource is properly loaded and does nothing.

With this model in mind, let's now consider the resource attributes.

Setting Resource Attributes

resChanged
When the resource map is loaded from disk, all the `resChanged` bits will be set to 0. When a resource changes in memory, pass the resource's handle to `ChangedResource()`. `ChangedResource()` sets the resource's `resChanged` bit and preallocates disk space to accommodate the changed resource.

Every time you call `ChangedResource()`, the Resource Manager allocates a small chunk of disk space (just until the resource file is closed). To avoid running out of disk space, call `WriteResource()` every once in a while to update the resource on disk and deallocate any extra disk space.

When a resource file is closed, if any of its resources have changed, the Resource Manager copies the resource map back to disk and copies all changed resources back to disk. So that your changes are saved when the resource file is updated, be sure to mark your resource as nonpurgeable as soon as you call `ChangedResource()`. Clearing the `resPurgeable` bit will *not* do this! Instead, you'll need to pass the resource handle to `HNoPurge()`. You can mark the resource as purgeable (by calling `HPurge()`) once you either close the resource file or write the resource back out via `WriteResource()` or `UpdateResFile()`. `UpdateResFile()` writes all the resources marked as changed back out to the resource file.

> Always use `ChangedResource()` to mark a resource as changed. Never access the bit directly via `GetResAttrs()` and `SetResAttrs()`. You *can* use `SetResAttrs()` to update any of a resource's other attributes. Don't touch Apple's private bits, though!

When you create a new resource via `AddResource()`, `AddResource()` **automatically calls** `ChangedResource()`.

resPreload

When you open a resource file, the file's resource map is copied into the application heap. Next, the Resource Manager checks each resource to see whether its `resPreload` bit is set. If the `resPreload` bit is set, the resource is immediately loaded into memory.

There are several good reasons for marking a resource as `resPreload`. One reason has to do with memory efficiency. If your resource will take a significant amount of memory, you might want to preload it. Preloading helps minimize heap fragmentation by loading your memory-intensive resources at one end of the heap. At the same time, it gives you a better picture of how much memory is at your disposal once your program starts running.

Another reason to preload a resource has to do with performance. Marking a processor-intensive resource like 'PICT' or 'snd' as preload lets you avoid awkward disk accesses in the middle of a performance-sensitive portion of your program. For example, if you're trying to play a sound the moment the user takes a specific action, you don't want the Resource Manager to pick that exact instant to have to do a time-consuming disk access because the sound resource it needs isn't loaded yet.

resProtected

The `resProtected` flag is sort of a poor man's read-only bit. It's not used very often. Marking a resource as protected prevents the Resource Manager from changing the resource's ID or name, from changing the resource's contents, or from removing the resource.

The `resProtected` bit is simple to defeat. You can turn it on and off using `SetResAttrs()`.

resLocked

When a resource is loaded, the Resource Manager checks to see whether the `resLocked` bit is set. If it is, the resource's handle is locked, locking the resource in place in the heap. Setting this bit doesn't lock the resource; it only causes the resource to be locked the next time it is loaded. It's important to understand that the `resLocked` bit is not the same as a handle's `isLocked` bit. The `resLocked` bit is in the resource map, not in the handle.

> Note that 680x0 code resources are always locked when they are in use.

resPurgeable

When a resource is loaded, the Resource Manager checks to see whether the `resPurgeable` bit is set. If it is, the resource's handle is marked as purgeable. As is the case with the `resLocked` bit, the `resPurgeable` bit is not the same as a handle's `isPurgeable` bit. Setting the `resPurgeable` bit doesn't affect the resource until the next time it is loaded.

Note that a locked handle cannot be purged. In other words, the `resLocked` bit overrides the `resPurgeable` bit.

If a resource is purgeable, it is up to you to make sure the resource has not been purged before you reference it. Remember, a resource's master pointer will be set to `nil` when a resource is purged. Use `LoadResource()` to bring a possibly purged resource back into memory.

`'MENU'` resources should not be purgeable (unless you plan on bypassing the standard Toolbox menu-handling mechanism).

Other than `'MENU'` resources, feel free to set any resource's `resPurgeable` bit. Remember, this bit just tells you that the resource will be marked as purgeable when it is loaded. At any time, you can guarantee that a resource will be in memory by loading the resource using `LoadResource()` and then immediately passing the resource's handle to `HLock()` or `HNoPurge()`.

If you have a large resource and you expect to use it frequently, set the `resPreload` bit and clear the `resPurgeable` bit. If you're going to load a resource and immediately make a local copy of the resource data, then go ahead and make the resource purgeable.

When in doubt, mark the resource as either locked or purgeable. It's better to safely run out of memory than to crash. For example, with error message strings, especially those that warn of "out-of-memory" errors, you definitely should read them in early (preferably pre-loaded) and then mark them as nonpurgeable until you don't need them anymore.

A Sample Program

The sample program StringLister serves two purposes. On one hand, it contains a useful set of 'STR#' management routines (courtesy of Doug McKenna) that you can use in your own programs. On the other hand, it serves as a sort of Resource Manager sandbox, providing an environment that you can use to test out your own resource code.

Running StringLister

Go into the Projects folder and then into the StringLister subfolder. Double-click on the StringLister application. A menu bar will appear featuring the , File, and Edit menus. The two items of interest are in the File menu.

Select Create 'STR#' File… from the File menu. A Standard File dialog that asks you to specify a file name and location will appear (Figure 6.9). Pick your spot, and then press the Save button.

Figure 6.9

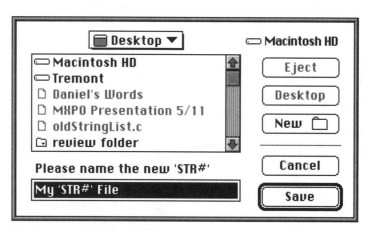

Naming your new resource file.

StringLister will create a new file with a creator of 'RSED' and a type of 'rsrc' (see the icon in Figure 6.10). Go to the Finder and double-click on your newly created file. ResEdit will launch and open your new resource file.

Your resource file contains a single 'STR#' resource, with an ID of 128. Figure 6.11 shows the list of strings that make up the string list resource.

FIGURE 6.10

My 'STR#' File

Your newly created resource file, as seen in the Finder.

FIGURE 6.11

```
▤▢▥▥▥▥▥ STR# ID = 128 from My 'STR#' File ▥▥▥
NumStrings      4
   1) *****
   The string    │This string should now be first!│
   2) *****
   The string    │String 1                        │
   3) *****
   The string    │String 2                        │
   4) *****
   The string    │String 3                        │
   5) *****
```

The list of strings in the 'STR#' resource created by StringLister.

Quit ResEdit and go back to StringLister. This time, select Create Prefs File from the File menu. StringLister will go out to your boot drive and find your Preferences folder, creating a file called StringLister Prefs in the Preferences folder. StringLister Prefs contains the same 'STR#' resource as your previous resource file. Double-click on it to check it out in ResEdit. Quit ResEdit once you're done admiring your handiwork.

One last thing. Now that you've already created a `StringLister Prefs` file, select Create Prefs File from the File menu one more time. StringLister should put up an alert telling you that the preferences file already exists.

Let's take a look at the source code.

The StringLister Source Code

StringLister is constructed from two different source code files. `StringList.c` contains a collection of 'STR#' management routines. `StringListerMain.c` is the heart and soul of StringLister and makes use of some of the routines from `StringList.c`. If you have a project that uses 'STR#' resources, just copy `StringList.c` into your project folder and use the routines as is.

StringListerMain.c

`StringListerMain.c` starts by including the files `<Folders.h>`, which contains all the constants used by `FindFolder()`, and `<GestaltEqu.h>`, which contains all the constants used by `Gestalt()`.

```
#include <Folders.h>
#include <GestaltEqu.h>
```

We'll get to these constants as they appear in the code:

```
#define kBaseResID          128
#define kMessageALRTid      128
#define kAboutALRTid        129

#define kSleep              60L
#define kNilFilterProc       0L

#define mApple              kBaseResID
#define iAbout              1

#define mFile               kBaseResID+1
#define iCreateFile          1
#define iCreatePrefs        2
#define iQuit               4
```

Only one global, `gDone`, is set to `false` when it's time to drop out of the main event loop:

```
Boolean    gDone;
```

Here are the function prototypes:

```
void      ToolboxInit( void );
void      MenuBarInit( void );
void      DoGestalt( void );
void      EventLoop( void );
void      DoEvent( EventRecord *eventPtr );
void      HandleMouseDown( EventRecord *eventPtr );
void      HandleMenuChoice( long menuChoice );
void      HandleAppleChoice( short item );
void      HandleFileChoice( short item );
void      CreateFile( void );
void      CreatePrefsFile( void );
void      WriteStringsToResFile( FSSpec *specPtr );
void      CreateStringList( void );
void      DoMessage( Str255 theString );
void      DoError( Str255 theString );
```

Here are the prototypes of the public functions from StringList.c, along with a typedef we'll need:

```
typedef Handle SLHandle;

SLHandle NewStringList(short resID);
SLHandle GetStringList(short resID);
SLHandle ReleaseStringList(SLHandle list);
Boolean  GetStringCopy(SLHandle list, short index, Str255 str);
Boolean  InsertStringInList(SLHandle list, short index, Str255 str);
void     DeleteStringsFromList(SLHandle list, short from, short count);
```

main() initializes the Toolbox, sets up the menu bar, checks to make sure some vital features are available, and then enters the main event loop:

```
/****************************** main ********/

void  main( void )
{
   ToolboxInit();
   MenuBarInit();
   DoGestalt();

   EventLoop();
}
```

There's nothing unusual about ToolboxInit() or MenuBarInit():

```
/******************************** ToolboxInit */

void ToolboxInit( void )
```

```
{
    InitGraf( &qd.thePort );
    InitFonts();
    InitWindows();
    InitMenus();
    TEInit();
    InitDialogs( 0L );
    InitCursor();
}


/***************** MenuBarInit **********************/

void  MenuBarInit( void )
{
    Handle        menuBar;
    MenuHandle    menu;

    menuBar = GetNewMBar( kBaseResID );

    if ( menuBar == NULL )
        DoError( "\pCouldn't load the MBAR resource..." );

    SetMenuBar( menuBar );

    menu = GetMHandle( mApple );
    AddResMenu( menu, 'DRVR' );

    DrawMenuBar();
}
```

DoGestalt() **checks to be sure that both the new Standard File package and** FindFolder() **are available:**

```
/***************** DoGestalt **********************/

void  DoGestalt( void )
{
    long response;
    OSErr   err;
```

We start by checking to see whether Gestalt() **is available:**

```
    err = Gestalt( gestaltVersion, &response );

    if ( err != noErr )
        DoError( "\pGestalt() is not available..." );
```

Next, we check for FindFolder()**:**

```
    err = Gestalt( gestaltFindFolderAttr, &response );

    if ( err != noErr )
       DoError( "\pError calling Gestalt()..." );

    if ( ! (response & (1L << gestaltFindFolderPresent)) )
       DoError( "\pThis machine does not support FindFolder()..." );

    err = Gestalt( gestaltStandardFileAttr, &response );
```

And finally, we check for the new Standard File routines:

```
    if ( err != noErr )
       DoError( "\pError calling Gestalt()..." );

    if ( ! (response & (1L << gestaltStandardFile58)) )
       DoError( "\pThe new Standard File routines \
           are not supported by this OS!" );
}
```

EventLoop(), DoEvent(), and HandleMouseDown() don't do anything unusual:

```
/***************************** EventLoop *********/

void  EventLoop( void )
{
    EventRecord     event;

    gDone = false;
    while ( gDone == false )
    {
       if ( WaitNextEvent( everyEvent, &event, kSleep, NULL ) )
          DoEvent( &event );
    }
}



/******************************** DoEvent      */

void  DoEvent( EventRecord *eventPtr )
{
    char     theChar;

    switch ( eventPtr->what )
    {
       case mouseDown:
          HandleMouseDown( eventPtr );
          break;
```

```
      case keyDown:
      case autoKey:
         theChar = eventPtr->message & charCodeMask;
         if ( (eventPtr->modifiers & cmdKey) != 0 )
            HandleMenuChoice( MenuKey( theChar ) );
         break;
   }
}


/*********************************** HandleMouseDown */

void  HandleMouseDown( EventRecord *eventPtr )
{
   WindowPtr      window;
   short       thePart;
   long        menuChoice;

   thePart = FindWindow( eventPtr->where, &window );

   switch ( thePart )
   {
   case inMenuBar:
      menuChoice = MenuSelect( eventPtr->where );
      HandleMenuChoice( menuChoice );
      break;
   case inSysWindow :
      SystemClick( eventPtr, window );
      break;
   }
}
```

HandleMenuChoice() **dispatches a selection from the** ■ **and File menus:**

```
/***************** HandleMenuChoice *********************/

void  HandleMenuChoice( long menuChoice )
{
   short menu;
   short item;

   if ( menuChoice != 0 )
   {
      menu = HiWord( menuChoice );
      item = LoWord( menuChoice );

      switch ( menu )
      {
```

```
            case mApple:
                HandleAppleChoice( item );
                break;
            case mFile:
                HandleFileChoice( item );
                break;
        }
        HiliteMenu( 0 );
    }
}
```

`HandleAppleChoice()` **handles the About alert or any other item selected from the menu:**

```
/***************** HandleAppleChoice ********************/

void   HandleAppleChoice( short item )
{
    MenuHandle   appleMenu;
    Str255       accName;
    short        accNumber;

    switch ( item )
    {
        case iAbout:
            NoteAlert( kAboutALRTid, NULL );
            break;
        default:
            appleMenu = GetMHandle( mApple );
            GetItem( appleMenu, item, accName );
            accNumber = OpenDeskAcc( accName );
            break;
    }
}
```

`HandleFileChoice()` **dispatches a selection from the File menu.**

```
/***************** HandleFileChoice ********************/

void  HandleFileChoice( short item )
{
    switch ( item )
    {
        case iCreateFile:
            CreateFile();
            break;
        case iCreatePrefs:
            CreatePrefsFile();
            break;
```

```
        case iQuit:
            gDone = true;
            break;
    }
}
```

CreateFile() is called when you select Create 'STR#' File... from the File menu. First, StandardPutFile() is called to prompt the user for the name and location of the new resource file:

```
/***************** CreateFile *******************/

void  CreateFile( void )
{
    StandardFileReply   reply;
```

The first parameter is a string that appears above the editable text field. The second parameter is the default string that appears *in* the editable text field. The third parameter is the address of the StandardFileReply, the structure that describes the file that was ultimately described by the user:

```
    StandardPutFile( "\p'STR#' file name:",
                "\pMy 'STR#' File", &reply );
```

If the user presses the Cancel button, reply.sfGood is false and we just return without creating the new file:

```
    if ( ! reply.sfGood )
        return;
```

If the user presses Save, we pass the FSSpec that was created to WriteStringsToResFile():

```
    WriteStringsToResFile( &(reply.sfFile) );
}
```

CreatePrefsFile() is called when you select Create Prefs File from the File menu. CreatePrefsFile() doesn't prompt you for a new resource file name. Instead, it uses FindFolder() to find the Preferences folder and creates the file there:

```
/***************** CreatePrefsFile *******************/

void  CreatePrefsFile( void )
{
```

```
OSErr err;
short foundVRefNum;
long  foundDirID;
FSSpec   spec;
```

This call to `FindFolder()` looks on the System disk (the disk with the current System Folder on it) for the current `Preferences` folder. It creates the `Preferences` folder if it doesn't already exist. Finally, `FindFolder()` returns the `Preferences` folder's volume reference number and directory ID:

```
err = FindFolder( kOnSystemDisk, kPreferencesFolderType,
        kCreateFolder, &foundVRefNum, &foundDirID );

if ( err != noErr )
{
   DoMessage( "\pError finding preferences folder!" );
   return;
}
```

The call to `FSMakeFSSpec()` turns the volume reference number, directory ID, and the specified file name into an `FSSpec`, which we then pass on to `WriteStringsToResFile()`, just as we did in the routine `CreateFile()`:

```
err = FSMakeFSSpec( foundVRefNum, foundDirID,
        "\pStringLister Prefs", &spec );

if ( err != fnfErr )
{
   DoMessage( "\pPrefs file already exists!" );
   return;
}

WriteStringsToResFile( &spec );
}
```

`WriteStringsToResFile()` starts by using `FSSpec` to create a new resource file:

```
/***************** WriteStringsToResFile ******************/

void  WriteStringsToResFile( FSSpec *specPtr )
{
   short refNum, err;
```

In addition to the FSSpec, FSpCreateResFile() takes a file creator, type, and script code. Passing a script code of nil specifies the default, Roman scripting system. Immediately after calling FSpCreateResFile(), we'll call ResError() to make sure the resource file was created properly. If the file already exists, we'll get an error code of dupFNErr. To force this error to happen, create the file and then create the file again in the same folder with the exact same name.

```
err = ResError();

if ( err == dupFNErr )
{
   DoMessage( "\pFile already exists!" );
   return;
}
```

If there is some other problem, we print this error message:

```
if ( err != noErr )
{
   DoMessage( "\pError creating resource file!" );
   return;
}
```

Once the file is created, we open it by passing the FSSpec to FSpOpenResFile().We open the file for both reading and writing, even though, in this case, we'll only be writing to the file:

```
refNum = FSpOpenResFile( specPtr, fsRdWrPerm );
```

If FSpOpenResFile() encounters any problems opening the file, it returns -1; otherwise, it returns a reference number for the newly opened file:

```
if ( refNum == -1 )
{
   DoMessage( "\pError opening new resource file!" );
   return;
}
```

Once the file is open, we call CreateStringList() to create a new string list resource. Next, we call CloseResFile() to close the resource file, which also has the effect of writing the string list resource back out to disk.

```
   CreateStringList();

   CloseResFile( refNum );

   .
   if ( ResError() != noErr )
      DoMessage( "\pError closing resource file!" );
}
```

CreateStringList() **makes use of Doug McKenna's string list utility routines to create a** 'STR#' **resource with an ID of 128. We insert three
strings, right in a row, and then insert a fourth string at the beginning of
the resource. When you open the newly created file using your favorite
resource editor, you should see something close to what was shown in
earlier Figure 6.11:**

> Spend some time playing with this routine. For example, rewrite the
> code to delete some strings from an existing resource. Or, try writing
> a 'STR#' resource browser that lets you scroll through and edit all the
> 'STR#' resources in a file.

```
/**************** CreateStringList ******************/

void  CreateStringList( void )
{
   SLHandle list;

   list = NewStringList( kBaseResID );

   InsertStringInList( list, 1, "\pString 1" );
   InsertStringInList( list, 2, "\pString 2" );
   InsertStringInList( list, 3, "\pString 3" );
   InsertStringInList( list, 1, "\pThis string should now be first!" );
}
```

DoMessage() **and** DoError() **each take a string parameter that
they display in an error message alert.** DoError() **exits the program
once the message is displayed, while** DoMessage() **just returns to the
calling routine:**

```
/**************** DoMessage ******************/

void  DoMessage( Str255 theString )
{
   ParamText( theString, "\p", "\p", "\p" );

   NoteAlert( kMessageALRTid, kNilFilterProc );
}
```

```
/***************** DoError *******************/

void  DoError( Str255 theString )
{
    ParamText( theString, "\p", "\p", "\p" );

    StopAlert( kMessageALRTid, kNilFilterProc );

    ExitToShell();
}
```

StringList.c

Since it was designed to be reused, `StringList.c` is heavily com-
mented. However, as we walk through the source code, let's ignore the
comments and focus on the routines.

All 'STR#' resources follow the same format. They start with a
2-byte word that specifies the number of strings in the resource.
Immediately following are the strings themselves, one after another,
with no padding. Each string is a standard pascal string — a length
byte, followed by that many bytes of string.

`StringList.c` starts with two `typedef`s that implement the 'STR#'
format. The first implements a 'STR#' resource in memory. Although
the structure only allocates a single byte for string storage, that allocation will be corrected once the actual number of bytes of needed
string storage is calculated. The correction is done by passing the
`SLHandle` along with its new size to `SetHandleSize()`:

```
typedef struct
{
    short     count;
    Byte      startOfStrings[1];
} StringList, **SLHandle;
```

The second `typedef` creates a type whose size can be used to
create a new, empty string list structure in memory:

```
typedef struct
{
    short     count;
} EmptyStringList;
```

The following macro looks weird if it appears on the left side of
an assignment statement, but it does provide an easier-on-the-eye way
to set or get the number of strings in a list:

```
#define NumberOfStrings(list) ( (*list)->count )
```

Here are the prototypes for the routines you'll use in your own code. Copy this list into your header file, as appropriate:

```
SLHandle NewStringList(short resID);
SLHandle GetStringList(short resID, short *whyNot);
void     ReleaseStringList(SLHandle *list);
Boolean  GetStringCopy(SLHandle list, short index, Str255 str);
Boolean  InsertStringInList(SLHandle list, short index, Str255 str);
void     DeleteStringsFromList(SLHandle list, short from, short count);
```

These routines are private to `StringList.c`; you'll never call them directly:

```
Byte     *GetStringAddr(SLHandle list, short index);
long     IndexToOffset(SLHandle list, short index);
```

`GetStringList()` tries to retrieve the 'STR#' with the specified resource ID from the current resource file. `whyNot` points to an error code that tells you what went wrong if `GetStringList()` returns `nil`:

```
SLHandle GetStringList( short resID, short *whyNot )
{
    SLHandle list;
```

Note that we call `Get1Resource()` so that we search only the current resource file. Feel free to change this code if you need to search your whole resource file list:

```
    list = (SLHandle)Get1Resource( 'STR#', resID );
    *whyNot = ResError();
```

For some reason, `ResError()` doesn't return an error if `Get1Resource()` can't find the resource—in which case, we have to set `whyNot` to `resNotFound` ourselves:

```
    if ( (list == nil) && (*whyNot == noErr) )
        *whyNot = resNotFound;
```

If some value is returned and an error is returned (or for some strange reason the resource is purged), return `nil`:

```
    if ( list != nil )
    {
        if ( *whyNot!=noErr || *list==nil)
```

```
        list = nil;
    }

    return( list );
}
```

NewStringList() **tries to load the specified** 'STR#' **resource. If the resource doesn't exist,** NewStringList() **creates a new one:**

```
SLHandle NewStringList( short resID )
{
    SLHandle list;
    short    whyNot;
```

First, we call GetStringList() **to see whether the resource exists:**

```
list = GetStringList(resID, &whyNot);
```

If the list isn't loaded because it doesn't exist, we make a new one by calling NewHandleClear(). NewHandleClear() **is just like** NewHandle() **except that it fills the new block with zeros:**

```
if (list == nil)
{
    if (whyNot == resNotFound)
    {
        list = (SLHandle)NewHandleClear( sizeof(EmptyStringList) );
        if (list != nil)
        {
```

If the new list is created properly, we turn it into a resource using AddResource(). **To save space,** "\p" **has been used for the resource name. Remember, the resource won't be added to the file until we either update or close the resource file:**

```
AddResource((Handle)list,'STR#',resID,"\p");
```

If we have a problem adding the resource, we dispose of the handle and set list **to** nil **to be returned later:**

```
        if (ResError() != noErr)
        {
            // Problem: back out and return nil
            DisposeHandle((Handle)list);
            list = nil;
        }
    }
}
```

If `GetStringList()` returns any other error, we just leave `list` as `nil` and return it that way:

```
     else
     {
     }
  }
```

If the resource already exists, we replace it with a new, empty string. You might want to change this code to suit your needs. For example, you might want to call `Unique1ID()` and generate a new resource with that ID, rather than overwriting an existing resource. For now, `NewStringList()` creates a new 'STR#' resource with the specified ID, whether it already exists or not:

```
   else
   {
      // Already exists and loaded:
      //   don't muck with handle itself, but zero its contents
      SetHandleSize( (Handle)list, sizeof(EmptyStringList) );

      NumberOfStrings(list) = 0;

      // And ensure that it gets written out in current form later
      ChangedResource((Handle)list);
   }

   return( list );
}
```

`ReleaseStringList()` calls `ReleaseResource()` to free up any memory allocated by the list. It also includes a nice safety precaution. By setting the handle to `nil`, we ensure that the list doesn't get released twice:

```
void ReleaseStringList(SLHandle *list)
{
   if ( list!=nil && *list!=nil )
   {
      ReleaseResource( (Handle)(*list) );
      *list = nil;
   }
}
```

`GetStringAddr()` returns the address of the start of the specified string:

```
static Byte *GetStringAddr(SLHandle list, short index)
{
    short len; Byte *p;
```

We start by setting p to the beginning of the first string (which should be 2 bytes into the struct):

```
p = (*list)->startOfStrings;
```

This while loop skips through index - 1 strings. Each time through the loop, you'll first skip the length byte and then skip len bytes to skip to the beginning of the next string. Note that if you pass in an illegal index, you're in trouble.

```
while (--index > 0)
{
len = *p++;
p += len;
}
```

Once we get to the string we want, we return its address. Note that this address is valid only until the Memory Manager moves the 'STR#' resource in memory, so be careful!

```
return( p );
}
```

IndexToOffset() converts an index to an offset in bytes from the beginning of the list:

```
static long IndexToOffset(SLHandle list, short index)
{
    long offset;
```

If the index is 1 or less, we return the size of a short. In other words, the smallest offset has to at least skip over the 2 bytes that specify the number of strings in the list:

```
if ( index <= 1 )
    offset = sizeof( (*list)->count );
```

If the index is greater than the number of strings in the list, we return an offset equal to the size of the string list, putting us right at the end of the list:

```
else if ( index > NumberOfStrings( list ) )
    offset = GetHandleSize( (Handle)list );
```

If the index is greater than 1 and legal, we subtract the list's starting address from the address of the begining of the indexed string:

```
else
    offset = ( GetStringAddr( list,index ) - (Byte *)(*list) );

return( offset );
}
```

`GetStringCopy()` **returns a copy of the specified string:**

```
Boolean GetStringCopy(SLHandle list, short index, Str255 str)
{
    register short len;
    register Byte *src, *dst;
```

If the index is invalid, we turn `str` into a zero-length string and **return** `false`:

```
    if ( list==nil || index<=0 || index>NumberOfStrings(list) )
    {
        str[0] = 0;
        return( FALSE );
    }
```

Otherwise, we set `src` to point to the beginning of the indexed string and `dst` to point to the beginning of the destination string and then copy `len` bytes from `src` to `dst` and **return** `true`:

```
    src = GetStringAddr(list,index); // src points to non-locked memory

    len = *src + 1;                  // Number of bytes to copy (256 max)
    dst = (Byte *)str;               // Where to place copy
    while (len- > 0)                 // For all bytes...
        *dst++ = *src++;             //    copy 'em on over

    return( TRUE );
}
```

`InsertStringInList()` **inserts a string into the list at the specified index. The string list handle is resized to accommodate the new string, and all strings after the insert are copied after the inserted string:**

```
Boolean InsertStringInList(SLHandle list, short index, Str255 str)
{
    short numStrings,len;
    long  size,offset,leftover;
    Byte *p;
```

If the list is `nil`, we return `false` (Just a reality check):

```
if ( list == nil )
  return( FALSE );
```

`numStrings` is the number of strings in the list, `size` is the size of the list in bytes, and `len` is the number of bytes occupied by the "to be inserted" string (which includes the length byte):

```
numStrings = NumberOfStrings( list );
size = GetHandleSize( (Handle)list );
len = 1 + *str;
```

Next, `offset` is set to the number of bytes into the list where the insertion will take place:

```
offset = IndexToOffset(list,index);
```

The handle is resized to accommodate the extra `len` bytes of the inserted string:

```
SetHandleSize((Handle)list,size+len);
```

If `MemError()` returns `noErr`, then we know the handle was resized correctly:

```
if (MemError() == noErr)
{
```

At this point, `size` is the size of the list before the resize. `leftover` is the number of bytes that need to be moved to make room for the new string. `p` is set to the address of the first byte to be moved. The call to `BlockMove()` moves `leftover` bytes from the insert point to the insert point plus the size of the new string:

```
leftover = size - offset;
p = ((Byte *)(*list)) + offset;
BlockMove(p,p+len,leftover);
```

Next, the string (including the length byte) is copied into the list at the insert point:

```
BlockMove(str,p,len);
```

Finally, the 2 bytes at the beginning of the list that hold the number of strings in the list are incremented to account for the new string. Doesn't the macro call on the left side of the += look weird?

```
    NumberOfStrings(list) += 1;
    return( true );
}

return( false );      // No room at the innsert
}
```

DeleteStringsFromList() **deletes** count **strings from the list, start-ing at the index specified in** from:

```
void DeleteStringsFromList(SLHandle list, short from, short count)
{
    long  size, fromOffset, toOffset, bytesToDelete;
    Byte  *p, *dst;
    short numStrings, len;
```

Another reality check follows:

```
if ( list==nil || from<=0 || count<=0 )
    return;
```

The next block of code makes sure count **is a legal value. If we try to delete more strings than are in the list, we clip** count **to the largest possible value. If clipping reduces** count **to 0 or less, we just return with-out deleting anything.**

```
numStrings = NumberOfStrings(list) + 1;

if ( (from+count) > numStrings )
{
    count = numStrings - from;
    if (count <= 0)
        return;
}
```

Once we make any necessary adjustments to count, **we then make sure the word that holds the number of strings in the list is accurate:**

```
NumberOfStrings(list) -= count;
```

Next, we set p **and** dst **to the address of the first string to be deleted and** fromOffset **to the number of bytes from the beginning of the list to the beginning of the first string to be deleted:**

```
p = dst = GetStringAddr( list, from );
fromOffset = p - ((Byte *)(*list));
```

Then, we step through the list, placing p at the end of the last string to be deleted. toOffset is the offset to the end of the last string to be deleted, and bytesToDelete is the number of bytes to delete from the list:

```
while (count- > 0)
{
    len = *p++;
    p += len;
}

toOffset = p - ((Byte *)(*list));

bytesToDelete = toOffset - fromOffset;
```

Finally, we move the block of bytes from the end of the deletion to the end of the list back over the bytes to be deleted and then resize the list handle accordingly:

```
size = GetHandleSize( (Handle)list );
BlockMove( p, dst, size - toOffset );

SetHandleSize( (Handle)list, size - bytesToDelete );
}
```

SUMMARY

There's much more to the Resource Manager than can be covered in a single chapter. If you have some specific issues that you would like me to deal with in future editions, drop me a line (my e-mail address is in Chapter 1) and let me know. In the meantime, if you have any questions, you can turn to the Resource Manager chapter of *Inside Macintosh: More Macintosh Toolbox*.

BIOGRAPHY

Douglas McKenna wrote his first computer program in 1969 and his first interactive graphics program in 1973, and he has continued programming (primarily in C) for the last two decades. The many large, interactive software applications and libraries that Doug has designed and implemented include an interactive graphic calculus explorer (1976); an adaptive telephone network simulator (1977); a C-to-Fortran source code translator (FabFor, 1978); IBM Research's first full-featured, bitmap font editor (McEdit, 1981); a PDP-11 Unix full-screen source code editor (EASE: Another Screen Editor, 1982); an early PostScript interpreter clone (1985); a graphical taxonomic database editor now being used to reclassify mammals (Unitaxon, 1989); significant portions of a recently released music notation editor (Nightingale, 1993); and all of his Eddy-award-winning Mac resource editor, Resorcerer, on which he has been working since his first ResEdit crash in 1987 and to which he is currently making further enhancements. A labor of love, Resorcerer is now in widespread use by professional Macintosh programmers and localizers around the world as a replacement for ResEdit.

For many years, Doug also worked as a computer artist, creating mathematical designs based on geometric fractal tiling patterns. His art shows in various parts of the country were entitled "Mathemaesthetics," an invented word that has since become the name of his software company. Like many computerists, Doug loves puns, anagrams, and other wordplay, and he is an accomplished piano player whose hobby is composing his own piano pieces. When not nursing an overused carpal tunnel while exploring the inner world of computers, Doug enjoys the outdoors of Boulder, Colorado, with his wife, Judith Houlding, and their three children, Caitlin, Alison, and Ian.

TOOLBOX
POTPOURRI

Chapter

7

Each of the previous chapters has been dedicated exclusively to a single topic. This chapter is a programmer's potpourri of useful tips and techniques that have been gathered from friends and colleagues. We'll begin with a pair of programs that will familiarize you with QuickTime, and then we'll move on to the Drag Manager, a cool directory scanner, some "smart-quote" routines, and a few Finder scripts.

Loading and Playing a QuickTime Movie

We'll start with two small programs, each of which plays a QuickTime movie in a window. One, VerySimplePlayer, allows the user to control the flow of the movie using the standard QuickTime controls. The other, MovieInWindow, just plays the movie through once without controls. You'll find both QuickTime programs in the `Projects` folder, inside the `QuickTime Projects` subfolder, along with the QuickTime clock movie from the QuickTime CD.

> Both of these programs were submitted by Apple's lead QuickTime engineer, Peter Hoddie. When he isn't busy putting new bugs into QuickTime, Peter spends his time fixing QuickTime bugs. Using this approach, he expects to remain employed indefinitely.

Running MovieInWindow

MovieInWindow, which plays a movie in a window without the standard QuickTime controls, uses QuickTime's Movie Toolbox at its highest level. The movie is played without regard to whether sound or video tracks are present. It is simply loaded into memory and then played completely from beginning to end. This example will work with any version of QuickTime. (For more information on QuickTime's Movie Toolbox, see *Inside Macintosh: QuickTime*.)

Make sure QuickTime is installed and then run MovieInWindow. When the Standard File dialog appears, find a QuickTime movie and click Open. A window will appear (Figure 7.1), and the movie will play. If the movie looks a little squashed, it is! (Check out VerySimplePlayer to see how to set up a smarter movie window.) If you want to dismiss the movie before it finishes playing, just click the mouse button in the movie window.

Let's take a look at the source code.

FIGURE 7.1

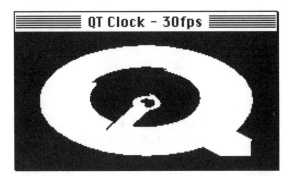

The QuickTime clock movie, as seen by MovieInWindow.

The MovieInWindow Source Code

`MovieInWindow.c` starts off with a pair of #includes. `<Movies.h>` contains the QuickTime constants and prototypes, and `<GestaltEqu.h>` contains the constants and prototype for `Gestalt()`:

```
#include <Movies.h>
#include <GestaltEqu.h>
```

Next come the function prototypes:

```
void main(void);
OSErr playMovieInWindow(WindowPtr theWindow, const FSSpec *theFile,
    const Rect *movieBox);
OSErr loadMovie(const FSSpec *theFile, Movie *theMovie);
```

`main()` begins with some local variables and some standard Toolbox initialization code:

```
void main(void)
{
    long                qtVers;
    StandardFileReply   reply;
    OSType              movieType = MovieFileType;
    Rect                bounds;
    WindowPtr           theWindow;

    InitGraf(&qd.thePort);
    InitFonts();
    InitWindows();
    InitMenus();
    TEInit();
```

```
InitDialogs(0L);
InitCursor();
MaxApplZone();
```

We'll then call Gestalt() to make sure QuickTime is installed.

```
if (Gestalt(gestaltQuickTime, &qtVers) != noErr) {
    SysBeep(1);
    return;
}
```

Next, we call EnterMovies() to initialize the Movie Toolbox. The Movie Toolbox provides the routines you'll need to work with QuickTime movies. Note that you can't call this routine if QuickTime isn't present, so don't place this call in your standard initialization routine:

```
EnterMovies();
```

Now, we prompt the user to select a QuickTime movie to play. StandardGetFilePreview() is part of the Movie Toolbox and gives the user a chance to a preview the currently selected file. Just like StandardGetFile(), StandardGetFilePreview() returns an FSSpec describing the file selected by the user:

```
StandardGetFilePreview(nil, 1, &movieType, &reply);
if (reply.sfGood == false) return;
```

Then, we create a window in which to play the movie. QuickTime is much more efficient playing into a color port. In this example, we set up a fixed-size window, 240 pixels wide and 120 pixels tall. We the movie fit into this window, regardless of its natural size. The next program, VerySimplePlayer, will size the window the right way. For the moment, bear with this ugliness:

```
SetRect( &bounds, 75, 75, 75+240, 75+120 );
theWindow = NewCWindow( nil, &bounds, reply.sfFile.name,
            true, 0, (WindowPtr)-1, false, 0 );
```

Once the window is set up, we play the movie by calling playMovieInWindow():

```
playMovieInWindow( theWindow, &reply.sfFile, &theWindow->portRect );
}
```

playMovieInWindow() loads the movie from theFile and then plays it in theWindow in the rectangle specified by movieBox. In this case, we're asking playMovieInWindow() to scale the movie to fill the entire window:

```
OSErr playMovieInWindow( WindowPtr theWindow,
        const FSSpec *theFile, const Rect *movieBox )
{
    OSErr        err;
    Movie        theMovie;
    CGrafPtr     savePort;
    GDHandle     saveGD;
```

We'll start by saving the current graphics context into `savePort` and making `theWindow` the current graphics context. When QuickTime loads a movie it automatically sets it to play in the current `GrafPort`. This makes it important to have a valid port set when you load a movie:

```
GetGWorld(&savePort, &saveGD);
SetGWorld((CGrafPtr)theWindow, nil);
```

Next, we load the movie from `theFile`:

```
err = loadMovie(theFile, &theMovie);
if (err) goto bail;
```

Now, we set the movie to play in our specified rectangle. Since this area may not accommodate the movie's natural size, the movie may not play as efficiently as possible (we'll solve this problem later in VerySimplePlayer).

```
SetMovieBox(theMovie, movieBox);
```

A QuickTime movie can be saved with the current frame set to any point in the movie. To ensure that we play the movie starting at the first frame, we rewind it:

```
GoToBeginningOfMovie( theMovie );
```

`MoviesTask()` is similar to the routine `SystemTask()` in that it gives a slice of time to the Movie Toolbox so that it can service your movie. The second parameter determines the size of this time-slice in milliseconds. If this value is 0, the Movie Toolbox gives your movie the minimum amount of time it can. By giving your movie this minimal attention before you begin to play it, you provide the Movie Toolbox with a chance to update the window so that the movie doesn't start with a jerk:

```
MoviesTask( theMovie, 0 );
```

`StartMovie()` starts the movie playing asynchronously, at its preferred playback rate. Before starting, it pre-rolls the movie to ensure that it will play smoothly:

```
StartMovie(theMovie);
```

At this point, we spin and wait for the movie to finish playing. If the user clicks the mouse, we also stop:

```
while ((IsMovieDone(theMovie) == false) && (Button() == false))
    MoviesTask(theMovie, 0);
```

Here's our error bailout label. If the movie runs with no problem, we also arrive at this line of code. In either case, we'll call `DisposeMovie()` to free up the memory used to implement the movie. Note that `DisposeMovie()` can take `nil` as a parameter so this call works even if we never loaded the movie:

```
bail:
    DisposeMovie(theMovie);
```

Finally, we restore the original graphics context:

```
    SetGWorld( savePort, saveGD );
}
```

`loadMovie()` loads the QuickTime movie from `theFile`:

```
OSErr loadMovie( const FSSpec *theFile, Movie *theMovie )
{
    OSErr    err;
    short    movieResRef;
```

First, we set the movie to `nil` in case of failure:

```
    *theMovie = nil;
```

Next, we open the movie file. Since we won't be doing any editing, we open it with read permission only:

```
    err = OpenMovieFile(theFile, &movieResRef, fsRdPerm);
```

If the file opens without a hitch, we call `NewMovieFromFile()` to load the movie into memory. Once the movie is in memory, we can close the file by calling `CloseMovieFile()`:

```
if (err == noErr)
{
    err = NewMovieFromFile( theMovie, movieResRef,
        nil, nil, newMovieActive, nil);
```

```
CloseMovieFile(movieResRef);
    }

    return err;
}
```

Once again, for the details on these calls, check out *Inside Macintosh: QuickTime*. In the meantime, the code just given should get you started.

Running VerySimplePlayer

VerySimplePlayer is a slightly more sophisticated program than MovieInWindows. It also loads a movie into a window but, rather than having the movie start playing, VerySimplePlayer provides the user with the standard QuickTime movie controller. The user uses this controller to start and stop the movie and to step through the movie frame by frame. As you examine the source code, note that the majority of the code involves the preparation of the movie and the movie controller. Once this controller is created, all you need to do is call `MCIsPlayerEvent()` each time you call `WaitNextEvent()`. The controller handles all its own events, without intervention on your part.

In most cases, using the movie controller works out pretty well. If you need more control than is afforded by `MCIsPlayerEvent()`, there is a set of routines that you can call in response to individual events (Figure 7.2).

FIGURE 7.2

> ### Movie Controller
> ### Event Handling Routines

Five routines you can use to dispatch movie controller events.

By using the movie controller, an application gains many standard human interface features, including automatic mouse and keyboard handling, balloon help, Drag Manager support, and optional editing support (including complete Undo). Nearly every feature of the movie controller can be turned on and off depending on your application's requirements.

(For more information on QuickTime's movie controller, see *Inside Macintosh: QuickTime Components*.)

Run VerySimplePlayer and, when prompted, open a movie. The movie will appear in a window sized to fit the movie's natural dimensions (Figure 7.3). Notice the controller that appears at the bottom of the window. Fool around with the controls. Play the movie a few times. Drag the window around on the screen. If you look carefully, you'll notice that when you drag the window, it drags smoothly in a vertical direction, but jumps a few pixels at a time in the horizontal direction. This effect becomes more apparent the lower your screen resolution (set your monitor to black and white to see this effect most clearly). You'll understand why when we walk through the code. You can hold down the command key to defeat this behavior.

Let's take a look at the source code, much of which will be familiar to you.

Figure 7.3

The QuickTime clock movie, as seen by VerySimplePlayer.

The VerySimplePlayer Source Code

This source code starts with the same #includes as MovieInWindow, and the function prototypes follow:

```
#include <Movies.h>
#include <GestaltEqu.h>

void main(void);
OSErr loadMovie(const FSSpec *theFile, Movie *theMovie);
pascal Boolean movieControllerEventFilter(MovieController
     theController, short action, void *params, long refCon);
```

This `main()` also begins with some locals and then initializes the Toolbox:

```
void main(void)
{
    long qtVers;
    OSErr err;
    StandardFileReply reply;
    OSType movieType = MovieFileType;
    Rect bounds;
    WindowPtr theWindow;
    Movie theMovie = nil;
    Boolean done = false;
    MovieController theController = nil;
    Rect maxBounds = {40, 40, 1000, 1000};

    InitGraf(&qd.thePort);
    InitFonts();
    InitWindows();
    InitMenus();
    TEInit();
    InitDialogs(0L);
    InitCursor();
    MaxApplZone();
```

Once again, we call `Gestalt()` to ensure that QuickTime is installed. This time, however, we check to be sure that version 1.5 or later is installed. Version 1.5 was the first version that included window alignment routines (see `DragWindowAligned()`, shown later in the code) as well as the function `MCSetActionFilterWithRefCon()`. This precaution isn't a big deal since no one runs QuickTime 1.0 anymore—but better safe than sorry, right?

```
    if ( (Gestalt( gestaltQuickTime, &qtVers ) != noErr )
        || (qtVers < 0x01508000))
    {
        SysBeep(1);
        return;
    }
```

As usual, we call `EnterMovies()` to initialize the Movie Toolbox and then prompt the user for a movie file to open by calling `StandardGetFilePreview()`:

```
EnterMovies();

StandardGetFilePreview( nil, 1, &movieType, &reply );
if (reply.sfGood == false) return;
```

Then, as before, we create a window in which to play the movie. This time, we make the window invisible. Since we'll be changing the window size later, we just use an arbitrary rectangle. Note that you should create a color window if there's a chance you'll be playing a color movie in it:

```
SetRect(&bounds, 75, 75, 75+160,75+120);
theWindow = NewCWindow( nil, &bounds, reply.sfFile.name,
              false, 0, (WindowPtr)-1, true, 0);
```

Next, we make the window the current `GWorld`, but, unlike what we did in MovieInWindow, we don't save the old `GWorld` first. Use whichever strategy makes sense for you, but be sure you make the movie window the current `GWorld` before you load the movie:

```
SetGWorld((CGrafPtr)theWindow, nil);
```

If we have trouble loading the movie, we bail out.

```
err = loadMovie(&reply.sfFile, &theMovie);
if (err) goto bail;
```

Now, we get the movie's natural bounding rectangle, which is the position it was in when it was last saved. We then move the rectangle so that its upper-left corner is at (0, 0), making it appear in the window's upper-left corner:

```
GetMovieBox(theMovie, &bounds);
OffsetRect(&bounds, -bounds.left, -bounds.top);
SetMovieBox(theMovie, &bounds);
```

Next, we create a new movie controller for the movie. `bounds` specifies the movie's bounding rectangle and determines the position of the controller. The last parameter allows you to set various flags that determine the position and appearance of the controller. The `mcTopLeftMovie`

flag tells the controller to position the movie in the upper-left corner
of bounds:

```
theController = NewMovieController(theMovie, &bounds,
                    mcTopLeftMovie);
```

We then resize the window to be large enough to display both the
movie and the controller:

```
MCGetControllerBoundsRect( theController, &bounds );
SizeWindow( theWindow, bounds.right, bounds.bottom, false );
```

AlignWindow() positions the movie at an optimal screen location
for high-performance video playback. It typically will move the window
only a pixel or two horizontally. We call ShowWindow() to make the window visible for the first time:

```
AlignWindow(theWindow, false, nil, nil);
ShowWindow(theWindow);
```

MCDoAction() asks the movie controller component to perform a
specified action. In this case, we're asking theController to set a
bounding rectangle that limits the resizing of the movie. If we don't
make this call, the movie controller will not have a grow box:

```
MCDoAction(theController, mcActionSetGrowBoxBounds, &maxBounds);
```

This time, we enable keyboard input for the controller:

```
MCDoAction(theController, mcActionSetKeysEnabled, (void *)true);
```

Next, we install a movie controller event filter that gets a shot at
each of the events handled by the controller. We'll use this procedure to
detect when the controller has been resized so that we can resize the
window. We'll pass the WindowPtr as the refCon parameter. It will be
passed on to our filter proc:

```
MCSetActionFilterWithRefCon( theController,
    movieControllerEventFilter, (long)theWindow );

while (!done)
{
    EventRecord theEvent;
```

At this point, we enter our main event loop. We pass a sleep value of 0 so that the movie gets lots of time to play (a more clever application might change the sleep value when the movie was paused):

```
WaitNextEvent(everyEvent, &theEvent, 0, nil);
```

We give the movie controller first crack at every event; otherwise, we process the event ourselves:

```
if (MCIsPlayerEvent(theController, &theEvent))
    continue;

switch (theEvent.what)
{
    case mouseDown:
        WindowPtr whichWindow;
        short part;

        part = FindWindow(theEvent.where, &whichWindow);
        switch (part)
        {
            case inGoAway:
                done = TrackGoAway(whichWindow, theEvent.where);
                break;
```

We use `DragAlignedWindow()` instead of our normal `DragWindow()` to make sure that the window stays aligned on the right word boundaries for optimal playback performance:

```
        case inDrag:
            DragAlignedWindow(whichWindow, theEvent.where,
                &qd.screenBits.bounds, nil, nil);
            break;
    }
    break;
```

We handle the update event here. The movie controller takes care of any areas covered by the movie or the movie controller. We take care of any other areas by erasing them to white. If we don't, then updates will not draw correctly for nonrectangularly shaped movies:

```
        case updateEvt:
            BeginUpdate((WindowPtr)theEvent.message);
            EraseRect(&((WindowPtr)theEvent.message)->portRect);
            EndUpdate((WindowPtr)theEvent.message);
            break;
        }
    }
```

Here's our bailout label. This time, we get rid of the movie controller, the movie, and the window. The order of disposing is important. For example, we don't want to throw away the window that the movie is in before disposing of the movie:

```
bail:
    DisposeMovieController(theController);
    DisposeMovie(theMovie);
    DisposeWindow(theWindow);
}
```

`loadMovie()` is the same as it was before.

```
OSErr loadMovie(const FSSpec *theFile, Movie *theMovie)
{
    OSErr err;
    short movieResRef;

    *theMovie = nil;

    err = OpenMovieFile(theFile, &movieResRef, fsRdPerm);
    if (err == noErr)
    {
        err = NewMovieFromFile(theMovie, movieResRef,
            nil, nil, newMovieActive, nil);

        CloseMovieFile(movieResRef);
    }

    return err;
}
```

Here's our controller event filter. The only action we care about is one that changes the size of the controller and, therefore, the size of the window:

```
pascal Boolean movieControllerEventFilter(MovieController
theController, short action, void *params, long refCon)
{
    if (action == mcActionControllerSizeChanged)
    {
        Rect bounds;
```

We retrieve the controller's current size (which also happens to be the same size as the window) and resize the window accordingly:

```
        MCGetControllerBoundsRect(theController, &bounds);
        SizeWindow((void *)refCon, bounds.right, bounds.bottom, false);
    }
```

We return `false`, indicating we didn't fully handle the action, so that normal processing will still occur:

```
return false;
}
```

WORKING WITH THE DRAG MANAGER

The next program is a simple implementation of the Drag Manager. You'll find the ReceiveDragDemo sources in the `Projects` folder, inside the subfolder named `ReceiveDragDemo f`.

> This code was contributed by Gregory Dow, best known as the designer of PowerPlant and the original TCL. Soon after buying his first Mac, Greg discarded eight years of chemical engineering education to become a Mac programmer. He now spends his time writing object-oriented class libraries and trying to discourage his five-year-old niece's penchant for dismantling floppy disks.

When you launch ReceiveDragDemo, a window containing an empty list will appear. Go to the Finder and click on a file (or set of files) and drag the selection to the Receive Drag Demo window. When the cursor enters the list rectangle, the drag area will be highlighted. If you release the mouse button with the cursor still in this area, the names of all the items in the selection will be added to the list (Figure 7.4). If you add enough items, the scroll bar will be enabled. You won't be able to drag items from the Receive Drag Demo window back out, and dragging items from anywhere other than the Finder will not produce anything approaching pleasant results. Once you get the hang of this code, there's plenty of room for customization.

Source Code Highlights

Rather than walking through the source code line by line, let's focus on the highlights. `main()` resides in the file `ReceiveDragDemo.h`. `main()` calls `MaxApplZone()` and `MoreMasters()`, initializes the Toolbox, sets up the menu bar, then calls `SetupWindows()`, which is just a single call to `CreateWindow()`. Both of these routines are defined in `PoohWindows.c`.

CreateWindow() creates a new window, allocates a handle to a `PoohInfoRecord`, then places the handle in the window's refCon field. The `PoohInfoRecord` is defined at the top of `PoohWindows.c` and contains a `ListHandle` and a `DragInfoRecord`. The `ListHandle` is the handle to the list associated with the window. The `DragInfoRecord` is defined in `DragManagerModule.h` and contains the fields we'll need to work with the Drag Manager.

FIGURE 7.4

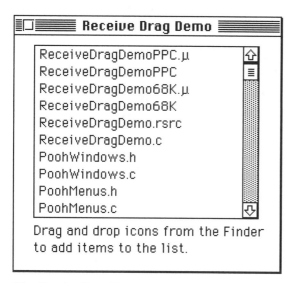

The Receive Drag Demo window, showing the files I dragged to it from the Finder.

At this point in time, the Drag Manager isn't part of *Inside Macintosh*. There's an excellent article in *develop* magazine, Issue 16, on using the Drag Manager with the Finder. The article was written by Dave Evans and Greg Robbins. Start by reading it. Then, plow through your developer CDs. They contain a bunch of great sample programs, each of which shows a slightly different approach to using the Drag Manager. Next, go to the CD in the back of this book and do a find using the word "drag". You'll turn up the *Drag Manager Programmer's Guide*, which lists the Drag Manager API, the *Drag and Drop Human Interface Guidelines*, as well as some cool source code.

Here's the code for `CreateWindow ()`:

```
WindowPtr     CreateWindow(void)
{
    WindowPtr     theWindow;
```

```
ListHandle    theListBox;
Rect          listBounds = {0, 0, 0, 1};
Point         cellSize = {0, 0};

PoohInfoHandle    poohInfo;
RgnHandle         receiveRgn;
Rect      receiveRect = listView;
```

We first create the window from the 'WIND' template, allocate the PoohInfoRecord, then stick the handle in the refCon field:

```
theWindow = GetNewWindow(WIND_Pooh, nil, (WindowPtr) -1);
poohInfo = (PoohInfoHandle) NewHandle(sizeof(PoohInfoRecord));
SetWRefCon(theWindow, (long) poohInfo);
```

Next, a new list is allocated and the handle stored in the PoohInfoRecord.

```
theListBox = LNew(&listView, &listBounds, cellSize, 0, theWindow,
                  true, false, false, true);
(**poohInfo).listBox = theListBox;
```

Next, we create a region coinciding with the visible portion of the list rectangle. This is the region that will highlight in response to a drag. Note that receiveRect was initialized using the global variable listView, which was initialized to the appropriate rectangle:

```
receiveRgn = NewRgn();
RectRgn(receiveRgn, &receiveRect);
```

After that, we set up the DragInfoRecord fields. We specify that our window can accept items of flavorTypeHFS (file or folder) within the rectangular region that coincides with the list box. We also specify that our ReceiveHFSDrag() function should be called for each item dragged and dropped into that region:

```
(**poohInfo).dragInfo.window = theWindow;
(**poohInfo).dragInfo.flavor = flavorTypeHFS;
(**poohInfo).dragInfo.receiveRgn = receiveRgn;
(**poohInfo).dragInfo.receiveFunc = ReceiveHFSDrag;
```

Then, we call InitDragInfo(). Since the PoohInfoRecord starts with the DragInfoRecord, when we cast the PoohInfoHandle to a DragInfoHandle, the receiving routine will only access only the DragInfoRecord.

```
InitDragInfo((DragInfoHandle) poohInfo);
```

Finally, we make the window visible and return the `WindowPtr`:

```
ShowWindow(theWindow);

return theWindow;
}
```

`InitDragInfo()` first checks to see whether the Drag Manager is installed. `IsDragManagerInstalled()` just calls `Gestalt()` using the `gestaltDragMgrAttr` attribute. To use the Drag Manager, you'll need to have installed either the `Macintosh Drag and Drop` extension or use System 7.5 or later; to use Finder dragging, you'll need Finder 7.1.1 or later:

```
OSErr   InitDragInfo( DragInfoHandle dragInfo )
{
    OSErr err = noErr;
    DragTrackingHandlerUPP   trackingProc;
    DragReceiveHandlerUPP    receiveProc;

    if (!IsDragManagerInstalled()) {
        return noErr;
    }
```

`NewDragTrackingHandlerProc()` creates a Universal Proc Pointer (UPP) for our drag tracking function. The drag tracking function tracks the movement of the cursor and uses visual feedback (highlighting) to indicate whether the current item can be dropped here. `InstallTrackingHandler()` installs `DragTrackingFunc()` as the drag tracking function for the specified window. A window's drag tracking function is called when the user drags an item over the window (we'll get into the details shortly):

```
trackingProc = NewDragTrackingHandlerProc(DragTrackingFunc);
(**dragInfo).dragTrackingProc = trackingProc;
err = InstallTrackingHandler(trackingProc,
    (**dragInfo).window, dragInfo);
if (err != noErr) {
    return err;
}
```

We follow a similar procedure to install our drag receive handler. The receive handler is called when a successful drag is made. The handler takes care of bringing the data into our window:

```
    receiveProc = NewDragReceiveHandlerProc(DragReceiveFunc);
    (**dragInfo).dragReceiveProc = receiveProc;
    err = InstallReceiveHandler( receiveProc,
        (**dragInfo).window, dragInfo);

    return err;
}
```

Let's take a look at our two drag handlers. We'll start with `DragTrackingFunc()`:

```
pascal OSErr DragTrackingFunc(
    DragTrackingMessage    theMessage,
    WindowPtr              theWindow,
    void                   *theRefCon,
    DragReference          theDragRef)
{
    OSErr         err = noErr;
    DragInfoHandle  dragInfo = (DragInfoHandle) theRefCon;
    DragAttributes  attributes;
```

As you saw earlier, `DragTrackingFunc()` was installed by `InitDragInfo()`. It will be removed by `KillDragInfo()`.

The first parameter, `theMessage`, takes one of five possible values:

1. `dragTrackingEnterHandler` tells you that a drag has entered one of the windows handled by this handler. A handler will get this message only once during a single drag.

2. `dragTrackingLeaveHandler` is called when the drag enters the focus of a different handler.

3. A handler will get a `dragTrackingEnterWindow` message every time the drag enters a window associated with the handler.

4. `dragTrackingLeaveWindow` tells the handler that the drag is leaving the window.

5. Our handler will get a series of `dragTrackingInWindow` messages as the drag progresses. The sequence of messages is typically as follows:

```
dragTrackingEnterHandler
dragTrackingEnterWindow
dragTrackingInWindow
        •
        •
        •
dragTrackingInWindow
```

```
dragTrackingLeaveWindow
dragTrackingLeaveHandler
```

The next parameter, theWindow, is the window that is the current focus of the drag. theRefCon is the reference constant that we'll use to pass our DragInfoHandle into the routine. theDragRef is like a serial number that uniquely identifies this particular drag.

Our second drag handler, GetDragAttributes(), returns a set of three flags that are embedded as bits in attributes and that provide information about the window and the application. If dragHasLeftSenderWindow is set, the drag has left the source window. If dragInsideSenderApplication is set, the drag is in a window that belongs to the source application. Finally, if dragInsideSenderWindow is set, the drag is inside the same window from which the drag started:

```
GetDragAttributes(theDragRef, &attributes);
```

At this point, we switch on theMessage. Since we don't do anything special when we enter or leave the handler, we ignore dragTrackingEnterHandler and dragTrackingLeaveHandler:

```
switch (theMessage)
{
```

If theMessage is dragTrackingEnterWindow, items have just been dragged into one of our windows. We call DragItemsAreAcceptable() to find out whether the items being dragged are acceptable by our window. DragItemsAreAcceptable() determines the number of dragged items using CountDragItems() and then retrieves an item reference number for each item using GetDragItemReferenceNumber(). Each reference number is passed to GetFlavorFlags() to determine whether the item's flavor (data type) is one acceptable to the receiving window:

```
case dragTrackingEnterWindow:
    currentDragIsAcceptable = DragItemsAreAcceptable(
            theDragRef, dragInfo );
    currentDragWasInReceiveRgn = false;
    break;
```

If theMessage is dragTrackingInWindow, items are being dragged in one of our windows. According to the Drag Manager's human interface guidelines, the area that can receive the drag is highlighted while the mouse is inside it. However, no highlighting occurs until the mouse leaves the area in which the drag started:

```
case dragTrackingInWindow:
    if (currentDragIsAcceptable) {
```

If the items are acceptable, we find out where the mouse is in our window:

```
PointmouseLocation;
GetDragMouse(theDragRef, &mouseLocation, nil);
GlobalToLocal(&mouseLocation);
```

If dragHasLeftSenderWindow is set *and* the drag is inside our receive region *and* we weren't already inside the receive region last time around, we highlight the drag region:

```
if (attributes & dragHasLeftSenderWindow) {
    if (PtInRgn(mouseLocation, (**dragInfo).receiveRgn)) {
        if (!currentDragWasInReceiveRgn) {
```

We call ShowDragHilite() to draw the highlighting in a region and HideDragHilite() to erase the highlighting in a drag region. The first parameter is the drag reference number, the second parameter is the drag region to be highlighted, and the third parameter is true for highlighting inside the region and false for highlighting outside the region:

```
ShowDragHilite(theDragRef, (**dragInfo).receiveRgn,
                true);
currentDragWasInReceiveRgn = true;
}
```

If the mouse is outside the drag receive region and we were inside the region last time around, we hide the highlighting:

```
} else {
    if (currentDragWasInReceiveRgn) {
        HideDragHilite(theDragRef);
        currentDragWasInReceiveRgn = false;
    }
}
}
}
break;
```

Finally, if the Message is dragTrackingLeaveWindow, **items have been dragged out of one of our windows or a drag has been completed. In this case, we must remove the current highlighting, if it exists:**

```
case dragTrackingLeaveWindow:
    /* Items have been dragged out of one of our windows, */
    /* or a drag has been completed. We must remove the */
    /* hiliting of the receive region. */
  if (currentDragIsAcceptable && currentDragWasInReceiveRgn) {
    SetPort((**dragInfo).window);
    HideDragHilite(theDragRef);
  }
  currentDragIsAcceptable = false;
  break;
}

return err;
}
```

The drag receive handler loops through each item in the drag and passes each item to a drag item processing function whose function pointer has been embedded in the DragInfoRecord whose handle was passed in as theRefCon:

```
pascal OSErr DragReceiveFunc(
    WindowPtr      theWindow,
    void        *theRefCon,
    DragReference      theDragRef)
{
    OSErr err = noErr;
    unsigned short itemCount;
    unsigned short itemIndex;
```

First, we retrieve the drag item processing function pointer from the DragInfoRecord:

```
DragItemReceiveFunc    receiveFunc =
(**((DragInfoHandle) theRefCon)).receiveFunc;
```

Then, we call the function for each dragged item:

```
CountDragItems(theDragRef, &itemCount);
for (itemIndex = 1; itemIndex <= itemCount; itemIndex++) {
    ItemReference    theItem;
    GetDragItemReferenceNumber(theDragRef, itemIndex, &theItem);
    err = (*receiveFunc)(theWindow, theDragRef, theItem);
    if (err != noErr) {
```

```
                 break;
        }
    }

    return err;
}
```

Back in `CreateWindow()`, we embedded a pointer to the function `ReceiveHFSDrag()` in the `DragInfoRecord`. `DragReceiveFunc()` called `ReceiveHFSDrag()` for every item in the drag. The three parameters passed to `ReceiveHFSDrag()` are the window receiving the drag, the drag reference number, and the item's index. If there were 10 items, `theItem` would range from 1 to 10:

```
static   OSErr ReceiveHFSDrag(
    WindowPtr       theWindow,
    DragReference   theDrag,
    ItemReference   theItem)
{
    OSErr      err = nil;
    HFSFlavor  hfsData;
    Size       dataSize = sizeof(HFSFlavor);
    ListHandle theListBox = GetListBox(theWindow);
    Cell       newCell = {0, 0};
```

`GetFlavorData()` takes a drag reference number, an item index, and a flavor and returns a data structure containing the data associated with the item. The data associated with `flavorTypeHFS` items contains, among other things, the item's `FSSpec`:

```
GetFlavorData(theDrag, theItem, flavorTypeHFS, (Ptr) &hfsData,
              &dataSize, 0);
```

We'll use the item's `FSSpec` to add the file's name to the list:

```
LDoDraw(false, theListBox);
LAddRow(1, 0, theListBox);
LSetCell(hfsData.fileSpec.name + 1, hfsData.fileSpec.name[0],
            newCell, theListBox);
LDoDraw(true, theListBox);
InvalRect(&listView);

return err;
}
```

Take some time to scan the rest of the code. More importantly, go through the references mentioned earlier in this section, especially the

Drag Manager Programmer's Guide. The Drag Manager is an essential part of the new Macintosh look and feel. If your applications don't support it, your users will know it.

SCANNING DIRECTORIES

This section contains some code that you'll use again and again. Scanning Module recursively scans a directory, passing each file it encounters to a routine of your choosing. You can use this code to search a hard drive for all QuickTime movies, AppleScript scripts, aliases, or whatever you like. Use it as the core of your own backup software. There are tons of possible applications.

> Scanning Module was written by Joe Zobkiw. If you've ever wandered into the music and MIDI forums on AOL or CompuServe, you might already know Joe. He's an accomplished musician and a great Mac programmer. Joe is the driving force behind a wide range of Macintosh software—from low-level network applications to lower-level system extensions. More importantly, Joe has an awesome CD collection and has done his part to make sure that I listen to the "right" music!
>
> As of this writing, Joe is spending the majority of his free time pushing his new Power Mac to the limits of speed and fury. When he isn't RISC-ing his life, Joe enjoys listening to tunes, playing with his synthesizers, chasing his dog, and cooking for his wife.

Running Scanning Module

Go into the `Projects` folder and then into the `Scanning Module` subfolder and launch Scanning Module. This particular incarnation of Scanning Module was hard-coded to search the active System Folder. For each file it finds, it displays the file's name, type, creator, creation date, and modification date (Figure 7.5). You can type command-period or Escape to quit the program.

Let's take a look at the source code.

The include file `<Folders.h>` is necessary because we call `FindFolder()` to locate the active System Folder. `"Scanning Module.h"` contains the function prototypes as well as the definition of the function pointer `ScanProc`:

```
#include <Folders.h>
#include "Scanning Module.h"
```

main() starts by initializing the Toolbox and drawing the empty menu bar:

```
void main(void)
{
    DialogPtr    d = nil;
    CInfoPBRec   cipb;
    OSErr        err = noErr;
    short        foundVRefNum;
    long         foundDirID;

    // initialize the Macintosh
    InitGraf(&qd.thePort);
    InitFonts();
    FlushEvents(everyEvent,0);
    InitWindows();
    InitMenus();
    TEInit();
    InitDialogs(0L);
    InitCursor();
    DrawMenuBar();
```

FIGURE 7.5

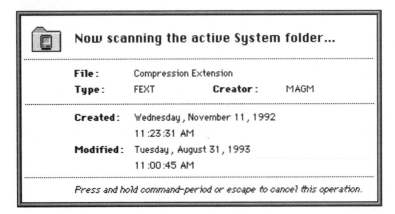

The Scanning Module window.

Next, we call FindFolder() to locate the active System Folder. We can used StandardGetFile() to prompt for a folder to open, but doing so opens several cans of worms. First off, we have to customize the code so that it will allow us to select a folder, as opposed to the standard behavior that only allows you to select a file. Next, we have to work out a satisfactory user interface because Apple has never come up with a consistent approach to selecting a folder. Rather than clouding the issue at hand, starting with the System Folder seems a better choice:

```
err = FindFolder(kOnSystemDisk, kSystemFolderType,
     kDontCreateFolder, &foundVRefNum, &foundDirID);

if (err == noErr) {
```

Then, we load the 'DLOG' resource, which will act as the basis for the progress dialog (Figure 7.6). This DLOG was created using Resorcerer:

```
d = GetNewDialog( 128, nil, (WindowPtr)-1 );
if (d == nil) { SysBeep(0); ExitToShell(); }

ShowWindow(d);
DrawDialog(d);
```

FIGURE 7.6

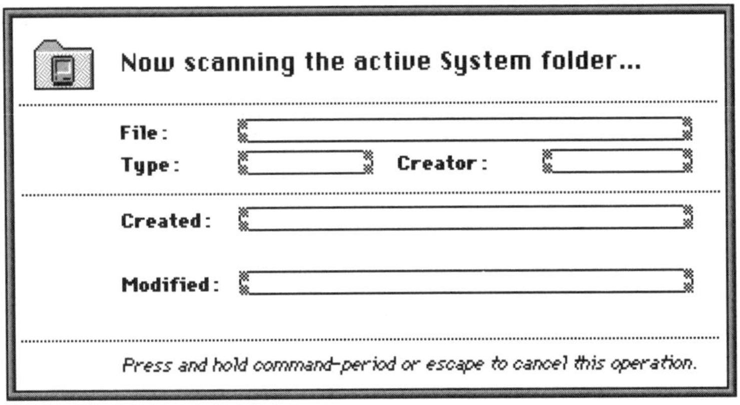

The progress dialog, showing all the hidden fields.

At this point, we'll load and display the watch cursor and then begin the scan by calling the recursive routine ScanDirectory(), which takes five parameters:

```
SetCursor(*GetCursor(watchCursor));
err = ScanDirectory(&cipb, foundVRefNum,
     foundDirID, DoScanStuff, (long)d);
```

The first parameter is a `CInfoPBRec` which is a union containing a parameter block that either describes a file or a directory. (We'll talk about the `CInfoPBRec` when we get into the `ScanDirectory()` code later in this section.) The second and third parameters are the volume reference number and directory ID of the folder to be scanned. As we descend, these will always reflect the current directory being searched. The fourth parameter is a pointer to the function we want called for each file. The last parameter is the reference constant that will be passed to the function. In this case, we're using the reference constant to hold a pointer to the dialog we just created.

If an error occurs or if the user cancels the scan by typing Escape or command-period, we beep once, nuke the dialog, flush all remaining events, and drop out of the program:

```
    if ((err != noErr) && (err != userCanceledErr))
        SysBeep(0);

    InitCursor();
    DisposeDialog(d);
    FlushEvents(everyEvent, 0);
    }
}
```

Here's the routine we call for every file we encounter. The first parameter is the parameter block that describes the file, and the second is a `refCon` containing a pointer to the dialog we'll be updating:

```
OSErr DoScanStuff(CInfoPBPtr cipbp, long refCon)
{
    short       iType;
    Handle       iHandle;
    Rect        iRect;
    long        someTime;
    unsigned char       type[5];
    unsigned char       creator[5];
    Str255              dateStr;
    Str255              timeStr;
```

First, we update the file name field:

```
    GetDItem((DialogPtr)refCon, 3, &iType, &iHandle, &iRect);
    SetIText(iHandle, cipbp->hFileInfo.ioNamePtr);
```

Next, we update the file type and creator:

```
type[0] = 4;
BlockMove(&cipbp->hFileInfo.ioFlFndrInfo.fdType,
     &type[1], sizeof(OSType));
GetDItem((DialogPtr)refCon, 7, &iType, &iHandle, &iRect);
SetIText(iHandle, type);

creator[0] = 4;
BlockMove(&cipbp->hFileInfo.ioFlFndrInfo.fdCreator,
     &creator[1], sizeof(OSType));
GetDItem((DialogPtr)refCon, 8, &iType, &iHandle, &iRect);
SetIText(iHandle, creator);
```

Now, we pick up the creation and modification dates.

```
IUDateString(cipbp->hFileInfo.ioFlCrDat, longDate, dateStr);
GetDItem((DialogPtr)refCon, 11, &iType, &iHandle, &iRect);
SetIText(iHandle, dateStr);
IUTimeString(cipbp->hFileInfo.ioFlCrDat, true, timeStr);
GetDItem((DialogPtr)refCon, 12, &iType, &iHandle, &iRect);
SetIText(iHandle, timeStr);

IUDateString(cipbp->hFileInfo.ioFlMdDat, longDate, dateStr);
GetDItem((DialogPtr)refCon, 13, &iType, &iHandle, &iRect);
SetIText(iHandle, dateStr);
IUTimeString(cipbp->hFileInfo.ioFlMdDat, true, timeStr);
GetDItem((DialogPtr)refCon, 14, &iType, &iHandle, &iRect);
SetIText(iHandle, timeStr);
```

Next, we delay a few ticks to make the items easier to read (feel free to adjust the delay to suit your own reading speed/patience; if you're going all out for speed, delete the line entirely):

```
Delay(3, &someTime);
```

Finally, we call `CommandPeriod()` to see whether the user hit Escape or command-period. If so, we return a `userCanceledErr`. Otherwise, we just return `noErr` and the scan can continue:

```
    return CommandPeriod() ? userCanceledErr : noErr;
}
```

`ScanDirectory()` is the heart of the program. The constant `kDirFlag` acts as a mask to determine whether the catalog entry being scanned is a file or a directory:

```
#define kDirFlag (1<<4)
```

```
OSErr ScanDirectory(CInfoPBPtr cipbp, short vRefNum, long dirID,
    ScanProc sp, long refCon)
{
    Str32     theString;
    StringPtr saveString;
    short     saveIndex;
    OSErr     err = noErr;
```

ScanDirectory() uses the directory ID passed into it to set up a
parameter block. We'll also set an index in the parameter block to 1, indicating that we're referring to the first file in the directory. We'll then
enter a loop, calling PBGetCatInfoSync() to retrieve the file or folder
specified in the parameter block. If the returned parameter block specifies a file, we'll pass it to our scanning procedure, DoScanStuff(). If the
parameter block specifies a directory, we'll pull out the directory ID and
pass it to ScanDirectory(). Either way, each time through the loop we'll
bump the index so that we refer to the next file in the directory.

> Note that if the directory being searched is deep enough, we can
> overflow the stack. If you think stack overflow is a real possibility, you
> can take precautions. First, stick a Debugger() call as the first line
> of ScanDirectory(). Run the program and have it search a series
> of nested folders at least 3 or 4 levels deep. Each time you drop into
> the debugger, check the stack pointer and compare it to the value of
> the stack pointer the last time around. This difference should remain
> constant each time you descend. Take the difference in bytes and
> divide it into your stack size, which will give you the maximum depth
> you can search before you overflow your stack. If you check the
> stack size at run time (not really a great thing to do), you can track
> your depth and then put up a warning to the user when you're asked
> to exceed the maximum depth. Taking this precaution is far better
> than crashing, right?

We start by initializing our parameter block. The first chunks of
fields on both sides on the union are the same, so it doesn't matter
whether we use hFileInfo or hDirInfo to access these fields. Setting
ioFDirIndex to 1 says that we want the first entry in this directory:

```
cipbp->hFileInfo.ioCompletion    = nil;
cipbp->hFileInfo.ioFDirIndex     = 1;
cipbp->hFileInfo.ioVRefNum v     = vRefNum;
cipbp->hFileInfo.ioNamePtr       = (StringPtr)theString;
```

As long as we don't run into an error and the user doesn't cancel,
we stay in this loop (note that we'll get an fnfErr when we run out of

catalog entries in the directory we're currently searching, which is how we'll normally drop out of the loop):

```
while (err == noErr) {
```

We start the loop by storing the current directory ID in the parameter block and then passing the parameter block to `PBGetCatInfoSync()`. If an error occurs, most likely we just ran out of entries (we already handled the last file or folder in this directory):

```
cipbp->hFileInfo.ioDirID = dirID;

err = PBGetCatInfoSync(cipbp);
if (err) goto exit;
```

We now increment the index so that the next time through the loop we'll look at the next entry in the current directory:

```
cipbp->hFileInfo.ioFDirIndex++;
```

If we're looking at a directory, we recurse:

```
if (cipbp->hFileInfo.ioFlAttrib & kDirFlag) {
```

Before we descend, we save the index and name so that we can restore them after we climb back up and continue exploring this directory:

```
// save before recursing
saveIndex = cipbp->hFileInfo.ioFDirIndex;
saveString = cipbp->hFileInfo.ioNamePtr;

// recurse within the directory
err = ScanDirectory(cipbp, vRefNum,
cipbp->hFileInfo.ioDirID, sp, refCon);

// restore after recursion
cipbp->hFileInfo.ioFDirIndex = saveIndex;
cipbp->hFileInfo.ioNamePtr = saveString;
```

If the candidate is a file, we pass it to `DoScanStuff()`:

```
} else {
if (sp != nil)
    err = (*sp)(cipbp, refCon);
}
```

```
        }

exit:
```

Here's where we arrive if we get an error. If the error is an `fnfErr` or an `afpAccessDenied` error, we return `noErr`, since these errors are a normal part of the process:

```
        if ((err == fnfErr) || (err == afpAccessDenied)) return noErr;
        else return err;
}
```

`KeyIsPressed()` returns `true` if the specified key is down. You'll probably want to integrate this routine and `CommandPeriod()` with your event-processing code:

```
short KeyIsPressed(unsigned short k)
{
        unsigned char km[16];

        GetKeys((long *) km);
        return ((km[k>>3] >> (k & 7) ) & 1);
}
```

`CommandPeriod()` returns `true` if the Escape key or command-period is pressed:

```
Boolean CommandPeriod(void)
{
        return ((KeyIsPressed(0x37) && KeyIsPressed(0x2f))
                        || (KeyIsPressed(0x35)));
}
```

Improving the Code

Here are a few tips for improving the code:

- At the end of the scanning procedure, you should verify that the file just checked is still at the same `ioFDirIndex` in the directory. Why would the `ioFDirIndex` change? If file sharing is turned on, a remote user might add a file to or delete a file from the directory you're scanning. If the `ioFDirIndex` changed, you should rescan the entire directory. Otherwise, you might miss a file or, worse, an entire directory.

- You might want to embed the `ScanDirectory()` parameters in a structure. In this way, you only push one argument on the stack when you recurse (we're currently using five arguments). Along the same lines, by reusing the same `CInfoPBRec`, you don't have to allocate one locally inside `ScanDirectory()`, which saves 108 bytes of stack space (the size of a `CInfoPBRec`) each time we recurse.

- You should change the declarations of the most frequently used variables so they are "register" based, which should give you a little more speed.

Note that, interestingly, when you compile this program native on a PowerPC, you won't see much of a speed increase. Why not? The File Manager is not currently native, and the File Manager is definitely the bottleneck here. On the other hand, if your scanning procedure performs some intense floating-point calculations for each file scanned, you'll see an incredible performance increase on the Power Mac.

INTERNATIONALIZING SMART QUOTES

The next project isn't really a program. Instead, it's a collection of routines that internationalize smart quotes, converting them into the proper glyphs for the local system. To find these routines, go into the `Projects` folder and then into the subfolder named `International f` and open the file named `International.c`.

....

This set of routines was conceived, written, and performed by Leonard Rosenthol, Director of Advanced Technology for Aladdin Systems. Leonard is probably the most quoted Macintosh programmer of all time and has had his coding fingers in a lot of pies, including such notable products as Aldus Persuasion, Mathematica, MicroPhone II, DTPrinter, and, most recently, the StuffIt family of products (his favorite is StuffIt Expander).

During those few spare cycles when he's not pumping out code or answering Mac programming questions, Leonard likes to read through his large collection of comic books or study a tome or two of Jewish law. He can be reached electronically at `leonardr@netcom.com` or `MACgician@aol.com`.

....

Some Smart Source Code

Let's start off with some globals to hold the different quote characters we'll use in the substitution process:

```
static char left2Quote[4], right2Quote[4], right1Quote[4];
```

Next is a routine for copying pascal strings:

```
unsigned char *pstrcpy (s1, s2)
register unsigned char *s1, *s2;
{
    register short i;

    for (i = 0; i <= *s2; ++i)
    s1 [i] = s2 [i];

    return (s1);
}
```

The next routine loads the *untoken table* from the System's 'itl4' resource. It is one of the many international mapping tables used by the Script Manager to track differences between script systems (to learn about the various 'itlx' resources, look up the routine IUGetIntl() in *Inside Macintosh* or THINK Reference):

```
static Boolean GetUntokenTable(UntokenTableHandle *x)
{
    Itl4Handle       itl4;
    UntokenTablePtr  p;

    itl4 = (Itl4Handle)IUGetIntl(4);

    if (itl4)
    {
        HLock((Handle)itl4);

        p = (UntokenTablePtr)( (char *)(*itl4) +
            ( (*itl4)->unTokenOffset ) );

        *x = (UntokenTableHandle)NewHandleSysClear(p->len);

        if ( x )
            BlockMoveData((Ptr)p,(Ptr)**x,p->len);

        HUnlock((Handle)itl4);

        return( TRUE );
    }
    else
    {
        return( FALSE );
    }
}
```

Now that we have an untoken table (which we loaded using
`GetUntokenTable()`), we use the routine `GetAToken()` to extract a specified token or character from the table (the list of legal tokens is found in
`<Script.h>`):

```
static char GetAToken( short whichToken,
    UntokenTableHandle tknTable, char *target)
{
    char  *tokenStr;

    if (tknTable)
    {
```

If the token index is bigger than the table, we return 0:

```
    if ( whichToken+1 > GetHandleSize((Handle)tknTable) )
        return 0;
```

Otherwise, we lock the table and make `tokenStr` point to the
beginning of the token:

```
    HLock( (Handle)tknTable );
    tokenStr = (char *)(*tknTable) +
            (*tknTable)->index[whichToken];
    HUnlock( (Handle)tknTable );
```

Finally, we copy the token into the parameter `target`. Remember,
`pstrcpy()` copies the second parameter into the first parameter:

```
        pstrcpy((unsigned char *)target,(unsigned char *)tokenStr);
    }
}
```

The following utility routine inserts a given substring into a "master" string (optionally removing any unneeded characters) at the specified position (you'll see this routine called when we get to
`SubstituteSmartQuotes()` at the end of this section):

```
static void InsertString(char *source,char *dest,
            short pos,short len)
{
```

First, the routine removes the needed `chars` from `dest`:

```
    if( (dest[0]-len) < pos )/* at end, just truncate */
        dest[0] = pos-1;
```

```
    else
    {
        BlockMoveData(&dest[pos+len],&dest[pos],255-pos);
        dest[0]-=len;
    }
```

Now, it makes room in dest for the source string.

```
BlockMoveData(&dest[pos],&dest[pos+source[0]],255-pos-source[0]);
```

Finally, it inserts the string:

```
BlockMoveData( &source[1], &dest[pos], source[0] );
dest[0] += source[0];
}
```

The next routine, LoadInternational(), uses the previous routines to load the untoken table, gets the left and right double-quote tokens and right single-quote (apostrophe) token from the untoken table, copying the tokens into the globals mentioned at the beginning of this section. In this particular sample, we load only the "smart-quote" tokens, but you may wish to load and store many others (such as the "thousands separator" used to display large numbers):

```
void LoadInternational(void)
{
    Intl0Hndl intl0 = (Intl0Hndl)IUGetIntl(0);
    UntokenTableHandle      myUntokenTable;

    pstrcpy((unsigned char *)left2Quote,"\p"");
    pstrcpy((unsigned char *)right2Quote,"\p"");
    pstrcpy((unsigned char *)right1Quote,"\p'");

    if (GetUntokenTable(&myUntokenTable))
    {
        char c;

        GetAToken(tokenLeft2Quote, myUntokenTable, left2Quote);
        GetAToken(tokenRight2Quote, myUntokenTable, right2Quote);
        GetAToken(tokenRight1Quote, myUntokenTable, right1Quote);

        DisposHandle((Handle)myUntokenTable);
    }
}
```

Assuming you've already called LoadInternational() (most likely at initialization time), here's the routine to call when you want to internationalize your program's strings to reflect the local system. Of course, you can add items to this set of tokens, but you'll definitely need to perform these three token substitutions since the U.S. ASCII values for smart quotes are not the local smart quotes for most international systems (such as Hebrew and Kanji, for example):

```
void SubstituteSmartQuotes(unsigned char *p)
{
    short i;

    for(i=1;i<=p[0];i++)
    {
        if( (char)p[i] == '"' )
        {
            InsertString( left2Quote, (char *)p, i, 1);
        }
        else if((char)p[i] == '"')
        {
            InsertString( right2Quote, (char *)p, i, 1 );
        }
        else if( (char)p[i] == ''' )
        {
            InsertString( right1Quote, (char *)p, i, 1 );
        }
    }
}
```

The code shown in this section gives you a glimpse at the process of internationalizing your code. When you're ready to introduce your product into the global market, invest in a copy of *Inside Macintosh: Text* and check out Chapter 6 on the Script Manager.

FINDER SCRIPTING

Our final entry in this chapter is a set of handy Finder scripts. You'll find all of these scripts in the `Projects` folder in Script Editor format. When you save them, make sure the "Never Show Startup Screen" checkbox is checked. Also, make sure the "Finder Scripting Extension" is installed (a few of the scripts won't compile without it). I keep aliases of these in my `Apple Menu Items` folder for easy access. You can also run them using Leonard Rosenthol's OSAMenu (it's on all the major on-line services).

Steve Michel, AppleScripter extraordinaire, introduced me to AppleScript through his writings, most notably his "Script Manager"

MacWEEK column. The Finder scripts in this section, along with scores of others, appear in the book *Finder Scripting Toolkit*, published by Heizer Software (January 1995). You can reach Steve at michel@netcom.com. Look for his "No Direction Home Page" Bob Dylan WWW site at Netcom soon.

The Scripts

This first script finds the original of a selected alias (or aliases):

```
tell application "Finder"
    copy selection to selectedFiles — list of selected files
    repeat with thisFile in selectedFiles
        if class of thisFile is alias file then
            if exists (original item of thisFile) then
                reveal original item of thisFile
            end if
        end if
    end repeat
end tell
```

This next very simple script closes all the windows except for the one in front:

```
tell application "Finder"
    close (every window whose index is not 1)
end tell
```

Scripts don't have to be long and complicated to be useful! This short script opens the disk or folder that contains the front window:

```
tell application "Finder"
    open container of folder of front window
end tell
```

Here's a script that opens the folders containing any selected aliases:

```
tell application "Finder"
    copy every alias file of selection to selectedFiles
                        — list of selected aliases
    repeat with thisFile in selectedFiles
        try
            — can we reveal the file?
            reveal original item of thisFile
        on error number errNum
            if errNum is 5038 then — original not there
                display dialog "The original of the alias '"¬
```

```
                & the name of thisFile & "' can't be found."
            end if
        end try
    end repeat
end tell
```

Since the previous script works with the current Finder selection, you need to run it from either the menu or OSAMenu. If you run it from the desktop as a Script Application, as soon as you double-click it, it becomes the selected item. On the other hand, you can also add an on open handler to the script, so you can drop aliases on top of it. The next example does just that.

This script is handy if you copy files to a floppy quite a bit. Save it as a Script application; when you drop a number of files or folders on it, it calculates the size of each item and reports the total:

```
on open theFiles
    sumSizes(theFiles)
end open

on run
    tell application "Finder"
        copy the selection to theFiles
    end tell
    sumSizes(theFiles)
end run

on sumSizes(theFiles)
    tell application "Finder"
        copy 0 to totalSize
        repeat with thisItem in theFiles
            if kind of thisItem is "alias" then
                copy totalSize +¬
                (size of original item of thisItem)¬
                to totalSize
            else
                copy totalSize + (size of thisItem) to totalSize
            end if
        end repeat
        copy (round (totalSize / 1024)) to totalSize
        display dialog "The selected items total "¬
        & (totalSize as string) & "K"
    end tell
end sumSizes
```

In a similar vein, the next script shows the Get Info window for the original of the selected aliases. It is particularly useful when you're working with aliases of applications:

```
tell application "Finder"
    — Let the Finder pick out the aliases
    copy every alias file of selection to selectedFiles
    repeat with thisFile in selectedFiles
        — trap for cases where the original item is not there
        if exists (original item of thisFile) then
            — it's there, so Get Info
            open information window of original item of thisFile
        end if
    end repeat
end tell
```

This final script uses script objects and the Save Script scripting addition to create scripts that restore your Finder windows to the state they were in when the script was saved:

```
script snapShotPlayer
    property theWindows : {}
    property windowBounds : {}
    tell application "Finder"
        close every window
        if the (count of theWindows) > 1 then
            repeat with x from (count of theWindows) to 1 by -1
                open item x of theWindows
                set the bounds of item x of theWindows to¬
                    item x of windowBounds
            end repeat
        else
            open item 1 of theWindows
            set the bounds of window 1 to windowBounds
        end if
    end tell
end script

on run
    copy (new file with prompt¬
        "Save the Window Snapshot as:"¬
        default name "Snapshot") to thefile
    tell application "Finder"
        copy every window to theWindows
        copy the bounds of every window to theBounds
    end tell
    set theWindows of snapShotPlayer to theWindows
    set windowBounds of snapShotPlayer to theBounds
    — what's cool is the saved script is editable!
    store script snapShotPlayer in thefile replacing yes
end run
```

Save both of these handlers in the same script; when you run the script, it creates a new script that re-creates the current setup of all open

Finder windows and prompts you to name the script. When you run the new script, the Finder recreates the window setup mirrored by the script. This script is really handy if you're working on different projects that require different Finder setups. You can also modify it to work with other scriptable applications.

Summary

You've reached the end of the road here, but definitely not the end of the book. Be sure to check out the appendices, especially the three Apple event strategy articles culled from the pages of *develop*.

The Macintosh programming landscape is changing. In many ways, Apple's new technologies are leveling the playing field, and giving smaller Mac developers the chance to break into the big time. If you are a smaller developer, your size is your advantage. While sheer inertia slows the pace of larger companies, you are nimble. Seize the day! Make your applications scriptable and recordable, or use the Drag Manager to add some real zing to your products.

The Mac universe has definitely changed. Welcome to the new frontier. . .

APPLE EVENT OBJECTS AND YOU
RICHARD CLARK

Appendix

Reprinted with permission of Apple Computer, Inc. from *develop*, The Apple Technical Journal, Issue 10. *develop* is a prize-winning quarterly journal that provides an in-depth look at code and techniques that have been reviewed for robustness by Apple engineers. Each issue comes with a CD that contains the source code for that issue, as well as all back issues, Technical Notes, sample code, and other useful software and documentation. Subscriptions to *develop* are available through APDA (1-800-282-2732), Apple Link DEV.SUBS, or Internet dev.subs@applelink.apple.com.

With Apple events, Apple has opened the door for applications to control each other and work collaboratively. However, before applications can communicate, they have to agree on the commands and data they'll support. Apple event objects form the basis of such a protocol—the Apple event object model. The object model is powerful, but still a source of confusion for many developers. This article provides an overview of the object model and answers several commonly asked questions, including "What is the Apple event object model?" and "How do I support it?"

One of the greatest strengths of the Macintosh—its graphical user interface—is also the basis of one of its greatest weaknesses—the difficulty of automating routine or repetitive tasks. "Give us batch files!" many users cried. The developers responded with macro programs such as QuicKeys and Tempo, which handle many of the routine tasks but can't always make a program do exactly what the user wants.

The problem is that macro programs are generally limited to manipulating an application's human interface and have limited information about the state of the application. This means that if some setting has been changed or something has been moved, running a particular macro might not have the desired effect. In other words, one Macintosh application cannot control another application reliably through the target application's human interface.

For one application to control another application reliably, all of the following must happen:

- The two applications must agree on a protocol for sending commands and data and agree on the specific information to be sent across this connection.

- The controlled application needs to provide a rich enough set of commands and sufficient access to its data so that meaningful work can be done.

- The protocols and command sets should be standardized so that many different applications can work together.

On the Macintosh, Apple events and the Apple Event Registry provide the standards that allow applications to control each other reliably. The Apple event, a standard protocol for sending commands and data between applications, was introduced as part of System 7. The Apple Event Registry defines standard Apple event commands and two standard data types—Apple event object and primitive. Apple event objects describe an application's internal data, and primitive types describe the data that can be sent between applications. In essence, the Registry forms the basis for a standard language that applications can use when sending or receiving Apple events.

One of the challenges in creating the Apple Event Registry was to keep the set of commands small while providing an adequate level of control between applications. The Registry does this by allowing the same command to apply to different Apple event objects within an application. The application of Apple events to Apple event objects is commonly referred to as the Apple event object model.

This article provides an overview of the object model and then discusses how you can add object model support to your application. The fundamentals of Apple events are given in Inside Macintosh Volume VI.

OBJECT MODEL BASICS

The Apple Event Registry defines an application's programmatic interface as a series of Apple event objects, where each object belongs to a particular object class. Each Apple event object is comprised of some data and a set of Apple event commands that operate on that data. In a traditional object-oriented fashion, new classes are defined by taking an existing class and adding new data and/or commands. Related classes are grouped together into suites.

The most commonly used objects (and their associated commands) are grouped together into the Apple event core suite. The commands in the core suite, which include Create Element, Delete, Get Data, and Set Data, cover the basic operations for any given object. The Apple event objects defined within the core suite include documents, windows, and the application itself. The core suite also includes some primitive classes such as long and short integers, Boolean values, and text. Every object model–aware application should support the core suite, and all Apple event objects defined within your application should support the core suite events.

The data portion of an Apple event object is broken into two parts: the object's properties and its elements:

• The properties of an object contain the attributes of the object— for example, its name and a 4-byte code designating its class.

- The elements of an object are the other objects (in other words, data) that it contains. For example, a drawing application contains one or more documents, and each document may contain several rectangles and a picture or two. When the Registry describes an object, it lists all the element classes of an object, but a particular object may contain only some (or no) elements of each class at run time. (The number of elements can change during run time. For example, the number of words in a window could increase due to user typing or an incoming Apple event.)

> Concepts from object-oriented programming (notably inheritance—the process of defining new classes in terms of other classes) are used in defining the Apple event object model, but supporting Apple event objects does not require the use of an object-oriented language or class library. You can use any language or implementation technique you want, as long as your application can understand the Apple events sent to it.

For more detail on the difference between a property and an element, see "Properties and Elements."

Figure A.1 shows three object classes that we'll use throughout the article; they've been derived from the Apple Event Registry and simplified for the purpose of illustration.

FIGURE A.1

	cDocument	cRectangle	cWord
Properties	pClass pDefaultType pName pIsModified	pClass pDefaultType pBounds	pClass pDefaultType pFont pSize pStyle
Elements	cFile cRectangle	(None)	cCharacter
Apple Events	Create Element Get Data Set Data Delete Open Close Print Save	Create Element Get Data Set Data Delete	Create Element Get Data Set Data Delete

Some Hypothetical Apple Event Object Classes

OBJECT SPECIFIERS

Most of the Apple events defined in the Apple Event Registry contain one or more object specifiers as parameters. An object specifier is similar to the instructions you might give someone who's looking for a particular house: turn left at the first signal, then look for Jones Street and turn right, then travel down to the third house on the right. Object specifiers can also be used to specify a group of objects—for example, every green house on Jones Street.

> In addition to the core suite, the *Apple Event Registry* includes other specialized suites for text processing, database manipulation, manipulating QuickDraw graphics, and the like. Application developers can define their own custom Apple event object classes and suites and submit them to the Apple Events Developer Association for standardization.

Or imagine you send an Apple event–aware word processor the object specifier "every Paragraph in the current Document that contains the Word 'Apple'." The application would search in stages, first finding the current document and then searching through the paragraphs one at a time to see if they contained the word "Apple." Object specifiers provide a powerful general mechanism for locating a particular object in an application.

The Apple event's direct parameter typically contains the object specifier, yielding such commands as "Close Document 3" and "Delete Word 3 of Document 'fred'." Passing an object specifier as part of a command allows the same command to be reused for different objects (New window, New document, or New rectangle) instead of inventing a unique command for each action-object pair (NewWindow, NewDocument, or NewRectangle).

Internally, an object specifier consists of a series of recursive "get a particular element of class x from object y" commands. For example, in the command "Close Document 1," the object specifier (Document 1) is represented as "the first object of class Document contained within the Application." Another way of looking at this is "(the first object of class Document in (the Application))" where the parentheses represent one object specifier embedded within another. In addition to specifying a single element, an object specifier can refer to a property of some object or to a set of objects. For example, your application may receive the object specifier for "the Bounds of Window 1" or "every Icon contained within Rectangle 1 of Window 5."

Properties and Elements

Each Apple event object contains exactly one of each of its properties (each of which has a name), so you might ask for the "Bounds of the frontmost Window" and receive back the pBounds property of the specified window. An object can contain zero or more of each of its element classes (each of which has a name), so you could ask for "every Paragraph in Document 1," where Paragraph is a valid element class for the document.

Many developers want to know when you should declare something as a property and when you should declare it as an element. You should make something (call it x) a property of an object when x describes something about that object. You should make something else (call it y) an element of an object if y is contained within the object.

Some developers use the rule "If there's only going to be one y in the object, make it a property." Alas, this rule isn't always correct. Let's assume that an application could display only one document window at a time. Should that document be an element or a property? According to the Registry's definition of an element, since the document is contained within the application, you should make it an element. If you make something an element based simply on the Registry's definition, your new classes will be consistent with the existing classes.

Another useful test is to ask "Can I delete this item?" If you can, it's not a property. (You can delete a window from within an application, so a window is an element of that application, not a property. But since you cannot delete the bounds of the window, the bounds is a property.)

Figure A.2 shows a simplified representation of two object specifiers. Object specifiers are stored as Apple event records, with one field each for the object class and the object's container (stored as a handle) and two fields for the element identifier. The two fields of the element identifier together represent the specific element to be selected. In part A of Figure A.2, the desired object class is cDocument, the container is 'null' (in other words, a descriptor that has type typeNull and a nil handle), and the element identifier is 1. The null container typically represents the application. In part B, the desired object class is cWord, the container is a handle to the object specifier from part A, and the element identifier is 5.

FIGURE A.2

(A) Close Document 1

Object class	cDocument
Object container	'null' (the application)
Element identifier	1

(B) Get Data Word 5 of Document 1

Object class	cWord		
Object container			
	Object class	cDocument	
	Object container	'null' (the application)	
	Element identifier	1	
Element identifier	5		

Simplified Representation of Object Specifiers

An actual object specifier is slightly more complicated than the ones shown in Figure A.2. In the examples given above, we've consistently referred to elements by number. However, you might want to refer to some object, such as a document, by name. In that case you would need to know that the two fields of the element identifier contain a key form and some key data.

Each different way you can refer to an element uses a different key form. When we refer to an element by number, we're using the "absolute position" key form. We could also specify a "name" key form, a "property" key form (to get a property of an object instead of one of its elements), and so on. A complete object specifier is shown in Figure A.3. A list of all standard key forms is given in the Apple Event Registry and in the Apple Event Manager chapter of the new, improved Inside Macintosh (preliminary draft) on the Developer CD Series disc.

FIGURE A.3

Close Window 1

Object class	cWindow
Object container	AEDesc: type 'null', no data
Key form	formAbsolutePosition
Key data	AEDesc: type 'long', value "1"

The Four Fields of an Object Specifier

HOW DO I DISPATCH AN APPLE EVENT CONTAINING OBJECT SPECIFIERS?

One of the side effects of the object model is that the same command will be executed differently depending on the type of object involved. Therefore the object class, event class, and event ID are required before you can dispatch an Apple event. Since the Apple Event Manager uses only two of these values when dispatching an Apple event (the event class and event ID), you'll need to write some additional dispatching logic.

We'll discuss three major ways of dispatching object-model Apple events: an event-first approach, an object-first approach, and a method that uses a lookup table to dispatch the events. These approaches all serve the same function—extracting an object specifier and using the combined object class, event class, and event ID to select one of the application's routines. They differ only in the way you structure your code.

An Event-First Approach

The event-first approach allows the Apple Event Manager to do most of the work. The Apple Event Manager calls a different handler for each event—for example, Get Data and Set Data—and that handler calls different routines depending on the object class given by the object specifier. Figure A.4 and the following sample code illustrate this approach.

```
pascal OSErr AESetDataHandler (AppleEvent *message, AppleEvent *reply,
    long refCon)
{
    OSErr      err;
    AEDesc     theObject, theToken;
```

```
err = AEGetKeyDesc(message, keyDirectObject, typeObjectSpecifier,
   &theObject);
if (err != noErr) return err;

err = AEResolve(&theObject, kAEIDoMinimum, &theToken);
AEDisposeDesc(&theObject);
if (err != noErr) return err;

/* The token is an Apple event descriptor. For now, we can */
/* assume that the token's descriptor type is the class of the */
/* object that should handle this event. */
switch (theToken.descriptorType) {

   case cWindow: case cDocument:
      err = Win_SetData(&theToken, message, reply);
   break;

   case cRectangle:
      err = Rect_SetData(&theToken, message, reply);
   break;

   case cWord:
      err = Word_SetData(&theToken, message, reply);
   break;

   default:
      err = errAEEventNotHandled;
}
AEDisposeDesc(&theToken);
return err;
}
```

For source-code samples that use the event-first technique, see the samples Quill and AEObject-Edition Sample in the Apple Events and Scripting Development Kit on the *Developer CD Series* disc.•

An application that processes events using the event-first approach goes through the following steps after it receives an Apple event and calls AEProcessAppleEvent (the numbers correspond to the numbers in Figure A.4):

1.   The Apple Event Manager locates the event in its dispatch table.

2.   The appropriate handler routine is called by the Apple Event Manager—in this example, it's Set Data. This handler routine needs to determine the object class before it can perform the appropriate action, so it calls AEResolve to convert the object specifier into a reference to a particular object.

3. AEResolve takes an object specifier as input, and calls one or more accessor routines to convert this object specifier into a token that refers to some object. (See the section "How Do I Resolve an Object Specifier?" for more information.)

4. The token is returned to the handler.

5. Once the handler knows the object class, it can call the appropriate object-specific routine. This routine typically accepts the token as one of its parameters.

FIGURE A.4

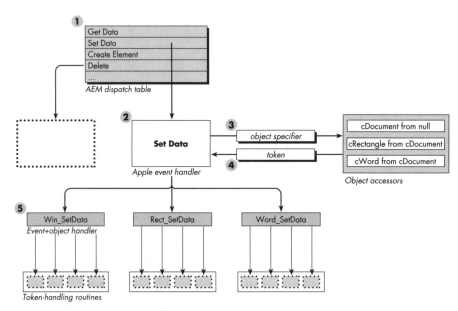

Event-First Approach to Dispatching Apple Events

Since many of the things you can do with a token fall into a few basic operations, such as reading, writing, inserting, or deleting the information represented by a token, you can choose to write a set of token-handling routines for each token type that you define. Token-handling routines are not required, but they are useful. (See the section "What Are Token-Handling Routines?" for more information.)

Due to its simplicity, the event-first approach is recommended for all applications written in a procedural programming style (as is typically done in C or Pascal). Its only real drawback is that if you add a new object class to your application, you have to modify a number of Apple event handlers to recognize the new class (one handler per event that the new object class supports).

If you have code spread across several source files, consider whether this could present a code maintenance problem. If so, the object-first approach might work better for your application.

An Object-First Approach

You can limit the amount of work required when adding a new object class by making each object class a self-contained unit. In this approach, an individual file (or group of files) contains all the code required to implement a single object class, including the event-dispatching code, object accessors, and token handlers. (For more information on token handlers, see the section "What Are Token-Handling Routines?")

Since the object includes its own event-dispatching code, you don't usually install a separate handler for each individual Apple event. Instead, you install one or more wild-card handlers that route the event to the appropriate object using the following algorithm:

1. Extract the parameter containing the object specifier.

2. Call AEResolve to convert this object specifier into a token.

3. Extract the object class from the token.

4. Call the event dispatcher within the appropriate object.

Since most Apple events carry their object specifiers in the direct parameter, a single wild-card handler works for all of these Apple events. However, there are some events that carry their object specifiers in different places, so you need to install specific handlers for these events. (For example, the Create Element event carries its object specifier inside an insertionLoc structure.) Using a single handler that uses the first object specifier it finds is inadequate, since some events use multiple object specifiers and an object specifier can appear anywhere another parameter can.

The handler that extracted the object specifier passes the token, the message, and the reply event to the object's central event dispatcher. This dispatcher then calls the appropriate routine, which typically calls one or more token-handling routines. This approach is illustrated in Figure A.5 and in the following sample code.

```
/* This is a typical Apple event handler that you install using */
/* a wild card (in this case, the class = 'core', and the event */
```

```
/* ID = '****'). This would go in a "common area" file, separate */
/* from the individual object implementation files. */
pascal OSErr AECoreSuiteHandler (AppleEvent *message, AppleEvent *reply,
   long refcon)
{
   OSErr     err;
   AEDesc    directParam, theToken;

   /* The following code works for all core Apple events except */
   /* Create Element. Either this routine would need to be modified */
   /* for Create Element, or a specific handler installed. */
   err = AEGetKeyDesc(message, keyDirectObject, typeWildCard,
      &directParam);
   if (err != noErr) return err;

   if (directParam.descriptorType == 'null') {
   /* AEResolve doesn't like null descriptors, so skip it. */
      theToken = directParam;
   }
   else {
      err = AEResolve(&directParam, kAEIDoMinimum, &theToken);
      AEDisposeDesc(&directParam);
      if (err != noErr) return err;
   }
   /* We assume the token's type is the class that handles this event. */
   switch (theToken.descriptorType) {
      /* Include one entry for each object class. */

      case 'null':
         /* This is the application object's token class. */
         err = AppEventDispatcher(&theToken, message, reply);
      break;

      case cDocument:
         /* See the example of this routine below.*/
         err = DocumentEventDispatcher(&theToken, message, reply);
      break;

      /* And so on for cRectangle, cWord, etc. */

      default:
         err = errAEEventNotHandled;
   }
   AEDisposeDesc(&theToken);
   return err;
} /* AECoreSuiteHandler */

/* ===In the Document Object file...=== */

OSErr DocumentEventDispatcher (AEDesc *theToken, const AppleEvent *message,
```

```
    AppleEvent *reply)
{
    OSErr         err = noErr;
    AEEventID   eventID;
    OSType        typeCode;
    Size          actualSize;

    /* Get the event ID. */
    err = AEGetAttributePtr(message, keyEventIDAttr, typeType,
        &typeCode, (Ptr)&eventID, sizeof(eventID), &actualSize);
    if (err != noErr) return err;

    switch (eventID) {

        case kAECreateElement:
            err = Doc_CreateElement(theToken, message, reply);
            break;

        case kAEGetData:
            err = Doc_GetData(theToken, message, reply);
            break;

        /* And so on for Set Data, Delete, Open, Close, Print, etc. */

        default:
            err = errAEEventNotHandled;
    }
    return err;
} /* DocumentEventDispatcher */
```

When an event is processed using the object-first technique, the application takes the following steps after it receives an Apple event and calls AEProcessAppleEvent (the numbers correspond to the numbers in Figure A.5):

1. The Apple Event Manager locates a handler routine in its dispatch table. The handler is usually installed with a wild-card value so that it's passed all (or most) events.

2. The appropriate handler routine is called. This routine acts as an object dispatcher—it determines the type of object involved and calls the code in the appropriate object's source file. This handler routine needs to determine the object class, so it calls AEResolve to convert the object specifier into a reference to a particular object.

3. AEResolve takes an object specifier as input, and calls one or more accessor routines to convert this object specifier into a token that refers to some object. (See the section "How Do I Resolve an Object Specifier?" for more information.)

FIGURE A.5

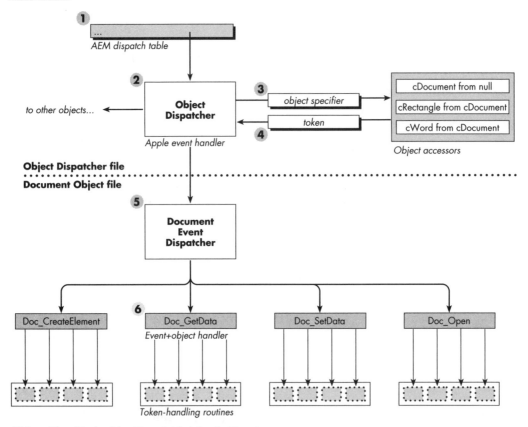

Object-First Method for Dispatching Apple Events

4. The token is returned to the handler.

5. Once the handler knows the object class, it can call the appropriate object's event dispatcher. The dispatcher looks at the event's class and ID and calls the appropriate routine.

6. The called routine performs a task specific to the event class, event ID, and object class. It typically accepts the token as one of its parameters.

This approach, or some variant of it, could be implemented using object-oriented programming and is recommended for object-oriented applications.

If you use the object-first approach in a procedural application, you can still get some of the benefits of object-oriented programming, since this technique can be used to implement a simple form of inheritance for Apple event objects. If a particular object's event dispatcher doesn't recognize an event, it can pass the event to its superclass' event dispatcher. If that dispatcher doesn't recognize the event, the request can be passed up the chain until the topmost dispatcher is reached (typically cObject). This minimizes the code required for adding a new object, since an object only needs to implement its unique events (and any standard events that it handles differently) and can pass all other events to its superclass.

One drawback to this approach is the overhead involved in dispatching the event. Each event goes through the Apple Event Manager, AEResolve, a pair of switch statements (one in the top-level Apple event handler, and another in the object's dispatch routine), and possibly a couple of superclass event dispatchers. Still, each of our approaches requires the initial use of the Apple Event Manager and a call to AEResolve, so the added overhead lies primarily in the switch statements.

Another drawback is that each Apple event typically has several parameters, and each Apple event handler needs to extract the set of Apple event–dependent parameters for that Apple event. This can lead to redundant code.

Table-based Dispatching

One way to lower the overhead associated with dispatching object-model Apple events involves building a dispatch table of your own to replace the Apple Event Manager's. The Apple Event Manager constructs a two-way hash table based on the event class and event ID. Since this isn't enough information to properly dispatch an object-model Apple event (you also need to know which object class will be responsible for handling the event), the solution is to construct your own table using a three-part index (event class, event ID, and object class) that contains the addresses of the appropriate routines.

As in the object-first example, this dispatcher should be "attached" to the Apple Event Manager through a wild-card handler in the Manager's regular dispatch table. (This is necessary since there's no other robust way to "unpack" an Apple event when it arrives from the outside world.) This handler would extract the event class and event ID attributes and would get the object specifier from the direct parameter. The handler would then call AEResolve and pass the object class (along with the event class and event ID) to your table lookup routine.

The only real problem occurs when the object specifier isn't contained in the direct parameter. The solution here is to install handlers for any events that don't contain their object specifiers in their direct parameters, and have these handlers call AEResolve and then jump directly into your table lookup routine.

The implementation of such a table-based dispatcher is left to you.

HOW DO I RESOLVE AN OBJECT SPECIFIER?

When an object-model Apple event is received, such as "Close Document 1," the object specifier (Document 1) is usually contained in the direct parameter of the event. Before the event can be processed, the object specifier needs to be resolved. Resolving an object specifier involves locating the specified information in memory so that the Apple event can act on this information.

While it's possible to parse an object specifier directly, object specifiers can be much more complicated than the simple examples shown here. The Apple event Object Support Library (OSL) helps you resolve an object specifier through a set of object accessor routines, which you write and then install. One type of accessor routine extracts one or more types of element from a given object, while other accessor routines extract a property from an object. When you ask the OSL to resolve an object specifier, it calls the appropriate accessor routines in the necessary order.

Figure A.6 shows how the OSL resolves the object specifier "Word 5 of Window 1." First, the accessor for the innermost specifier (Window 1) is called. This accessor returns a token, which is an Apple event descriptor (AEDesc) referring to some data in your application. The returned token and the next part of the object specifier to be processed are then passed to the appropriate accessor. This process is repeated until the object specifier has been fully resolved, and the final result is returned to your application.

HOW DO I IMPLEMENT AN OBJECT ACCESSOR?

Each accessor routine should accept one part of an object specifier and return a token. An accessor routine has the form

```
pascal OSErr MyAccessor (DescType desiredClass, const AEDesc *container,
   DescType containerClass, DescType keyForm, const AEDesc *keyData,
   AEDesc *value, long refCon);
```

and is passed the desiredClass, containerClass, keyForm, and keyData
fields directly from the part of the object specifier being resolved. The
container is either the token returned from the last accessor called or
an AEDesc of type 'null' containing a null handle (if this is the first accessor in the series to be called).

All accessors have to perform essentially the same functions:

1.   Check that the specified key form is valid.

2.   Locate the requested information.

3.   Construct a return token.

The following code illustrates this process using a simple "extract a
Window from a null container" accessor. (In most applications, this accessor extracts both windows and documents from the null container since
most applications maintain a one-to-one correspondence between documents and windows.)

```
pascal OSErr WindowFromNull (DescType desiredClass,
   const AEDesc *containerToken, DescType containerClass,
   DescType keyForm, const AEDesc *keyData, AEDesc *theToken,
   long theRefcon)
{
   WindowPtr      wp;
   long           count;

   /* 1. Make sure we can handle this request. We only handle */
   /* object specifiers of the form "Window 1", "Window 2", etc. */
   if ((keyForm != formAbsolutePosition) return errAEBadKeyForm;

   /* 2. Extract the window number and find the window. */
   count = **(long**)(keyData->dataHandle);
   wp = FrontWindow();
   while (count > 1) {
       if (wp == 0L) return errAENoSuchObject;
       wp = (WindowPtr)((WindowPeek)wp)->nextWindow;
       --count;     /* Count down by 1. */
   };

   /* 3. Create the token. */
   /* The token is an AE descriptor of type 'cwin' (window). */
   /* The AEDesc contains a handle to a WindowPtr. */
   return AECreateDesc(desiredClass, (Ptr)&wp, sizeof(wp), theToken);
} /* WindowFromNull */
```

FIGURE A.6

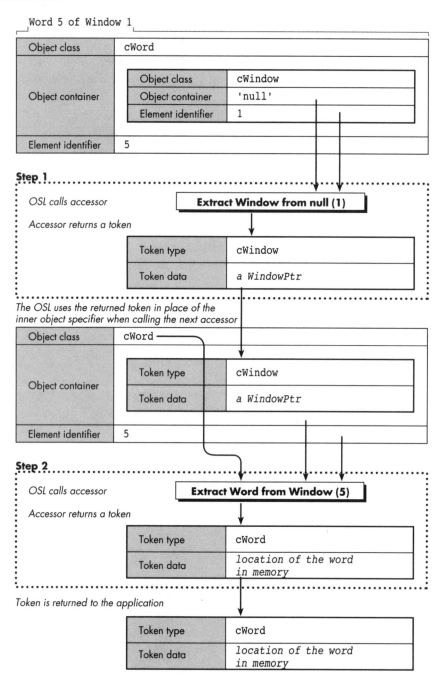

Resolving an Object Specifier

While the preceding code contains many of the features of an object accessor, it's far from complete. For example, it doesn't handle formName, which is one of the more common key forms. It also assumes that the value for a formAbsolutePosition parameter will be a positive integer. In fact, the value could be a negative number (with -1 signifying the last element of the container, -2 signifying the next to the last element, and so on), or one of the special constants representing the first, last, middle, any, or every element of the container.

To make the formAbsolutePosition code complete, you need to add a routine that looks at the key data for one of the special values and converts the key data into a positive integer or returns a flag indicating that every element should be returned. Such a routine would look something like this:

```
OSErr GetWindowIndex (const AEDesc *keyData, long *index, Boolean *getAll)
{
    long        numWindows;
    long        rawIndex;

    /* There are three flavors of formAbsolutePosition key: */
    /* typeLongInteger/typeIndexDescriptor, typeRelativeDescriptor, */
    /* and typeAbsoluteOrdinal. */

    /* 1. Initialize some values. */
    *getAll = false; *index = 1;
    numWindows = CountUserWindows(); /* A private routine */

    /* 2. Get the number out of the key. If it's not an absolute */
    /* value, convert it to one. */
    rawIndex = **(long**)(keyData->dataHandle);
    switch (keyData->descriptorType) {

        case typeLongInteger:
            if (rawIndex < 0)
            /* A negative value means "the Nth object from the end," */
            /* i.e., -1 = the last object. */
                rawIndex = numWindows + rawIndex + 1;
            /* A positive value is an absolute value, so do nothing. */
        break;

        case typeAbsoluteOrdinal:
            /* kAEFirst, etc. are special 4-byte constants. */
            if (rawIndex == kAEFirst)        rawIndex = 1;
            else if (rawIndex == kAELast)    rawIndex = numWindows;
            else if (rawIndex == kAEMiddle)  rawIndex = numWindows / 2;
            else if (rawIndex == kAEAll)        *getAll = true;
```

```
        else if (rawIndex == kAEAny) {  /* Select a random window. */
            if (numWindows <= 1)    /* 0 or 1 */
                rawIndex = numWindows;
            else
            /* Get a random number between 1 and numWindows. */
                rawIndex = 1 + ((unsigned long)Random() % numWindows);
        }
        else return errAEBadKeyForm;
    break;
    }
    return noErr;
} /* GetWindowIndex */
```

To install an accessor, use the AEInstallObjectAccessor routine:

```
pascal OSErr AEInstallObjectAccessor (DescType desiredClass,
    DescType containerType, accessorProcPtr theAccessor,
    long accessorRefcon, Boolean isSysHandler)
```

In the "extract a Window from a null container" example, the call to the AEInstallObjectAccessor routine would look like this:

```
err = AEInstallObjectAccessor(cWindow, 'null',
    (accessorProcPtr)WindowFromNull, 0, false);
```

You can also install accessor routines to get one of the properties of an object (use the special constant 'prop' in specifying the desired type), or you can supply a wild card for either the container or the desired type. Most developers install one accessor routine for each of the element types supported by a particular object, and one accessor routine to handle all of the properties of that object.

WHAT SHOULD I PUT INTO A TOKEN?

As noted earlier, accessors communicate with each other and with the application using application-specific tokens. Most Apple events that contain an object specifier end up resolving the object specifier into a token and then manipulating the data represented by that token. Since the format of each object class is different, you'll typically write Read Token Data and Write Token Data routines for each object class that your application supports. (You might also choose to write Create Token Data (Create Element) and Delete Token Data routines if more than one Apple event in a given object needs to create or delete information.) What you put into these token-handling routines depends completely on the contents of your tokens.

Each token is stored in an Apple event descriptor—a data structure containing a 4-byte type code and a handle to some data, where the contents of the handle are completely up to you. While this raises the question of what should go into the handle, many developers decide to invent a different token data type for each object class or set of related object classes.

In this approach, a window token would contain a WindowPtr, a text token would contain a handle to some text, and so on. Since tokens are used for both elements and properties, each token might also contain a 4-byte property code.

Here's how the tokens might look for the object classes defined in Figure A.1:

```
struct DocumentTokenBody {
    WindowPtr       theWindow;
    Boolean     useProperty;
    DescType        propertyCode;
};

struct RectTokenBody {
    Rect            *theRect;           /* Use a pointer so we can read */
                                        /* and write the rectangle. */

    long            elementNumber;      /* See token-handling examples */
                                        /* below. */

    Boolean     useProperty;
    DescType        propertyCode;
    WindowPtr       parentWindow;       /* The window that holds this */
                                        /* rectangle. */
};

struct WordTokenBody {
    Handle          theText;
    long            startingOffset;  /* How many bytes in does the text */
                                     /* start? */
    long            textLength;         /* How many bytes long? */
    Boolean     useProperty;
    DescType        propertyCode;
    TEHandle        parent;             /* The location from which we took */
                                        /* this text. */
};
```

These three sample tokens demonstrate several things you should keep in mind when designing your own tokens:

- Each token contains a reference to the data—not a copy of the data itself. This allows the same token to be used for both reading and writing the data.

- Each token contains a field for the property code. If the application received the object specifier "the Name of Document 1," the returned token would contain a pointer to the document's window and the Name property code—'pnam'. The token-handling routines have to include code to support property tokens.

- Since each token format is different, you'll need to write the token-handling routines (Read/Write and, optionally, Insert/Delete) for each token type.

- The Word and Rectangle tokens contain references to the objects that contain them. This is important, since changing the text or the rectangle could affect the document containing the information and there's no way to get either a partially resolved object specifier or the intermediate products of the resolution. Therefore, if you need to know the parent of a particular token, you must store a copy of that information in the child token yourself, since the OSL may dispose of the original parent token. (You may need to supply a custom DisposeToken callback if your tokens contain handles or pointers to other data.)

The guidelines given above cover the contents of the token's handle, but they don't say anything about the descriptorType field. When you return a token from an accessor routine, you must put the proper type code into the descriptorType field of the AEDesc. This is required because the OSL uses the returned token type from one step of the resolution process to guide the next step. Having the accessor routines control the resolution process actually insulates outside Apple event sources from having to know about your specific implementation details.

Throughout the article, we've assumed that the token type in the token is the same as the external data type specified by the object specifier. However, your code can put anything in the token type field as long as you write the matching object accessors for those token types.

For example, let's say that you've written a word-processing program, and another application sends the request "Get Data Word 2 of Paragraph 2 of Window 1" where the italicized part is an object specifier. The returned type would probably be some styled text. However, if the requester had sent "Get Data Word 1 of the Name of Window 1," your application would have to access a completely different form of text (a simple Str255) and might return some nonstyled text.

Internally, the data type that represents text within a document can be different from the data type representing a simple string. Instead of forcing the user to use two different terms for the same thing (documentWord and plainTextWord, perhaps), the application can make this determination at run time. Figure A.7 shows how an application might resolve the two preceding examples.

FIGURE A.7

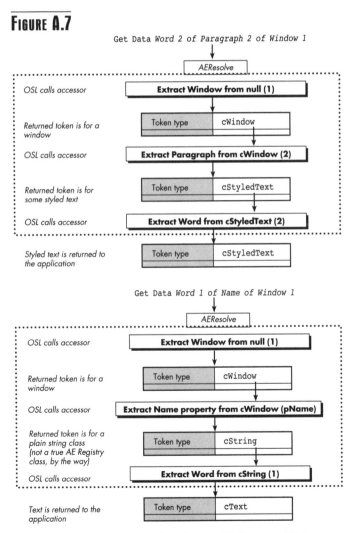

Controlling Object Specifier Resolution with Returned Tokens

WHAT ARE TOKEN-HANDLING ROUTINES?

Token-handling routines are optional routines (in other words, routines not explicitly required by the object model or OSL) that perform common editing operations on the data referred to by a token. Generally, when you have a token, you want to read, write, insert, or delete the data the token refers to. Here are Read Token Data and Write Token Data handlers for the cRectangle object class:

```
struct RectTokenBody {
    Rect         *theRect;     /* Use a pointer so we can read */
                               /* and write the rectangle. */
    long         elementNumber;
    Boolean      useProperty;
    DescType     propertyCode;
    WindowPtr    parentWindow;  /* The window that holds this rectangle. */
};

typedef struct RectTokenBody RectTokenBody;
typedef RectTokenBody *RectTokenPtr, **RectTokenHandle;

OSErr ReadRectToken (const AEDesc *theToken, AEDesc *result)
{
/* This routine gets called by the Get Data Apple event handler (or any */
/* other handler that needs to read some data and possibly return it to */
/* the user). If the useProperty flag is true, we return the requested */
/* property, otherwise we return the default representation for this */
/* class (we'll use the cQDRect primitive type for this). */
    RectTokenPtr    tokenPtr;
    DescType        descCode;
    OSErr           err;

    HLock(theToken->dataHandle);
    tokenPtr = (RectTokenPtr)*theToken->dataHandle;
    if (tokenPtr->useProperty) {
      switch (tokenPtr->propertyCode) {

          case pClass:
             /* Tell the world that this is a rectangle. */
             descCode = cRectangle;
             err = AECreateDesc(typeType, (Ptr)&descCode,
                 sizeof(descCode), result);
          break;

          case pBounds:
             /* Return the bounds of this rectangle, as a QuickDraw */
```

```
            /* rectangle. */
            err = AECreateDesc(typeQDRectangle,
                (Ptr)&tokenPtr->theRect, sizeof(Rect), result);
        break;

        /* More property codes go here... */

        default:
            err = errAENoSuchObject;
    }
  }
  else {
      /* Return the default representation. In this simple example, */
      /* it's a QuickDraw rectangle. */
      err = AECreateDesc(typeQDRectangle, (Ptr)&tokenPtr->theRect,
                                   sizeof(Rect), result);
  }
  return err;
}


OSErr WriteRectToken (const AEDesc *theToken, const AEDesc *theData)
{
/* This routine gets called by the Set Data Apple event handler (or */
/* any other handler that needs to change a property or some value */
/* of the object). If the useProperty flag is true, we check to see */
/* if the property is writable and modify it, otherwise we change */
/* the contents of this object. */

    RectTokenPtr        tokenPtr;
    AEDesc              thisRectDesc;
    OSErr               err;

    HLock(theToken->dataHandle);
    tokenPtr = (RectTokenPtr)*theToken->dataHandle;
    if (tokenPtr->useProperty) {
      switch (tokenPtr->propertyCode) {
          case pClass: /* This is a read-only property. */
              err = errAEWriteDenied;
          break;

          case pBounds: /* Set the bounds of this rectangle. */
              /* Make sure we have a QuickDraw Rectangle. */
              err = AECoerceDesc(theToken, typeQDRectangle,
                  &thisRectDesc);
              if (err != noErr) return err;
              /* Copy the data into our rectangle. */
              BlockMove(*thisRectDesc.dataHandle, &tokenPtr->theRect,
                  sizeof(Rect));
              AEDisposeDesc(&thisRectDesc);
```

```
        break;

        /* More property codes go here... */

        default:
            err = errAENoSuchObject;
        }
    }
    else {
        /* Change the default representation (the bounds of this */
/* rectangle). */
        err = AECoerceDesc(theToken, typeQDRectangle, &thisRectDesc);
        if (err != noErr) return err;
        /* Copy the data into our rectangle. */
        BlockMove(*thisRectDesc.dataHandle, &tokenPtr->theRect,
            sizeof(Rect));
        AEDisposeDesc(&thisRectDesc);
    }
    return err;
}
```

The contents of the Create Element and Delete Token Data routines are completely application-specific and are not illustrated here. Typically, the Create Element routine takes a token for the element's container and an index position within that container, and returns an object specifier describing the new element. (This object specifier may be returned as the result of a Create Element Apple event, or may be resolved so that you can insert some data into the newly created element.)

> The cRectangle class used in this code is simplified. Remember that if you're implementing the real cRectangle class from the Apple Event Registry, you'll need to support many more properties and a more complex default representation.

COMBINING OBJECTS AND EVENTS

Once you've created the object event dispatcher code, the object accessor routines, the token formats, and the token handlers, your last task is to write the actual event-handling routines. (These are different from the routines that you install into the Apple Event Manager's dispatch table; event-handling routines do the work for a specific event as handled by a specific object class.) While the exact content of these routines is application dependent, they do have some features in common:

- Routines that need to return something to the outside world can use a Read Token Data handler to convert an internal token into an externally usable form, and can use the other token manipulation routines as needed.

- Each routine should accept both the event and the reply record as parameters. The results from an event are typically placed into the direct parameter of the reply record. When your event has finished execution, the Apple Event Manager will send the reply back to the client application.

MOVING ON

Writing an object model application isn't difficult; once you've implemented an object or two (including the accessors and tokens) and a couple of events, you should have a good understanding of the issues. I hope that this article has given you a good idea of where and how to begin adding the object model to your application. If you still need help there are several options: reading the related documentation (see the box below); looking at the sample code on the Developer CD Series disc (the samples Quill and AEObject-Edition Sample in the Apple Events and Scripting Development Kit and the sample code provided with this article); talking with other programmers; training through Apple's Developer University; and using the on-line support available through AppleLink, CompuServe, and other means.

Good luck! We all look forward to seeing the exciting things that can be done when applications can work both cooperatively and under the control of scripting environments.

Related Reading

- *Inside Macintosh Volume VI* (Addison-Wesley, 1991) provides fundamental information about Apple events. Chapter 1 gives an overview of interapplication communication and explains the relationship of the Apple Event Manager to other parts of System 7. Chapter 6 provides a complete description of Apple events, explains how to send and receive Apple events, and includes reference information for all Apple Event Manager routines.

- The Apple Event Manager chapter of the new, improved Inside Macintosh (preliminary draft) on the *Developer CD Series* disc provides information about Apple event objects and object classes.

- *Apple Event Registry: Standard Suites,* on the *Developer CD Series* disc, describes standard Apple events, Apple event data types, and Apple event object classes. A printed version of the Apple Event Registry is available from APDA (#R0130LL/A).

BIOGRAPHY

RICHARD CLARK is an instructor and course designer in Apple's Developer University, is no stranger to projects both large and small. (He claims that both of his recent projects—the new Advanced System 7 class and Daniel Guy Clark—took around nine months and developed a life of their own.) When he's not playing with his new son, you can find him dancing in local Renaissance Faires, stunt kite flying, searching for the ultimate chocolate recipe, and dreaming up horrible new puns.

THANKS TO OUR TECHNICAL REVIEWERS

Kevin Calhoun, Donn Denman, C. K. Haun, Eric House, Bennet Marks •

BETTER APPLE EVENT CODING THROUGH OBJECTS
ERIC M. BERDAHL

Appendix

Reprinted with permission of Apple Computer, Inc. from *develop*, The Apple Technical Journal, Issue 12. *develop* is a prize-winning quarterly journal that provides an in-depth look at code and techniques that have been reviewed for robustness by Apple engineers. Each issue comes with a CD that contains the source code for that issue, as well as all back issues, Technical Notes, sample code, and other useful software and documentation. Subscriptions to *develop* are available through APDA (1-800-282-2732), Apple Link DEV.SUBS, or Internet dev.subs@applelink.apple.com.

In "Apple Event Objects and You" in develop Issue 10, (Appendix A) Richard Clark discusses a procedural approach to programming for Apple events and goes into details of the Apple event object model. This article reveals a few simple truths about the significance of Apple events and the Apple event object model, focusing on how the object model maps onto a typical object-oriented application. It also provides an object-oriented C++ framework for adding scripting support.

It's every developer's worst nightmare: Your team has just spent the last two years putting the finishing touches on the latest version of Turbo WhizzyWorks II NT Pro, which does everything, including make coffee. As a reward for your great work, the team is now preparing to do some serious tanning development on an exotic island. Then, Marketing comes in with "one last request." They promise it's the last thing they'll ask for before shipping, and in a weak moment, you agree that one last little feature won't hurt your itinerary. "Good," quips the product manager, "then as soon as you add full scripting support, you can enjoy your vacation."

You know that to add scripting support, you need to delve into Apple events. You think this requires learning about Apple events, the Apple event object model, and scripting systems. Further, you think Apple events must be designed into your application from the ground up and can't possibly be added without a complete redesign. Which of the following is the appropriate reaction to Marketing's request?

A. Immediately strangle your sales manager and plead justifiable homicide.

B. Look around while laughing hysterically and try to find the hidden Candid Camera.

C. Change jobs.

D. Feign deafness.

E. None of the above.

Unfortunately, there's no correct answer, but the scenario is all too real as developers are increasingly being asked to add scripting support to their applications. The design of Apple events and the Apple event object model can provide the user with more power than any other scripting system. However, to access the power of the design you need to work with the complex interface provided by the Apple Event Manager. By its nature, this interface collapses to a procedural plane of programming that prevents developers from fully taking advantage of the object-oriented design inherent in the Apple event world. The Apple event object model is difficult to implement without some fancy footwork on the part of your framework. But remember the words of Marshall Brodeen, "All magic tricks are easy, once you know the secret." With this in mind, join me on a trip through the rabbit hole into AppleEventLand.

Marshall Brodeen, a.k.a. Wizzo the Wacky Wizard from station WGN's "Bozo's Circus," was a television spokesman for T.V. Magic Cards.•

WHAT ARE APPLE EVENTS AND THE OBJECT MODEL?

Whenever I give presentations on Apple events, the audience has an overwhelming urge to ignore the theory and jump into coding. Resist the urge. For most developers Apple events provide an unfamiliar perspective on application design. To appreciate the significance of Apple events and the object model, it's important to understand their underlying concepts and background. So, although you'll be reading about code later, a little theory needs to come first.

At the most basic level, Apple events are a program-to-program communication (PPC) system, where program is defined as a piece of code that the Macintosh can see as an application (in other words, that has a real WaitNextEvent-based event loop). However, billing Apple events as PPC is akin to describing an F-16 as merely a plane. To fully understand how Apple events are more than simple program-to-program communication, you need to take a look at the Apple event object model.

The object model isn't really defined in a pithy paragraph of Inside Macintosh, but is instead a holistic approach to dealing with things that users call objects. In a literal sense, the object model is a software developer's description of user-centric objects or cognitive objects.

Cognitive Theory

Cognitive science tells us that people interact with the world through objects. A printed copy of develop is an object, a plant in the corner of your office is an object, and a can of Coke Classic on your desk is an object. Each of the objects has properties, behaviors, and parts. Some properties exist for each of the objects (for example, each one has a name) and other properties make sense for only some of the objects (for example, page size makes sense only when applied to develop). Behaviors are quite similar to properties in their ephemeral binding to objects. Only Coke will fizz, but all three objects will decompose. However, they each decompose in a different way. Further, each object can be separated into arbitrary parts that are themselves objects. The plant can be separated into branches, which can in turn be separated into leaves. The plant itself can also be separated into leaves, so leaves are contained by both branch objects and plant objects.

Back Inside the Computer

Now, since a user will someday interact with your software, and since users interact with the world in terms of cognitive objects, it makes sense to model software in terms of cognitive objects. Hence, the object model describes objects in a rather ghostlike fashion whereby objects have behaviors and properties and contain other objects. Although the object model defines an inheritance for each category of objects (for example, Journal might inherit from OpenableThing which might inherit from Object), it's used only for the purpose of grouping similar behaviors. Just as in the mind, the only thing that's important is the identity of a specific object in existence at a given time—its categorization is purely a detail of implementation.

Gee, this sounds a lot like what real programmers mean when they talk about objects. Strangely enough, real objects and cognitive objects are quite related. Many references cite cognitive theory as justification for beginning to program in an object-oriented style. Object-oriented code tries to get closer to the language of the native operating system of the human mind than traditional procedural approaches, and the format of an Apple event object mirrors natural language to a surprisingly large degree. It comes as no surprise, then, that Good Object Design lends itself quite easily to slipping in support for Apple event scripting.

APPLE EVENT OBJECTS AND SCRIPTING

The motivation for you to provide object model support is so that your users can "script" your application. There are a variety of solutions available today that allow advanced users to write things that resemble DOS batch files or UNIX® shell scripts. These entities are commonly called scripts, but in the context of Apple events a script is something with greater potential. Whenever a user thinks "I want to sharpen the area around the rose in this picture," a script has been formed. If this seems too simplistic, consider it again. Script here refers to the earliest conception of a user's intent to do something. It's not relegated to the world of the computer and does not imply any given form or class of forms; an oral representation (voice interface a la the Knowledge Navigator) is equally as valid as a written one (traditional scripting systems). From this perspective, the definition of script takes the user to a greater depth of control over applications than previously dreamed of, allowing access to the very engine of your application by the very engine of the user. This is the great empowering ability of Apple events: they enable users to use their native operating system—the mind—with little or no translation into computerese.

OBJECT-ORIENTED PROGRAMMING OBJECTS

The biggest problem with Apple event objects is the interface provided by the Apple Event Manager. Instead of allowing you to write real object-oriented source code using a given class library that implements basic Apple event and object model functionality, the Apple Event Manager requires you to register every detail programmatically. You must declare what classes exist, which methods exist and where, and what relationships are possible within and between classes. Although at first this flexibility seems advantageous, many developers find it a problem later when they have to declare everything again at run time. Anyone with secret desires to design an object-oriented runtime environment and a compiler/linker combination to support that environment will feel quite at home with Apple event coding.

Good Object Design is sometimes lumped together with pornography as being difficult to define, "but I'll know it when I see it." Others consider the search for G.O.D. as a holy crusade. Rather than giving a thoroughly useless description for G.O.D., here I refer the interested reader to *Developing Object-Oriented Software for the Macintosh* by Alger and Goldstein (Addison-Wesley, 1992).•

The second biggest problem with Apple event objects is that programs aren't written in the Apple event (user) world. Instead, they're often written in object-oriented programming languages like LISP and C++. What's needed is a good generic interface to translate objects from the user world of natural language into the world of LISP or C++ objects. Scripting systems do some of the work by delivering Apple event objects to applications in the form of object specifiers, a strange data structure that resembles a binary form of natural language stuffed into the familiar Apple event generic data structure AEDesc. However, object-oriented applications ship objects around in the form of . . . well . . . objects! So, you need translation from binary natural language to actual objects. Easy, huh? (Don't hurt me yet—this will seem fairly straightforward after reading a bit further.)

AEDesc is the basic Apple event data structure described in *Inside Macintosh Volume VI,* Chapter 6, "The Apple Event Manager."•

Presenting a new interface should solve the problem of the Apple Event Manager interfaces. Presenting that new interface in terms of the familiar object-oriented class libraries should solve the problem of different paradigms. So, if these two problems are approached with an object perspective, it's clear that some of the classes in your program need to include a set of methods that implement object model protocols. Application domain classes must be able to return objects contained within them and to perform generic operations on themselves. It turns out that if your classes also provide the ability to count the number of a specific type of object they contain, you can provide a rudimentary, yet powerful, parsing engine for transforming objects from the Apple event world into the traditional object programming world.

Further analysis indicates that only those application domain classes that correspond to object model classes need this protocol. This indicates that the protocol for providing Apple event object model support is probably appropriate to provide in a mixin class (a class that's meant to be multiply inherited from). In this way, only those classes that need to provide object model support must provide the necessary methods. In the sample application discussed later, that class is called MAppleObject. MAppleObject plays a key role in UAppleObject, a generic unit that can be used to provide Apple event object model support to any well-designed C++ application.

Apple provides a convenient solution to the user versus programming language problem in the form of the Object Support Library (OSL). The OSL has the specific responsibility of turning an object specifier into an application's internal representation of an object. (See "A Sample OSL Resolution" for an example of how the OSL actually works.) The OSL implements a generic parsing engine, applying a few simple assumptions about the state of the application's design to the problem. However, for all the power provided by the engine within the OSL, it lacks an object-oriented interface. Instead, it uses a paradigm like that provided by the Apple Event Manager, requiring the application to register a set of bottleneck routines to provide application-specific functionality. As with the Apple Event Manager, you must write routines that implement runtime dispatching to the individual objects your application creates instead of using the natural method-dispatching mechanisms found in your favorite object-oriented language, whatever it may be.

The nicest thing about the OSL is that, like the Apple Event Manager itself, it applies itself quite well to being wrapped with a real object-oriented interface (although you have to write it yourself, sigh). Curiously, the OSL solves both problems—poor interface and cognitive versus object-oriented programming differences. With a nice object-oriented framework, you can write your code once, in the fashion to which you're accustomed. I won't lie to you by telling you the job becomes easy, but it does change from obscure and harrowing to straightforward and tedious.

A Sample OSL Resolution

Here's a short example to give you a feel for how the OSL actually works. Don't read too much into the details of object resolution, but do try to understand the flow and methodology the OSL applies to resolve object specifiers. Also, don't worry too much about how the OSL asks questions; the protocol you'll actually be using in UAppleObject hides such details from you.

Figure B.1 on the next page gives an overview of the process. Consider the simple object specifier "the third pixel in the first scan line of the image called 'Girl with Hat,'" and an Apple event that says "Lighten the third pixel in the first scan line of the image called 'Girl with Hat' by twenty gray levels." On receiving this Apple event (Lighten) the application notes that the direct object of the event (the third pixel in the first scan line of the image called "Girl with Hat") is an object specifier and asks the OSL to resolve it into a real object.

At this point the parsing engine in the OSL takes over, beginning a dialog with your application through a set of preregistered callback routines. Notice that the object specifier bears a striking resemblance to a clause of natural language — English in this case. This is not unintentional. Apple event objects are cognitive objects, and cognitive objects are described by natural language — hence the parallels between object specifier formats and natural language. Further, the parsing engine inside the OSL operates like a high school sophomore parsing sentences at the chalkboard. But I digress . . .

To continue, the OSL asks the null object to give it a token for the image called "Girl with Hat." (Tokens are the Coin of the Realm to the OSL.) So the null object looks through its images to find the one named "Girl with Hat" and returns a token to it.

The OSL then turns around and asks the image called "Girl with Hat" to give it a token for the first scan line. After getting this token, the OSL has no further use for the image token, so it's returned to the application for disposal. In effect, this says, "Uh, hey guys, I'm done with this token. If you want to do anything like free memory or something, you can do it now." Notice how polite the OSL is.

Next, the OSL asks the scan line for a token representing the third pixel, which the line handily returns. Now it's the scan line token's turn to be returned to the application for recycling. The OSL has no further use for the scan line token, so the application can get rid of it if necessary.

Finally, having retrieved the token for the third pixel of the first line of the image called "Girl with Hat," the OSL returns the token with a "Thanks, and come again." The application can then ask the object represented by the token to lighten itself (remember that was the original Apple event), and dispose of the token for the pixel.

As you can see, the OSL operates by taking an unreasonable request, "give me the third pixel of the first line of the image called "Girl with Hat," and breaks it into a number of perfectly reasonable requests. Thus, your application gets to take advantage of its innate knowledge of its objects and their simple relationships to answer questions about complex object relationships.

FIGURE B.1

Resolving an Object Specifier

OBJECT MODEL CONCEPTS

There are two basic concepts defined in the object model. One is containment, which means that every object can be retrieved from within some other object. In the language of the object model, every object is contained by another object. The only exception to this rule is the single object called the null object. The null object is commonly called the application object, and may or may not be contained by another object. In practice, a null object specifier is like a global variable defined by the object model. The application implicitly knows which object is meant by "null object." Object resolution always begins by making some query of the null object.

For example, with a simple image processor, it would be appropriate to state that pixels are contained by scan lines, scan lines by images, and images by windows. It's also appropriate to have pixels contained by images and windows. Windows themselves have no natural container, however. Therefore, they must be contained by the null object. One way you can decide whether these relationships make sense for your product is to ask if a user could find it useful to do something to "the eighth pixel of the second scan line" or to "the twentieth pixel of the image." If statements like these make sense, a containment relationship exists.

The second basic concept of the object model is behavior. Behavior is quite simple; it means that objects must be able to respond to an Apple event. Behavior correlates directly with the traditional object programming concept of methods of a class. In fact, as you'll see, the actual Apple event–handling method of Apple event objects is usually a switch statement that turns an Apple event into a dispatch to the C++ method that implements the Apple event's functionality.

Taken together, the concepts of containment and behavior define the limits for objects in the model of the Apple event world. The object model resembles the programming worlds of Smalltalk or LISP, where everything is an object. Everything. For those familiar with these paradigms where even integers, characters, and floating-point numbers are full first-citizen objects, the Apple event world will be a refreshing change from traditional programming in C++ and Pascal.

FINDING THE OBJECTS

The overriding concept in designing object model support in your application is to do what makes sense for both you—as the developer—and the user.

1. It's best to begin by deciding what objects exist in your application. To decide what objects exist, do some user testing and ask the users what objects they see and what objects they think of while using your application. If this isn't possible, just pretend you're a user and actually use your application, asking yourself those same questions. For example, if you ask users for a list of objects in an image processing application (and refrain from biasing them with computer mumbo jumbo) they'll probably list such things as window, icon, image, pixel, area, scan line, color, resolution, and menu

FIGURE B.2

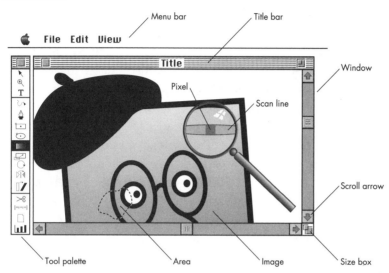

Objects the User Sees

bar. (Figure B.2 shows types of objects a user might list.) Guess
what? In reality, those probably are object model classes that an
image processing application could support when it supports the
object model. Since the objects you'll want to support are user-level
kinds of entities, this makes perfect sense.

2. After deciding what objects exist in your application, run another
    series of user tests to determine the relationships between different
    objects. For example, what objects does a window contain? Menus?
    Pixels? Areas? Color? What objects does an area contain? Pixels?
    Scan lines? Windows? This is just as simple as it seems. Just ask the
    question, "Does this object contain that object?" If you get immedi-
    ate laughter, move on. Positive answers or thoughtful looks indicate
    a possible relationship.

3. Finally, determine what properties and behaviors each object class
    will have. These questions can be asked during the same user test
    as in step 2 because the answers users will give are closely related.
    Will you be able to ask windows for their names or pixels for their
    colors? How about asking windows to move or close? Can you ask
    pixels to change color or make a copy?

    You may have noticed that this approach falls into the category of
Good Object Design. Undoubtedly, anyone who does object-oriented

design has gone through a similar process when developing an application. Resist the temptation to design the application's internal structure using G.O.D. and be done with it, because the object model design is different from the application design. When designing the application, you typically analyze structure from the perspective of eventually implementing the design. Thus, you impose design constraints to make implementation easier. For example, you probably don't keep representations of images, areas, and pixels, but choose one model for your internal engine—a reasonable solution for a programmer looking at the problem space. A typical image processing program usually has real classes representing images, and probably has an area class, but may not have a pixel class or scan line class. Pixels and scan lines may be implemented by a more basic representation than classes—simple indices or pointers into a PixMap, for example.

However, when you design object model support, you have a very different perspective. You're designing classes based on user expectation and intention, not on programmer constraints. In object model design of an image processor, you do have TImage, TArea, TScanLine, and TPixel classes, regardless of your internal representation. This is because a user sees all these classes. The TImage and TArea may be the same as your internal engine's TImage and TArea, and probably are. After all, there's little reason to ignore a perfectly usable class that already exists. However, the TPixel and TScanLine classes exist only to provide object model support. I call classes that exist only to provide object model support ephemeral classes.

Undeniably, the most useful tool for finding objects is user testing. Another important source of information is the Apple Event Registry. The Apple Event Registry describes Apple event classes that are standardized in the Apple event world. The Registry lists each class along with its inheritance, properties, and behaviors. It's also the last word on the values used to code object model support. For example, constants for predefined Boolean operators and class types are listed in detail. As you follow the process for finding the objects in your application, you can use the elements found in the Registry as a basis for your investigation and for later implementation. For example, if your user tests reveal that a pixel class is appropriate for your application and a Pixel class is documented in the Registry, you should probably use the behaviors and properties documented there as a basis for your application's TPixel class. Doing so allows your application to work well with existing scripts that manipulate pixels and allows your users to have a consistent scripting experience across all pixel-using applications.

> The Apple Event Registry is on the *Developer CD Series* disc and is available in print from APDA (#R0130LL/A).

OSL Concepts

In addition to the principles imposed by the object model itself, the OSL makes a few reasonable assumptions about what applications provide to support their objects. Since the object model requires that objects be able to retrieve contained objects, the OSL allows an object to count the number of objects of a given type contained within them. So, if an image contains scan lines, the image object needs to be able to count the number of scan line objects contained within it. Of course, in some circumstances, the number of objects that are contained can't be counted or is just plain big (try asking how many TSand objects are contained in a TBeach object). In this case, the OSL allows the object to indicate that the number can't be counted.

Additionally, the OSL allows applications to apply simple Boolean operators to two objects. The operators themselves are a part of the Apple Event Registry. They include the familiar operators like less than, equal to, and greater than as well as some more interesting relations like before, after, over, and under. The requirement for these operators is that they have Boolean results. This means that if object1 and object2 have operator applied to them, the expression object1 operator object2 is either true or false. Of course, there's no requirement that every class implement every operator, only those that make sense. It makes little sense to ask if an object of type TColor is greater than another, but brighter than is another story.

During resolution of an Apple event, the OSL asks for tokens of objects between the application object and the final target to be returned (as described earlier in this article in "A Sample OSL Resolution"). To a programmer, they look like AEDescs being passed around, but the OSL treats them specially:

• The OSL guarantees that it will never ever look in the data portion of the token, the dataHandle field of the AEDesc. It may peek at the descriptorType field from time to time, but the data itself is golden. This becomes a critical point when applying the OSL engine to an object-oriented interface. The token data of Apple event objects should be "real" object references in whatever programming language is appropriate, and keeping the data completely private to the application makes this possible.

- The application must be able to recognize the token when it appears again. Thus, if the application returns a token for the image "Girl with Hat" to the OSL, the application must be able to recognize the significance of having that token passed back by the OSL.

- The OSL asks only that we guarantee the validity of a token during the resolution of the current object specifier.

Since the data contained in the AEDescs is private, the OSL must provide a system for the application to know when a token is being created and when it's being terminated. Creation of tokens is provided through the containment accessor protocol. Termination is provided by a callback routine which does the actual token disposal and which the application registers with the OSL. This callback is invoked from AEDisposeToken and comes in handy when applying the object model to C++ classes.

There are also a number of features that are beyond the scope of this article. One of these is the OSL concept of marking objects. This means that objects are labeled as belonging to a particular group. The contract the OSL makes with the application is that the OSL will ask whenever it needs a new kind of mark, and the application will recognize whether any object is marked with a particular mark. Further, given the mark itself, the application will be able to produce all the objects with that mark. If this sounds particularly confusing, just consider mark objects as typical list objects. Given a list and an object, it's quite natural to answer the question, "Is this object in this list?" Further, it's quite natural to answer the question, "What are all the objects contained in this list?"

The framework for adding Apple event support described later in the section "Inside UAppleObject" satisfies the basic OSL requests for counting objects, applying Boolean operators, and handling tokens. However, it doesn't handle marks. The intrepid reader could add support for this feature with a little thought.

CLASS DESIGN

To incorporate object model support into your applications, you need a class library that implements the object model classes you want to support—for example, the TWindow, TImage, TArea, and TPixel classes described earlier. These classes exist because they represent Apple event objects the application will support. Then you create a mapping of Apple event objects to the C++ classes that implement them (see Figure B.3). For the sake of argument, say that TWindow, TArea, and TImage are also part of the class library used to implement the non–object-model portions of the program. The TPixel class is an ephemeral class. What these four classes have in common is a mixin class, MAppleObject, that provides the hooks for adding object model functionality (see the next section, "Inside UAppleObject," for more details).

FIGURE B.3

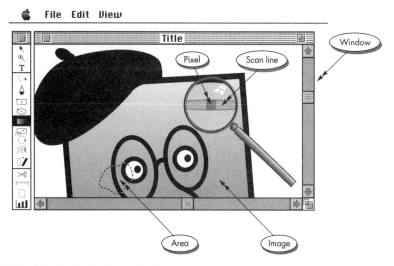

The Objects As Implemented

MAppleObject must include protocol that implements the object model and OSL concepts. Given an MAppleObject, there should be protocol for returning an object contained within MAppleObject. This accessor method is expected to return an object that satisfies the containment request. It also needs to inform the framework if the returned object is an ephemeral object—some might say that such an object is lazy evaluated into existence. As a practical matter, this informs the framework whether an object needs to be deleted when the OSL disposes of the object's token (as described in "A Sample OSL Resolution"). Obviously, it would be undesirable to have the framework delete the TImages because the application depends on them for its internal representation. It would be equally stomach-turning to have all the TPixels pile up in the heap, never to be deleted.

> The naming convention I use for classes differentiates between classes that are intended to be instantiated directly and those that are intended to be used as a mixin class. Classes that are directly instantiable begin with an uppercase T — TPixel, for example. Similarly, mixin classes begin with an uppercase M — MAppleObject, for example.

Since TPixel objects don't actually exist until they're lazy evaluated into existence, you're free to design their implementation in a wide variety of ways. Remember that one of the contracts the OSL makes with the application is that tokens need to be valid only during the resolution of the current object specifier. Well, consider that the implementation of images is just a handle of gray values. Normally, if someone suggested that a pixel be implemented as an index into a block of data, you'd throw temper tantrums. "What!" you'd yell, "What if the pixel is moved in the image! Now the index is stale." This is not an issue for tokens, because they're transient. Since pixels won't be added during the resolution of an object specifier, such a representation is fine. Of course, if you'd prefer a more robust implementation, that's fine, too, but remember that the OSL doesn't impose such robustness on you.

MAppleObject must also include a protocol to implement the comparison operators, counting protocol, and behavior dispatching. As a practical matter, these methods will likely be large switch statements that call other, more meaningful, methods depending on the details of the request. For example, the counting protocol might key on the kind of objects that should be counted and invoke methods specialized to count contained objects of a specific class.

> TPixel objects don't actually exist until someone — usually the OSL — asks for them. Before that, pixels are hidden within other objects, probably TImage or TArea objects. However, when someone asks for a pixel object, suddenly a TPixel is lazy evaluated into existence.

Finally, each class provides protocol for telling clients which object model class the object represents. This is necessary for the framework to be able to communicate with the OSL. During the resolution conversation the OSL holds with the framework, the framework returns descriptors of each object the OSL asks for. These descriptors are required to publish to the OSL the type of the object returned from the request.

INSIDE UAPPLEOBJECT

UAppleObject is a framework whose main contribution is the class MAppleObject. MAppleObject provides the basis for integrating Apple event objects and Apple event object support into object-oriented applications. UAppleObject also includes a dispatcher, TAppleObjectDispatcher, and the 'aedt' resource. You drop the UAppleObject files into your application and immediately begin subclassing to provide Apple event functionality.

Exception Handling in UAppleObject

Developers familiar with the details of Apple event implementation are no doubt aware that the Apple Event Manager deals exclusively with error code return values, as does the rest of the Toolbox. When the Apple Event Manager invokes a developer-supplied callback routine, that routine commonly returns an integer error code. This style of error handling is found nowhere in UAppleObject. Instead, UAppleObject uses the UMAFailure unit to provide exception handling. UMAFailure is a unit available on the Developer CD Series disc that provides both a MacApp-style exception-handling mechanism for non-MacApp programs and excellent documentation for its use.

Wherever UAppleObject is invoked through a callback routine that expects an error code to be returned, all exceptions are caught and the exception's error code is returned to the Toolbox. Therefore, when an error occurs, call the appropriate FailXXX routine provided by UMAFailure—for example FailMemError, FailNIL, or FailOSErr. In the UAppleObject documentation, calling one of these routines is referred to as throwing an exception.

MAppleObject

The major workhorse of UAppleObject is MAppleObject, an implementation of the basic Apple event object functionality. MAppleObject is an
abstract mixin class that provides the protocol necessary for the
UAppleObject framework to resolve Apple event objects and handle
Apple events.

```
class MAppleObject
{
public:
            MAppleObject();
            MAppleObject(const MAppleObject& copy);
    virtual ~MAppleObject();

    MAppleObject& operator=(const MAppleObject& assignment);

    virtual DescType GetAppleClass() const = 0;

    virtual long CountContainedObjects(DescType ofType);
    virtual MAppleObject* GetContainedObject(DescType desiredType,
        DescType keyForm, const AEDesc& keyData, Boolean& needDisposal);
    virtual Boolean CompareAppleObjects(DescType compareOperator,
        const MAppleObject& toWhat);
    virtual void DoAppleEvent(const AppleEvent& message,
        AppleEvent& reply, long refCon);

    static void SetDefaultAppleObject(MAppleObject* defaultObject);
    static MAppleObject* GetDefaultAppleObject();

    static void GotRequiredParameters(const AppleEvent& theAppleEvent);

    static void InitAppleObject(TAppleObjectDispatcher* dispatcher = nil);
};
```

GetAppleClass

```
DescType GetAppleClass() const = 0;
```

GetAppleClass is an abstract method that returns the object model type
of an object. Every MAppleObject subclass should override this method
to return the object model type specific to the individual object.

CountContainedObjects

```
long CountContainedObjects(DescType ofType);
```

CountContainedObjects should return the number of objects of the indicated type that are contained within the receiver object. This is usually
done by counting the number of objects your subclass knows how to
access and adding it to the number of objects the parent class finds (in
other words, call the inherited version and add it to the number you find
yourself). If the number of objects is too large to be enumerated in a
signed 16-bit integer, CountContainedObjects may throw the
errAEIndexToo-Large exception.

GetContainedObject

```
MAppleObject* GetContainedObject(DescType desiredType, DescType keyForm,
    const AEDesc& keyData, Boolean& needDisposal);
```

GetContainedObject is a generic method for obtaining an object
contained by the receiver. Subclasses always override this method to
provide access to the subclass's contained objects. The desiredType,
keyForm, and keyData arguments indicate the specific object to be
returned as the function result. If the resulting object is one used in the
framework of the application, GetContainedObject should return false in
the needDisposal argument.

The alternative is for GetContainedObject to create the resulting
object specifically for this request; in this case, it returns true in the
needDisposal argument. If needDisposal is true, the UAppleObject
framework deletes the result object when it's no longer needed.

CompareAppleObjects

```
Boolean CompareAppleObjects(DescType compareOperator,
    const MAppleObject& toWhat);
```

CompareAppleObjects performs the logical operation indicated by the
arguments, returning the Boolean value of the operation. The semantics
of the operation is this compareOperator toWhat. So, if the compare-
Operator parameter were kAEGreaterThan, the semantics of the method
call would be this is greater than toWhat. Subclasses always override this
method to provide the logical operations they support.

DoAppleEvent

```
void DoAppleEvent(const AppleEvent& message, AppleEvent& reply,
    long refCon);
```

When an object is identified as the target of an Apple event, it's sent the DoAppleEvent message. The message and reply Apple event records are passed in the corresponding arguments. If the direct parameter to the message is typeObjectSpecifier, the object specifier is guaranteed to resolve to the receiver; otherwise the receiver is the application object. Additional modifiers for the event can be extracted from the message, and the reply should be filled in by DoAppleEvent, if appropriate. The refCon parameter is the shortcut number registered with the UAppleObject framework (see the section "The 'aedt' Resource"). Subclasses always override DoAppleEvent to dispatch their supported Apple events to appropriate methods.

SetDefaultAppleObject and GetDefaultAppleObject

```
void MAppleObject::SetDefaultAppleObject(MAppleObject* defaultObject);
MAppleObject* MAppleObject::GetDefaultAppleObject();
```

GetDefaultAppleObject returns the MAppleObject currently registered as the null container. Similarly, SetDefaultAppleObject registers a particular object as the null container. Usually, the object serving as null container doesn't change during the lifetime of the application—it's always the application object. In this case, just call SetDefaultAppleObject from within your application object's constructor. But remember that any Apple event that arrives when no null container is registered falls on the floor and is returned to the Apple Event Manager with the errAEEventNotHandled error.

GotRequiredParameters

```
void MAppleObject::GotRequiredParameters(const AppleEvent&
    theAppleEvent);
```

GotRequiredParameters is here for convenience. To do Apple event processing "right," each Apple event handler should check that it has received everything the sender sent. Almost every good Apple event sample has this routine and calls it from within the handlers. Since all handling is done from within an MAppleObject method, it makes sense for this protocol to be a member function of MAppleObject. However, the member function really doesn't need access to the object itself, and could actually be called from anywhere, so it's a static member function.

InitAppleObject

```
void MAppleObject::InitAppleObject(TAppleObjectDispatcher* dispatcher =
    nil);
```

InitAppleObject must be called once after the application initializes the
Toolbox and before it enters an event loop (specifically, before
WaitNextEvent gets called). This method installs the given object dis-
patcher, or creates a TAppleObjectDispatcher if nil is passed.

TAppleObjectDispatcher

The second element of UAppleObject is TAppleObjectDispatcher.
Together with MAppleObject, TAppleObjectDispatcher forms a complete model of Apple events, the objects themselves, and the Apple
event engine that drives the object protocol. TAppleObjectDispatcher is
responsible for intercepting Apple events and directing them to the
objects that should handle them. A core feature of this engine is the ability to resolve object specifiers into "real" objects.

```
class TAppleObjectDispatcher
{
public:
    TAppleObjectDispatcher();
    virtual ~TAppleObjectDispatcher();

    virtual void Install();

    virtual MAppleObject* ExtractObject(const AEDesc& descriptor);
    virtual void StuffDescriptor(AEDesc& descriptor, MAppleObject* object);

    virtual void HandleAppleEvent(const AppleEvent& message,
        AppleEvent& reply, long refCon);

    virtual void AccessContainedObjects(DescType desiredClass,
        const AEDesc& container, DescType containerClass, DescType form,
        const AEDesc& selectionData, AEDesc& value, long refCon);
    virtual long CountObjects(const AEDesc& containerToken,
        DescType countObjectsOfType);
    virtual Boolean CompareObjects(DescType operation, const AEDesc& obj1,
        const AEDesc& obj2);
    virtual void DisposeToken(AEDesc& unneededToken);

    virtual MAppleObject* GetTarget(const AppleEvent& message);

    virtual void SetTokenObjectDisposal(MAppleObject* tokenObject,
        Boolean needsDisposal);
```

```
virtual Boolean GetTokenObjectDisposal(const MAppleObject*
    tokenObject);

virtual MAppleObject* ResolveSpecifier(AEDesc& objectSpecifier);

virtual void InstallAppleEventHandler(AEEventClass theClass,
    AEEventID theID, long refCon);

static TAppleObjectDispatcher* GetDispatcher();
};
```

Install

```
void Install();
```

Install is called when the dispatcher object is actually installed (at
InitAppleEvent time). It's responsible for reading the 'aedt' resources for
the application and declaring the appropriate handlers to the Apple
Event Manager as well as registering with the OSL. Overrides should call
the inherited version of this member function
to maintain proper functionality. This method may be overridden to provide functionality beyond that supplied by TAppleObjectDispatcher—to
provide for mark tokens, for example, which are left as an exercise for
the reader. (Don'cha just hate it when articles do this to you?)

ExtractObject and StuffDescriptor

```
MAppleObject* ExtractObject(const AEDesc& descriptor);
void StuffDescriptor(AEDesc& descriptor, MAppleObject* object);
```

One of the key abstractions provided by TAppleObjectDispatcher is the
packaging of MAppleObjects into tokens for communication with the
Apple Event Manager and OSL. ExtractObject and StuffDescriptor are
the pair of routines that carry the responsibility for translation.
ExtractObject returns the MAppleObject contained within the token
descriptor, while StuffDescriptor provides the inverse function. These
functions are extensively used internally, but are probably of little interest to clients. Subclasses that override one method should probably override the other as well.

HandleAppleEvent

```
void HandleAppleEvent(const AppleEvent& message, AppleEvent& reply,
    long refCon);
```

HandleAppleEvent is called whenever the application receives an Apple event. All responsibility for distributing the Apple event to an object is held by this member function. HandleAppleEvent is rarely overridden.

> The TAppleObjectDispatcher implementation registers a static member function as the actual handler of the Apple event. This static member function calls the dispatcher's HandleAppleEvent method polymorphically. Thus, you'll most likely get the behavior you want out of an override of HandleAppleEvent.

AccessContainedObjects

```
void AccessContainedObjects(DescType desiredClass,
    const AEDesc& container, DescType containerClass, DescType form,
    const AEDesc& selectionData, AEDesc& value, long refCon);
```

At times during the resolution of an object specifier, MAppleObjects are asked to return objects contained within them. AccessContainedObjects is called when the parsing engine makes that query (in other words, it's the polymorphic counterpart of the OSL's object accessor callback routine). The method is responsible for getting the MAppleObject container, making the appropriate inquiry, and returning the result, properly packed. AccessContainedObjects is rarely overridden.

CountObjects

```
long CountObjects(const AEDesc& containerToken,
    DescType countObjectsOfType);
```

At times during the resolution of an object specifier, it may be helpful to find out how many of a particular object are contained within a token object. This method is called when the parsing engine makes that query (in other words, it's the polymorphic counterpart of the OSL's count objects callback routine). It's responsible for finding the MAppleObject corresponding to the token, making the inquiry of the object, and returning the answer.

CompareObjects

```
Boolean CompareObjects(DescType operation, const AEDesc& obj1,
    const AEDesc& obj2);
```

At times during the resolution of an object specifier, it may be helpful to compare two objects to determine if some logic relationship (for example, less than, equal to, before, or after) holds between them.

CompareObjects is responsible for making the inquiry of the appropriate MAppleObject and returning the result (in other words, it's the polymorphic counterpart of the OSL's compare objects callback routine). The semantics of the operation is obj1 operation obj2. So, if the compareOperator parameter were kAEGreaterThan, the semantics of the method call would be obj1 is greater than obj2. This method is rarely overridden.

DisposeToken

```
void DisposeToken(AEDesc& unneededToken);
```

DisposeToken is called when the OSL determines that a token is no longer necessary. This commonly occurs during resolution of an object specifier. DisposeToken is responsible for acting appropriately (in other words, it's the polymorphic counterpart of the OSL's object disposal callback routine). For the implementation in TAppleObjectDispatcher, this means the routine checks to see if the object is marked as needing disposal, and deletes the object if necessary.

GetTarget

```
MAppleObject* GetTarget(const AppleEvent& message);
```

GetTarget is responsible for looking at the Apple event and determining which object should receive it. Notably, GetTarget is used by HandleAppleEvent. The TAppleObjectDispatcher implementation sends the Apple event to the default object unless the direct parameter is an object specifier. If the direct parameter is an object specifier, it's resolved to an MAppleObject, which is then sent the Apple event. This method is rarely overridden.

SetTokenObjectDisposal and GetTokenObjectDisposal

```
void SetTokenObjectDisposal(MAppleObject* tokenObject,
    Boolean needsDisposal);
Boolean GetTokenObjectDisposal(const MAppleObject* tokenObject);
```

Any MAppleObject can be marked as needing disposal or not needing it. SetTokenObjectDisposal and GetTokenObjectDisposal manage the internal representation of the table that keeps track of such information. You may want to override them both (never do it one at a time) to provide your own representation.

ResolveSpecifier

```
MAppleObject* ResolveSpecifier(AEDesc& objectSpecifier);
```

ResolveSpecifier returns the MAppleObject that corresponds to the object specifier passed as an argument. Under most circumstances, you don't need to call this routine since it's called automatically to convert the direct parameter of an Apple event into an MAppleObject. If, however, in the course of handling an Apple event, you find another parameter whose descriptorType is typeObjectSpecifier, you'll probably want to resolve it through this routine. Remember that objects returned from ResolveSpecifier may need to be deleted when the application is done with them. To accomplish this, you may either stuff the object into an AEDesc by calling StuffDescriptor and then call AEDisposeToken, or ask whether the object needs to be deleted by calling GetTokenObject-Disposal and delete it if true is returned.

InstallAppleEventHandler

```
void InstallAppleEventHandler(AEEventClass theClass, AEEventID theID,
    long refCon);
```

InstallAppleEventHandler is very rarely overridden. It's responsible for registering an Apple event with the Apple Event Manager, notifying the manager that the application handles the Apple event.

GetDispatcher

```
TAppleObjectDispatcher* GetDispatcher();
```

This static member function returns the dispatcher object that's currently installed. It's useful for calling TAppleObjectDispatcher member functions from a global scope.

The 'aedt' Resource

The last piece of the UAppleObject puzzle is the 'aedt' resource. The definition of this resource type is in the Types.r file distributed with MPW. Developers familiar with MacApp's use of the 'aedt' resource already know how it works in UAppleObject because UAppleObject uses the same mechanism.

The 'aedt' resource is simply a list of entries describing the Apple events that an application handles. Each entry contains, in order, the event class, the event ID, and a numeric reference constant. The event class and ID describe the Apple event the application supports and the numeric constant is used internally by your application. The constant should be different for each supported Apple event. This allows your application to recognize the kind of Apple event at run time by looking at the refCon passed to DoAppleEvent.

When installed via the Install method, a TAppleObjectDispatcher object looks at all 'aedt' resources in the application's resource fork, registering all the Apple events in them. Thus, additional Apple event suites can be signified by adding resources instead of adding to one resource. For example, the Rez code to define an 'aedt' resource for the four required Apple events is as follows:

```
resource 'aedt' (100) {{
    'aevt', 'oapp', 1;
    'aevt', 'odoc', 2;
    'aevt', 'pdoc', 3;
    'aevt', 'quit', 4;
}};
```

When the Open Document Apple event ('aevt', 'odoc') is sent to the application, the refCon value to DoAppleEvent is 2. Since you've assigned a unique numeric constant to each different Apple event, a refCon value of 2 can be passed to DoAppleEvent only when the Apple event is Open Document.

To add the mythical foobar Apple event ('foo ', 'bar ') to the application, mapped to number 5, you may either add a line to the resource described above or add another resource:

```
resource 'aedt' (101) {{
    'foo ', 'bar ', 5;
}};
```

Extending CPlusTESample

So far this sounds all well and good. The theory behind adding Apple event object support holds together well on paper. The framework, UAppleObject, has been written and works. The only thing left is to put my money where my mouth is and actually use UAppleObject to demonstrate the addition of Apple events to an Apple event–unaware application. The subject of this foray into the Twilight Zone is CPlusTESample in the Sample Code folder on the Developer CD Series disc. TESample serves as the basis for adding scripting support for object model classes.

> UAppleObject is easier to implement in dynamic languages like Smalltalk or Macintosh Common Lisp. However, these packages don't yet lend themselves to creating commercial applications (no flames, please). The only language that has the requisite malleability and marketability is Uncle Barney's love child. Sorry, folks.

CPlusTESample is attractive for a number of reasons. First, it's a simple application that could support some nontrivial Apple events. Second, it's written in an object-oriented style and contains a decent design from the standpoint of separating the user interface from the engine and internal representation. Finally, it's written in C++, a necessary evil for the use of UAppleObject.

To prove that CPlusTESample actually had the necessary flexibility to add Apple events, I began by adding font, font size, and style menus to the original sample. Adding these features required little modification to the original framework aside from the addition of methods to existing classes. Thus, I was satisfied that the underlying assumptions and framework could hold the paradigm shift of adding Apple event support.

In identifying the objects of the program, I chose windows and text blocks as the central object classes. If I were more gutsy, I would have attempted to actually define words and characters. However, the ancient programmer's credo crept in—it was more work than I was willing to do for this example. Further complicating this decision was the fact that CPlusTESample is built on TextEdit. Therefore, the obvious concepts of paragraphs and words translated exceptionally poorly into the internal representation, TEHandles. Characters would have been simpler than either paragraphs or words, but I copped out and left it as an exercise for the reader.

The relationships between classes are very straightforward. Windows are contained by the null object and text blocks are contained by windows. However, since I had a concept of window, it became interesting to define various attributes contained in windows: name, bounding box, and position. So, object model classes were defined for names, bounding boxes, and positions.

Behaviors were similarly straightforward. Text blocks, names, bounding boxes, and positions had protocol for getting their data and setting their data. Thus, an Apple event could change a name or text block or could ask for a position or bounding box.

In the end, six classes were defined to implement the object model classes: TESample, TEDocument, TWindowName, TWindowBounds, TWindowPosition, and TEditText. TESample is the application class and functions as the null object. TEDocument implements the window class and is used as the internal representation of the document and all its data. The remaining four classes are ephemeral classes that refer to a specific TEDocument instance and represent the indicated feature of that instance.

From that point, it was straightforward to write methods overriding MAppleObject to provide the containment, counting, comparison, and behavior dispatching. You can check out CPlusTESample with Apple event support added on the Developer CD Series disc.

Implementing a Class

This section shows how UAppleObject helps you write cleaner code by looking at one of the CPlusTESample classes in detail—TEditText, the text class. User testing revealed the need for a class to represent the text found inside a CPlusTESample window, so I created a TEditText class whose objects are contained within some window class. Additionally, users wanted to retrieve and set the text represented by the text class. The Apple Event Registry defines a text class that roughly resembles the text class I wanted to provide in my CPlusTESample extension. Therefore, I decided to use the Registry's description as a basis for my TEditText class.

TEditText provides object model support for the user's concept of text, indicating that it should inherit from MAppleObject. TEditText objects don't contain any other objects, so there's no need to override the CountContainedObjects or GetContainedObject methods. However, TEditText objects do respond to Apple events. The Registry says that text objects should provide access to the text data itself through the Set Data and Get Data Apple events. Therefore, TEditText should include methods to implement each Apple event and should override DoAppleEvent to dispatch an Apple event to the appropriate method. After taking all this into account, here's what TEditText looks like:

```
Class TEditText : public MAppleObject
{
public:
   TEditText(TEHandle itsTE);

   virtual void DoAppleEvent(const AppleEvent& message,
      AppleEvent& reply, long refCon);
   virtual DescType GetAppleClass() const;

   virtual void DoAppleGetData(const AppleEvent& message,
      AppleEvent& reply);
   virtual void DoAppleSetData(const AppleEvent& message,
      AppleEvent& reply);
private:
   TEHandle    fTEHandle;
};
```

The constructor is relatively simple to implement. Since
CPlusTESample uses TextEdit records internally, it's natural to implement TEditText in terms of TextEdit's TEHandle data structure.
Therefore, TEditText keeps the TEHandle to which it refers in the
fTEHandle instance variable.

```
TEditText::TEditText(TEHandle itsTE)
{
   fTEHandle = itsTE;
}
```

UAppleObject requires each MAppleObject instance to describe its
object model class type through the GetAppleClass method. Since all
TEditText objects represent the Registry class denoted by typeText,
TEditText's GetAppleClass method is exceptionally straightforward,
blindly returning the typeText constant.

```
DescType TEditText::GetAppleClass() const
{
   return typeText;
}
```

DoAppleEvent is also straightforward. It looks at the refCon parameter to determine which Apple event–handling method should be
invoked. This method represents a large part of the remaining tedium
for Apple event coding. Each class is responsible for translating the inte-
ger-based Apple event specifier, refCon in this example, into a polymorphic method dispatch such as the invocation of DoAppleSetData or

DoAppleGetData. The nice part of this implementation is that subclasses of TEditText won't need to implement DoAppleEvent again if all the subclass needed was the Set Data or Get Data protocol. Instead such a subclass would simply override the DoAppleSetData or DoAppleGetData method and let the C++ method-dispatching mechanisms do the work.

```
void TEditText::DoAppleEvent(const AppleEvent& message,
   AppleEvent& reply, long refCon)
{
   switch (refCon)
   {
   case cSetData:
      this->DoAppleSetData(message, reply);
      break;
   case cGetData:
      this->DoAppleGetData(message, reply);
      break;
   default:
      MAppleObject::DoAppleEvent(message, reply, refCon);
      break;
   }
}
```

DoAppleGetData and DoAppleSetData are the Apple event–handling methods of the TEditText class. To developers familiar with the traditional Apple Event Manager interfaces, these methods are the UAppleObject equivalents of what the Apple Event Manager calls Apple event handlers. Each method follows a general pattern common to most remote procedure call protocols, of which Apple events are an advanced form.

First, the Apple event–handling method reads additional information from the message Apple event. The DoAppleGetData method doesn't happen to need any additional information because the entire meaning of the message is found in the identity of the Apple event itself. However, DoAppleSetData needs one additional piece of information—the text that should be stuffed into the object.

Next, the handler method calls GotRequiredParameters, passing the message Apple event as the sole argument. GotRequiredParameters ensures that the handler has retrieved all the information that the Apple event sender has sent. (For a discussion of why this is necessary, see *Inside Macintosh Volume VI,* Chapter 6.)

Third, the handler method will do whatever is necessary to perform the Apple event and create necessary reply data. The Get Data

Apple event requires the TEditText object to fill the reply Apple event with the text it represents. Therefore, the DoAppleGetData method should retrieve the text contained in the TEHandle and pack it into an appropriate Apple event descriptor, putting that descriptor into the reply Apple event. In contrast to Get Data, the Set Data Apple event requires no reply, but does require that the text represented by the TEditText object be changed to reflect the text contained by the message Apple event. Thus, the DoAppleSetData method should contain code that sets the text contained in the object's TEHandle to the text retrieved from the message Apple event.

```
void TEditText::DoAppleGetData(const AppleEvent& message,
      AppleEvent& reply)
{
    // Note: This method uses no additional parameters.

    // Make sure we have all the required parameters.
    GotRequiredParameters(message);

    // Pack the text from the TEHandle into a descriptor.
    CharsHandle  theText = TEGetText(fTEHandle);
    AEDesc    textDesc;
    HLock((Handle) theText);
    OSErr theErr = AECreateDesc(typeText, (Ptr) *theText,
        GetHandleSize((Handle) theText), &textDesc);

    // Unlock the handle and check the error code, throwing an
    // exception if necessary.
    HUnlock((Handle) theText);
    FailOSErr(theErr);

    // Package the reply.
    theErr = AEPutParamDesc(&reply, keyDirectObject, &textDesc);

    // Dispose of the descriptor we created and check the reply from
    // packaging the reply, throwing an exception if necessary.
    OSErr ignoreErr = AEDisposeDesc(&textDesc);

FailOSErr(theErr);

}

void TEditText::DoAppleSetData(const AppleEvent& message,
    AppleEvent& /* reply */)
{
    // Get the text data descriptor from the message Apple event.
    AEDesc    textDesc;
```

```
    FailOSErr(AEGetParamDesc(&message, keyAETheData, typeText,
        &textDesc));

    // Make sure we have all the required parameters.
    GotRequiredParameters(message);

    // Use the data in the text descriptor to set the text of TEHandle.
    HLock(textDesc.dataHandle);
    TESetText(*textDesc.dataHandle, GetHandleSize(textDesc.dataHandle),
        fTEHandle);
    HUnlock(textDesc.dataHandle);

    // Dispose of the text descriptor we created above.
    OSErr   ignoreErr = AEDisposeDesc(&textDesc);
}
```

It's Up to You

This article set out to reveal the deep significance of Apple events and the object model and to find a strategy for developing an object-oriented framework to take advantage of the Apple event object model design. Along the way, it danced around cognitive theory and discussed how cognitive theory applies to user perception of software. You've seen how object programming resembles such cognitive models to a more-than-trivial degree. And you've seen how those similarities can be leveraged to give workable, programmable models of user concepts within Turbo WhizzyWorks II NT Pro.

You've also seen the difficulties presented by the Apple Event Manager interface. Although Apple event objects and the object model are unarguably tied to user models and user-centric models, the Apple Event Manager is not. The UAppleObject framework presented here works with the object model and the Apple Event Manager to reduce generic user scripting to a tedious but straightforward task.

In the midst of all this detail, don't forget the payoff—providing a mechanism for users to interact with your applications using a level of control and precision previously undreamed of. The rest, as they say, is in your hands.

BIOGRAPHY

ERIC M. BERDAHL (AppleLink BERDAHL) is a refugee from Chicago, recently deported to the West Coast to join Taligent. Having lived most of his life in a suburb of the Windy City, he exhibits a psychosis common to that area of the country—fanatic loyalty to the Cubs. His formula for success includes bucking the establishment and blindly following one's heart over one's head. The jury's still out on whether that formula works, but it's been effective so far. He's the current president of MADA, an international developer's association devoted to providing cutting-edge access to information about object technologies. MADA conferences are a real blast, too (just ask Eric about his grass skirt). In his copious spare time, he collects comic books, catches up on the Cubs' latest follies, and chases a neurotic flying disc around a grassy field (some call it Ultimate).

Thanks to Our Technical Reviewers

Richard Clark, C. K. Haun, Chris Knepper

DESIGNING A SCRIPTING IMPLEMENTATION

CAL SIMONE

Appendix

This is a preliminary draft of an article that
will appear in Issue 21 of *develop*, the Apple
Technical Journal. Reprinted with permission
of Apple Computer, Inc. *develop* is a prize-
winning quarterly journal that provides an in-
depth look at code and techniques that have
been reviewed for robustness by Apple engineers. Each issue comes with a CD that contains the source code for that issue, as well as
all back issues, Technical Notes, sample code,
and other useful software and documentation. Subscriptions to *develop* are available
through APDA (1-800-282-2732),
Apple Link DEV.SUBS, or Internet
dev.subs@applelink.apple.com.

C

Now that AppleScript is fast becoming an important core technology of the Macintosh Operating System, more and more developers are making their applications scriptable or improving their scriptability. The way you design your scripting implementation can make the difference between satisfaction and frustration for users who want to script your application. The tips in this article will help you do it right.

A well-designed user interface enables users to discover your application's capabilities and take full advantage of them. Likewise, the way you design your scripting implementation determines the degree of success users will have in controlling your application through scripting—writing simple, understandable, and, in most cases, grammatically correct sentences.

And just as the consistency of its user interface has been perhaps the most important factor in the Macintosh computer's ongoing adoption and success, consistency is an essential part of the world of scripting. It's highly important for users (by which I mean anyone who writes scripts, including power users, solutions providers, consultants, in-house developers, resellers, and programmers) to feel as if they're using a single language, regardless of which application they're scripting. As a developer, you have a responsibility to extend the AppleScript language in a consistent manner.

My purpose in this article, which might be considered a first attempt at some human scriptability guidelines, is to offer conventions, suggestions, and general guidelines that you can follow to maintain consistency with the AppleScript language. I also give some suggestions for redoing a poorly done scripting implementation. (I'm assuming you're already convinced that you should make your application scriptable; if you're not, see "Why Implement Scriptability?") The result of doing all this work is that the AppleScript language feels consistent across applications of different types produced by different vendors.

Why Implement Scriptability?

If you're still wondering why you should implement scriptability in your application, consider these reasons:

- Scripting gives users a way to control your application through a different interface. This alternate interface allows users to incorporate your application into multi-application scenarios, as well as to automate tedious, repetitive tasks.
- Allowing your application to be controlled through Apple events enables Apple Guide to give your users truly active assistance.

- Implementing scripting prepares your application for OpenDoc by ensuring that your part handlers will be able to mesh smoothly with other parts.
- Making your application scriptable ensures that as speech recognition matures, you'll be able to give users the option of voice control.

It's important to implement AppleScript support in your core application, rather than through an external API, as some databases such as 4th Dimension and Omnis do. When your core application isn't Apple event–aware, two things happen: (1) no dictionary resides in the application itself, and (2) functionality is usually limited. Users have difficulty doing decent scripting of these applications, by and large. If you simply *must* support Apple events through an external API, at least support the dynamic terminology mechanism for your extensions.

The bottom line is this: If your application isn't scriptable soon, you'll be left out in the cold. If you do the work now, not only will you open up more uses for your application in the "big picture," but you'll also be that much closer to implementing what you need in order to support several other technologies. Don't put it off!

FIRST, SOME BASIC CONCEPTS

A good scripting implementation consists of two parts:

- An Apple event *object model hierarchy*, which describes the objects in your application and the attributes of those objects.

- A *semantic vocabulary*, also called a *terminology*, consisting of the terms used in the construction of command statements. Your vocabulary is stored in your application's 'aete' resource, known to users as the *dictionary*.

Your terms, and the organization of those terms in your dictionary, directly affect the ability of users to explore and control your application through scripting. Creating a vocabulary through which users can effectively and easily script your application takes time and careful effort. Don't expect to spend six months implementing Apple events and then simply to throw together a dictionary at the last second.

It's important to note that a well-designed Apple event structure greatly increases the ease of scripting your application. In a minute I'll say more about that, but first let's look at the basic anatomy of an AppleScript command statement.

ANATOMY OF A COMMAND

You should design your scripting implementation so that users will be guided into using a clean, natural-language sentence structure. To help you begin to visualize the kinds of sentences your users should be encouraged to write, let's look at AppleScript's syntactic statement structure (say that three times fast!). All application-defined commands are in the form of imperative sentences and are constructed as follows:

verb [noun] [keyword and value] [keyword and value] . . .

These elements of sentence construction can be thought of as parts of speech that make up a human-oriented computer language. Here are a couple of examples of commands:

```
close the front window saving in file "Goofballs:Razor"
set the font of the first word in the front window to "Helvetica"
```

Let's dissect these:

close	verb, corresponding to kAECloseElement
the front window	noun, corresponding to keyDirectObject (typeObjectSpecifier)
saving in	keyword, corresponding to keyAEFile
file "Goofballs:Razor"	value, of typeFSS
set	verb, corresponding to kAESetData
the font of the first word	noun, corresponding to keyDirectObjectin the front window (typeObjectSpecifier)
to	keyword, corresponding to keyAEData
"Helvetica"	value, of typeWildCard

Note that for application-defined commands, a *verb*—for example, close or set—is the human language representation for the action described by an Apple event (which I often shorten to just *event*), so there's a general correspondence between Apple events and verbs. In this article, I identify Apple events by the event's name, its 4-byte ID, or the constant name for the ID. For example, the Close Element event has the ID 'clos' and the constant name kAECloseElement, and corresponds to the AppleScript verb close; the Set Data event has the ID 'setd' and the constant name kAESetData, and corresponds to the AppleScript verb set.

Your ability to guide users toward writing clean, natural-language statements depends a great deal on your use of the object model, as I explain next.

Why Use the Object Model?

Supporting the object model facilitates scripting by enabling the use of familiar terms for objects and actions. In the last couple of years, some important applications that don't implement the object model have shipped, and most of them range from difficult to impossible to script. Let's explore a couple of examples of how using the object model can make scripting a lot easier.

> Apple events and the object model are covered extensively in "Apple Event Objects and You" in *develop* Issue 10 and "Better Apple Event Coding Through Objects" in Issue 12 (Appendices A and B).

The following script is the result of a lack of defined objects in the application we'll call My Charter. The lack of defined objects leads to a vocabulary in which every noun-verb combination must be covered by verbs alone—a vocabulary that doesn't relate to other applications and that forces users to learn a new set of commands.

```
tell application "My Charter"
   Plot Options myOptions
   Set Axis Lengths for X 100 for Y 100
   Output PICT
   Plot chart "pie"
end tell
```

By contrast, this script describing the same operation in much more familiar terms results when the application uses familiar objects and characteristics of objects (properties):

```
tell application "My Charter"
   make new chart
   tell chart 1
      set the type to pie
      set the x axis to 100
      set the y axis to 100
   end tell
end tell
```

As illustrated by this script, a principal indication of solid use of the object model is that the most common verbs used in scripts are make, set, and get.

Users are more likely to remember the terms for objects than commands. Moreover, from the user interface, they often use Command-key shortcuts for the actions instead of looking at the menu items once they get comfortable using your application. If you don't implement the standard commands, they'll probably need to go back to your application's menus to find out that the menu command is, for instance, Plot Chart. You can help them by making the scripting terms intuitive. For instance, they already know what a chart is, and they're familiar with the standard AppleScript verbs make and set, which they're using to script other applications. Thus, the second script above will feel like an extension of the same language used in scripting other applications, while the first script won't.

Now consider this partial list of custom verbs from a popular mail application that doesn't follow the object model:

AddAttachment	SetSubject	GetSubject
AddTo	SetText	GetText
AddCC	SetReceipt	GetReceipt
AddBCC	SetPriority	GetPriority
AddToAtPO	SetLog	GetLog

Notice some patterns here? All of them start with Add, Set, or Get—and this isn't even a complete list of all the commands in this application starting with these verbs. It's definitely time for this application to go with the object model. Most of the above commands can be replaced by set and get commands applied to properties such as subject, receipt, priority, log, and so forth.

DESIGNING YOUR OBJECT MODEL

Now that you know how important the object model is to scriptability, let's look at how to get started with your design. As you approach the design of your object model, keep in mind both your application's objects and the character of the commands you expect your users to write.

DECIDE WHICH OBJECTS TO INCLUDE

Base the design of your object model only partly on your application's objects. Keep in mind that the objects in an object model aren't necessarily the same as the programmatic objects in an object-oriented program but rather represent tangible objects that the *user* thinks about when working with your application.

Generally, you won't want the user to script interface elements, such as dialog box items (whose meaning should be expressed through verbs, or properties of the application or your objects), but rather objects that either contain or represent the user's data (which I'll call *containers* and *content objects*). For example, an object model might incorporate documents (containers); graphic objects (containers or content objects); forms (containers) and the elements of a form, such as fields (content objects); cells in a spreadsheet or database (content objects); and text elements, like paragraphs, words, and characters (content objects).

You should think carefully about whether to make something an object or a property; this is discussed later in the section "Other Tips and Tricks."

Think from Actions to Objects

When you design your commands, the primary thing to keep in mind is how you want the script command statements to read or to be written. The character of the commands you expect your users to write should determine your object model, *not* the other way around.

As programmers, we have the notion that an object "owns" its methods; we think in terms of sending messages to an object. For instance, the following C++ code fragment sends several messages to one object:

```
CDocument::Print
CDocument::Close
CDocument::Save
CDocument::Delete
```

By contrast, users think about doing some action to an object. So when you think about scripting, you should think about allowing verbs to be applied to many different types of objects, as illustrated here:

```
print document "Fred"
print form ID 555
print page 4
```

Examine the actions that users take with your application and the objects that the actions are taken on. This will lead you naturally to an effective object model design.

Start—but Don't End—with Object Commands

One place to start your scripting implementation is to implement your menu commands as verbs for scripting. You can use this as a push-off point, but because your menu commands most likely don't supply all the functionality of your application, you shouldn't limit yourself to *only* implementing menu commands.

Before I say any more about this approach, you should note these two very important caveats:

- Keep in mind that the philosophy of AppleScript is to allow the user to script the *meaning* behind an action, not the physical act of selecting a menu item or pushing a button. This perspective should be the foundation for your entire design.

- When you use the standard events, often there's a set <property> scripting equivalent that's better than creating a new verb to match a particular menu item. Menu commands are designed for user interface work and don't always provide the best terminology for scripting. Thinking in terms of make, set, and get can sometimes be more useful than creating verbs that mimic menu commands.

That said, let me elaborate on the idea of implementing menu commands and beyond. Ideally, you should allow users to achieve through scripting everything that they can with your user interface. To accomplish this, you should think of capabilities you would like users to be able to script that go beyond your menu commands, such as capabilities accessible only from tools in a palette or actions resulting from a drag and drop operation. On the other hand, it's not entirely necessary to make the capabilities available from your user interface identical to those controllable through scripting. Scripting is a different interface into your program, so it's OK to do things a bit differently.

For example, you don't have to create exactly one script statement corresponding to each user action. If a single menu item or button in your application results in a complex action or more than one action, it might produce clearer scripting or give more flexibility to allow the user to perform individual portions of the action through separate statements in a script. Conversely, it can also be better to combine more than one action into one statement, especially when the set of actions is always performed in the same sequence.

Also, actions that aren't even possible from the user interface can often be made scriptable. For example, the Scriptable Text Editor allows a script to make a new window behind the front window, something that the user normally can't do. You could also provide a method of accomplishing a task that's too complex or impossible to express through manipulation of objects on the screen.

Make an Early Blueprint

These two exercises can help you get started with designing your hierarchy and your command scheme:

* Write down in real human sentences as many commands as you can think of to control your application. Refer to these sentences later when you're thinking about what Apple events and objects to include in your implementation.

* Make an early version of your 'aete' resource (see "Tools for Developing an 'aete'"). You can then do your coding based on this.

   I would recommend that you go back and do both of these exercises again periodically throughout your development cycle. Use the combination of your 'aete' resource and the sentences as a blueprint during your implementation work.

Tools for Developing an 'aete'

To assemble your 'aete' resource, you can choose from these tools:

* The aete editor stack—This HyperCard stack is a commonly used tool. It's a good way to assemble your 'aete' if it's not too large.
* The Rez files—The Rez source files can easily be changed and can handle any size 'aete', so this is the tool of choice for developers who do serious work with resources. You'll need AEUserTermTypes.r and AERegistry.r as include files. In addition, you can refer to AppleEvents.r, AEObjects.r, AEWideUserTermTypes.r, and ASRegistry.r. You can use the files EnglishTerminology.r and EnglishMiscellaneous.r to examine the standard registry suites.
* Resource editors—Any resource editor *except* ResEdit will suffice. This is one situation in which ResEdit isn't really useful unless your 'aete' is microscopic; you can't open your resource using the 'aete' template if it's more than about 2K in size. Resorcerer includes a pretty decent 'aete' editor, considering the complexity of this resource—but be warned, the editor is equally complex.

   The aete editor stack and the include files for Rez are available on this issue's CD and as part of the AppleScript Software

Development Toolkit from APDA. Resource editors with good 'aete' editors are commercially available.

Details of the structure and format of an 'aete' resource can be found in *Inside Macintosh: Interapplication Communication*.

Make the Containment Hierarchy Obvious

Your object model design includes an *object containment hierarchy*, a scheme indicating which objects are contained in which other objects. When you design your containment hierarchy, think again about the user's experience when writing scripts. Make it easy for the user to determine that objects of class y are contained in objects of class x, which is in turn contained in the application. For instance, Figure C.1 shows part of the object containment hierarchy for an imaginary application that contains text windows, folders, and a connection. The windows can contain one or more paragraphs, words, or characters; paragraphs can contain words or characters; and words can contain characters. Note that even though only one connection is possible for this particular application, connection is an object class contained by the application, as opposed to being merely a property of the application.

It's important to connect up all the appropriate pieces of your containment hierarchy. It's *especially* important to hook up the main classes of objects—such as windows, documents, and other special objects not contained by other objects—to the *top level* of the hierarchy by listing them as elements of your application. Never "orphan" a class! Every

FIGURE C.1

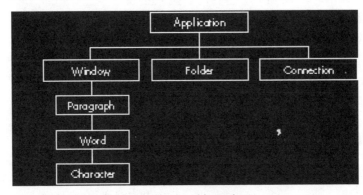

Part of a typical object containment hierarchy

object class (except the application) must be listed as an element of *something*. Most classes or objects are contained by another object. If any object can't be contained by another object, it *must* be contained by the application.

ASSEMBLING YOUR VOCABULARY

After you've taken a shot at writing down the kinds of commands suggested by your application's capabilities and the object model, it's time to think about how to assemble your vocabulary. The AppleScript terms (commands, objects, and properties) that you'll use in your vocabulary fall into two categories:

- standard terms—those drawn from the standard Apple Event Registry suites and other well-defined suites
- extended terms—those you'll create to represent actions or objects specific to your application

To ensure that your scripting implementation will have as much consistency across applications as the user interface, you should use the standard terms whenever possible. As you've seen, this is inextricably tied to good object model design. See "Registry Suites" for descriptions of each suite. Unless you have a excellent reason, don't vary from the standard terms associated with these suites.

Registry Suites

The Apple event suites listed below (which include those defined in the *Apple Event Registry* as well as additional standard suites) are collections of events, objects, properties, and other terms common to most applications. For the sake of consistency with other scripting implementations, you should draw on these suites as much as possible as you design your vocabulary.

- The Required suite (kCoreEventClass = 'aevt') consists of the four events that the System 7 Finder uses to launch and terminate an application and to open and print documents. Note that while the Required suite's ID is 'reqd' (kAERequiredSuite), its four Apple events have the suite ID 'aevt'. Note also that in the early days, Apple originally referred to the Apple events in the Required suite as the core events (even including "core" in the C and Pascal constant names), creating some confusion with the Core suite.

Please *don't* refer to the events in the Required suite as "core events."

- The Core suite (kAECoreSuite = 'core') consists of 17 events (14 main and 3 extra) and 8 objects that encompass much of the functionality that most applications support, including creating, deleting, opening, closing, and counting objects, as well as getting and setting properties. In an object model–based application, a great deal of the work in AppleScript is done through the Apple events in the Core suite. For an example of the standard implementation of this suite, see the Scriptable Text Editor's dictionary. Applications generally support most but not all of the Core suite. Note that the Core suite's ID is 'core', and while most of its events have that suite ID, the Open, Print, and Quit events have the suite ID 'aevt'.
- The Text suite (kAETextSuite = 'TEXT') defines the object classes used in text handling, such as characters, words, and paragraphs, normally the direct objects of events defined in the Core suite. No Apple events are defined in this suite.
- The Table suite (kAETableSuite = 'tbls') defines the essential object classes used in table handling, such as rows, columns, and cells, normally the direct objects of events defined in the Core suite. Again, no Apple events are defined in this suite.
- The Database suite (kAEDBSuite = 'dbst') consists of the Group and Sort events; transaction-related events; the host, DBMS, database, session, and key objects; and extended definitions for the Table suite objects. It focuses the functionality of the Table suite specifically toward database activity.
- Miscellaneous Standards (kAEMiscStandards = 'misc') is a collection of additional Apple events, including editing events such as Cut, Paste, Undo, Redo, Select, and Revert, and the menu, menu item, and text item objects. This isn't used as a suite; only individual events or small groups of events are used.

Other Apple event suites that are used less frequently include the following:

- the Scheduling suite, used for applications such as calendars, appointment books, and alarm programs
- the Telephony suite, used by any application that handles phone numbers, including PIM, database, forms, and scheduling applications
- the Mail suite, based on the AOCE Mailer and used in mail-capable applications to mail documents
- the Collaborative Information suite, used in applications that

access AOCE catalog services or manage contact or human resources information

- the System Object suite (which isn't actually a suite), used for terminologies defined in Apple's scripting additions

The Word Services, QuickDraw, and QuickDraw Supplemental suites are generally *not* used in scripting.

To look up the accepted human-language constructs for the Required, Core, Text, Table, and QuickDraw suites, see the file EnglishTerminology.r (also available for French and Japanese); for the Database suite, see Database.aete.r; and for Miscellaneous Standards, see EnglishMiscellaneous.r (also available for French and Japanese). These files, which present the standard terms in the form of 'aete' resource templates (in Rez form), can be found on this issue's CD and are included in the AppleScript Software Development Toolkit.

Using Standard Terms

When it comes to implementing the standard suites, you have three options:

- supporting an entire suite as is

- supporting an entire suite and overriding or adding to it

- supporting part of a suite

Supporting an entire suite.

When you want to support *all* the events, parameters, classes, properties, and so on, of a suite, you should include the entire suite in your 'aete' resource. Listing 1 is an example of the Rez code you'll use to indicate that an entire suite (in this case, the Required suite) is supported. The four empty arrays in this listing are indicative of the fact that when you want a whole suite intact, you don't supply any events, classes, and so on. The entire suite will appear in your dictionary.

Listing 1: Sample Rez code supporting an entire suite

```
"Required Suite",    /* The entire suite, as is */
"Terms that every application should support",
kCoreEventClass,    /* 'reqd' */
1,
1,
{  /* array Events: 0 elements */
},
```

```
{  /* array Classes: 0 elements */
},
{  /* array ComparisonOps: 0 elements */
},
{  /* array Enumerations: 0 elements */
},
```

Note that whenever you use the 4-byte suite ID for a *suite itself* (as opposed to the suite ID for the individual events in a suite), *all* the standard definitions for that suite will automatically appear in your dictionary. Do *not* use this technique if you're implementing only a few of a suite's Apple events or objects. And note that this technique works only for the Required, Core, Text, Table, and QuickDraw suites, which are in AppleScript's 'aeut' resource. For all other suites, you'll need to include all the details of the suite in your 'aete' resource if you support it in its entirety.

> Supporting only the Required suite doesn't qualify your application as Apple event–aware or scriptable. To qualify as being scriptable, your application must support more than just the Required suite.

Supporting an entire suite to be modified.

When you want to support a whole suite and then add to or otherwise modify it, use the Rez code in Listing 2 as a model. In this example, the entire Core suite is supported, and a new copies parameter is added to the print command. You can use the same technique to add property definitions to a standard object class. Just as in the previous example, here we don't specify any of the suite's details except the ones we're overriding or adding.

Listing 2: Sample Rez code supporting an entire suite to be modified

```
"Standard Suite",    /* The entire suite, plus an extra parameter */
"Common terms for most applications.",
kAECoreSuite,        /* 'core' */
1,
1,
{  /* array Events: 1 element */
   /* [1] */
   "print",          /* This is the event being extended. */
   "Print the specified object(s)",
   kCoreEventClass,
   kAEPrint,
```

```
...
{   /* array OtherParams: 1 element */
    /* [1] */
    "copies",     /* This is the parameter being added. */
    'NCOP',
    'shor',
    "The number of copies to print.",
    ...
  }
},
{   /* array Classes: 0 elements */
},
{   /* array ComparisonOps: 0 elements */
},
{   /* array Enumerations: 0 elements */
},
```

Supporting part of a suite.

On the other hand, when you want to implement only part of a suite, you need to explicitly define the subset of the suite's events and objects that you support. For example, let's say you implement only seven of the events in the Core suite (which nearly everyone implements only partially; these seven are the minimum Core events you should support). You'll create a new suite with a unique ID—your application's signature, perhaps, or, as used by the Scriptable Text Editor, 'CoRe' (note the alteration from all lowercase). Then you'll include the events and objects you want. Listing 3 shows how to do this in Rez code. Note that you should retain the original suite ID of 'core' for the individual Apple events (except for Open, Print, and Quit, which get 'aevt', as mentioned earlier in "Registry Suites"), both in your 'aete' and in your Apple event handlers.

> The format for Rez listings in *Inside Macintosh* puts one element on each line, as I've done in Listings 1 and 2. To conserve space, I'll now begin putting more elements on each line, which is also a permissible format.

Listing 3: Sample Rez code supporting a partial suite

```
"Subset of the Standard Suite",  /* Only seven of the Core events */
"Common terms used in this application",
'CoRe',    /* Note uppercase alteration of the 'core' suite ID. */
1,
1,
{   /* array Events: 7 elements */
```

```
/* [1] */
"count", "Return number of elements of a particular class ...",
kAECoreSuite, kAECountElements,
...
/* [2] */
"delete", "Delete an element from an object",
kAECoreSuite, kAEDelete,
...
/* [3] */
"exists", "Verify if an object exists",
kAECoreSuite, kAEDoObjectsExist,
...
/* [4] */
"get", "Get the data for an object",
kAECoreSuite, kAEGetData,
...
/* [5] */
"make", "Make a new element",
kAECoreSuite, kAECreateElement,
...
/* [6] */
"quit", "Quit an application program",
kCoreEventClass,  /* Open, Print, and Quit have 'aevt' suite ID. */
kAEQuitApplication,
...
/* [7] */
"set", "Set an object's data",
kAECoreSuite, kAESetData,
},
{  /* array Classes ...
```

Using Extended Terms

Whenever possible in your scripting implementation, you should use constructs and terms that are already in use. But sometimes you need to express concepts unique to your application. When you do, it's important to keep in mind the style of what's already been done in the AppleScript language, and in other applications.

The terms you create that aren't in the standard suites are actually extensions to AppleScript. The nature of these terms will directly affect the experience your users will have in scripting your application. You should create terms that give users the feeling that they're working within a unified language.

Keep in mind that creating new object classes or properties is generally better than creating new verbs. If you do need to create your own verbs or use terms unique to your application, it's better to try to do it in the spirit of what's been done before instead of inventing your own "language within a language." Users shouldn't feel as if they're jumping between what appear to be separate "pseudo-languages" for each application.

Although early documentation from Apple suggested creating one custom suite containing your Core suite subset lumped together with your custom verbs, I don't always recommend this. If you're adding a lot of vocabulary, either new events or objects, you can make your dictionary more understandable by keeping the Core subset in one suite and defining your own new verbs in a separate suite. In fact, it's OK to make more than one custom suite if you have a great many new verbs or objects and if you can separate them into distinct functional groupings.

Make sure that the names for your new suites clearly indicate that they're custom suites or specific to your application. And when you create ID codes for your new events, objects, and such, remember that Apple reserves the use of all 4-byte codes that contain only lowercase letters, so you should use at least one uppercase letter in the codes. There isn't yet a way to register your codes, but the Webster project (described at the end of this article in "Resources") aims to serve that end.

A Word about Do Script and Do Menu—Don't!

One of the easiest methods of gaining the appearance of scriptability is to implement the Do Script event. Do Script enables users to pass statements or groups of statements written in your own internal scripting language to your application for execution. If you have an internal scripting language already, Do Script can be OK as a first step. Just don't stop there—in the end, it's useful as a supplement to the rest of your scriptability, but not as a substitute.

The drawbacks to Do Script are that (1) new users must learn a new language—yours—in addition to AppleScript, and (2) Do Script is a one-way communication in most cases—the script can control your application, but it acts much more like a puppeteer than a team leader. In the end, Do Script defeats the purpose of a single language for controlling all applications.

Another easy method of appearing to be scriptable is to implement a Do Menu event, in which a user can simulate pulling down a menu and selecting menu items. Again, this is no substitute for real scriptability.

By the way, if you're thinking about creating a *new* scripting language internal to your application, think again. The world doesn't need yet another private application-specific language. AppleScript is there for you, with all of its rich expressiveness, to use as your own. The benefit is that by the time you complete your scripting support, some of your users will already be familiar with AppleScript.

CONVENTIONS, TIPS, AND TRICKS

Here are some concepts and techniques that you can use to make your vocabulary more helpful to the script writer. Included are well-known tricks as well as techniques that aren't often considered. Adhering to these guidelines will make scripting cleaner and promote a consistent language "look and feel" across applications.

STYLISTIC CONVENTIONS

Begin terms with lowercase.

Begin all the terms in your dictionary with lowercase letters, except for proper names like PowerTalk. It may seem trivial, but it's actually quite important. If you use uppercase letters to begin your object names, for example, you'll end up with strange-looking commands that contain a mixture of uppercase and lowercase letters:

```
make new History
set the Title of the first History to ...
```

Using all lowercase letters gives a more consistent look:

```
make new history
set the title of the first history to ...
```

Separate all terms.

If you have terms that consist of more than one word, separate the words. Don't turn them into Pascal-like names:

```
ReplaceAll
set the TransferProtocol to ConvertFromMainframe
```

Instead, make them flow naturally:

```
replace all
set the transfer protocol to convert from mainframe
```

Use familiar terms, but avoid reserved words.

Generally speaking, you'll want to identify your object classes with terms your users are already familiar with. When it comes to your verbs, you can use many of your menu items, and for the rest use terms that will be familiar and that lend themselves to starting clean and natural statements. Plain human language is always preferable to C- or Pascal-style identifiers.

On the other hand, when you attempt to use familiar terms, keep in mind that the list of words that could potentially conflict with your dictionary is constantly growing and also depends on which scripting additions and applications are currently running on a particular computer. As a result, there's no official list of reserved words to avoid. Choose your terms with extreme care—remember, you're actually extending the language and what you do here will affect the future.

In summary, try to provide words that are familiar to users without running into conflicts with existing terminology. Don't make up new terms to express something when there's a clean way to do it using existing terminology: where possible, use terms analogous to those already in use to represent constructs (verbs, parameters, objects, properties, and enumerators) in your application. Conversely, don't use existing terms to represent something that differs from a term's accepted use.

Enumerations, Lists, Records, and Type Definitions
Use lots of enumerations.

Very few developers have made effective use of enumerations. An *enumeration* is a set of constants, usually representing a fixed set of choices. In AppleScript, these constants, known as *enumerators*, are identified (like everything else) by 4-byte ID codes. Use an enumeration as the type for a parameter or property whenever there's a choice to be made from a specific list of possibilities, and make sure you use natural language. For example,

```
set status to 1
```

   or

```
set status to "warm"
```

   isn't as helpful to the script writer as

```
set status to warm
```

This subtle change makes a great deal of difference. In the dictionary, the enumeration is displayed as "hot|warm|cool|cold," as opposed to "integer" or "string," and the user can easily see there's a choice. To accomplish this, you would create an enumeration with the enumerators hot, warm, cool, and cold, and use the 4-byte enumeration ID as the type for the status property, as shown in Listing 4. The dictionary entry for this property will read "status hot|warm|cool|cold," instead of "status integer" or "status string."

Listing 4: Creating and using an enumeration

```
{  /* array Properties: ...
       /* [1] */
       "status",
       'Psta',          /* Note uppercase in your IDs. */
       'Esta',          /* the enumeration's ID */
       "the status",
       reserved,
       singleItem,
       enumerated,     /* use "enumerated" */
       ...
   },
       ...
{  /* array Enumerations: 1 element */
   /* [1] */
   'Esta',
   {  /* array Enumerators: 4 elements */
       /* [1] */
       "hot", 'Khot', "A hot condition",
       /* [2] */
       "warm", 'Kwrm', "A warm condition",
       /* [3] */
       "cool", 'Kcoo', "A cool condition",
       /* [4] */
       "cold", 'Kfrz', "A cold condition"
   }
},
```

It's an extremely common mistake among developers to try using ordinal values as enumerators, but it simply won't work. Unlike in C or Pascal, you can't use ordinal values—you must use 4-byte ID codes.

Set the list flag to indicate lists in parameters and properties.
If you're normally expecting a list of items as a parameter or a property, set the list flag (kAEUTListOfItems) in the parameter or property definition flags; the dictionary entry will then show "list of <whatever>." (Note

that this is different from defining a parameter's or a property's type as list, which you should do when you want to indicate a mixed-type list or a list of lists.) An interesting possibility is to combine lists with enumerations, to indicate that the user can specify more than one choice, as in

```
set the applicability of filter 1 to {incoming, outgoing, ...}
```

Define record labels in a record definition.
To document the labels for the elements that make up a record, create a record definition in your dictionary. A record definition is actually a fake "class" in which the "properties" represent the labels in the record. Although there won't really be any objects in your application with this record type's class, your users can determine what labels are appropriate in order to fill in a record used as a parameter or a property value. Record definitions can also be helpful for users to interpret a record passed back as a result.

To create a record definition, invent a name for your record type and create a new class in your 'aete' resource with the record type name as the class name. Define all the possible labels as properties. As an example, Listing 5 shows the "class" definition you would create in your 'aete' resource for a record that looks like the following:

```
{name:"Fred", age:3, status:warm}
```

In this case, you would also define the enumeration for status with the enumerators hot, warm, cool, and cold. The record type would appear in the dictionary as follows:

> class person info: A record containing information about a person
> > person info
> > > name string—the name
> > > age short integer— age in years
> > > status hot|warm|cool|cold—current status

This technique should generally be used in conjunction with the Abstract Class suite, described in the next section.

Listing 5: Class definition for our sample record definition

```
{   /* array Classes: 1 element */

/* [1] */
"person info", 'CPIN',
"A record containing information about a person",
{   /* array Properties: 3 elements */
```

```
/* [1] */
"name", 'pnam', 'itxt', "the name",
reserved, singleItem, notEnumerated,
...
/* [2] */
"age", 'AGE ', 'shor', "age in years",
reserved, singleItem, notEnumerated,
...
/* [3] */
"status", 'Psta', 'Esta', "current status",
reserved, singleItem, enumerated,
...
},
{   /* array Elements: 0 elements */
},
```

Put abstract class and primitive type definitions in special suites.
There are two suites you can use to organize your dictionary better: the
Type Definitions suite and the Type Names suite. These suites are used
in special situations where you want to define object and type classes
that are used in your terminology but that won't ever be actual instantiable objects in your application.

In the case of the record definition classes described in the previous section, you need to define abstract classes that don't refer to real
objects. You'll also need to do this in the case of extra classes defined for
property inheritance, which aren't instantiable as objects in your application. To include these record or type definitions, create a Type
Definitions suite (also known as an Abstract Class suite) with the ID
'tpdf' (kASAbstractClassSuite; note that this constant isn't defined in any
.r files, so you'll need to define it yourself) and include your abstract
class and record definitions.

On some occasions you may want to add terms to your vocabulary
that you don't want to show up in your dictionary. For example, you
might need to provide the terms for primitive types, such as integer and
point, to make AppleScript work properly, but users are already familiar
with these elemental terms and don't need to see them defined. In this
case, make a Type Names suite with the ID 'tpnm' (kASTypeNamesSuite)
and include your types as classes in this suite. Well-behaved editors such
as Apple's Script Editor and Scripter from Main Event will suppress the
display of this suite.

To sum up, if you want these definitions to be visible to the user,
include them in your Type Definitions suite. If you want them to be hid-

den, include them in the Type Names suite. Use of these suites will help keep the rest of your suites less cluttered.

Notes on Direct Objects

Be explicit about direct objects.

Some developers have relied on a default or current target, such that commands that don't include a specific object target will act on the frontmost window or the last explicitly set object. There are three reasons to be careful here:

- Users of multiple applications may be confused by different assumptions surrounding the notion of a current object used as the target.

- If your Apple events act just on the current object, your users can only act on some other object by explicitly making it the current object. In the case where the current object is considered to be the frontmost window, there's no way to script other windows.

- Another script (or the user!) could make a different object the current object while a script is running.

The moral of this story is that it's best to be explicit at all times about the object that will be acted on.

Make the target the direct object.

One of our goals in scripting is to maintain a natural imperative command style throughout. However, there's one situation in which a technical issue might make it difficult to preserve this style. From the scripting point of view, you'd really like to allow the user to write something like the following:

```
attach <document-list> to <mail-message-target>
```

The problem is that OpenDoc requires the target to be in the direct parameter. In the preceding script, the target is in the to parameter, not the direct parameter. To make this compatible with OpenDoc, you'll need to change the attach verb to attach to and swap the direct parameter and the to parameter, like this:

```
attach to <mail-message-target> documents <document-list>
```

Help your users figure out which objects to use with a verb.

Due to limitations in the 'aete' resource, there's no provision for indicating which Apple events can act on which objects. The AppleScript compiler will accept any combination of verbs and objects, even though some of these combinations have no meaning to your application and will result in runtime errors. To help your users determine which objects work with which verb, you can employ the following trick.

Define the parameter's type as an enumeration instead of an object specifier. Use a # as the first character of the 4-byte ID for the enumeration. Then define the enumerators as the object classes that are appropriate for the event. You can use the same enumeration for more than one event; you can define different enumerations with different sets of object enumerators for different events; and you can even indicate the same object class in more than one enumeration. For example, instead of

```
close reference
```

a dictionary entry incorporating this technique would read

```
close window|connection|folder
```

This entry indicates to the user that the only objects that make sense for the close command are from the object classes window, connection, and folder.

Other Tips and Tricks
Think carefully about objects versus properties.
Often, most of the work in a script is accomplished through creating objects and setting and getting properties, so use properties liberally. Be mindful that in certain cases, what initially might seem to be good candidates for objects might, on more careful examination, be represented as properties of another object, particularly when there's only one of such an object in your application. On the other hand, don't make something a property just because there's only one of it (such as a single object class belonging to an application or a containing object).

It's not always clear which is the better way to go—object or property. Some examples may help you understand how to decide this. Certain Finder objects have properties but are themselves properties of the application or the desktop container. The selection, an object of the abstract "selection-object" class, has properties such as the selection's contents. However, the selection-object class is never actually used in scripts; selection is listed as a property of the application and other selectable objects, so that a script writer doesn't need to form an object specifier, and the class name can be used as the object itself ("selection" instead of "selection 1").

As another example, a tool palette, which would normally be an object class, might be one of several objects of the palette class, or it might be better listed as a property of the application. This would depend on whether you had several named palettes (palette "Tools," palette "Colors") or wanted separate identifiers for each palette (tool palette, color palette). It could also depend in part on whether there were properties (and perhaps elements) of the palettes. In this particular case, using the tool palette and color palette properties is more localizable than including the name of the palette in the script. If you translate the program into some other language, it's a fair bet that the tool palette won't be named "Tools" anymore. However, your 'aete' resource will have been localized and thus tool palette will be transformed into the correct name for the object.

Try to be careful when deciding whether to make something a property or an object—users can end up writing

```
<property> of <property> of <object>
```

or even

```
<property> of <object> of <property> of <object>
```

and may become confused by real objects that appear to be datalike or that normally would be elements but are presented as properties. Make something a property only when it's meaningful rather than for convenience; otherwise, the concept of an object model hierarchy becomes eroded.

Whether something is a property or an object really depends on the specifics of your application. Still, in a large number of cases, objects are things that can be seen or touched, while properties are characteristics of the objects or the application. A good rule of thumb is: If the item in question is a characteristic of something else, it's probably a property.

Use inheritance to shrink your 'aete'.
If you've got a large 'aete' resource, or large groups of properties used in multiple classes, you can reduce the size and repetitiousness of your 'aete' by defining those sets of properties in an abstract or base class. Then classes that include those property definitions can include an inher-

itance property, with the ID code 'c@#^' (pInherits), as their first property. The human name for this property should be <Inheritance> (be sure to include the angle brackets as part of the name). The inclusion of this property will indicate to the user that this class inherits some or all of its properties from another class.

As an example, in QuarkXPress, several of the object classes have a large number of properties. Without inheritance, there would have been up to a hundred properties in the dictionary's list of properties for some of the classes! By creating abstract base classes in the 'aete' (defined in the application's Type Definitions suite) and inheriting from these, the application uses the same sets of properties (some quite large) in several different classes. The size of the 'aete' resource was reduced from 67K to 44K, and the lists of properties for many of the classes were reduced to just a few, including the inheritance property.

On the other hand, because this method produces a hierarchy that's smaller but more complex (and therefore slightly more confusing), I recommend using it only in situations where inheritance applies to more than one class. If you plan to use inheritance in only one place in your 'aete', or if your 'aete' isn't particularly large, it's probably better just to repeat all the properties in each class without using inheritance.

Be cautious when you reuse type codes.
If you use the same term for more than one "part of speech" in your dictionary, use the same 4-byte code. For example, if you use input as a parameter, again as a property, and later as an enumerator, use the same type code for each of the various uses.

By contrast—and this is very important because it's the single most common source of terminology conflicts—don't use the same type code for more than one event, or more than one class, and so on. If you do, AppleScript will change the script to show the last event or class defined with that code, changing what the user wrote in the script. This is usually not the desired effect, unless you specifically want synonyms.

If you do want synonyms, you can create them this way. For instance, in HyperCard the term "bkgnd field" is defined before "background field." The former can be typed and will always be transformed into the latter at compile time, so that the latter is always displayed. Just be careful not to have the script appear to change terminology indiscriminately—it's unsettling to the user.

The section "ID Codes and the Global Name Space" later in this article discusses additional considerations having to do with type codes.

Avoid using *is* in Boolean property and parameter names.
Because is can be used to mean "=" or "is equal to," and because it's a
reserved word, you should avoid using it in human names for properties
and parameters, such as is selected, is encrypted, or is in use. It's better,
and less awkward, to use selected, encrypted, and in use or used. In a
script, writing

```
if selected of thing 1 then ...
```

    or

```
tell thing 1
  if selected then...
end tell
```

    is better than writing

```
if is selected of thing 1 then ...
```

    or

```
tell thing 1
  if is selected then ...
end tell
```

However, it's OK to use has or wants (which have none of the
problems presented by is), as in

```
if has specs then ...
```

    or

```
set wants report to true
```

When you name your Boolean parameters, keep in mind that
AppleScript will change true and false to with and without. If the user
writes

```
send message "Fred" queuing true
```

    it compiles to

```
send message "Fred" with queuing
```

Control the number of parameters.
Sometimes you may find yourself implementing a verb that contains lots
of options, for which you might be tempted to make separate Boolean

parameters. When the number of parameters is small, it looks good to be able to say "with a, b, and c." Excessive use of this technique, however, can lead to unwieldy dictionary entries for these events with long lists of parameters. There are two solutions to this:

- Make a parameter or parameters that accept a list of enumerators for the option or set of options.

- Break the command into separate commands with more focused functionality, reducing the number of options for each event.

For example, suppose a statistics package creates a single command to perform any type of analysis with lots of parameters, like this:

analyze <reference>	75 Boolean parameters indicating various analysis options

It would be better to split the analysis capability into multiple commands, followed by small groups of Boolean parameters, forming a suite, such as

cluster <reference>	small number of Boolean parameters indicating clustering options or list of enumerators
correlate <reference>	small number of Boolean parameters indicating correlation options or list of enumerators
fit curve <reference>	small number of Boolean parameters indicating curve-fitting options or list of enumerators

and so on.

Use replies meaningfully.

In your dictionary, including a reply in an event's definition helps the user understand the behavior of an application-defined command and its role in the communication between a script and your application. However, you shouldn't include a reply definition if the only possible reply is an error message (except in the rare case where the error message is a normal part of the event's behavior).

When you return an object specifier as a reply, as in the case of the make command, it's up to you to decide which reference form to use. *Reference forms* (the various ways objects can be described in a script), also known as *keyforms,* include the following:

- name ("Fred", "Untitled 1")

- absolute (first, second, middle, last)

- relative (after word 2, behind the front window)

- arbitrary (some)

- ID (ID 555)

- range (4 through 6)

- test (whose font is "Helvetica")

> For more information on reference forms, see *Inside Macintosh: Interapplication Communication* and the *AppleScript Language Guide.*

Most scriptable applications to date implement the absolute reference form, such as window 1, as the reply to a make command. If your users are likely to change the position of this object during a script, you might consider using the name form instead. When you absolutely want a unique value, reply with the ID form, as in window ID -5637. The ID reference form ensures a unique value but usually means much less to the user.

Deciding which reference forms to use for object specifiers comes into play in applications that are recordable, as well.

Approaches to Recording Commands

If your application will be recordable, take note. Some early adopters of AppleScript recordability assumed that their users would only record an action and play it back to see an example of how to script it. Their early scripting implementations were done quickly, often without supporting the object model. Later they realized that users would actually write scripts, sometimes from scratch, using the dictionary as their guide. As a result, most have redone their implementations to clean them up or use the object model. Don't use recordability as an excuse to take the easy route and implement quickly. You'll end up wanting to redo it later, but you won't be able to because your installed base will be too large. Instead, implement the object model the first time.

There are two approaches to recording commands. One approach is to send something as close as possible to what the user would write to the recorder. This isn't necessarily a mirror image of the user's actions but produces recorded statements that more closely resemble what a user will write.

```
open folder "Goofballs" in disk "Razor"
```

The other approach is to duplicate the actions of users. This is the method used in the Scriptable Finder. In this method, what's recorded is that the user makes a selection and then acts on that selection.

```
select folder "Goofballs" in disk "Razor"
open selection
```

In the first case, the recorded statement helps the user understand how to write the command (my personal favorite). In the other case, there's a relationship between what the user did and what was recorded. Either method is useful—it depends on your objectives.

As is the case with returning object specifiers as replies (discussed above), you decide which reference forms to use for object specifiers that get recorded.

ID Codes and the Global Name Space

One of the areas of greatest confusion among AppleScript developers is AppleScript's global name space and its implications for choosing ID codes for properties and enumerators. In this name space are all the terms used in all the scripting additions (see "If You're Writing a Scripting Addition . . .") installed on a user's computer and all the terms defined by AppleScript as reserved words. Properties and enumerators must have either unique or identical codes, depending on the situation. (Events, parameters, and classes that are defined within an application's dictionary aren't affected by this requirement.)

....

IF YOU'RE WRITING A SCRIPTING ADDITION . . .

Scripting additions (otherwise known as *osaxen*, the plural of *osax*, for OSA extension) add new core functionality to AppleScript by extending the AppleScript language. If you're writing a scripting addition, either for general purposes or for use with a particular application, you should be aware of a growing problem: the increasingly crowded name space for commands. When the number of additions was small, it was simple; each command (term) generally had only one usage. Now the situation is beginning to get out of hand.

The problem stems from three issues:

• Unlike applications, which generally go through a fairly significant development cycle, many osaxen have been written by programmers who aren't commercial application developers. As a result, there tend to be a great many more osaxen than scriptable applications.

- The name space for osax terminology is global in the sense that these gems are accessible from any script running on your computer. You might think of all the osax dictionaries being lumped together as though they were a single large application's dictionary (really a "system-level" dictionary). So when two or more osaxen use the same terms in slightly (or radically) different ways, trouble abounds. Only one of them will capture AppleScript's attention, and you, the osax author, can't control which will win out.
- If an application command is named the same as an osax command, the application command will be invoked inside a **tell** block, while the osax will be invoked outside the **tell** block. On the other hand, an osax command executed inside a **tell** block for an application that doesn't define the same command name will invoke the osax. Users writing scripts will undoubtedly make errors.

It's impossible to completely avoid every term used in every application, but where possible, try not to use terms that are likely to be used by application developers. Remember that a user may load up a computer with any number of osax collections, without realizing that there are four different **rename file** osaxen among the horde (or should I say herd?). And remember that if, for example, you define an **open file** command as an osax, the command **open file "curly"** is ambiguous. A user might want the Open event, **open (file "curly")**, or an osax command, **(open file) "curly"**. Again, be extra careful when defining system-level terms.

A different problem exists in the special case where a set of osaxen is marketed for use with a special application, such as plug-ins or database connectivity. In this case, you should name your commands so that they are unmistakably associated with their host application. One possible solution is to begin the command names with a prefix indicating that they should only be used with the particular application.

As noted earlier, you can reuse terms for different "parts of speech"—for example, for a parameter, a property, and an enumerator—but then you must use the same 4-byte ID code. By extension, if the term you want to use for a property or an enumerator is defined in the global name space, you *must* use the 4-byte code already defined there. For example, if you want to use the property modification date, you must use the code 'asmo', which is defined in the File Commands scripting addition. This applies across different parts of speech, so if, for instance, the term you want to use for a parameter is already defined in the global name space as a property, you must use the same code. If you use a different code, scripts that include your term may not compile, or they may compile but send the wrong code to your application when executed.

Conversely, if you want to make up a new 4-byte ID code for your own property or enumerator, you need to take reasonable precautions to avoid using a code that corresponds to another term in the global name space. If you don't use a new code, you can't be sure which term is represented by that code in scripts that contain the code. So, for example, you shouldn't use the code 'asmo' unless you're referring to the modification date property.

How can you identify potential conflicts? One way is by using a script editor, MacsBug (with the aevt dcmd and the atsend macro), and the templates on the AppleScript Developer CD, notably the templates for the Apple Event Manager traps. Together, these tools enable you to catch an Apple event as it's sent and to examine it. Here's what you do:

1. Use the Formatting menu item in the editor to set the colors of the AppleScript styles so that you can see if a term parses as an application-defined variable or as a script-defined variable.

2. Type in your desired terminology and compile.

3. If it parses as a script-defined variable, it's free and you can use it with your own unique code to represent your own term. If it parses as an application-defined term, go on to the next step.

4. Break into MacsBug, type "atsend," and go. Execute the script and the code for the property or enumerator will be displayed. You can then use this term in a manner consistent with standard terminology or definitions in scripting additions—the appropriate ID code will be generated by AppleScript. You must still include this term, along with the ID code you just discovered, in your 'aete' resource so that users will see the term in your dictionary. Then things will still work if the scripting addition that defines the term is subsequently removed.

It's Not too Late to Clean Up Your Act

Let's say you took a first stab at scriptability, implemented it in your application, and shipped it. Perhaps you did the expedient thing and didn't implement the object model. Or maybe you implemented totally new terms in your dictionary. Don't be afraid to redo some of your scripting implementation—it's still early enough in the scripting game to clean up your vocabulary or to go the distance and support the object model. It's *much* better to do it now, when there are only 50 or 100 people struggling to script your application. The overwhelming majority of your users will breathe a sign of relief and thank you profusely for making their lives easier, even if they have to modify some of their existing scripts.

Two well-known developers have each recently done a relatively full scripting implementation and have indicated to their users that this is the first version, that some of it is experimental and is likely to change. A number of others have retraced their steps, rethinking their approach, and on occasion switched to object model support. I'll give two examples of applications where changing a scripting implementation made a significant difference.

Eudora: Cleaning Up Vocabulary

As one of the most widely distributed applications in the history of the Macintosh, Eudora by Qualcomm is used by a vast number of people to manage their Internet mail. Eudora originally used completely nonstandard terms. For example, this script created a new message and moved it to a specific mail folder:

```
tell application "Eudora"
    CreateElement ObjectClass message InsertHere mailfolder "Good stuff"
    Move message 1 InsertHere mailfolder "Other stuff"
end tell
```

This was an easy cleanup job, involving only changes to the dictionary. Standard human terms were substituted for Apple event constructs, as can be seen in this script that now accomplishes the same thing as the preceding script:

```
tell application "Eudora"
    make new message at mail folder "Good stuff"
    move message 1 to mail folder "Other stuff"
end tell
```

Your terms don't have to be quite this far afield for you to consider a scripting facelift.

Stuffit: Switching to the Object Model

By contrast, in the case of StuffIt from Aladdin, the developer revamped the application, replacing a non-object model implementation with one that supports the object model. This revision produced a dramatic increase in the ease of scriptability.

Here's a synopsis of the original implementation:

- Required suite: OpenApp, OpenDocs, PrintDocs, QuitApp

- StuffIt suite: Stuff, UnStuff, Translate, Copy, Paste, Clear, Get Max Number of Archives, Get Current Number of Archives, Stack Windows, Tile Windows, Get Version

- Selection suite: Select, Select All, DeSelect All, Select By Name, View Selected Items, Rename Selected Items, Delete Selected Items, Get Selected Count, Get Selected Name . . .

- Archive suite: New Archive, Create New Folder, Open Archive, Close Archive, Verify Archive, Get Archive Pathname, Get Archive Name, Set/Get Archive Comment, Set/Get Archive View, Stuff Item, UnStuff Item, Change Parent, Save

- Item suite: Get Item Count, Get Item Type, Get Item Name (and 14 others beginning with "Get Item"), Rename Item, Delete Item, Copy Items, Move Items

Notice the redundancy of Set, Get (more than 20 occurrences), Rename, Delete, Stuff, UnStuff, and Select. Also, notice that the command names look much like Apple event names. It was extremely hard to figure out how to script this application.

Once the object model was implemented, the scheme became a lot simpler:

- Required suite
    Events: open, print, quit, run

- Core suite
    Events: make, delete, open, and so on (the 14 main events)
    Classes: application, document, window

- StuffIt suite
    Miscellaneous events: cut, copy, paste, select
    Custom events: stuff, unstuff, view, verify, segment, convert
    Classes: archive, item, file, folder

- Type Definitions suite
    3 special record types used as property types in other classes

Each of the classes has a multitude of properties, where most of the action takes place. All the redundancies have been removed (the verbs can be remembered and used naturally), and statements can be written that resemble those written for other applications. The entries in the Type Definitions suite are record types used for properties. The result of this redesign is that the dictionary is now smaller and more understandable. A script to access all the items in an archive that was originally 68 lines long is now only 20 lines!

The Journey Begins

Making your application scriptable is an art. Think of AppleScript as a living, growing human language. As you've seen, there are standard terms and object model constructs that you can use when designing your application's scripting implementation, for those capabilities that are common to many or all applications. In the end, though, a unique treatment is usually necessary to fully express the particular capabilities of each application, and your scripting implementation should be carefully constructed accordingly.

I hope this article has convinced you to do the following:

- Make AppleScript *your* application's language. Remember, AppleScript isn't just for programmers—many users will want to write and record scripts to control your application.

- Develop a sense of style. Consider the character of what your users will end up writing in their scripts. "Clean and elegant" (like a user interface) will serve your users well. Use human terms that can be easily understood by a nonprogrammer.

- Strive for consistency. Follow the conventions, suggestions, and general guidelines outlined here, for the sake of semantic consistency across applications.

- Choose your terms carefully. Consider whether and how the terms you use in your vocabulary will affect the name space for AppleScript.

On the other hand, if you aren't comfortable designing a semantic vocabulary or if you're having trouble formulating a clear picture in your mind of a natural-language sentence structure, don't attempt to do it yourself. As in the case of graphic and interface design, it might be better to engage the services of an expert.

If you do undertake designing a scripting implementation yourself, you'll find it to be a rewarding experience, one that can enable your users to accomplish things never before possible. Happy implementing!

Resources

- *Inside Macintosh: Interapplication Communication* (Addison-Wesley, 1993), Chapters 3 through 10. (*Inside Macintosh* Volume VI is *not* recommended.)

- "Apple Event Objects and You" by Richard Clark, *develop* Issue 10.

- "Better Apple Event Coding Through Objects" by Eric M. Berdahl, *develop* Issue 12.

- *Apple Event Registry: Standard Suites*, available on this issue's CD or in print from APDA.

- AppleScript Software Development Toolkit, available from APDA.

- *AppleScript Language Guide* (Addison-Wesley, 1993). Also in the AppleScript Software Development Toolkit.

- The Webster Project. This master database, containing terms used in scriptable applications and scripting additions, assists in resolving naming collisions across applications and serves to regularize the common terms used by applications of different types. I'm designing and implementing this; contact me at AppleLink MAIN.EVENT for more information.

BIOGRAPHY

CAL "MR. APPLESCRIPT" SIMONE (AppleLink MAIN.EVENT) has dedicated his life to bringing scripting to the masses. He can usually be found moving fast through the Worldwide Developers Conference or MAC-WORLD Expo, a cloud of dust in his wake. A founder of Main Event Software of Washington, DC, he designed the Scripter authoring and development environment for AppleScript and sometimes teaches AppleScript at corporate sites. An honorary member of the Terminology Police as a result of having reviewed scripting vocabularies for more than two dozen third-party products, Cal is available to look at *yours*. He lives about a mile from the White House and was fond of saying of President Bush, "I don't bother him, and he doesn't bother me."

Thanks to our technical reviewers

C. K. Haun, Don Olson, and Jon Pugh, and to Michael Bayer.

NERD'S GUIDE TO FRONTIER

DAVE WINER

USERLAND SOFTWARE

Appendix

D

FRONTIER

This article is a top-level technical overview of the UserLand Frontier scripting system, written for experienced C or Pascal programmers. The goal is to show how the language and the environment work, but not to be a complete tutorial in using Frontier.

Frontier is an integrated collection of development tools built around a scripting language and disk-based storage system. Frontier provides a script editor/debugger, table editor, menubar editor, documentation tools and a comprehensive set of built-in verbs that allow you to customize and automate the Macintosh file system, operating system, networks, utilities and scriptable applications.

Frontier scripts can be saved to the Finder desktop, can be linked to menu items, and can run in the background. Scripts can also be embedded in a small application to allow collections of files, folders and disks to be dropped onto the script.

Frontier 1.0 shipped in January 1992; version 2.0 shipped in October 1992. All the examples in this article work with Frontier 2.0.

In the following sections we break out each of the major features in Frontier and discuss them using sample scripts to demonstrate the features.

THE USERTALK SCRIPTING LANGUAGE

UserTalk is a full-featured language, with looping, if-then-else, case statements, local and persistent variables, subroutines, error recovery and automatic type coercion. UserTalk's syntax is most like C or Pascal. The language is very tightly integrated with Frontier's object database, discussed in the "Storage System" section, below.

The goal of the language is to make it easy to write utilities that operate at the system level; launching and communicating with applications, managing the file system and operating system and other system resources, and moving information around a network.

Hello World

There's a long tradition of introducing languages with a simple "Hello World" program. Here's what Hello World looks like in UserTalk:

```
msg ("Hello World!")
```

This displays the string in Frontier's main window:

```
☐ ▼                    Hello World!                    ♪
```

Built-in Verbs

Let's look at a more comprehensive script that creates aliases of all applications on all hard disks in the Apple Menu Items folder:

```
local (appleFolder = file.getSpecialFolderPath ("", "Apple Menu Items",
        true))
fileloop (f in "", infinity) «scan over all disks, to infinite depth
    if file.type (f) == 'APPL' «it's an application
        local (name = file.fileFromPath (f)) «copy the file's name
                                              «into a local
        if dialog.yesNo ("Create alias of "" + name + "" in Apple
                    Menu Items folder?")
            file.newAlias (f, appleFolder + name + " alias")
```

The script loops over all files, and when it finds one whose type is 'APPL', it displays a "yesNo" dialog asking if you want to create the alias. If you click on Yes, the script calls the Frontier built-in `file.newAlias` verb to create the alias in the Apple Menu Items folder.

"fileloop" is a special construct in UserTalk, it allows you to iterate over all the files on a disk or in a folder. If the path is the empty string, fileloop will loop over all mounted disks. By saying we want to go to infinite depth, the loop will visit all files in all sub-folders, no matter how deeply nested.

We could have hard-coded a path to the Apple Menu Items folder, but by calling `file.getSpecialFolderPath` this script will work on any Macintosh, in any country. For example, in the Fredonia version of

System 7, this call will return "Sturgeon:Smidgadzchen Festerest:Apfel Menu Gethingies". (With apologies to the good citizens of Freedonia...)

`file.getSpecialFolderPath`, `file.type`, `file.fileFromPath`, `dialog.yesNo` and `file.newAlias` are examples of calls to built-in verbs. Generally, if the Macintosh OS provides an API for a system-oriented operation, Frontier provides a simple scripting API for that operation.

As examples, Frontier 2.0 includes built-in verbs that allow you to:

- Launch an application, data file, control panel, or desk accessory. Loop over all running applications. Bring an application to the front. Access the desktop database.

- Move, copy, delete or rename files and folders. Get and modify file/folder attributes such as the creation date, modification date, file type and creator, size, file comment, version information, icon position. Determine whether a file is visible or not visible, locked or unlocked, busy or not. Reconcile the changes between two versions of the same folder.

- Manage the resource fork of any file. Read and write text files and data files. Access the system clock. Move data in and out of the clipboard.

Frontier is itself completely scriptable and includes built-in verbs to manage its object database script, outline, text and picture windows.

INTERAPPLICATION MESSAGING

Scripts that drive applications look very much like scripts that drive the file system and operating system.

Here's a script that creates a StuffIt archive containing compressed versions of all files on all disks modified after May 15, 1993:

```
local (archive = "System:Desktop Folder:Changed Files.sit")
if file.exists (archive)
    file.delete (archive)
StuffIt.launch ()
StuffIt.newArchive (archive, false) «create a 3.0-format archive,
                                 «not 1.5.1
StuffIt.bringToFront ()
fileloop (f in "", infinity)
    if file.modified (f) > date ("May 15, 1993")
        StuffIt.stuffItem (f)
StuffIt.closeArchive (archive)
```

The new archive appears on the desktop. We delete the file if it already exists. Then we launch StuffIt Lite 3.0, create the new archive, and loop over all files on all disks. If a file's modification date is greater than May 15, 1993, we add the file to the archive. When the loop completes, we close the archive.

The verbs `StuffIt.newArchive`, `StuffIt.stuffItem`, and `StuffIt.closeArchive` result in an Apple Event being sent to the StuffIt application. But this fact is invisible to the script writer. You call StuffIt from a script exactly as if you were calling a built-in verb. The only difference is that you have to launch the StuffIt application in order to call it.

Here's what the script for `StuffIt.stuffItem` looks like:

```
on stuffItem (path) «return true if StuffIt was able to add
                    «the file to the current archive


    return (appleEvent (StuffIt.id, 'SIT!', 'Stuf', 'path',
        string (path)) == 0)
```

More information on the built-in appleEvent verb is included in the Q&A section at the end of the article.

Object Model Scripting

Some applications implement the richer "object model" style of Apple Events. Scripts that drive object model applications can look very different from scripts that drive simpler scripting APIs, as illustrated in the previous example.

Here's a script that opens a FileMaker Pro 2.0 database containing information about the 50 states in the United States. It creates a text file that lists each state and its capital on a separate line:

```
local (textfile = "System:States Text", database = "System:States
        Database")
file.new (textfile) «create the file, its length is 0 bytes
file.setType (textfile, 'TEXT') «it's a text file
file.setCreator (textfile, 'ttxt') «it can be opened by TeachText
file.open (textfile) «open the data fork of the file
app.startWithDocument ("FileMaker", database)
with FileMaker, objectModel «use FileMaker and object model vocabularies
    local (i)
```

```
      show (record [all]) «select all records
      for i = 1 to count (layout [1], record) «loop over all the records
          local (stateName, stateCapital)
          stateName = get (record [i].cell ["Name"])
          stateCapital = get (record [i].cell ["Capital"])
          file.write (textfile, stateCapital + tab + stateName + cr)
file.close (textfile)
FileMaker.quit ()
```

In this example, we create a text file on the disk named System, set
its type and creator, and open its data fork. We launch the FileMaker
application, telling it to open the States Database.

We access FileMaker's terminology by including the FileMaker-
related script code inside the "with" statement. When we refer to `count`
`(layout [1], record)` we're asking FileMaker for the number of records
when viewed thru the first layout. We make sure all the records are
selected. Then we loop over all the records in the database, copying the
state name and capital into locals, then writing a line to the text file.
After looping over all the records, we close the text file and quit the
FileMaker application.

SCRIPT EDITOR

Frontier has a full-featured, integrated script editor.

Here's what the first sample script looks like in a Frontier script
editing window:

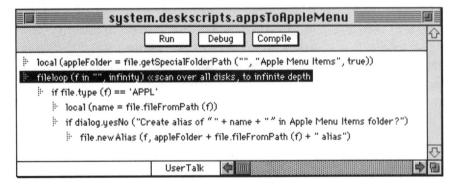

Frontier scripts are outlines. You could collapse the `fileloop` statement to show none of its sub-heads, or one of them, or all of them. You
can control the level of detail you want to view. Outlining also helps you

edit the structure of your scripts. Drag a headline to a new location, and all the sub-heads move with it. Programs are hierarchies. Outliners are hierarchy editors. It makes a lot of sense to have a script editing tool that understands hierarchic program structure.

One of the fallouts of this design is that structure symbols such as curly braces and semi-colons are unnecessary when you edit a script using Frontier's script editor. The structure of the outline is the structure of the program and vice versa.

The window title shows the object database address for this script. It's located in the deskscripts sub-table of the system table. Its name is appsToAppleMenu. Details on the object database are in the "Storage System" section, below.

This screen shot was taken using a development version of Frontier that supports multiple scripting components. To the left of the horizontal scrollbar is a popup menu that allows you to select the scripting component to run the script. This allows you to edit an AppleScript script within Frontier and call it from any other script. In fact, you can edit a script in any OSA-compatible scripting language. This includes a new version of CE Software's QuicKeys macro utility, currently in development.

You can find and replace within a single script and over groups of scripts. Options include case insensitive searching, wrap around, find only language identifiers or whole words. Here's a screen shot of Frontier's Find & Replace window:

The script editor is itself scriptable, so you can write tools that automate script development.

DEBUGGER

The script editor also provides the interface for debugging. Here's what a script editing window looks like after you click on the Debug button:

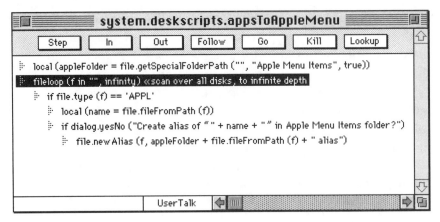

The buttons at the top of the window are handled by Frontier's integrated script debugger. You can step from statement to statement, go into a script call, step out from a script call, follow statement execution, resume normal execution, or halt the script. You can examine and edit all local and global variables in the storage system while any number of scripts are running. You can set a breakpoint at any statement.

For example, if you set a breakpoint on the `file.newAlias` call, and clicked on Lookup with the name `appleFolder` selected, as shown below:

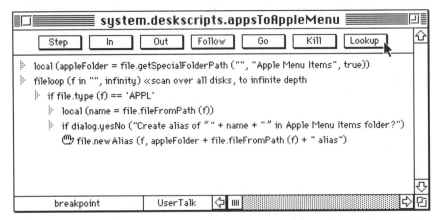

You'd see the top-level stack frame for this script. This table is fully editable:

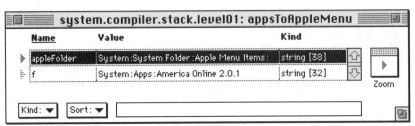

To resume running the script, bring the script window to the front and click on Follow or Go.

When a syntax or runtime error occurs, you can jump to the line where the error occurred, with all script editing features enabled. You can view all local and global variables before terminating the script.

STORAGE SYSTEM

Frontier's built-in storage system is called the object database. It can store small objects like a user's name, or the time of the last backup; or larger objects like a list of users, a standard form letter, or a table of electronic mail accounts. It makes it easy for scripts to communicate with each other, especially scripts running in different threads. The object database is a permanent data structure, so you don't have to worry about complicated file formats for your scripts.

The object database starts with a top-level table is called "root." Start by clicking on the flag in the Frontier's main window. It reveals four buttons:

Click on Object DB button. Frontier opens the "root" table:

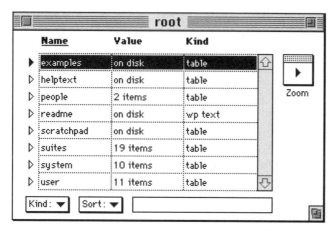

There are eight items at the top level of the database. Some are still on disk. Frontier only reads in tables as they are needed. If you double-click on the wedge next to examples, the sub-table opens:

```
examples
    Name          Value              Kind
├ age            38                 number
▷ counter        on disk            script
├ dir            up                 direction
▷ docs           1 item             table
├ flag           true               boolean
├ frequency      15000              number
▷ IQ             139.02904          double
├ haircolor      25,37,91           rgb
▷ letter         on disk            wp text
▷ list           on disk            outline
├ mouseat        388,29             point
├ name           Bull Mancuso       string [12]
├ nextchar       M                  char
▷ picture        3588 bytes         picture
├ ptrtext        @root.readme       address [11]
├ sysLargestBlock 0x600E00005846434E0 binary [XFCN]
├ windowat       10,30,110,230      rect

Kind: ▼   Sort: ▼
```

Zoom

Values can be small things like booleans, characters and numbers; or large things like strings, word processing text, outlines or scripts. Frontier supports over 20 built-in types, and has a general type called "binary" which allows you to store types which Frontier doesn't directly support.

The Kind popup menu allows you to change the type of an object. The Sort popup allows you to change the order in which objects are displayed in the window.

The storage system uses a 31-bit internal address, so files can be huge, limited only by available disk space. Even though the database is disk-based, Frontier has a Save command, and even a Revert command, allowing you to roll back to the previous version of the database.

From scripts, you use dot-syntax to traverse the table hierarchy. For example, to add 1 to the number "age" stored in the "examples" table you say `examples.age = examples.age + 1`. You could also say `examples.age++`.

Because database paths can get long, UserTalk has a "with" statement, like Pascal's, that lets you easily work with deeply-nested tables.

The following script launches MacWrite, brings it to the front, opens and prints a document and quits:

```
with system.verbs.apps.MacWrite
    launch ()
    bringToFront ()
    printDocument ("System:Business Plan")
    quit ()
```

Frontier has another mechanism to help simplify deeply nested values, the paths table. Like Unix or MS-DOS, the paths table defines a set of object database tables that are globally accessible. Because `system.verbs.apps` is in the paths table, it's possible to re-write the previous script as:

```
MacWrite.launch ()
MacWrite.bringToFront ()
MacWrite.printDocument ("System:Business Plan")
MacWrite.quit ()
```

Another special table is `system.agents`. Any script in `system.agents` is executed once per second. Here's a very simple agent that adds 1 to a counter once a second and displays the result in Frontier's main window:

```
    msg (scratchpad.count++)
If you want to count once a minute:
    msg (scratchpad.count++)
    clock.sleepFor (60)
```

Agent scripts are used to monitor folders, especially on shared disks. A server running Frontier or Frontier Runtime can run an agent script that watches the folder. When a file appears in the special folder, the agent script processes it in some fashion.

In addition to agent scripts, there are special tables for scripts that run on startup and shutdown, or scripts that respond to incoming Apple Event messages. Even the interpreter's runtime stack is accessible thru the object database hierarchy.

Much of the culture of Frontier is implemented as scripts stored in the object database, so you can examine and customize the scripts and add your own. When we upgrade Frontier, we only upgrade the parts of the database that we created, and leave the parts that are subject to customization untouched.

MENUBAR EDITOR, MENU SHARING

Like Frontier's script editor, the menu editor works with an outline. The outline is hot-wired to the actual Macintosh system menu bar. When you make a change in the menu editor it's immediately reflected in the system menu bar. In the following screen shot, the script writer is editing the Graphics sub-menu of the Work menu in Frontier's menu bar:

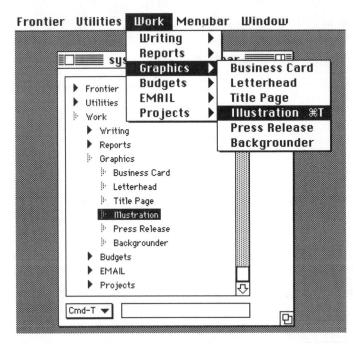

The outline hierarchy is reflected in hierarchical menus. Each main heading is a menu, each sub-head is a command or a sub-menu. To edit the script linked into each menu item, click on the Script button (it's hidden in the screen shot above). A script window opens.

This menu editor can also be used to add commands to applications that support the Apple Event-based menu sharing protocol. Examples include Think C and Symantec C++ 6.0, Quark XPress 3.2, Storm Technologies PicturePress 2.0, and StuffIt Deluxe 3.0 and StuffIt Lite 3.0 from Aladdin Systems. Thru the FinderMenu extension, included with Frontier 2.0, you can add commands to the Finder's menu bar.

To see how menu sharing works from a script writer's perspective, open the table at `system.menubars`:

Name	Value	Kind
▷ readme	on disk	wp text
▷ BARC	on disk	menu bar
▷ DOCS	on disk	menu bar
▷ DRPa	on disk	menu bar
▷ GEOL	38 items	menu bar
▷ IOWA	on disk	menu bar
▷ MWPR	on disk	menu bar
▷ SHUI	on disk	menu bar
▷ SIT!	on disk	menu bar
▶ KAHL	on disk	menu bar
▷ UBAS	on disk	menu bar
▷ XPR3	on disk	menu bar
▷ fMNU	124 items	menu bar

system.menubars

This table associates a menubar object with a Macintosh application that supports menu sharing. KAHL contains the shared menu for Think Project Manager. XPR3 contains the shared menu for Quark XPress 3.2. When one of these applications launches, it sends a series of Apple Events to Frontier to request its shared menus. When the user selects one of the commands, the application sends a message to Frontier to run the script that the user selected.

Frontier Software Developer Kit (or Frontier SDK) includes the Menu Sharing Toolkit which makes it easy for developers to open their menubars to script writers. It can be downloaded from any of UserLand's on-line services and is included in the Frontier 2.0 package. All UserLand developer toolkits are royalty-free and provided in full C source code.

SCRIPTS ON THE DESKTOP

Desktop Scripts

Desktop scripts are files that contain a script that runs when the file is double-clicked on. The script can be programmed to operate on the folder it was launched from.

To create a new desktop script, choose the New Desktop Script command in Frontier's UserLand menu. A new script is created in the `system.deskscripts` table. To export it, choose the Export a Desktop Script command from the Export sub-menu of the UserLand menu.

The following desktop script searches the folder it was launched from for TeachText files. When it finds one the script changes its creator id so that Microsoft Word will open it.

```
local (f, folder)
folder = file.folderFromPath (system.deskscripts.path)
fileloop (f in folder, infinity)
    if file.creator (f) equals 'ttxt'
        file.setCreator (f, 'MSWD')
```

Before a desktop script runs, Frontier sets up `system.deskscripts.path` so that it contains the full path to the desktop script file. The script can loop over all files in a folder, or store information in the resource fork of the script file.

Here's what a desktop script looks like in the Finder:

Change to Word

TeachText Files

If you run the script in the same folder as the TeachText Files folder, it changes all the TeachText files to Word files.

Droplet Scripts

Droplets are small applications that have an embedded script that runs once for each file, folder or disk icon that's dropped onto the application.

Frontier communicates with the droplet script through the `system.droplet` table. The script can also use this table to store values that persist across calls to the script. In the following example, the droplet keeps track of the amount of disk space it reclaimed in `system.droplet.bytessaved`.

Here's a droplet script that searches the folders dropped on it for Think C project files. It opens each project, removes all objects, and closes the project. It automatically launches Think Project Manager if it's not running. As it finishes, it reports the amount of disk space reclaimed:

```
if system.droplet.startup
    system.droplet.bytessaved = 0 «keeps track of space we
                                   «reclaimed
```

```
if system.droplet.closedown
    if system.droplet.bytessaved > 0 «report to the user
        dialog.notify (string.kBytes (system.droplet.
                        bytessaved) + " reclaimed.")
    delete (@system.droplet.bytessaved)
    return
on checkfile (f)
    if think.isProjectFile (f)
        local (origfilesize = file.size (f))
        think.openProject (f)
        think.removeObjects ()
        think.closeProject (true)
        system.droplet.bytessaved = system.droplet.bytessaved +
                            (origfilesize - file.size (f))
if file.isFolder (system.droplet.path)
    local (f)
    fileloop (f in system.droplet.path, infinity)
        checkfile (f)
else
    checkfile (f)
```

This is what a droplet looks like on the desktop:

Remove Objects   Project Files

Drag the Project Files folder onto the Remove Objects icon. Here's what you see:

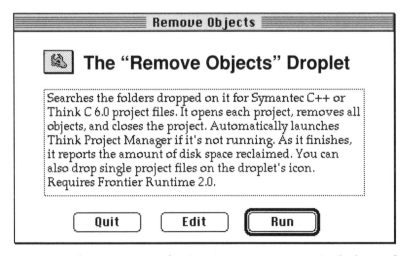

Droplets are menu-sharing-aware, so you can include configuration commands in the droplet's menu bar, implemented as scripts.

A full tutorial and reference guide, sample code, and source for the Droplet Developer Kit is available in the Extras folder of Frontier SDK.

DocServer

DocServer is the on-line documentation tool for Frontier script writers. Each "page" in the DocServer database describes one of the UserTalk language verbs. The example below shows the docs for the `file.exists` verb. Information on the syntax, parameters, action and returned value of the verb are included.

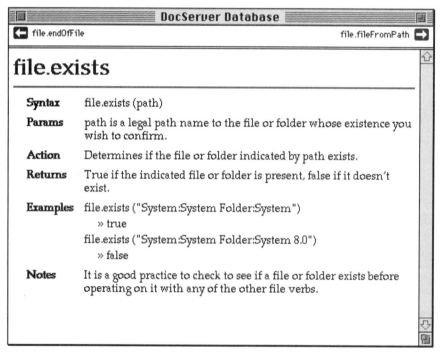

DocServer is connected to Frontier thru Apple Events. If you select a name in Frontier, and hold down the Control key while double-clicking on it, DocServer will display the documentation for that verb.

DocServer is an open tool. Other developers are encouraged to provide Apple Event verb documentation in DocServer format.

ARCHITECTURE & ECONOMICS

Frontier scripts can run over AppleTalk-compatible networks, sending messages to other copies of Frontier or Runtime, or to other Apple Event-aware applications.

Scripts are re-usable. Scripts can call other scripts, passing parameters and receiving returned values. Script writers can add new verbs to the language.

Scripts can be compiled into an intermediate non-human-readable form. In an upcoming release of Frontier it will be possible to distribute scripts in this form.

Compiled machine code can be stored in the object database and called exactly as scripts are called. Two communication protocols are supported: the well-known HyperCard 1.0 XFCN protocol and a new and more powerful protocol known as UCMD, which is compatible with the AppleScript OSAX protocol. Toolkits for developing both kinds of code resources is included in Frontier SDK 2.0.

The language is case-insensitive. `fileFromPath` is the same identifier as `filefrompath` and `FiLeFRoMPAtH`.

Frontier is multi-threaded. Each script runs in its own thread, and can use the object database to communicate with each other and for synchronization.

On-line support is provided thru CompuServe, America Online and AppleLink. Support forums are staffed by Frontier's lead developers. Sample scripts, toolkits, and documentation, all without additional charge, can be downloaded from UserLand's on-line support services:

- CompuServe: Type GO USERLAND at any ! prompt.

- America Online: Keyword USERLAND.

- AppleLink: UserLand Discussions under Third Parties.

Frontier Runtime runs scripts, but has no interactive script editing or debugging features. It's available as an inexpensive shareware package, with a 30-day free trial period. Network site licenses are available for as little as $20 per machine for networks with more than 10 Runtime users. Runtime can be bundled with commercial applications that support Apple Events for $100 per year, no royalty. All prices are in U.S. dollars.

A special shareware Scripting Starter Kit (SSK) is available for Think C and Symantec C++ 6.0 developers. It can be downloaded from any of UserLand's on-line services.

Frontier is a commercial product with a suggested retail price of $249.

Both Frontier and Frontier Runtime require System 7.0 or greater. Frontier requires a minimum of 1024K, Frontier Runtime requires 512K.

Q&A

Why would I add Frontier capability over AppleScript?

Both AppleScript and Frontier build on the same protocol: Apple Events. It's impossible to support one without supporting the other.

The only extra protocol we ask you to support is menu sharing. You should add it because script writers want it, and it's very easy to implement.

How do I make verbs for my app?

Suppose your app, named mathApp, implements a single Apple Event that takes one parameter, a long. It multiplies it by two, and returns the result.

Create a new table for your application at `system.verbs.apps.mathApp`. Create a new script in that table, call it "doubler". Here's what the script looks like:

```
on doubler (x)
    return (appleEvent ('MIKE', 'CUST', 'DOUB', '—', long (x)))
```

It returns the value of a call to Frontier's built-in appleEvent verb. 'MIKE' is the creator id of mathApp, 'CUST' is the class of the verb, 'DOUB' is the verb identifier. The next two parameters provide the key, '—', and the value of the single long parameter to the Apple Event.

A script writer can then call your verb exactly as if it built into the language. Here's an example that displays 24 in a standard alert dialog:

```
dialog.alert (mathApp.doubler (12))
```

Full details are provided in Frontier SDK 2.0, Extras folder, Frontier Install File Creator sub-folder.

How long does it take to add menu sharing to my app?

You add calls to Menu Sharing Toolkit routines in five places:

1. Where you initialize Macintosh toolkits. [Add a call to InitSharedMenus to set up globals and install handlers for messages sent by the menu sharing server.]

2. In your menu handling routine. [Call SharedMenuHit to filter out shared menu selections. If it returns false, process the menu selection normally, if it returns true, it was a shared menu command, return to your main event loop.]

3. In your keystroke handler. [Call CancelSharedScript if the user hits cmd-period and SharedScriptRunning returns true. Otherwise, process the keystroke as you normally would.]

4. In your event handler. [On receipt of a null event, call CheckSharedMenus to load the shared menus, or reload them if they changed.]

5. In each Apple Event handler. [Call the toolkit routine SharedScriptCancelled . If it returns true, your handler should returns noErr immediately.]

If you're working in Think C or Symantec C++ it could take as little as 20 minutes to find these places and add the calls. There's a reasonably good chance it will work the first time, as it has for many others.

A full tutorial and reference guide, sample code, and source for the Menu Sharing Toolkit is available in the Toolkits folder of Frontier SDK.

FINAL NOTE

If you have any questions, comments or suggestions, please get in touch through one of UserLand's on-line services. If you're an AppleLink user, check out the UserLand Discussion Board under the Third Parties icon. On CompuServe, visit the UserLand Forum in the Computing Support section, or enter GO USERLAND at any ! prompt. On America Online, enter the keyword USERLAND.

ABOUT THE AUTHOR

Dave Winer is founder and president of UserLand Software. He and Doug Baron are the lead developers at UserLand. Dave has been a commercial software developer since 1979, and shipped his first product, the ThinkTank outliner for the Apple II in 1983. The IBM PC version shipped in 1984. As founder and president of Living Videotext, Inc., he shipped one of the first Macintosh applications, ThinkTank 128, in mid-1984, and in 1986 shipped the award-winning MORE 1.0, followed by MORE 1.1c in 1987. Living Videotext merged with Symantec shortly after that and Dave moved on to start the development of Frontier. Frontier 2.0 received MacUser's Eddy award for best development tool of 1992.

EXTENDING APPLESCRIPT™ WITH SCRIPTING ADDITIONS

DONALD OLSON

Appendix

Reprinted with permission of
MacTech Journal

E

Not everything is handled in vanilla AppleScript—here's how you add to it.

A BRIEF HISTORY . . .

In the beginning, the high priests made AppleScript. It had conditionals and flow controls and pretty printing. It had script objects with properties and methods. It talked to applications and integrated their functionality. It conversed across the network. It was an OODL. And the high priests proclaimed it good.

But the people of AppleScript soon saw something amiss in the design. "Where is the ask/answer dialog and the lowly beep?" the people asked. "Where are the standard file and PPC Browser dialogs?" they demanded.

The high priests declared, "These things you ask for are not part of a pure language such as AppleScript. You must look to applications for the relief you seek!"

There was much wailing and gnashing of teeth in the land of AppleScript. "We must have the simple beep and the friendly ask/answer dialogs so that we may talk amongst ourselves without the use of special applications," the people protested. "It is an abomination to our hard drives that we must have so many tiny applications to do our bidding!"

So the priests conferred. "The people of AppleScript want to add new functionalities to our language" they said. "We will not allow the purity of AppleScript, the language, to be sullied with such things as user interface elements and noises. We, therefore, will provide a mechanism which allows the people to add syntax and dialogs and data transformations to AppleScript without requiring that they be made a permanent part of our language. And we will give them a basic set of these extensions to appease their needs."

And low, the high priests unveiled Scripting Additions to the people of AppleScript.

The people rejoiced. "We have our beep, our ask/answer and it is good! Scripting Additions are loaded on demand, are available to the entire system, and yet, do not fill up our system heap!"

"But, oh high priest, " one of the AppleScript people said, "this minimal set of scripting additions does not have all that I need. How may I write such scripting additions myself so that I can achieve the total integration AppleScript promises?"

"Oh AppleScript people, I will bring down from the mountain of VirtualTables the coding instructions and the commandments of Scripting Addition programming. Use this information wisely, and your Scripting Additions will prosper."

"Heed me well, people of AppleScript. Scripting Additions are part of our new OSA scripting language AppleScript. Scripting Additions provide a mechanism for extending the language and functionality of AppleScript. They are similar to XCMD's for HyperCard and UCMD's for Frontier."

MacTech Editor:"Hellooow, Donald!"

Article Author:"Um, uh, yea Neil?"

MacTech Editor:"This mythology stuff is fun, but can we get on with the article??"

Article Author:"Article?? Oh! Sorry! Ok, here we go…"

THE PARTS

Scripting Additions are implemented as Apple Event handlers or coercions that AppleScript loads on demand. In order to write Scripting Additions, you need a basic understanding of the Apple Event Manager (AEM) .

The AEM is a collection of routines that provide a mechanism for sending and receiving messages (called AppleEvents) between applications either on the local machine or over an AppleTalk network. Each message contains a pair of identifiers that serve to inform the receiving application of the action to be taken as a result of this message. These identifiers are called the class and id of the message. Since the class and id specify the action to be taken, it is common to call the class and id the verb of the message.

Data may also be associated with the verb of the message. This data is placed in structures called descriptors and added as parameters to the Apple event. The AEM provides a set of routines for adding or extracting parameters from a message. Since there may be more than one parameter associated with a message, each parameter has a unique identifier called a keyword associated with it. Since a verb normally has a focus for the action it is to take, there is a standard parameter called the direct parameter (or direct object) which is used to specify the object the verb is to act on.

An example of an Apple Event message is the open document message that is sent by the Finder when you double click on one or more documents associated with an application. The class of the open document event is kCoreEventClass and the id is kAEOpenDocuments. It has one parameter, the keyDirectObject (a.k.a. the direct parameter), which contains an AppleEvent list containing aliases to the documents that the application is to open.

When an application receives an Apple event (high level event) in its event queue, it calls the AEM routine AEProcessAppleEvent. This causes the AEM to attempt to dispatch the AppleEvent to an Apple event handler that is installed by the application in the AEM application dispatch table. The AEM dispatches based on the class and id of the event. In our example above, the application would need to have installed a handler with the class kCoreEventClass and the id kAEOpenDocuments in order to successfully deal with the open documents Apple event.

What, you ask, does this have to do with writing a Scripting Addition?

The AEM provides not only a dispatch table for AppleEvents for each application that installs handlers, it also maintains a dispatch table for system handlers as well. System handlers, unlike application specific handlers, are available to all applications on the machine where they are installed. This is where AppleScript installs Scripting Additions. If the AEM does not find a match in the application dispatch table, or if the handler returns one of two special errors (errAEEventNotHandled or errAENoSuchObject), the AEM attempts to find a match in this system dispatch table and thus, OSAX are invoked.

Coercions work in a similar fashion. In coercions, class and id are not used. The 'from' and 'to' data types are used instead. The AEM maintains application and system dispatch tables for coercions as well.

Now that we've had a very brief overview of Apple events, let's dive into the parts of a Scripting Addition.

The Scripting Additions File.

The file that contains the various resources that make up a Scripting Addition is created with the type 'osax' and the creator 'ascr'. This allows the Finder to associate the Scripting Additions icon (stored in AppleScript) with each OSAX file.

The ' osax' resource.

Each Scripting Addition file has at least one code resource of type 'osax' that contains the event or coercion handler for the Scripting Addition. It's the name of the 'osax' resource that tells AppleScript the type of Scripting Addition and the class and id of the event handler; or the from and to types for a coercion OSAX. The naming scheme works like this: The first four characters of the 'osax' resources name tells AppleScript the type of OSAX. It will be 'AEVT' for event handlers and 'CSDS' or 'CSPT' for coercion handlers. 'AEVT' stands for "Apple Event", 'CSDS' stands for "coerce from descriptor", and 'CSPT' stands for "coerce from pointer".

For example, an 'osax' resource named "AEVTaevtodoc" would install an Open document handler. An 'osax' resource named "CSDSscptTEXT" would install a coercion from the type 'scpt' (the data type for an AppleScript compiled script) to 'TEXT' which is the type for text.

Other Resources . . .

Both event and coercion OSAX can have other resources included in there files. An event handler that puts up a dialog might have 'DLOG' and 'DITL' resources. A coercion handler might have a resource that contains conversion information for the coercion to use. The Scripting Addition mechanism in AppleScript makes the OSAX's resource file the current when prior to dispatching to the OSAX code. An OSAX can therefore access any resource in the following resource chain: OSAX -> [target application] -> System. If no target is specified in the script (i.e. no 'tell application' block is used), the target application is the script editor in use.

Event handlers require one resource that coercion handlers do not require. The 'aete' or Apple event terminology extension resource. This is the resource that provides the language syntax for your event.

The 'aete' Resource.

It is the 'aete' resource that AppleScript uses to determine the syntax for your OSAX command. In the aete you describe the Apple event and all its parameters along with a corresponding grammatical equivalent for each. In fact, the way I like to design my OSAX's is by starting with the AppleScript syntax for the verb, write the aete to match the syntax, and then actually writing the code.

WRITING A SCRIPTING ADDITION

Design your syntax first

Let's design an OSAX that plays a QuickTime movie in a modal dialog. Let's see, how about the syntax: 'play movie <the path to the movie> [at <point or rectangle>]'? That sounds about right. This gives the user the ability to specify the movie to play and optionally position the window on the screen. (We're purposely not going to add support for the controller in this implementation. That we'll leave as an exercise for the reader…)

Here's what the event for the preceding syntax looks like:

play movie—this is the verb so let's assign the class and id for this.

class: 'OLIE'—this happens to be my nick name, you should use the signature of your application that you've registered with DTS or some other 4 character code that will differentiate your OSAX. Remember, lower case is reserved for the System (read Apple Computer).

id: 'QTIM'—Try to use something descriptive here.

<the path to the movie>—The direct parameter of an Apple event is defined as not having an associated language label. This is because the object the verb is acting on implies that the object to act on will be described next. Since our verb 'play movie' requires that we describe which movie we're to play, we'll use the direct parameter for the path to the movie to play.

keyword: '——'—The direct parameter.

type: typeAlias—For the path we'll use typeAlias. For a discussion about aliases versus other addressing forms, see the section 'Tips, tricks and gotchas' below.

[at <point or rectangle>]—our first 'named' parameter.

keyword: 'LOCA'—This can be a list of 2 or 4 integers or a record that contains labels for the positions of the point or rectangle; For example: 'play movie alias "Cool Disk:Cooler Folder:Hot Movie" at {qttop: 15, qtleft:30}'. This is nice for the user since they don't need to remember the ordering for the point or rectangle coordinates. Notice that we don't simply use 'top' and 'left' for our record labels, instead we use the prefix 'qt'. This is because of a conflict with terminology defined for the text suite included in AppleScript itself.

'left' and 'right' are already defined as formating options for a block of text. See Section V below for a discussion of other possible syntax clashes.

type: typeAEList/typeMyRectangle –Since the data can be either be a list or a record, we need to define this parameter with each of the possible data types. The type typeMyRectangle is a custom type that we define as a class. See Section V below for more information on using classes to define custom data types.

We could also use the wild card type for the 'at' parameter. We choose not to however because it can add a level of ambiguity to the syntax of the OSAX since it implies that any data type can be passed in for that parameter.

Build Your 'aete' Second

Now take a look at the listing "SAPlayMovie.r" to see the above design work in an 'aete'. Notice how we've filled in the other fields of the aete. In particular, pay close attention to the class definition near the bottom. Here is where we declare the record for our 'at' parameter. We define the rectangle record type to be a class of type 'rect' with properties for the top, left, bottom and right coordinates.

Also notice that we've declared the 'at' parameter twice: once with the type list, and once with the type of the class definition for our rectangle record. This way AppleScript knows both of the allowed types for the 'at' parameter.

The formal definition for an 'aete' resource is found in the file "AEUserTermTypes.r".

```
/*
    SAPlayMovie.r written by Donald O. Olson
    A simple QuickTime Scripting Addition written
    to illustrate writing Scripting Additions.

    Copyright ®1993 Donald O. Olson
    All rights reserved.
*/

#include "Types.r"
#include "SysTypes.r"
#include "AEUserTermTypes.r"

#define typeMyRectangle 'RECT'
```

```
resource 'vers' (1) {
    0x1,
    0x0,
    final,
    0x0,
    verUS,
    "1.0",
    "1.0, Copyright ® 1993 Donald Olson"
    ". All rights reserved."
};

resource 'vers' (2) {
    0x1,
    0x0,
    final,
    0x0,
    verUS,
    "1.0",
    "(by Donald Olson)"
};

/* This string gets displayed if the user double clicks on us. */

resource 'STR ' (-16397) {
    "This document can not be opened or printed."
    " It extends the functionality of AppleScript™"
    "and should be placed in the Scripting Additions"
    "folder found in the Extensions folder of your"
    " System Folder."
};

resource 'aete' (0, "play movie") {
    /*
        The major and minor version fields refer to the
        'aete' definition.
    */
    0x1,    /* major version in BCD   */
    0x0,    /* minor version in BCD   */
    english,/* language code */
    roman,    /* script code */
    { /* array Suites: 1 elements */
        /* [1] */
        "The Olson OSAX Suite.",    /* suite name */
        /* Suite Description */
        "A collection of fine Scripting Additions"
        " for work and play.",   /* suite description */
        'OLIE',        /* suite ID */
        1,                /* suite level */
        1,                /* suite version */
        {  /* array Events: 1 elements */
```

```
/* [1] */
"play movie",    /* event name */
/* event description    */
"Play a QuickTime movie in a modal dialog.",
'OLIE',        /* Our Class */
'QTIM',        /* Our ID */
noReply,           /* No Reply */
/* Reply comment. */
"No reply is returned by this event.",
replyOptional,   /* Reply not required. */
singleItem,          /* Reply is a single item. */
notEnumerated,       /* Reply is not enumerated */
reserved, reserved, reserved, reserved, reserved,
reserved, reserved, reserved, reserved, reserved,
reserved, reserved, reserved,
'alis',           /* Direct param is alias. */
/* Comment for direct parameter. */
"Pass in path to the QuickTime movie to play.",
directParamRequired,
singleItem,
notEnumerated,
doesntChangeState,
reserved, reserved, reserved, reserved,
reserved, reserved, reserved, reserved,
reserved, reserved, reserved, reserved,
{  /* array OtherParams: 2 elements */
    /* [1] */
    "at",    /* Optional parameter */
    'LOCA',  /* Its keyword. */
    'list',  /* Its type. */
    /* Comment for optional parameter. */
    "Point to use to position movie or rectangle"
    " to play move in. Must be in order 'left,"
    " top, right, bottom.",
    optional,        /* Optional parameter */
    listOfItems,     /* Must be a list. */
    notEnumerated,   /* is not enumerated */
    reserved, reserved, reserved, reserved,
    reserved, reserved, reserved, reserved,
    reserved, reserved, reserved, reserved,
    reserved,
    /* [2] */
    /*
        We define our optional parameter
        twice so that we can allow two
        different data types.
    */
    "at",               /* Optional parameter */
    'LOCA',             /* Its keyword. */
```

```
            typeMyRectangle,        /* Its type. */
            /* Comment for optional parameter. */
            "Point to use to position movie or rectangle"
            " to play move in. Must be in order 'left,"
            " top, right, bottom.",
            optional,           /* Optional parameter */
            listOfItems,        /* Must be a list. */
            notEnumerated,      /* is not enumerated */
            reserved, reserved, reserved, reserved,
            reserved, reserved, reserved, reserved,
            reserved, reserved, reserved, reserved,
            reserved
        }
    },
    {   /* array Classes: 1 elements */
        /* [1] */
        /*
            This is how we define our custom
            record. We define a class 'rectangle'
            with the custom keyword typeMyRectangle.
            We then define properties of this class
            for each of our records labels.
        */
        "rectangle",                /* Name of our class. */
        typeMyRectangle,            /* Type of our class. */
        /* Comment for optional parameter. */
        "This is a custom class definition used to "
        "define the record we use to position our "
        "movie's window.",
        {/* array Properties: 4 elements */
        /* [1] */
            "qttop",                /* Name of property. */
            'TOP ',                 /* Keyword */
            typeMyRectangle,        /* Its type. */
            "Top of rectangle.",    /* Comment field. */
            reserved,
            singleItem,
            notEnumerated,
            readOnly,
            reserved, reserved, reserved, reserved,
            reserved, reserved, reserved, reserved,
            reserved, reserved, reserved, reserved,
        /* [2] */
            "qtright", /* Name of property. */
            'RGHT', /* Keyword */
            typeMyRectangle,    /* Its type. */
            /* Comment field. */
            "Right side of rectangle.",
            reserved,
```

```
            singleItem,
            notEnumerated,
            readOnly,
            reserved, reserved, reserved, reserved,
            reserved, reserved, reserved, reserved,
            reserved, reserved, reserved, reserved,
            /* [3] */
            "qtleft",        /* Name of property. */
            'LEFT',             /* Keyword */
            typeMyRectangle,    /* Its type. */
            "Left side of rectangle.",/* Comment field. */
            reserved,
            singleItem,
            notEnumerated,
            readOnly,
            reserved, reserved, reserved, reserved,
            reserved, reserved, reserved, reserved,
            reserved, reserved, reserved, reserved,
            /* [4] */
            "qtbottom",  /* Name of property. */
            'BOTM',    /* Keyword */
            typeMyRectangle,/* Its type. */
            "Bottom of rectangle.", /* Comment field. */
            reserved,
            singleItem,
            notEnumerated,
            readOnly,
            reserved, reserved, reserved, reserved,
            reserved, reserved, reserved, reserved,
            reserved, reserved, reserved, reserved
        },
        {  /* array Elements: 0 elements */
        }
    },
    {  /* array ComparisonOps: 0 elements */
    },
    {  /* array Enumerations: 0 elements */
    }
  }
};
```

Write Your Code Third

Writing OSAX is very straight forward: follow all the rules for writing standalone code resources and all will be swell.

Our samples will be written in 'C', but Scripting Additions can be written in any language that can compile your work into a code resource.

```
/////////////////////////////////////////////////////////////
//
//   SAPlayMovie.c written by Donald O. Olson
//   A simple QuickTime Scripting Addition written
//   to illustrate writing Scripting Additions.
//
//   Copyright ®1993 Donald O. Olson
//   All rights reserved.
//
/////////////////////////////////////////////////////////////

// Our includes
#include <Movies.h>
#include <Memory.h>
#include <Fonts.h>
#include <OSEvents.h>
#include <limits.h>
#include <Menus.h>
#include <Processes.h>
#include <String.h>
#include <Resources.h>
#include <Packages.h>
#include <AppleEvents.h>
#include <Errors.h>
#include <GestaltEqu.h>
#include <Files.h>

// Our optional parameters keyword
#define keyLocation    'LOCA'

// Our rectangle records keywords
#define keyRight    'RGHT'
#define keyLeft     'LEFT'
#define keyTop      'TOP '
#define keyBottom   'BOTM'

#define kLeft      1 // Our list of points are in the
#define kTop       2  // order shown
#define kRight     3
#define kBottom    4

// Used to position movie on screen
#define kDefaultOffset  100
#define kBogusNumber    UINT_MAX

/*
   Our prototypes, could be in a .h file but are included here
   for ease of use.
*/
```

```
OSErr PlayTheMovie( FSSpec myFSSpec, AEDesc theLocationDesc);
OSErr SetMovieRect( AEDesc theLocationDesc, Movie theMovie,
        Rect *ourRect);

///////////////////////////////////////////////////////////
//
//   main()
//   The entry to our Scripting Addition.
//   Remember to declare it pascal!!
//
///////////////////////////////////////////////////////////

pascal OSErr main( AppleEvent *theEvent,
        AppleEvent *theReply,
        long theRefCon)
{
  OSErr     theErr = noErr;
  FSSpec    theFSSpec;
  DescType  typeCode;
  long      theGestaltReturn = 0;
  Size   actualSize;
  AEDesc theLocationDesc;

  /* Is QuickTime present? */
  theErr = Gestalt(gestaltQuickTime, &theGestaltReturn);
  if(theErr) return theErr; // If not, bail.

  /*
    Grab the movie file's path from the direct parameter.
    We declared the direct parameter to be an alias in our
    aete.  Since the AEM will coerce an alias to a FSSpec for
    us, and that's what the OpenMovieFile call wants, we'll
    ask for it as an FSSpec.
  */

theErr = AEGetParamPtr( theEvent, keyDirectObject,
        typeFSS, &typeCode, (Ptr)&theFSSpec,
        sizeof(FSSpec), &actualSize);
if(theErr) return theErr;

  /*
    Now get the location parameter, if it's present.
    We don't check errors for this call since the AEM
    will return the descriptor with the descriptorType
    field set to typeNull if there is an error.  We check
    for NULL in the PlayTheMovie function.
  */

  theErr = AEGetParamDesc(            theEvent, keyLocation,
```

```
                        typeWildCard, &theLocationDesc);

    /* Start up the movie tools */
    if(EnterMovies()) return theErr; // Bail on error.

      theErr = PlayTheMovie(theFSSpec, theLocationDesc);
      ExitMovies();  // Close our connection to the movie tools

      return theErr; // And return our error.
}


///////////////////////////////////////////////////////////
//
//   PlayTheMovie() Opens and plays Movie File
//   This code is based on the SimplePlayer sample
//   that comes with the QuickTime Developers Disk.
//
///////////////////////////////////////////////////////////

OSErr  PlayTheMovie(FSSpec myFSSpec, AEDesc theLocationDesc)
{
  Movie        theMovie;
  Rect         dispBounds;
  WindowPtr movieWindow = NULL;
  OSErr        theErr = noErr;
  short     resRefNum;
  long        duration = 60, finalTick;

  /* Open the movie file */
  if(OpenMovieFile(&(myFSSpec), &resRefNum, 0)) {
    SysBeep(1);   // Signal our error
    return theErr;// And bail
  }

  if(NewMovieFromFile( &theMovie, resRefNum,
          NULL, NULL,0, NULL )) {
    SysBeep(1);  // Signal our error
    return theErr;  // And bail
  }

  /* Get the bounds for the movie. */

  GetMovieBox( theMovie, &dispBounds);

  /*
    If the user passed in a location or size for the window,
    let's grab it now.
  */
```

```
if(theLocationDesc.descriptorHandle != NULL) {
  // Use the values sent to us by the user.
  theErr = SetMovieRect( theLocationDesc, theMovie,
      &dispBounds);
if(theErr) return theErr;
} else {
  OffsetRect(   &dispBounds,-dispBounds.left,-dispBounds.top);
  SetMovieBox(theMovie, &dispBounds);
  // Make sure window not under menu bar
  OffsetRect(&dispBounds,kDefaultOffset,kDefaultOffset);
}

/*
    Any time you are going to put up a dialog be sure to
  call AEInteractWithUser. The AppleEvent Manager will
  take care of posting notification and/or layer switching
  as needed.
*/

theErr = AEInteractWithUser(kAEDefaultTimeout, NULL, NULL);
if(theErr) return theErr;

/* Set up our window */
movieWindow = NewCWindow(  0L, &dispBounds,
          (StringPtr)myFSSpec.name,
          true,0,(WindowPtr)-1L,false,0L);
if(movieWindow == NULL) {
  // Whoops, no window so BAIL;
  SysBeep(1);
  return memFullErr;
}

ShowWindow(movieWindow);      // Make the window visible
SetPort(movieWindow);      // Set the part
// Set up the movie world
SetMovieGWorld(theMovie,NULL,NULL);

/* Now we're ready to play the movie */
GoToBeginningOfMovie(theMovie);// Rewind movie
PrerollMovie(theMovie,0,0);  // Get the movie ready to play
SetMovieActive(theMovie,true);  // Activate movie
StartMovie(theMovie);          // Start playing

/*
  Play the movie to the end unless the mouse button has
been pressed
*/
while ( !IsMovieDone(theMovie) && !Button())
  MoviesTask(theMovie,0);
```

```
    FlushEvents(everyEvent, 0);      // Clean up spurious events
    Delay(duration, &finalTick); // Pause on the final frame
    /* Clean up and go home */
    DisposeMovie(theMovie);             // Get rid of the movie
    CloseMovieFile(resRefNum);      // Close movie file
    DisposeWindow(movieWindow);        // And dispose our window
    return theErr;
}


/////////////////////////////////////////////////////////////
//
//    SetMovieRect
//    Set the position and bounding rectangle of
//    our movie window.
//
/////////////////////////////////////////////////////////////

OSErr SetMovieRect( AEDesc theLocationDesc, Movie theMovie,
        Rect *ourRect) {
    long        numberOfListItems = 0;
    OSErr        theErr = noErr;
    AEKeyword    theAEKeyword;
    DescType     typeCode;
    Size         actualSize;
    long          pointLeft, pointTop,
                 pointRight = kBogusNumber, // We use pointRight
                 pointBottom;     // to see if we've gotten a point
                                  // or a rectangle

    /* Did we get passed a list? */
    if(theLocationDesc.descriptorType == typeAEList) {

    /* Get the data handle size to determine if point or rect */
    theErr = AECountItems( &theLocationDesc,
                          &numberOfListItems);
    if(theErr) return theErr; // Bail on error!
    /* Must be two or four items in list */
    if(numberOfListItems != 2 && numberOfListItems != 4)
        return paramErr;

    /* If it's a point, just move the window. */
    if(numberOfListItems == 2) {
        theErr = AEGetNthPtr( &theLocationDesc, kLeft,
            typeLongInteger, &theAEKeyword, &typeCode,
            (Ptr)&pointLeft, sizeof(pointLeft), &actualSize);
        if(theErr) return theErr; // Just in case…

        theErr = AEGetNthPtr( &theLocationDesc, kTop,
            typeLongInteger, &theAEKeyword, &typeCode,
```

```
    (Ptr)&pointTop, sizeof(pointTop), &actualSize);
    if(theErr) return theErr; // Just in case…
} else if(numberOfListItems == 4) { // It's a rectangle
    theErr = AEGetNthPtr(  &theLocationDesc, kLeft,
        typeLongInteger, &theAEKeyword, &typeCode,
    (Ptr)&pointLeft, sizeof(pointLeft), &actualSize);
    if(theErr) return theErr; // Just in case…

    theErr = AEGetNthPtr(  &theLocationDesc, kTop,
        typeLongInteger, &theAEKeyword, &typeCode,
    (Ptr)&pointTop,sizeof(pointTop), &actualSize);
    if(theErr) return theErr; // Just in case…

    theErr = AEGetNthPtr(  &theLocationDesc, kRight,
    typeLongInteger, &theAEKeyword, &typeCode,
    (Ptr)&pointRight, sizeof(pointRight), &actualSize);
    if(theErr) return theErr; // Just in case…

    theErr = AEGetNthPtr(  &theLocationDesc, kBottom,
        typeLongInteger,&theAEKeyword, &typeCode,
    (Ptr)&pointBottom, sizeof(pointBottom), &actualSize);
  if(theErr) return theErr; // Just in case…

  }
/* Is it a record? */
} else if(theLocationDesc.descriptorType == typeAERecord) {
    /* Get the points out by key names */

    theErr = AEGetKeyPtr(  &theLocationDesc, keyLeft,
        typeLongInteger, &typeCode, (Ptr)&pointLeft,
    sizeof(pointLeft), &actualSize);
    if(theErr) return theErr; // Must have these two

    theErr = AEGetKeyPtr(  &theLocationDesc, keyTop,
        typeLongInteger, &typeCode, (Ptr)&pointTop,
        sizeof(pointTop), &actualSize);
    if(theErr) return theErr; // Must have these two

    theErr = AEGetKeyPtr(  &theLocationDesc, keyRight,
        typeLongInteger, &typeCode, (Ptr)&pointRight,
        sizeof(pointRight), &actualSize);
    // Ignore this error

    theErr = AEGetKeyPtr(  &theLocationDesc, keyBottom,
        typeLongInteger, &typeCode, (Ptr)&pointBottom,
        sizeof(pointBottom), &actualSize);
    // Ignore this error too, but clear our variable
    theErr = noErr;
```

```
    }

    if(pointRight == kBogusNumber) // We got a new origin...
        SetRect( ourRect, pointLeft, pointTop,
(ourRect->right—ourRect->left) + pointLeft,
(ourRect->bottom—ourRect->top) + pointTop);
        else                // We got a new rectangle...
            SetRect( ourRect, pointLeft, pointTop,
pointRight, pointBottom);

    /* Set topleft to 0,0 */
    OffsetRect(ourRect,-ourRect->left,-ourRect->top);

    /* Set the movie box to the new rect. */
    SetMovieBox(theMovie, ourRect);
    OffsetRect(ourRect,pointLeft, pointTop);
    return theErr;
}
```

Compiling

To compile in MPW, use the following build commands:

```
C -b "SAPlayMovie.c" -d SystemSevenOrLater
Rez -a -o "play movie" -t osax -c ascr 'SAPlayMovie.r'
Link -p -w -t osax -c ascr -rt osax=6991 -m MAIN -sg "AEVTOLIEQTIM" -
ra "AEVTOLIEQTIM"=resSysHeap,resPurgeable Γ
    "SAPlayMovie.c.o" Γ
    "{CLibraries}"StdCLib.o Γ
    "{Libraries}"Runtime.o Γ
    "{Libraries}"Interface.o Γ
    -o "play movie"
```

To compile in Symantec THINK C, include SAPlayMovie.c, SAPlayMovie.r and MacTraps in your project. Set your project type as shown. Make sure that the resource attributes Purgeable and System Heap are set to true.

Write Some Test Scripts Fifth

```
play movie (choose file) at {100, 100}
play movie (choose file) at {qttop: 100, qtleft: 100,
qtright:250, qtbottom, 250}
```

○ Application   File Type | osax |

○ Desk Accessory

○ Device Driver   Creator | ascr |

◉ Code Resource   ☐ Multi-Segment

Name | AEVTOLIEQTIM |

Type | osax | ID | 6991 |

☐ Custom Header   Attrs | 60 |

[Cancel]   [OK]

WRITING A COERCION SCRIPTING ADDITION

Writing a coercion OSAX is simpler than writing an event OSAX. The design work is to simply notice that you need to coerce one data type to another. The one decision you need to make is whether the coercion should be coerce from pointer or coerce from descriptor. In general, always use a coerce from pointer coercion since it means AppleScript need not build an AEDesc to pass into your coercion.

Write Your Code

We're going to write a sample coercion here that takes a script object and coerces it to text. We'll do this by taking advantage of a few calls in the Open Scripting Architecture that will do the work of de-compiling a script object into its representative text form. And, this is an example of when you would want to use the coerce from descriptor form.

```
//////////////////////////////////////////////////////////////////
//
//   CoercescptToText.c written by Donald O. Olson
//   A simple Coercion Scripting Addition written
//      to illustrate writing Scripting Additions.
//
//   Copyright ®1993 Donald O. Olson
```

```
//      All rights reserved.
//
///////////////////////////////////////////////////////////

#include <Memory.h>
#include <Fonts.h>
#include <OSEvents.h>
#include <Menus.h>
#include <Processes.h>
#include <String.h>
#include <Resources.h>
#include <Packages.h>
#include <AppleEvents.h>
#include <Errors.h>
#include <GestaltEqu.h>
#include <Files.h>
#include <OSA.h>


#define typeStyledText          'STXT'


///////////////////////////////////////////////////////////
//
//   main()
//      This is the interface for a coerce from descriptor
//      coercion.  Remember to declare it 'pascal'!!!
//
///////////////////////////////////////////////////////////

pascal OSErr main( AEDesc *scriptDesc, DescType toType,
        long refcon, AEDesc *resultDesc)
{
    OSErr           theErr = noErr;
    OSAError        theOSAErr;
    ComponentInstance     gASComponent = 0;
    OSAID           resultingID = 0;
    long            modeFlags = 0;

    /*
       Open an instantiation of the
       Generic Scripting Component
    */
    gASComponent = OpenDefaultComponent(kOSAComponentType,
        kOSAGenericScriptingComponentSubtype);

    /* Checking errors here! */
    if(((long)gASComponent == (long)badComponentInstance) ||
       ((long)gASComponent == (long)badComponentSelector)) {
       theErr = invalidComponentID;
```

```
        goto CLEANUP;    // Yea! A valid use for a 'goto'!!
    }

    /* Load script in scriptDesc into a scriptID */
    theOSAErr = OSALoad(  gASComponent, scriptDesc,
               modeFlags, &resultingID);

        if( theOSAErr != noErr) {
        theErr = theOSAErr;
        goto CLEANUP;
    }

    /*
        Now get the source.  Since AppleScript can coerce any
        of the various text forms to a text object (which is
        what we claim to be returning, let's just return the
        styled text and let AppleScript do the secondary
    coercion for us.
    */

    theOSAErr = OSAGetSource( gASComponent, resultingID,
               typeStyledText, resultDesc);

    if(  theOSAErr != noErr) theErr = theOSAErr;

    CLEANUP:;
    if(resultingID != 0) OSADispose(gASComponent, resultingID);
    if(gASComponent != 0) CloseComponent(gASComponent);

    return theErr;
}
```

Compiling

To compile in MPW, use the following build commands:

```
C -b "CoercescptToText.c" -d SystemSevenOrLater
Link -p -w -t osax -c ascr -rt osax=9999 -m MAIN -sg "CSDSscptctxt" -ra
"CSDSscptctxt"=resSysHeap,resPurgeable Γ
   "CoercescptToText.c.o" Γ
   "{CLibraries}"StdCLib.o Γ
   "{Libraries}"Runtime.o Γ
   "{Libraries}"Interface.o Γ
   -o "ScriptToTextCoercion"
```

To compile in Symantec THINK C, include CoercescptToText.c
and MacTraps in your project. Set your project type as shown. Make
sure that the resource attributes Purgeable and System Heap are set to
true.

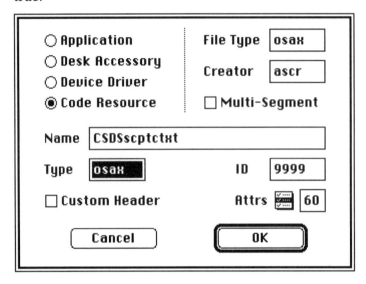

Write Some Test Scripts

Here's a sample script to use to test our coercion.

```
script Fred
   property foo : 3
   property bar : 3
   on fumble()
      beep 2
      return "Whoops!"
   end fumble
end script
```

Fred as Text

Executing this script will return the following as a result of the coercion:

```
"property foo : 3
property bar : 3
on fumble()
   beep 2
   return \"Whoops!\"
end fumble"
```

This is correct since this is the script associated with the script object. The script declaration is not stored as part of the script object.

TIPS, TRICKS AND GOTCHAS

Wildcard classes and multiple verbs

The Apple Event Manager allows the use of wildcards for either the class or id for event handlers, and the 'from' and 'to' types for coercions. When the AEM does not find a direct match and event or coercion, it looks to see if it can find a partial match with an entry in the table that uses a wildcard entry for either or both of its keys. For example: if I have an entry in our AEM dispatch table for the class 'OLIE' and the id '****' and we recieve an event with the class 'OLIE' and the id 'TEXT', as long as there is not a match for the id 'TEXT' in the dispatch table somewhere, the wildcard entry will be called.

We can use this ability in OSAX to have one 'osax' code resource that handles several different yet related events or coercions.

For events, the way to do this is to define either the class or id with the '****' wildcard type. For example, I want to write a cd player OSAX that shares a large amount of the same code. I'll define the OSAX's name like this "AEVTCDPL****". In the 'aete' for the OSAX I'll define as many verbs as I need using the class 'CDPL' with unique id's for each verb. In the 'osax' code for the handler I'll extract the id using the call AEGetAttributePtr with the key keyEventIDAttr. This returns the id of the event. Simply case off the id to the appropriate code.

We can do the same thing with coercions. To declare a wildCard to text coercion (coerce anything to text) we would name the 'osax' code resource "CSPT****TEXT". The big difference here is that the from type is passed in as a parameter to the coercion handler so we can case directly off of that.

Globals and the refCon

If you need to use global data in your OSAX, or if you need a place to keep a handle to some data around, you can use the refCon field of your event or coercion handler. When AppleScript installs your handler it initializes your refCon to NULL. You can then test for NULL the first time you are called to determine if you have initialized your globals or data.

To set the refCon field you use a two step process. First, you call AEGetEventHandler for event handlers or AEGetCoercionHandler for coercions. In both cases set the isSystem parameter to true. Second, you use AEInstallEventHandler or AEInstallCoercionHandler. Make sure that you use the procPtr returned to you from the AEGet… call since the Scripting Addition mechanism uses a special loading scheme to load your handler or coercion and to make its resource available in the current resource chain.

Movable Modals and Other Windows

While it is possible to write OSAX that have moveable windows, it is not recommended. The normal method for doing movable modal dialogs requires a hook into the host application's event loop to assure that update events are handled appropriately. Since there is no simple way to pass update events to an application, only use modal windows in OSAX.

Conflicts with Verbs, Properties, Enums, and Such

There are potentially three different terminology caches in use by AppleScript at any given time. AppleScript has an internal terminology cache that is available System wide. This terminology contains the Required Suite, the Core Suite, and the AppleScript Suite. AppleScript also keeps terminology caches for each running application that has been targeted in a 'tell' block. The last terminology cache is the OSAX cache.

There is a 'terminology inheritance' chain that is in affect that can cause OSAX to have terminology conflicts. The path is as follows: the targeted application (if any), AppleScript, and last, the OSAX. The fact that the OSAX is last is the biggest reason there are conflicts.

Terminology conflicts will normally display themselves at compile time. An example of a compile time conflict occurs when you target the Scriptable Text Editor with a script that uses the offset OSAX. Offset is also defined as a property of many of the text based classes such as paragraph, word and character. The following script demonstrates the problem:

```
tell app "scriptable text editor"
   offset of "1" in "123"
end tell
```

This returns the error "Can't get '1' in '123'. Access not allowed." Another example is the 'play movie' OSAX we wrote above. Since 'left' and 'right' are already defined as properties of the text class (align left, align right), compiling our OSAX will fail with the first colon after the the first declaration of 'left' or 'right' selected and the error message "Expected ',' or '}' but found ':'." displayed for our enjoyment. We solved the problem in the ugliest fashion possible by pre-pending 'qt' to each of our four parameters.

This is a very difficult problem for OSAX authors to deal with. There are only so many descriptive verbs that apply to the desktop metaphor used so extensively by Macintosh programs. Without additional support from AppleScript to resolve these kinds of conflicts, the best thing an OSAX developer can do is test their work against as many scriptable applications as possible.

More Than One 'osax' Code Resource in a File

You can place more than one OSAX in a Scripting Addition file. It may make sense to place 'families' of OSAX together. One example is the File Commands Scripting Additions file. It contains four different commands that all are related in that they manipulate the file system in some fashion.

With more than one OSAX in Scripting Addition file, replacing just one of the commands with a newer or more powerful version necessitates replacing the entire old file or doing surgery to remove the old command and replace it with the new. And since the terminology for a collection of OSAXs in the same file must contain all of there syntax, updating the syntax of one requires working with the collections 'aete'. This is out of the skill range for most users and certainly not very friendly.

Errors, Error Strings and the AEM

The Apple Event Manager will add the error you return from your event handler as an attribute of the reply Apple event. This is the key keyErrorNumber. If you wish AppleScript to display a descriptive string with errors you return, add the error string to the reply as an attribute with the key keyErrorString. AppleScript has error strings for most common errors returned by the Toolbox so it may not be necessary to add an error string for most errors returned from your Scripting Addition.

Class/Property Definitions for Record Labels

If you need to return a custom record type to AppleScript from either your command or coercion OSAX, create a custom class and define properties for the labels you need for your record. Simply use the id of the class you've created as the return data type for your command OSAX. In your OSAX, bundle up the record as an AERecord with each of the parameters being keyed off of the properties defined in your custom class. See the file "SAPlayMovie.r" for an example of this in a command OSAX.

AEInteractWithUser

Anytime you display a dialog or window from an OSAX, be sure to call AEInteractWithUser immediately before the window is shown. If the AEInteractWithUser call fails, do not display your window. Return the error returned from AEInteractWithUser instead.

'osiz' Resource—New for AppleScript 1.1

Starting with AppleScript 1.1, an OSAX may contain an additional resource to give AppleScript more information about the OSAX(s) in the OSAX file. The 'osiz' contains two flags for OSAX writers use.

The first flag specifies whether or not the OSAX mechanism opens the resource fork of the OSAX file about to be invoked. Set this flag to dontOpenResourceFile if the OSAX does not have owned resources. In other words, if the OSAX do not rely on using a resource that resides in the same file as the osax code resource, specify dontOpenResourceFile. If, on the other hand, the OSAX does use owned resources, such as dialogs or sounds, set this flag to openResourceFile. The default setting if no 'osiz' resource is included in the OSAX file is openResourceFile.

The second flag specifies whether or not the OSAX mechanism dispatches events that originate remotely. Set this flag to acceptRemoteEvents if you wish the OSAX to be accessable by both local and remote machines. If the OSAX is potentially dangerous, or might require a large number of CPU cycles for a protracted time, it might be appropriate to set the flag to dontAcceptRemoteEvents. The default setting if no 'osiz' resource is included in the OSAX file is acceptRemoteEvents.

The 'osiz' resource is defined as follows:

```
type 'osiz' {
  boolean openResourceFile,
      dontOpenResourceFile;
  boolean acceptRemoteEvents,
      dontAcceptRemoteEvents;
  boolean reserved;
```

```
    boolean reserved;
    boolean reserved;
    boolean reserved;
    boolean reserved;
    boolean reserved;
    boolean reserved;
    boolean reserved;
    boolean reserved;
    boolean reserved;
    boolean reserved;
    boolean reserved;
    boolean reserved;
    boolean reserved;
    boolean reserved;
    boolean reserved;
    boolean reserved;
    boolean reserved;
    boolean reserved;
    boolean reserved;
    boolean reserved;
    boolean reserved;
    boolean reserved;
    boolean reserved;
    boolean reserved;
    boolean reserved;
    boolean reserved;
    boolean reserved;
    boolean reserved;
    boolean reserved;
    boolean reserved;
};
```

PROTOTYPES FOR EVENT HANDLERS AND THE TWO FORMS OF COERCIONS

In 'C':

```
pascal OSErr MyEventHandler(  AppleEvent *theEvent,
        AppleEvent *theReply, long theRefCon)

pascal OSErr MyCoerceFromPtr(DescType fromType,
        Ptr dataPtr, Size dataSize, DescType toType,
        long refcon, AEDesc *resultDesc)

pascal OSErr MyCoerceFromDesc (AEDesc *fromDesc,
        DescType toType, long refcon, AEDesc *resultDesc)
```

In Pascal:

```
FUNCTION MyEventHandler(  theEvent, theReply: AppleEvent;
     theRefCon: LONGINT):OSErr;

FUNCTION MyCoerceFromPtr( fromType: DescType;
     dataPtr: Ptr; dataSize: Size;
     toType: DescType; refcon: LONGINT;
     VAR resultDesc: AEDesc):OSErr;

FUNCTION MyCoerceFromDesc ( fromDesc: AEDesc;
     toType: DescType; refcon: LONGINT;
```

BIOGRAPHY

Donald Olson is an engineer at Apple Computer and has been working with Apple events since their infancy. When he is not trying to convince the world that AppleScript is the most important technology to come out of Apple since the introduction of the Mac, Donald hangs out with his wife Theresa and children Matthew and Jessica.

Donald has worked on the HyperCard, Apple Event Manager, and AppleScript teams. Now, as a senior software engineer, he is working on the OpenDoc project. If he is not writing code or waiting for compiles to finish, Donald likes to cruise with his family, go for long bicycle rides, and make obnoxious noises with his electric guitar.

The Required Apple Events
Dave Mark

Appendix

F

In last month's column, I told you about a new class library we'll be using as the basis for much of the software featured in this column. I hope to bring you some Sprocket material starting next month. In the meantime, we've gotten a lot of requests for some code that handles the four required Apple events. That's what this month's column is all about.

THE REQUIRED APPLE EVENTS

In the old days (before System 7), when a user double-clicked on a document, the Finder first looked up the document's creator and type in its desktop database to figure out which application to launch. It then packaged information about the document (or set of documents if the user double-clicked on more than one) in a data structure, launched the appropriate application and passed the data structure to the application. To access this data structure, the application called the routine CountAppFiles() (to find out how many documents it needs to open or print) then, for each one, it called GetAppFiles() (to get the information necessary to open the file) and either opened or printed the file.

That model is no longer supported in the Power Mac interface files. It's also way outdated. While existing applications which use the AppFiles method are supported as a compatibility feature of the system, any new code written these days should support the current Apple event scheme. When you mark your application as a modern, with-it application supporting high-level events, launching an application follows a different path. When a user opens a document, the Finder still uses the file's creator and type to locate the right application to launch, but that's where the similarity ends. Once the application is launched, the Finder sends it a series of Apple events.

- If the application was launched by itself, with no documents, the Finder sends it an Open Application Apple event. This tells the application to do its standard initialization and assume that no documents were opened. In response to an Open Application Apple event, the application will usually create a new, untitled document.

- If a document or set of documents were used to launch the application, the Finder packages descriptions of the documents in a data structure know as a descriptor, adds the descriptor to an Open Document Apple event, then sends the event to the application.

When the application gets an Open Document event, it pulls the list of documents from the event and opens each document.

- If the user asked the Finder to print, rather than open a document or set of documents, the Finder follows the exact same procedure, but sends a Print Document Apple event instead of an Open Document event. In response to a Print Document Apple event, the application prints the document rather than opening it.

- Finally, if the Finder wants an application to quit (perhaps the user selected Shutdown from the Special menu) it sends the application a Quit Application Apple event. When the application gets a quit application event, it does whatever housekeeping it needs to do in preparation for quitting, then sets the global flag that allows it to drop out of the main event loop and exit.

These events are the four required Apple events. As the name implies, your application must handle these events. There are a couple of other situations where your application might receive one of these events.

For starters, any application can package and send an Apple event. If you own a recent copy of QuicKeys, you've got everything you need to build and send Apple events. If you install AppleScript, you can use the Script Editor to write scripts that get translated into Apple events. If you make your application recordable (so that the user can record your application's actions using the Script Editor, or any other Apple event recording application) you'll wrap all of your program's actions in individual Apple events. This means that when the user selects Open from the File menu, you'll send yourself an Open Document Apple event. If the user quits, you'll send yourself a Quit Application event.

In addition to the events described above, there are other situations in which the Finder will send you one of the four required Apple events. If the user double-clicks on (or otherwise opens) one of your application's documents, the Finder will package the document in an Open Document Apple event and send the event to your application. The same is true for the Print Document Apple event.

The user can also drag a document onto your application's icon. If your application is set up to handle that type of document, your application's icon will invert and, when the user let's go of the mouse, the Finder will embed the document in an Open Document Apple event and send the event to your application. Note that this technique can be used to launch your application or to request that your application open a document once it is already running.

APPLE EVENT HANDLERS

Apple events are placed in an event queue, much like the events you already know, love, and process, such as mouseDown, activateEvt, and updateEvt. So far, the events you've been handling have all been low-level events, the direct result of a user's actions. The user uncovers a portion of a window, an updateEvt is generated. The user clicks the mouse button, a mouseDown is generated.

Apple events, on the other hand, are known as high-level events, the result of interprocess communication instead of user-process communication. As you process events retrieved by WaitNextEvent(), you'll take action based on the value in the event's what field. If the what field contains the constant updateEvt, you'll call your update handling routine, etc. If the what field contains the constant kHighLevelEvent, you'll pass the event to the routine AEProcessAppleEvent():

```
switch ( eventPtr->what )
{
    case mouseDown:
        HandleMouseDown( eventPtr );
        break;
    case keyDown:
    case autoKey:
        theChar = eventPtr->message & charCodeMask;
        if ( (eventPtr->modifiers & cmdKey) != 0 )
            HandleMenuChoice( MenuKey( theChar ) );
        break;
    case updateEvt:
        DoUpdate( eventPtr );
        break;
    case kHighLevelEvent:
        AEProcessAppleEvent( eventPtr );
        break;
}
```

AEProcessAppleEvent() passes the event to the Apple event handler you've written specifically for that event. To handle the four required events, you'll write four Apple event handlers. You'll install the handlers at initialization time by passing the address of each handler (in

the form of a universal-procedure-pointer) to AEInstallEventHandler().
AEProcessAppleEvent() calls your handler for you automatically. Once
your handler is installed your work is done.

This Month's Program: AEHandler

This month's program, AEHandler, provides a skeleton you can use to
add the required Apple events to your own programs. We'll start off by
creating the AEHandler resources. Create a folder called AEHandler in
your development folder. Launch ResEdit and create a new file called
AEHandler.π.rsrc in the AEHandler folder.

1   Create an MBAR resource with an ID of 128 containing the MENU
     IDs 128, 129, and 130.

2   Use the specs in Figure F.1 to create three MENU resources with
     IDs of 128, 129, and 130.

Figure F.1.

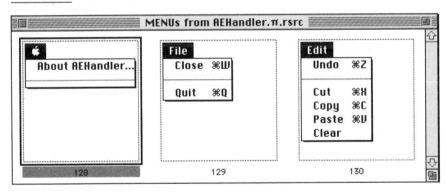

Three MENUs used by AEHandler.

3   Create a WIND resource with an ID of 128, having a top of 41, a left
     of 3, a bottom of 91, and a right of 303. Use the standard document
     proc (left-most in a ResEdit editing pane).

4   Copy the standard error alert from one of our previous programs. If
     you don't have one, create an ALRT with an ID of 128, a top of 40,
     left of 40, bottom of 156, and right of 332. Next, create a DITL with
     an ID of 128 and two items. Item 1 is an OK button with a top of
     86, a left of 219, a bottom of 106, and a right of 279. Item 2 is a sta-
     tic text item just like the one shown in Figure F.2.

FIGURE F.2

```
┌────────────────────────────────────────────────────────┐
│ ▤▢▤▤▤   Edit DITL item #2 from AEHandler.π.rsrc  ▤▤▤▤▤  │
├────────────────────────────────────────────────────────┤
│                                                         │
│              Text:   ┌──────────────────────────────┐   │
│                      │ ^0                            │   │
│     ┌─────────────┐  │                              │   │
│     │ Static Text ▼│  │                              │   │
│     └─────────────┘  │                              │   │
│                      └──────────────────────────────┘   │
│                                                         │
│  ☒ Enabled      Top:  ┌─────┐    Bottom:  ┌─────┐      │
│                       │ 5   │             │ 71  │      │
│                       └─────┘             └─────┘      │
│                 Left: ┌─────┐     Right:  ┌─────┐      │
│                       │ 67  │             │ 283 │      │
│                       └─────┘             └─────┘      │
└────────────────────────────────────────────────────────┘
```

The static text item for the error alert.

That covers the standard resources. Next come the resources that link specific document types to our application and that tie a set of small and large icons to our application. The Finder uses these resources to display an icon that represents our application in different situations (a large icon when the app is on the desktop, a small icon to display in the right-most corner of the menu bar when our app is front-most). The Finder uses the non-icon resources to update its desktop database.

5   Create a new BNDL resource with a resource ID of 128. When the BNDL editing window appears in ResEdit, select Extended View from the BNDL menu. This gives you access to some additional fields.

6   Put your application's four-byte signature in the Signature: field. Every time you create a new application, you'll have to come up with a unique four-byte string unique to your application. To verify that the signature is unique, you'll need to send it to the AppleLink address DEVSUPPORT. If you don't have a signature handy, feel free to use mine (DM=a). I've registered it for one of my applications but since it's not an application I distribute, you won't run into any conflicts.

7   Put 0 in the BNDL's ID field.

8   Put a copyright string in the © String field. This string will appear in the Finder's get info window for your application.

9   Select New File Type from the Resource menu. Use the specifications in Figure 3 to fill out the information for the APPL file type. This ties the first row of icons to the application itself. To edit the

FIGURE F.3

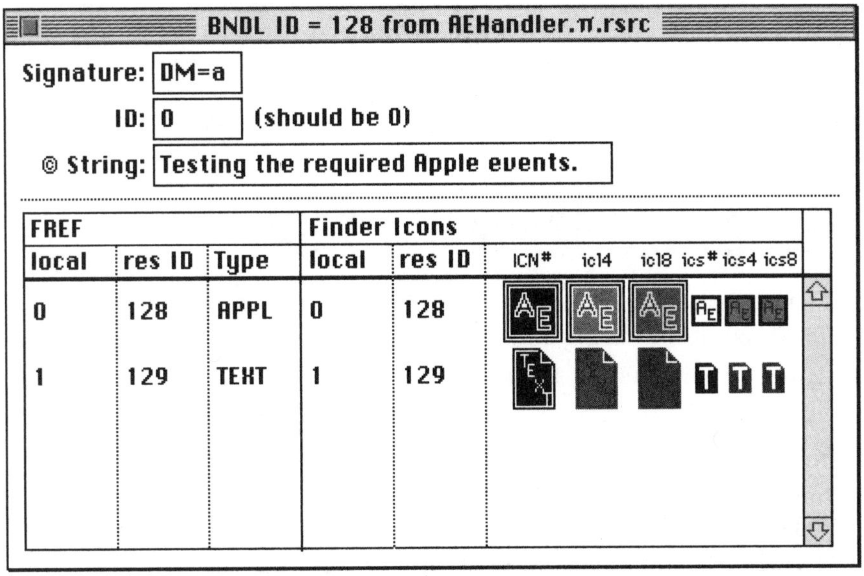

```
┌─────────────────────────────────────────────────────────────┐
│ ▣ ▨▨▨▨▨▨▨  BNDL ID = 128 from AEHandler.π.rsrc  ▨▨▨▨▨▨▨ │
├─────────────────────────────────────────────────────────────┤
│  Signature: │DM=a│                                           │
│         ID: │0   │     (should be 0)                         │
│    © String: │Testing the required Apple events.│            │
│  ┌────────────────────┬──────────────────────────────────┐  │
│  │ FREF               │ Finder Icons                     │  │
│  │ local │res ID│Type │ local │res ID│ICN# icl4 icl8 ics# ics4 ics8│
│  │                    │                                  │  │
│  │  0    │ 128  │APPL │  0    │ 128  │                   │  │
│  │                    │                                  │  │
│  │  1    │ 129  │TEXT │  1    │ 129  │                   │  │
│  │                    │                                  │  │
│  └────────────────────┴──────────────────────────────────┘  │
└─────────────────────────────────────────────────────────────┘
```

The AEHandler BNDL resource.

icons, double-click on the icon area and ResEdit will open an icon family editing window.

10   Back in the BNDL editing window, select New File Type again to add a second row of file types to the BNDL window. This time use the specs in Figure 3 to fill out the info for files of type TEXT. By doing this, we've told the finder that files with the signature 'DM=a' and of type 'TEXT' belong to the application AEHandler. Once again, double-click on the icon family to edit the individual icons.

If your application will support file types belonging to other applications, create file type entries in the BNDL resource for them as well, but don't edit the icons – leave them blank.

In addition, be aware that the Finder uses the file type entries to determine what files can drop launch your application. Right now, the Finder will only let you drop launch files with the signature 'DM=a' and of type 'TEXT' on AEHandler. To make AEHandler respond to all file types, create a new file type entry with the file type '****'. Don't edit the icons – leave them blank.

11   Save your changes and close the resource file.

12   In ResEdit, create a new resource file called test.text.

13   Select Get Info for test.text from the File menu.

14   When the info window appears, set the file's type to TEXT and its creator to whatever signature you used (if you used mine, it's DM=a).

That's it. Save your changes, quit ResEdit, and let's create the project.

CREATING THE AEHANDLER PROJECT

Pick your favorite development environment and create a new project called AEHandler.π, saving it in the AEHandler folder. Immediately edit your project type info (In THINK C, select Set Project Type... from the Project menu. In Code Warrior, pick the Project icon in the Preferences dialog). Set the project's creator to the creator you used (mine was 'DM=a'). Next, be sure to set the High-Level Event Aware flag in the SIZE resource flags. If you don't do this, the Apple Event Manager won't call your handlers!

Next, add either MacTraps or MacOS.lib to your project. Then, create a new source code file, save it as AEHandler.c and add it to your project. Here's the source code:

```
#include <GestaltEqu.h>
#include <AppleEvents.h>

#define kBaseResID              128
#define kErrorALRTid            128
#define kWINDResID              128

#define kVisible        true
#define kMoveToFront            (WindowPtr)-1L
#define kSleep                  60L
#define kNilFilterProc     0L
#define kGestaltMask            1L
#define kKeepInSamePlane        false

#define kWindowStartX           20
#define kWindowStartY           50

#define mApple                  kBaseResID
#define iAbout                  1

#define mFile                   kBaseResID+1
#define iClose                  1
#define iQuit                   3
```

Globals

```
Boolean    gDone;
short      gNewWindowX = kWindowStartX,
               gNewWindowY = kWindowStartY;
```

Functions

```
void      ToolboxInit( void );
void      MenuBarInit( void );
void      AEInit( void );
void      AEInstallHandlers( void );
pascal OSErr DoOpenApp(       AppleEvent *event,
                                   AppleEvent *reply, long refcon );
pascal OSErr DoOpenDoc(       AppleEvent *event,
                                   AppleEvent *reply, long refcon );
OSErr  CheckForRequiredParams( AppleEvent *event );
pascal OSErr DoPrintDoc(      AppleEvent *event,
                                   AppleEvent *reply, long refcon );
pascal OSErr DoQuitApp(       AppleEvent *event,
                                   AppleEvent *reply, long refcon );
void             OpenDocument( FSSpec *fileSpecPtr );
WindowPtr CreateWindow( Str255 name );
void             DoCloseWindow( WindowPtr window );
void      EventLoop( void );
void      DoEvent( EventRecord *eventPtr );
void      HandleMouseDown( EventRecord *eventPtr );
void      HandleMenuChoice( long menuChoice );
void      HandleAppleChoice( short item );
void      HandleFileChoice( short item );
void      DoUpdate( EventRecord *eventPtr );
void      DoError( Str255 errorString );
```

main

```
void    main( void )
{
    ToolboxInit();
    MenuBarInit();
    AEInit();

    EventLoop();
}
```

ToolboxInit

```
void    ToolboxInit( void )
{
    InitGraf( &qd.thePort );
    InitFonts();
    InitWindows();
    InitMenus();
    TEInit();
    InitDialogs( 0L );
    InitCursor();
}
```

MenuBarInit

```
void    MenuBarInit( void )
{
    Handle      menuBar;
    MenuHandle  menu;

    menuBar = GetNewMBar( kBaseResID );

    if ( menuBar == NULL )
        DoError( "\pCouldn't load the MBAR resource..." );

    SetMenuBar( menuBar );

    menu = GetMHandle( mApple );

    AddResMenu( menu, 'DRVR' );

    DrawMenuBar();
}
```

AEInit

```
void    AEInit( void )
{
    OSErr   err;
    long    feature;

    err = Gestalt( gestaltAppleEventsAttr, &feature );

    if ( err != noErr )
        DoError( "\pError returned by Gestalt!" );

    if (    !( feature
```

```
                            & ( kGestaltMask << gestaltAppleEventsPresent ) ) )
            DoError("\pThis configuration does not support Apple events...");

    AEInstallHandlers();
}
```

AEInstallHandlers

```
void    AEInstallHandlers( void )
{
    OSErr               err;

    err = AEInstallEventHandler( kCoreEventClass,
                                        kAEOpenApplication,
                NewAEEventHandlerProc( DoOpenApp ), 0L, false );

    if ( err != noErr )
        DoError( "\pError installing 'oapp' handler..." );

    err = AEInstallEventHandler( kCoreEventClass,
                kAEOpenDocuments,
                NewAEEventHandlerProc( DoOpenDoc ), 0L, false );

    if ( err != noErr )
        DoError( "\pError installing 'odoc' handler..." );

    err = AEInstallEventHandler( kCoreEventClass,
                kAEPrintDocuments,
                NewAEEventHandlerProc( DoPrintDoc ), 0L, false );

    if ( err != noErr )
        DoError( "\pError installing 'pdoc' handler..." );

    err = AEInstallEventHandler( kCoreEventClass,
                kAEQuitApplication,
                NewAEEventHandlerProc( DoQuitApp ), 0L, false );

    if ( err != noErr )
        DoError( "\pError installing 'quit' handler..." );
}
```

DoOpenApp

```
pascal OSErr    DoOpenApp( AppleEvent *event,
                                    AppleEvent *reply, long refcon )
{
    OpenDocument( nil );

    return noErr;
}
```

DoOpenDoc

```
pascal OSErr    DoOpenDoc( AppleEvent *event,
                                AppleEvent *reply, long refcon )
{
    OSErr       err;
    FSSpec      fileSpec;
    long        i, numDocs;
    DescType    returnedType;
    AEKeyword   keywd;
    Size        actualSize;
    AEDescList  docList = { typeNull, nil };

    // get the direct parameter—a descriptor list—and put
    // it into docList
    err = AEGetParamDesc( event, keyDirectObject,
                                typeAEList, &docList);

    // check for missing required parameters
    err = CheckForRequiredParams( event );
    if ( err )
    {
        // an error occurred:  do the necessary error handling
        err = AEDisposeDesc( &docList );
        return  err;
    }

    // count the number of descriptor records in the list
    // should be at least 1 since we got called and no error
    err = AECountItems( &docList, &numDocs );

    if ( err )
    {
        // an error occurred:  do the necessary error handling
        err = AEDisposeDesc( &docList );
        return  err;
    }

    // now get each descriptor record from the list, coerce
    // the returned data to an FSSpec record, and open the
    // associated file
    for ( i=1; i<=numDocs; i++ )
    {
        err = AEGetNthPtr( &docList, i, typeFSS, &keywd,
                                &returnedType, (Ptr)&fileSpec,
                                sizeof( fileSpec ), &actualSize );

        OpenDocument( &fileSpec );
    }
```

```
    err = AEDisposeDesc( &docList );

    return err;
}
```

CheckForRequiredParams

```
OSErr   CheckForRequiredParams( AppleEvent *event )
{
    DescType    returnedType;
    Size        actualSize;
    OSErr       err;

    err = AEGetAttributePtr( event, keyMissedKeywordAttr,
                    typeWildCard, &returnedType,
                    nil, 0, &actualSize);

    if ( err == errAEDescNotFound )   // you got all the required
                                      //parameters
        return noErr;
    else
        if ( err == noErr )   // you missed a required parameter
            return errAEParamMissed;
        else                          // the call to AEGetAttributePtr failed
            return err;
}
```

DoPrintDoc

```
pascal OSErr   DoPrintDoc(   AppleEvent *event,
                                AppleEvent *reply, long refcon )
{
    return noErr;
}
```

DoQuitApp

```
pascal OSErr   DoQuitApp(   AppleEvent *event,
                                AppleEvent *reply, long refcon )
{
    SysBeep( 20 );
    gDone = true;

    return noErr;
}
```

OpenDocument

```
void    OpenDocument( FSSpec *fileSpecPtr )
{
    WindowPtr   window;

    if ( fileSpecPtr == nil )
        window = CreateWindow( "\p<Untitled>" );
    else
        window = CreateWindow( fileSpecPtr->name );
}
```

CreateWindow

```
WindowPtr   CreateWindow( Str255 name )
{
    WindowPtr   window;
    short            windowWidth, windowHeight;

    window = GetNewWindow( kWINDResID, nil, kMoveToFront );

    SetWTitle( window, name );

    MoveWindow( window, gNewWindowX, gNewWindowY,
                        kKeepInSamePlane );

    gNewWindowX += 20;
    windowWidth = window->portRect.right
                            - window->portRect.left;

    if ( gNewWindowX + windowWidth > qd.screenBits.bounds.right )
    {
        gNewWindowX = kWindowStartX;
        gNewWindowY = kWindowStartY;
    }

    gNewWindowY += 20;
    windowHeight = window->portRect.bottom
                            - window->portRect.top;

    if ( gNewWindowY + windowHeight >
                                    qd.screenBits.bounds.bottom )
    {
        gNewWindowX = kWindowStartX;
        gNewWindowY = kWindowStartY;
    }

    ShowWindow( window );
```

```
    SetPort( window );

    return window;
}
```

DoCloseWindow

```
void    DoCloseWindow( WindowPtr window )
{
    if ( window != nil )
        DisposeWindow( window );
}
```

EventLoop

```
void    EventLoop( void )
{
    EventRecord    event;

    gDone = false;
    while ( gDone == false )
    {
        if ( WaitNextEvent( everyEvent, &event, kSleep, nil ) )
            DoEvent( &event );
    }
}
```

DoEvent

```
void    DoEvent( EventRecord *eventPtr )
{
    char    theChar;

    switch ( eventPtr->what )
    {
        case mouseDown:
            HandleMouseDown( eventPtr );
            break;
        case keyDown:
        case autoKey:
            theChar = eventPtr->message & charCodeMask;
            if ( (eventPtr->modifiers & cmdKey) != 0 )
                HandleMenuChoice( MenuKey( theChar ) );
            break;
        case updateEvt:
            DoUpdate( eventPtr );
            break;
```

```
            case kHighLevelEvent:
                AEProcessAppleEvent( eventPtr );
                break;
        }
}
```

HandleMouseDown

```
void    HandleMouseDown( EventRecord *eventPtr )
{
    WindowPtr       window;
    short           thePart;
    long            menuChoice;

    thePart = FindWindow( eventPtr->where, &window );

    switch ( thePart )
    {
        case inMenuBar:
            menuChoice = MenuSelect( eventPtr->where );
            HandleMenuChoice( menuChoice );
            break;
        case inSysWindow :
            SystemClick( eventPtr, window );
            break;
        case inGoAway:
            if ( TrackGoAway( window, eventPtr->where ) )
                DoCloseWindow( window );
            break;
        case inContent:
            SelectWindow( window );
            break;
        case inDrag :
            DragWindow( window, eventPtr->where, &qd.screenBits.bounds );
            break;
    }
}
```

HandleMenuChoice

```
void    HandleMenuChoice( long menuChoice )
{
    short   menu;
    short   item;

    if ( menuChoice != 0 )
    {
```

```
        menu = HiWord( menuChoice );
        item = LoWord( menuChoice );

        switch ( menu )
        {
            case mApple:
                HandleAppleChoice( item );
                break;
            case mFile:
                HandleFileChoice( item );
                break;
        }
        HiliteMenu( 0 );
    }
}
```

HandleAppleChoice

```
void    HandleAppleChoice( short item )
{
    MenuHandle  appleMenu;
    Str255      accName;
    short       accNumber;

    switch ( item )
    {
        case iAbout:
            SysBeep( 20 );
            break;
        default:
            appleMenu = GetMHandle( mApple );
            GetItem( appleMenu, item, accName );
            accNumber = OpenDeskAcc( accName );
            break;
    }
}
```

HandleFileChoice

```
void    HandleFileChoice( short item )
{
    switch ( item )
    {
        case iClose:
            DoCloseWindow( FrontWindow() );
            break;
        case iQuit:
```

```
        gDone = true;
        break;
    }
}
```

DoUpdate

```
void    DoUpdate( EventRecord *eventPtr )
{
    WindowPtr  window;

    window = (WindowPtr)eventPtr->message;

    BeginUpdate(window);
    EndUpdate(window);
}
```

DoError

```
void    DoError( Str255 errorString )
{
    ParamText( errorString, "\p", "\p", "\p" );

    StopAlert( kErrorALRTid, kNilFilterProc );

    ExitToShell();
}
```

Running AEHandler

Save your code, then build AEHandler as an application (In Metrowerks, just run the application) and then run it. An untitled window should appear. If it didn't, go back and check your SIZE resource to make sure the High-Level-Event Aware flag is set.

As you look through the code, you'll see that the untitled window is created by the Open Application handler. Now double click on the file test.text. A window titled test.text should appear. This window was created by the Open Documents handler.

With AEHandler still running, go into the Finder and select Shutdown from the Special menu. The Finder should bring AEHandler to the front and send it a Quit Application Apple event. Our Quit Application handler beeps once then sets gDone to true. When you quit normally, you won't hear this beep.

IDG License Agreement

Important: Please read this carefully before opening the software packet. This is a legal agreement between you (either an individual or an entity) and IDG Books Worldwide, Inc. (IDG). By opening the accompanying sealed packet containing the software disk, you acknowledge that you have read and accept the following IDG License Agreement. If you do not agree and do not want to be bound by the terms of this Agreement, promptly return the book and the unopened software packet to the place you obtained them for a full refund.

1   License. This License Agreement (Agreement) permits you to use one copy of the enclosed Software program(s) on a single computer. The Software is in "use" on a computer when it is loaded into temporary memory (that is, RAM) or installed into permanent memory (for example, hard disk, CD ROM, or other storage device) of that computer.

2.   Copyright. The entire contents of this disk and the compilation of the Software are copyrighted and protected by both United States copyright laws and international treaty provisions. The individual programs on the disk are copyrighted by their respective owners. You may only (a) make one copy of the Software for backup or archival purposes, or (b) transfer the Software to a single hard disk, provided that you keep the original for backup or archival purposes. None of the material on this disk or listed in this Book may ever be distributed, in original or modified form, for commercial purposes.

3.   Other Restrictions. You may not rent or lease the Software. You may transfer the Software and user documentation on a permanent basis provided you retain no copies and the recipient agrees to the terms of this Agreement. You may not reverse engineer, decompile, or disassemble the Software except to the extent that the foregoing restriction is expressly prohibited by applicable law. If the Software is an update or has been updated, any transfer must include the most recent update and all prior versions.

4.   Limited Warranty. IDG Warrants that the Software and disk are free from defects in materials and workmanship for a period of sixty (60) days from the date of purchase of this Book. If IDG receives notification within the warranty period of defects in material or workmanship, IDG will replace the defective disk. IDG's entire liability and your exclusive remedy shall be limited to replacement of the Software, which is returned to IDG with a copy of your receipt.

This Limited Warranty is void if failure of the Software has resulted from accident, abuse, or misapplication. Any replacement Software will be warranted for the remainder of the original warranty period or thirty (30) days, whichever is longer.

5. No Other Warranties. To the maximum extent permitted by applicable law, IDG and the author disclaim all other warranties, express or implied, including but not limited to implied warranties of merchantability and fitness for a particular purpose, with respect to the Software, the programs, the source code contained therein and/or the techniques described in this Book. This limited warranty gives you specific legal rights. You may have others which vary from state/jurisdiction to state/jurisdiction.

6. No Liability For Consequential Damages. To the extent permitted by applicable law, in no event shall IDG or the author be liable for any damages whatsoever (including without limitation, damages for loss of business profits, business interruption, loss of business information, or any other pecuniary loss) arising out of the use of or inability to use the Book or the Software, even if IDG has been advised of the possibility of such damages. Because some states/jurisdictions do not allow the exclusion or limitation of liability for consequential or incidental damages, the above limitation may not apply to you.

METROWERKS LICENSE AGREEMENT

"METROWERKS AND METROWERKS' LICENSOR(S), AND THEIR DIRECTORS, OFFICERS, EMPLOYEES OR AGENTS (COLLECTIVELY METROWERKS) MAKE NO WARRANTIES, EXPRESS OR IMPLIED, INCLUDING WITHOUT LIMITATION THE IMPLIED WARRANTIES OF MERCHANTABILITY AND FITNESS FOR A PARTICULAR PURPOSE, REGARDING THE SOFTWARE. METROWERKS DOES NOT WARRANT, GUARANTEE OR MAKE ANY REPRESENTATIONS REGARDING THE USE OR THE RESULTS OF THE USE OF THE SOFTWARE IN TERMS OF ITS CORRECTNESS, ACCURACY, RELIABILITY, CURRENTNESS OR OTHERWISE. THE ENTIRE RISK AS TO THE RESULTS AND PERFORMANCE OF THE SOFTWARE IS ASSUMED BY YOU. THE EXCLUSION OF IMPLIED WARRANTIES IS NOT PERMITTED BY SOME JURISDICTIONS. THE ABOVE EXCLUSION MAY NOT APPLY TO YOU."

"IN NO EVENT WILL METROWERKS AND METROWERKS' LICENSOR(S), AND THEIR DIRECTORS, OFFICERS, EMPLOYEES OR AGENTS (COLLECTIVELY METROWERKS) BE LIABLE TO YOU FOR ANY CONSEQUENTIAL, INCIDENTAL OR INDIRECT DAMAGES (INCLUDING DAMAGES FOR LOSS OF BUSINESS PROFITS, BUSINESS INTERRUPTION, LOSS OF BUSINESS INFORMATION, AND THE LIKE) ARISING OUT OF THE USE OR INABILITY TO USE THE SOFTWARE EVEN IF METROWERKS HAS BEEN ADVISED OF THE POSSIBILITY OF SUCH DAMAGES. BECAUSE SOME JURISDICTIONS DO NOT ALLOW THE EXCLUSION OR LIMITATION OF LIABILITY FOR CONSEQUENTIAL OR INCIDENTAL DAMAGES, THE ABOVE LIMITATIONS MAY NOT APPLY TO YOU. Metrowerks liability to you for actual damages from any cause whatsoever, and regardless of the form of the action (whether in contract, tort (including negligence), product liability or otherwise), will be limited to exceed the cost of the replacement of the media on which the software is distributed.

SOFTWARE LICENSE

PLEASE READ THIS LICENSE CAREFULLY BEFORE USING THE SOFTWARE. BY USING THE SOFTWARE, YOU ARE AGREEING TO BE BOUND BY THE TERMS OF THIS LICENSE. IF YOU DO NOT AGREE TO THE TERMS OF THIS LICENSE, PROMPTLY RETURN

THE UNUSED SOFTWARE TO THE PLACE WHERE YOU OBTAINED IT AND YOUR MONEY WILL BE REFUNDED.

1. License. The application, demonstration, system and other software accompanying this License, whether on disk, in read only memory, or on any other media (the "Software") the related documentation and fonts are licensed to you by Metrowerks. You own the disk on which the Software and fonts are recorded but Metrowerks and/or Metrowerks' Licensor retain title to the Software, related documentation and fonts. This License allows you to use the Software and fonts on a single Apple computer and make one copy of the Software and fonts in machine-readable form for backup purposes only. You must reproduce on such copy the Metrowerks copyright notice and any other proprietary legends that were on the original copy of the Software and fonts. You may also transfer all your license rights in the Software and fonts, the backup copy of the Software and fonts, the related documentation and a copy of this License to another party, provided the other party reads and agrees to accept the terms and conditions of this License.

2. Restrictions. The Software contains copyrighted material, trade secrets and other proprietary material. In order to protect them, and except as permitted by applicable legislation, you may not decompile, reverse engineer, disassemble or otherwise reduce the Software to a human-perceivable form. You may not modify, network, rent, lease, loan, distribute or create derivative works based upon the Software in whole or in part. You may not electronically transmit the Software from one computer to another or over a network.

3. Termination. This License is effective until terminated. You may terminate this License at any time by destroying the Software, related documentation and fonts and all copies thereof. This License will terminate immediately without notice from Metrowerks if you fail to comply with any provision of this License. Upon termination you must destroy the Software, related documentation and fonts and all copies thereof.

4. Export Law Assurances. You agree and certify that neither the Software nor any other technical data received from Metrowerks, nor the direct product thereof, will be exported outside the United States except as authorized and as permitted by the laws and regulations of the United States. If the Software has been rightfully obtained by you outside of the United States, you agree that you will

not re-export the Software nor any other technical data received from Metrowerks, nor the direct product thereof, except as permitted by the laws and regulations of the United States and the laws and regulations of the jurisdiction in which you obtained the Software.

5. Government End Users. If you are acquiring the Software and fonts on behalf of any unit or agency of the United States Government, the following provisions apply. The Government agrees: (i) if the Software and fonts are supplied to the Department of Defense (DoD), the Software and fonts are classified as "Commercial Computer Software" and the Government is acquiring only "restricted rights" in the Software, its documentation and fonts as that term is defined in Clause 252.227-7013(c)(1) of the DFARS; and (ii) if the Software and fonts are supplied to any unit or agency of the United States Government other than DoD, the Government's rights in the Software, its documentation and fonts will be as defined in Clause 52.227-19(c)(2) of the FAR or, in the case of NASA, in Clause 18-52.227-86(d) of the NASA Supplement to the FAR.

6. Limited Warranty on Media. Metrowerks warrants the diskettes and/or compact disc on which the Software and fonts are recorded to be free from defects in materials and workmanship under normal use for a period of ninety (90) days from the date of purchase as evidenced by a copy of the receipt. Metrowerks' entire liability and your exclusive remedy will be replacement of the diskettes and/or compact disc not meeting Metrowerks' limited warranty and which is returned to Metrowerks or a Metrowerks authorized representative with a copy of the receipt. Metrowerks will have no responsibility to replace a disk/disc damaged by accident, abuse or misapplication. ANY IMPLIED WARRANTIES ON THE DISKETTES AND/OR COMPACT DISC, INCLUDING THE IMPLIED WARRANTIES OF MERCHANTABILITY AND FITNESS FOR A PARTICULAR PURPOSE, ARE LIMITED IN DURATION TO NINETY (90) DAYS FROM THE DATE OF DELIVERY. THIS WARRANTY GIVES YOU SPECIFIC LEGAL RIGHTS, AND YOU MAY ALSO HAVE OTHER RIGHTS WHICH VARY BY JURISDICTION.

7. Disclaimer of Warranty on Apple Software. You expressly acknowledge and agree that use of the Software and fonts is at your sole risk. Except as is stated above, the Software, related documentation and fonts are provided "AS IS" and without warranty of any kind and Metrowerks and Metrowerks' Licensor(s) (for the purposes of provisions 7 and 8, Metrowerks and Metrowerks' Licensor(s) shall be col-

lectively referred to as "Metrowerks") EXPRESSLY DISCLAIM ALL OTHER WARRANTIES, EXPRESS OR IMPLIED, INCLUDING, BUT NOT LIMITED TO, THE IMPLIED WARRANTIES OF MER-CHANTABILITY AND FITNESS FOR A PARTICULAR PURPOSE. [LICENSEE NAME] DOES NOT WARRANT THAT THE FUNCTIONS CONTAINED IN THE SOFTWARE WILL MEET YOUR REQUIRE-MENTS, OR THAT THE OPERATION OF THE SOFTWARE WILL BE UNINTERRUPTED OR ERROR-FREE, OR THAT DEFECTS IN THE SOFTWARE AND THE FONTS WILL BE CORRECTED. FURTHER-MORE, [LICENSEE NAME] DOES NOT WARRANT OR MAKE ANY REPRESENTATIONS REGARDING THE USE OR THE RESULTS OF THE USE OF THE SOFTWARE AND FONTS OR RELATED DOCU-MENTATION IN TERMS OF THEIR CORRECTNESS, ACCURACY, RELIABILITY, OR OTHERWISE. NO ORAL OR WRITTEN INFORMA-TION OR ADVICE GIVEN BY [LICENSEE NAME] OR AN [LICENSEE NAME] AUTHORIZED REPRESENTATIVE SHALL CREATE A WARRANTY OR IN ANY WAY INCREASE THE SCOPE OF THIS WARRANTY. SHOULD THE SOFTWARE PROVE DEFECTIVE, YOU (AND NOT [LICENSEE NAME] OR AN [LICENSEE NAME] AUTHO-RIZED REPRESENTATIVE) ASSUME THE ENTIRE COST OF ALL NECESSARY SERVICING, REPAIR OR CORRECTION. SOME JURIS-DICTIONS DO NOT ALLOW THE EXCLUSION OF IMPLIED WAR-RANTIES, SO THE ABOVE EXCLUSION MAY NOT APPLY TO YOU.

8. Limitation of Liability. UNDER NO CIRCUMSTANCES INCLUDING NEGLIGENCE, SHALL [LICENSEE NAME] BE LIABLE FOR ANY INCIDENTAL, SPECIAL OR CONSEQUENTIAL DAMAGES THAT RESULT FROM THE USE OR INABILITY TO USE THE SOFTWARE OR RELATED DOCUMENTATION, EVEN IF [LICENSEE NAME] OR AN [LICENSEE NAME] AUTHORIZED REPRESENTATIVE HAS BEEN ADVISED OF THE POSSIBILITY OF SUCH DAMAGES. SOME JURISDICTIONS DO NOT ALLOW THE LIMITATION OR EXCLUSION OF LIABILITY FOR INCIDENTAL OR CONSEQUEN-TIAL DAMAGES SO THE ABOVE LIMITATION OR EXCLUSION MAY NOT APPLY TO YOU.

    In no event shall Metrowerks' total liability to you for all damages, losses, and causes of action (whether in contract, tort (including negligence) or otherwise) exceed that portion of the amount paid by you which is fairly attributable to the Software and fonts.

9. Controlling Law and Severability. This License shall be governed by and construed in accordance with the laws of the United States

and the State of California, as applied to agreements entered into and to be performed entirely within California between California residents. If for any reason a court of competent jurisdiction finds any provision of this License, or portion thereof, to be unenforceable, that provision of the License shall be enforced to the maximum extent permissible so as to effect the intent of the parties, and the remainder of this License shall continue in full force and effect.

10. Complete Agreement. This License constitutes the entire agreement between the parties with respect to the use of the Software, the related documentation and fonts, and supersedes all prior or contemporaneous understandings or agreements, written or oral, regarding such subject matter. No amendment to or modification of this License will be binding unless in writing and signed by a duly authorized representative of Metrowerks.

INDEX

CompuServe

The Information Service You Won't Outgrow

Calling all Macintosh Developers

If you're looking for additional information on how to program for the Macintosh, visit the MAUG support forums on CompuServe. To access these valuable services, GO MAUG.

How will you benefit from accessing the MAUG support forums on CompuServe?

- Talk directly with the author of Ultimate Mac Programming, Dave Mark, in Section 11 of the Macintosh Developer's Forum (GO MACDEV).

- Ask questions and gain helpful tips and tricks from fellow Macintosh developers, company representatives and magazine editors 24 hours a day, 7 days a week.

- Download the latest updates, fixes, and patches for popular software toolkits.

- Access libraries full of freeware and shareware programs.

- Get utilities, driver files, and more...

MAUG(R)...the nicest place your Macintosh can take you.

FREE CompuServe Membership offer for Macintosh Developers!

Access the CompuServe folder on the CD-ROM included with this book to get all of the tools you need to become a CompuServe member today. You'll

find a free copy of the CompuServe Information Manager interface software, our sign-up program, and a README file with instructions to become a CompuServe member. You'll also receive your first month of basic services free (an $8.95 value), as well as a complimentary subscription to *CompuServe Magazine.*

In order to become a CompuServe member, you'll need to complete the sign-up process using the software provided on the enclosed CD-ROM. Make sure you use the following information to complete the sign-up process:

Agreement Number (Name):
     MACPROGRAM

Serial Number: 9999

Don't delay!

Sign up now to join the largest and most prestigious international network of personal computer users. You'll have instant access to more than 2000 products and services and over 2.4 million CompuServe members worldwide. Get computer support from over 750 hardware and software manufacturers (including Adobe, Apple, Aldus, Borland, Lotus, Microsoft, Novell, Symantec, and WordPerfect). Access airline schedules and fares, weather information, investment services, research databases, national and international news wires, and much more.

Become a CodeWarrior now!

Order the commercial version of Metrowerks CodeWarrior, the premier software development package for 68K and Power Macintosh computers. Once you register, you'll receive updates for one year as part of your CodeWarrior subscription.

CodeWarrior Bronze CD-ROM $99

This CD comes with C, C++, and Pascal compilers and other tools for developing 68K Macintosh software.

CodeWarrior Gold CD-ROM $399

This CD comes with C, C++, and Pascal compilers and other tools for developing 68K and native Power Macintosh software.

All CodeWarrior compilers run native on the 68K and PowerPC processors. Both CodeWarrior CD-ROMs come with compilers, debuggers, profilers and other tools, the Metrowerks PowerPlant™ application framework, over 3000 pages of on-line documentation, example source code, and many third party tools, demonstrations, and offers.

To order, call Metrowerks Mail Order (800) 377-5416 (USA only)
or (419) 281-1802 (outside USA).
To order by fax, fill out this form and fax to (419) 281-6883.
For sales and site licensing information, call (512) 346-1935, or e-mail sales@metrowerks.com (internet).

	QTY	Cost Each	Total
CodeWarrior Gold			
CodeWarrior Bronze			
CodeWarrior Gold Academic			
Total			
Tax, Shipping & Handling			
Total Payment			

Name

Company or Educational Institution

Address

Address

City   State/Province   ZIP/Postal Code

Telephone Number   Fax Number

E-mail Address

☐ VISA
☐ MasterCard

Exp. Date (M/Y)

Credit Card Number

Cardholder's Signature

1. Dave Mark, noted author, demystifies programming for those new to the Mac.

2. In-depth coverage of System Software Technologies, Object Oriented Programming, Visual Programming, Databasing ...

3. Mike Scanlin's monthly contest will challenge even the most experienced programmer!

4. Chris Espinosa talks about Apple – from the inside. Where it has been and where it is going.

5. Get information from the experts and Apple on how to make the transition to Power Macintosh.

6. Articles from industry leaders that will improve your code writing.

7. Workshop articles including languages from Assembly and C to Pascal, FORTRAN, and others.

8. Technical support for Symantec's products.

9. Impartial insider reviews of the latest development tools.

10. Legal issues specific to programming – from the release of new software to copyrights.

11. Interesting, not so conventional programming ideas.

12. Ideas to help you clean up, use shortcuts on, and organize your work.

13. Comments on the industry and pertinent notable events.

14. An open forum for developers to share their thoughts, dilemmas, solutions and opinions.

15. Recent releases, product updates, company mergers, shipping dates ...

16. Valuable developer tools and reference materials at discounted prices.

17. Your opportunity to share information or tips useful to other programmers – see it in print & get paid for it!

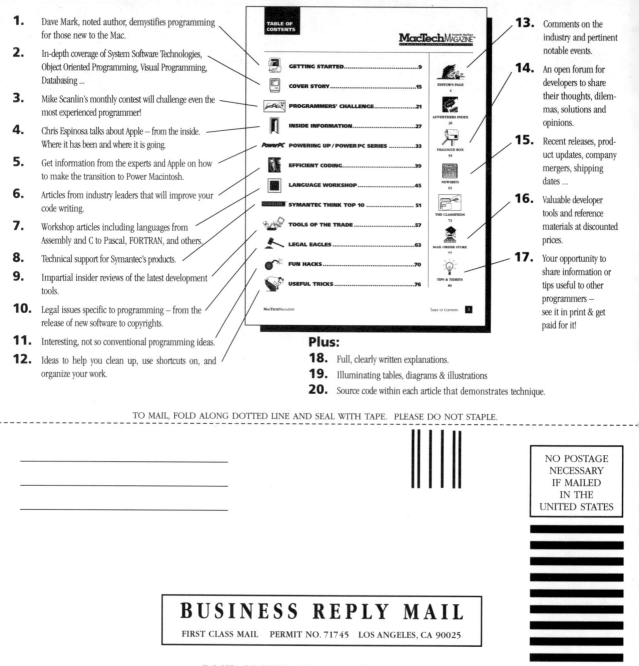

Plus:

18. Full, clearly written explanations.

19. Illuminating tables, diagrams & illustrations

20. Source code within each article that demonstrates technique.

TO MAIL, FOLD ALONG DOTTED LINE AND SEAL WITH TAPE. PLEASE DO NOT STAPLE.

NO POSTAGE
NECESSARY
IF MAILED
IN THE
UNITED STATES

BUSINESS REPLY MAIL

FIRST CLASS MAIL   PERMIT NO. 71745   LOS ANGELES, CA 90025

POSTAGE WILL BE PAID BY ADDRESSEE

XPLAIN CORPORATION
P O BOX 250055
LOS ANGELES CA 90099-3873

IDG BOOKS WORLDWIDE REGISTRATION CARD

RETURN THIS REGISTRATION CARD FOR FREE CATALOG

Title of this book: **ULTIMATE MAC PROGRAMMING**

My overall rating of this book: ❏ Very good [1] ❏ Good [2] ❏ Satisfactory [3] ❏ Fair [4] ❏ Poor [5]

How I first heard about this book:

❏ Found in bookstore; name: [6]

❏ Advertisement: [8]

❏ Word of mouth; heard about book from friend, co-worker, etc.: [10]

❏ Book review: [7]

❏ Catalog: [9]

❏ Other: [11]

What I liked most about this book:

What I would change, add, delete, etc., in future editions of this book:

Other comments:

Number of computer books I purchase in a year: ❏ 1 [12] ❏ 2-5 [13] ❏ 6-10 [14] ❏ More than 10 [15]

I would characterize my computer skills as: ❏ Beginner [16] ❏ Intermediate [17] ❏ Advanced [18] ❏ Professional [19]

I use ❏ DOS [20] ❏ Windows [21] ❏ OS/2 [22] ❏ Unix [23] ❏ Macintosh [24] ❏ Other: [25]_____
(please specify)

I would be interested in new books on the following subjects:
(please check all that apply, and use the spaces provided to identify specific software)

❏ Word processing: [26]

❏ Data bases: [28]

❏ File Utilities: [30]

❏ Networking: [32]

❏ Other: [34]

❏ Spreadsheets: [27]

❏ Desktop publishing: [29]

❏ Money management: [31]

❏ Programming languages: [33]

I use a PC at (please check all that apply): ❏ home [35] ❏ work [36] ❏ school [37] ❏ other: [38] _____

The disks I prefer to use are ❏ 5.25 [39] ❏ 3.5 [40] ❏ other: [41]_____

I have a CD ROM: ❏ yes [42] ❏ no [43]

I plan to buy or upgrade computer hardware this year: ❏ yes [44] ❏ no [45]

I plan to buy or upgrade computer software this year: ❏ yes [46] ❏ no [47]

Name: _____ Business title: [48] _____ Type of Business: [49] _____

Address (❏ home [50] ❏ work [51]/Company name: _____)

Street/Suite# _____

City [52]/State [53]/Zipcode [54]: _____ Country [55] _____

❏ **I liked this book!** You may quote me by name in future
IDG Books Worldwide promotional materials.

My daytime phone number is _____

IDG BOOKS

THE WORLD OF
COMPUTER
KNOWLEDGE

 # YES!

Please keep me informed about IDG's World of Computer Knowledge.
Send me the latest IDG Books catalog.